P9-DEP-676

Presidents of the United States Chronology

1. George Washington (no affiliation), 1789–1797

2. John Adams (Federalist), 1797–1801

3. Thomas Jefferson (Democratic-Republican), 1801–1809

4. James Madison (Democratic-Republican), 1809–1817

5. James Monroe (Democratic-Republican), 1817–1825

6. John Quincy Adams (National Republican), 1825–1829

7. Andrew Jackson (Democrat), 1829–1837

8. Martin Van Buren (Democrat), 1837–1841

9. William Henry Harrison (Whig), 1841

10. John Tyler (Whig), 1841–1845

11. James K. Polk (Democrat), 1845–1849

12. Zachary Taylor (Whig), 1849–1850

13. Millard Fillmore (Whig), 1850–1853

14. Franklin Pierce (Democrat), 1853–1857

15. James Buchanan (Democrat), 1857–1861

16. Abraham Lincoln (Republican), 1861–1865

17. Andrew Johnson (Democrat), 1865–1869

18. Ulysses S. Grant (Republican), 1869–1877

19. Rutherford B. Hayes (Republican), 1877–1881

20. James Garfield (Republican), 1881

21. Chester A. Arthur (Republican), 1881–1885

alpha
books

22. Grover Cleveland (Democrat), 1885–1889

23. Benjamin Harrison (Republican), 1889–1893

24. Grover Cleveland (Democrat), 1893–1897

25. William McKinley (Republican), 1897–1901

26. Theodore Roosevelt (Republican), 1901–1909

27. William H. Taft (Republican), 1909–1913

28. Woodrow Wilson (Democrat), 1913–1921

29. Warren G. Harding (Republican), 1921–1923

30. Calvin Coolidge (Republican), 1923–1929

31. Herbert Hoover (Republican), 1929–1933

32. Franklin Delano Roosevelt (Democrat), 1933–1945

33. Harry S. Truman (Democrat), 1945–1953

34. Dwight Eisenhower (Republican), 1953–1961

35. John F. Kennedy (Democrat), 1961–1963

36. Lyndon Baines Johnson (Democrat), 1963–1969

37. Richard Nixon (Republican), 1969–1974

38. Gerald R. Ford (Republican), 1974–1977

39. Jimmy Carter (Democrat), 1977–1981

40. Ronald Reagan (Republican), 1981–1989

41. George Bush (Republican), 1989–1993

42. Bill Clinton (Democrat), 1993–2001

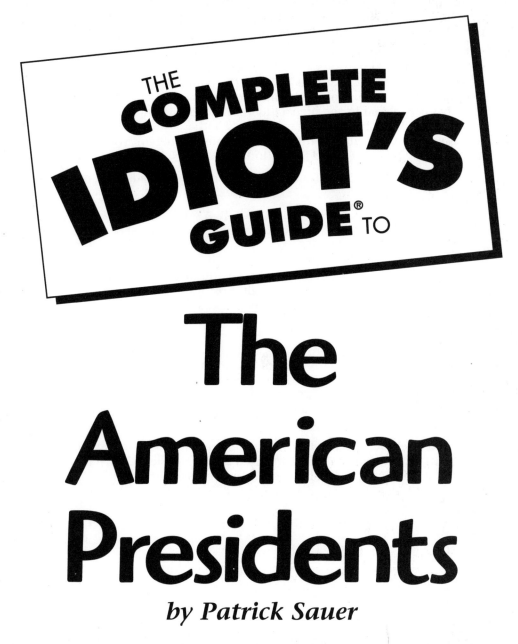

THE COMPLETE IDIOT'S GUIDE® TO

The American Presidents

by Patrick Sauer

alpha books

Macmillan USA, Inc.
201 West 103rd Street
Indianapolis, IN 46290

A Pearson Education Company

Publisher
Marie Butler-Knight

Product Manager
Phil Kitchel

Managing Editor
Cari Luna

Acquisitions Editor
Randy Ladenheim-Gil

Development Editor
Tom Stevens

Copy Editor
Krista Hansing

Illustrator
Jody P. Schaeffer

Cover Designers
Mike Freeland
Kevin Spear

Book Designers
Scott Cook and Amy Adams of DesignLab

Layout/Proofreading
Bob LaRoche
Gloria Schurick

Contents at a Glance

Contents

xiii

Foreword

Supermodels, movie stars, and boy bands come and go, but the most enduringly popular figures in the American limelight are 42 middle-aged white men, all except one of them Protestants and all of them confirmed wearers of suits. Even years and decades after their deaths, we as a people cannot get enough about these guys. We want to be able to examine every detail of their lives, ideas, and actions, and we love to hear presidential celebrity gossip, especially if sex is involved.

Year after year, the presses pour out millions of words of biography, history, and political analysis about presidents' actions and personal lives. Cable television's C-SPAN has recently devoted hundreds of hours of programming to explaining and narrating the lives of the presidents. A random Internet search will turn up thousands of sites related to U.S. presidents. Any artifact related to John F. Kennedy will fetch thousands—or hundreds of thousands—of dollars at public auction.

Why all this interest in a group of middle-aged white men who definitely do not make up a politically correct historical category?

The answer is quite simple: Even the most modestly talented or character-challenged president holds enormous power. The U.S. Constitution vests the executive power of the nation in the president—and in our own day, this has come to mean not only political and economic power, but literally the power to destroy the world with thermonuclear weapons.

In earlier times, the power of a president was somewhat less dramatic but was still hugely important. Thomas Jefferson's gutsy unilateral action purchased a gigantic addition to the nation, and James K. Polk's determination to have his own way expanded the territory of the United States all the way to the Pacific Ocean. Abraham Lincoln—by general consensus, the foremost among all presidents—altered the nation forever by his prosecution of the Civil War and his declaration of the Emancipation Proclamation. Teddy Roosevelt brought us into world affairs, and his cousin, Franklin Delano Roosevelt, towered as one of the greatest figures of the twentieth century when he led us through the Great Depression and most of World War II. The list goes on.

Granted, some of the presidents seem like dim nonentities—few contemporary Americans known much about Franklin Pierce or Benjamin Harrison, and Millard Fillmore is best known as joke fodder for his unusual cognomen—but even the most inept and obscure are important to learn about. For example, did Andrew Johnson's impeachment have lessons for Bill Clinton? Why were Franklin Pierce and James Buchanan reviled by abolitionists? Were James Monroe or George Bush affected as presidents by their wartime experiences as young men? These and similar questions fuel our endless fascination with presidents.

The Complete Idiot's Guide to the American Presidents gives readers a concise and lively look at our presidents: the heroes, the geniuses, the tragic figures, the weak characters, and the occasional buffoons.

L. Edward Purcell

L. Edward Purcell is a historian with 17 books to his credit as author or collaborator. He is a graduate of Simpson College and the University of Iowa, and for several years he was editor-in-chief of the State Historical Society of Iowa. He has taught at a number of colleges and universities and has been a consultant to historical museums. He now lives in Lexington, Kentucky.

Introduction

The President of the United States is now generally regarded as the leader of the free world, but it certainly hasn't always been that way. In fact, the growth of the office is a microcosm of the growth of the nation. The United States has long been a country of contradictions: brilliant in its adherence to the principles of democracy, liberty, and personal freedom, yet simultaneously allowing institutional corruption to subvert many of those very principles upon which the nation was built. The country has produced many sagacious thinkers, innovators, and statesmen, but it also has suffered at the hands of those in power who had not a whit of foresight or ethics. The United States of America has been called the most glorious mess imaginable, which could easily be the sign over the door to the Oval Office.

Before you begin to look into the lives of the men who have led this country for better or worse, through sickness and health, through good times and bad, and, sadly, on a few occasions, until death do us part, keep in mind that *The Complete Idiot's Guide to the American Presidents* is strictly an overview. Hopefully it will spark your interest in one of the men who called the White House home or will steer you to a general understanding of the predominant issues of the day. Ideally, this book will help plant the seed in a young child's brain to believe that "someday I am going be president of the United States"—which, of course, will lead them to place their *left* hand on the *Idiot's Guide* during the swearing-in and invite me to don a tux at the Inaugural Ball.

What You'll Learn in This Book

The Complete Idiot's Guide to the American Presidents is a primer into the lives of the 41 men who have dared to serve in the most unique political position in the world. Each chapter briefly covers their lives, tells how they reached the top, and focuses on the major events that have come to define their presidencies. I have divided the book into categories that loosely follow boxing divisions, but this isn't an unbending definitive ranking. I compared rankings from a variety of sources and tried to place each President of the United States into a consensus category based on his impact on the executive office.

Part 1, "Undisputed Champions," covers the "Big Four": George Washington, Abraham Lincoln, Franklin Roosevelt, and Thomas Jefferson. Each of these men shaped the executive office for the betterment of the nation and steered the country through its greatest crises. They are the presidential deities in the religion of democracy.

Part 2, "Heavyweights," lists the presidents of the United States who brought dignity, class, ethics, passion, and ideas to the Oval Office but may not have faced as great a dilemma or left a singly important footprint on the office as the "undisputed champions." This category does contain the three most entertaining characters to ever dwell in the White House: Harry Truman, Teddy Roosevelt, and Andrew Jackson.

Part 3, "Middleweights," looks at those who have balanced their terms with major highs and lows—notably Lyndon Johnson and Ronald Reagan—or those who had a few important moments but didn't change the office in any great manner—like John Quincy Adams and Rutherford B. Hayes. For the most part, these presidents either balanced their positives and negatives or left the presidency in decent shape.

Part 4, "Club Fighters," looks at the men who either had a minimal impact as President of the United States—including Jimmy Carter or Chester A. Arthur—or leaders who led the country down a dubious road—such as James Madison and Herbert Hoover. These aren't the best of the best, but they didn't leave the office in total disrepute, either.

Part 5, "Tomato Cans, Never Coulda' Been Contenders, and Still in Training," is the catch-all category that encompasses those who weakened the White House through political inertia—James Buchanan and Calvin Coolidge—or the stain of scandal—Andrew Johnson and Richard Nixon. It includes the Presidents of the United States who died before seeing their first term through, either by an assassin's bullet (James Garfield) or because of some bad fruit (Zachary Taylor). Last, we'll look at the two men who deserve some distance between their years in the executive office and our constitutional right to point out their flaws, shortcomings, and successes: George Bush and Bill Clinton.

More for Your Money!

In addition to all the explanation and information, this book contains other political, historical, familial, and comical nuggets to enhance your enjoyment of learning about the leaders of the free world. Here's how you can recognize these features:

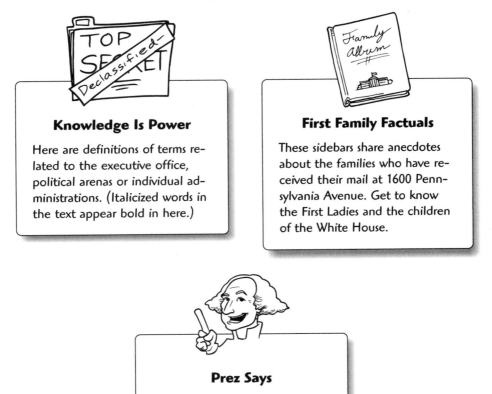

Knowledge Is Power

Here are definitions of terms related to the executive office, political arenas or individual administrations. (Italicized words in the text appear bold in here.)

First Family Factuals

These sidebars share anecdotes about the families who have received their mail at 1600 Pennsylvania Avenue. Get to know the First Ladies and the children of the White House.

Prez Says

These are the words straight out of the mouths of presidents of the United States themselves.

Commander in Chief Lore

Here you'll find surprising facts, anecdotes, trivia, and information about the lives of the presidents.

Acknowledgments

I would like to thank Randy Ladenheim-Gil, Christy Wagner, and Tom Stevens for their assistance in bringing this book to fruition; Mom for taking me to see Jimmy Carter when I still considered myself "undecided"; Daniel because I said I would; Gerald Boschert for historical perspective; and Kim for listening to a constant stream of unnecessary trivia about a bunch of dead white guys.

Unless otherwise noted, all photos are from the American Memory collection of the Library of Congress.

Special Thanks to the Technical Reviewer

The Complete Idiot's Guide to the American Presidents was reviewed by an expert who double-checked the accuracy of what you'll learn here, to help us ensure that this book gives you everything you need to know about the American presidents. Special thanks are extended to Jennifer Wood.

Trademarks

All terms mentioned in this book that are known to be or that are suspected of being trademarks or service marks have been appropriately capitalized. Alpha Books and Macmillan USA, Inc. cannot attest to the accuracy of this information. Use of a term in this book should not be regarded as affecting the validity of any trademark or service mark.

Part 1
Undisputed Champions

"You have heard the story, haven't you, about the man who was tarred and feathered and carried out of town on a rail? A man in the crowd asked him how he liked it. His reply was that if it was not for the honor of the thing, he would much rather walk."

—President Abraham Lincoln responding to a friend inquiring as to how he enjoyed being president from Lincoln Talks: A Biography in Anecdote, *by Emmanuel Hertz*

Sadly, in the end Honest Abe met a fate much worse than a tar and feathering, but it grew out of his dedication to preserving the Union while abolishing slavery, the "original sin" of America that spat in the eye of the famous words that "all men are created equal." Those words came from another of the "Undisputed Champions," Thomas Jefferson, and his story can be found in this section along with George Washington's and Franklin Delano Roosevelt's.

Chapter 1

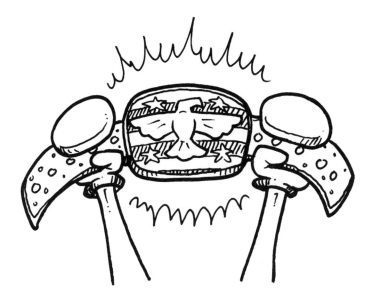

Setting the Presidential Precedence with George Washington

In This Chapter

➤ Why George Washington deserves to be called the Father of Our Country

➤ It's unanimous, Washington becomes president

➤ The man who wouldn't be king

Consider for a moment this question: What would the United States of America look like today if a man other than George Washington had been the elected leader of the infant democracy? The merits of his presidency have been the subject of debate, and there is a large school of thought that Washington wasn't in the same intellectual league as Benjamin Franklin, Thomas Jefferson, or John Adams. True or not, it's a specious argument of the "what if" sort. It might be better to paraphrase another president's tagline and ask not what George Washington didn't do for the country, but rather ask what George Washington *did* for the country.

If the President of the United States is now generally regarded as the leader of the free world, it certainly hasn't always been that way, and the growth of the office is a microcosm of the growth of a nation. The United States has long been a country of contradictions: brilliant in its adherence to the principles of democracy, liberty, and personal freedom, while simultaneously allowing institutional corruption to subvert many of those very principles upon which the nation was built. The United States has produced many of the world's leading thinkers, innovators, and statesmen, but it has also suffered at the hands of some of those in power who didn't have a whit of morality. The United States of America has been called the most glorious mess imaginable, which could easily be the sign over the door to the Oval Office.

George, George, George of the Valley (Strong as He Could Be)

In 1775, at the Second Continental Congress, George Washington was elected general and commander of the Continental Army. He was chosen because of his military know-how and commitment to colonial freedom, but also because he was a Southerner. His election was a political maneuver designed to bond the Southern colonies with their Northern counterparts in the rebellion against the British. Washington accepted the position and rejected any compensation for it. He asked only to be repaid for his expenses.

Little is known about George Washington's childhood, but he was a strong outdoorsman from Westmoreland County, Virginia, who worked in the wilderness as a surveyor in his teenage years. But nothing could have prepared him for the long, cold winter in Valley Forge, Pennsylvania. Washington encamped his army at Valley Forge on December 19, 1777, in a strategic spot that could keep the British armies resting comfortably in check and that also could provide a defense for Congress, which was in session in York, Pennsylvania. Contrary to all the famous paintings, it was a mild winter, and rain was the biggest factor. Still, Washington's troops were faced with inhumane circumstances. They had little food, clothing, or shelter, and disease ravaged the soldiers. It is estimated that more than 2,500 men died of typhus, dysentery, and/or pneumonia. On one occasion, the provisions ran out before Christmas, and some men went totally without any semblance of a holiday meal. Desertion also cut the ranks of men from 11,000 to about half that number, but many soldiers believed that Washington would see them through the disaster.

Congress was slow to react to requests for supplies, and the situation never rose above desperation, even though well-stocked bases were located in Lancaster and Redding, Pennsylvania. Profiteering was the main reason that supplies didn't reach Washington's troops, whether due to farmers selling to British soldiers in Philadelphia, or due to Boston merchants demanding profits of 1,500 percent or higher for government clothing. Americans love to mythologize the past, but this was clearly a case of citizens selling out their soldiers for a fast buck. Add in the standard bureaucratic snafus within the quartermaster and commissary departments that slowed a stream of supplies, and it becomes clear that the strength of Washington's character is a main reason the troops remained united.

Prez Says

"The preservation of the sacred fire of liberty and the destiny of the republican model of government are justly considered as deeply, perhaps as finally stalked, on the experiment and trusted to the hands of the American people."

—Excerpt from George Washington's inaugural address

Commander in Chief Lore

Washington knew when his troops arrived at Valley Forge that the most pressing need was shelter, so he planned an operation for building huts. Each troop was given exact directions for building the huts, every regiment was divided into units of 12, and each was equipped with the tools to build a hut for that number of men. To light a fire under the lazy and the slow, Washington offered a $12 prize to the unit in each regiment that built its hut quickest and best. He offered another $100 to any man—officer or soldier—who could devise a cheaper and quickly assembled covering for the huts. These instructions were not universally followed, however, which led to much unnecessary suffering.

Meanwhile, in York, some members of Congress were trying to replace Washington with General Horatio Gates, in a plot called the Conway Cabal. Gates was a commander whose army had defeated the British in the Second Battle of Saratoga, New York, which helped convince the French King Louis XVI to join an alliance with the Americans; this alliance would become the major turning point in the Revolutionary War. The efforts failed, however, after Washington sent a public letter to Gates detailing the hardships his troops endured. His congressional supporters rallied to thwart the Conway Cabal.

Amid all these calamities, George Washington persevered and remained steadfastly devoted to the American cause. This is often regarded as the darkest period of the American Revolution, but Washington's dedication to his men helped hold the army together. In February 1778, Baron Friedrich Wilhelm von Steuben, a Prussian officer who volunteered his services, came in and reorganized Washington's troops and lifted both morale and order by instituting new military tactics. The men survived, and Washington eventually led the army against Lord Cornwallis. On October 19, 1781, Cornwallis surrendered after a 20-day siege at Yorktown, Virginia, effectively ending the Revolutionary War (although a formal peace treaty wouldn't come for almost two years).

Commander in Chief Lore

One falsehood about Valley Forge is that Episcopalian Washington got down on his knees in prayer and that a devout Quaker who happened by abandoned his belief that guns and the gospel couldn't co-exist. The Quaker thought that if a man of God like Washington fought for America, then it must be a pious cause. It is an oft-told tall tale from the mind of Parson Weems, an Episcopalian minister and writer who published a biography of Washington in 1800. Washington was particularly pious and was not given to referring to Jesus in public or private. In fact, he didn't even partake in the communion sacrament at his church. The supposed "Valley Forge Prayer" was printed on a stamp in 1928 and unveiled as the central stained-glass piece in 1955 in a private congressional chapel in the Capitol. Even without the mythology, however, the winter at Valley Forge serves as a great example of how deeply committed George Washington was to the creation of our burgeoning republic.

Other Presidential Firsts

➤ **First president to center his belief system in Providence (i.e., fate):** George Washington.

➤ **First president born after World War II:** Bill Clinton.

➤ **First president to be born in a hospital:** Jimmy Carter, in the Wise Sanitarium in Plains, Georgia.

➤ **First president to use the handshake as a means of greeting foreign dignitaries and other guests:** Thomas Jefferson (and where would "pressing the flesh" be without him?).

➤ **First president who was an ardent golfer:** William Howard Taft, but he was too fat to bend down, so his caddie had to place his golf ball on the tee.

➤ **First president born in the nineteenth century:** Millard Fillmore (January 7, 1800).

➤ **First president born in the twentieth century:** John F. Kennedy (May 29, 1917).

➤ **First president over 65 to be elected president:** William Henry Harrison (68), followed by James Buchanan (65) and Ronald Reagan (69).

Getting Off on the Good Foot

On February 4, 1789, the first *electoral college* gathered in New York City, and George Washington was unanimously elected President of the young nation.

The presidency was not Washington's first unanimous election to a position—he also was unanimously elected President of the Constitutional Convention in Philadelphia in 1787, where he pushed for a strong federal government. He followed up by promoting the ratification of the Constitution in Virginia. Washington was always a staunch supporter of the Constitution, and later he refused to appoint anyone to his staff who was a known opponent of the document.

Washington's unanimous election to president of the Constitutional Convention was a remarkable achievement in personal restraint, considering that there was strong support to name him king of an American monarchy after his leadership in the Revolutionary War. He stuck to his belief in the founding of a democracy, and his lone formal request at the Constitutional Convention came on the last day, September 17, 1787. He asked the delegates to add an amendment increasing the number of representatives in Congress to provide a broader base for the democracy. He then returned to Mount Vernon and waited to hear of the ratification of the Constitution. He made no public statements, but within nine months, New Hampshire became the ninth state to ratify the Constitution, and a new government was hatched.

Knowledge Is Power

The **electoral college** is the assembly elected by the voters to perform the formal duty of electing the President and Vice President of the United States. The electors of each state, equal in number to its members in Congress, are expected to cast their votes for the candidates selected by the popular vote in their state.

The formal inauguration took place on April 30, 1789, on a balcony at Federal Hall in New York City, the capital of the United States at the time. Washington spontaneously added the phrase "so help me God" to the Oath of Office. This was the beginning of a position of leadership that has remained in place, unabated, through scandal and triumph for more than 200 years. Looking at the position of the president of the United States, as compared to leadership positions of other nations throughout history, offers a glimpse at what an amazing feat it has been that the office itself remains unscathed.

There have been no strong coup d'état attempts, no movements to institute a monarch or an emperor, no dictators rising up from the ashes of discontent to force their will, and not even a call to split the powers between a prime minister and a head of state. Consider, for example, Russia at the dawn of a new century. In the last 100 years, Russia has gone from Czar Nicholas II to the Communist regimes, running the gamut from the tyrannical Stalin to the reformist Mikhail Gorbachev. Certainly, the three branches of the United States government and its system of checks and balances has kept the office from amassing too much power, but it is still a credit to the unique responsibilities spelled out in the document that Washington revered, the Constitution.

George Washington, first president of the United States.

Knowledge Is Power

The **Federalists** were a political faction before the rise of the party system that advocated a solitary federal union of the American colonies, and it dominated politics from 1789 to 1801. Its supporters came primarily from the moneyed elite of the cities and included Alexander Hamilton, James Madison, and John Jay.

Perhaps no other man besides George Washington could have brought together both *Federalists* and those who opposed a strong central government.

Washington was a war hero, and people responded to him because of this. If he had had an enormous ego, he could have enlisted the majority of the colonialists to support whatever type of position he felt he deserved. So, by following Article II, Section I, of the Constitution, "The Executive Power shall be vested in a President of the United States of America," he made possible the conception of the office. On the flip side, Washington may have been the only man respected enough to be given the opportunity to try out this new President of the United States thing. Would the Southern states have trusted Alexander Hamilton? Would the Northern Federalists have supported the "radical" Thomas Jefferson? The answer in both cases is a soundly theoretical, no way.

Commander in Chief Lore

Mount Vernon was Washington's beloved home in Fairfax County, Virginia, 15 miles south of the capital that bears his name. He inherited the 8,000 acres in 1752 from his half-brother, Lawrence, who had named it after British Admiral Edward Vernon, whom he had served under. After the Revolutionary War, George Washington and wife Martha moved into the three-story wood building, built in 1743 and much smaller than when Washington first inherited it. He once wrote to a friend that his manner of living was plain and that he was content because a glass of wine and a bit of mutton were always ready, but soon the presidency would get in the way. Washington retired to Mount Vernon in the spring of 1797, but he enjoyed the quiet life for only a little more than two years. He died on December 14, 1799, of what his doctors diagnosed as quinsy, a severe inflammation of the tissue surrounding the tonsils.

George Washington was the right man for the job, and that may have been his greatest attribute. He was dedicated to the cause of a union that adhered to the Constitution, but he was detached enough to let the experiment play out on its own. A Dr. Frankenstein may have tinkered with the newly created monster known as the United States until it unraveled and imploded long before it got a chance to show the world what it could be. Washington never actively sought any position, but he knew that his post-war status would help the baby nation get off on the good foot. Washington became the hardest-working man in presidential business.

George Washington and Original Sin

The American terrain was infinitely stained by the "original sin" of slavery, and historians in the last few years have pored over Washington's role in the ugly historical period. There is no doubt that Washington was raised in an atmosphere founded upon slavery. He received 10 slaves on his twenty-first birthday, and Mount Vernon used slaves throughout his lifetime. For what it's worth, Washington was regarded as a benevolent owner, although the slave quarters at Mount Vernon were reported to be miserable.

To his credit, in his later years, Washington understood the contradictions of a "free" society that allowed its citizens to own slaves. On December 30, 1775, in Cambridge,

Washington granted the enlistment of black soldiers in the Continental Army, with the official understanding that slaves would be granted their freedom in return for service.

This was an important and often overlooked moment in civil rights because many white citizens had never been on an equal plane with black soldiers before. Washington was quoted as saying that nobody wanted the abolishment of slavery more than him, but he never spoke words like that in public and didn't have any ideas as to how to change the status quo. In fact, slavery was never much of a consideration during his presidency and never became a confrontational issue. In his will, Washington liberated his slaves upon Martha's death and challenged his state's legal ban on the schooling of blacks.

Ultimately, Washington seemed personally conflicted by slavery, but publicly he didn't take the initiative to do anything about it. A modicum of pressure came from Quakers and other abolitionist groups, but although Washington sympathized with their definition of true liberty, he didn't acknowledge or aid their cause. Is it possible he could have helped to eliminate slavery with the bully pulpit? That is impossible to say, but it *is* fair to say that slavery became an even greater factor in Southern life until the Civil War because the economy of the new country heavily relied on southern agriculture.

A common theory is that Washington's main goal was to keep the Union intact—plain and simple. Because Southern states were the most vociferously anti-Federalist, one wonders what would have happened with a presidential mandate that subverted their economic base. A civil war, maybe? And, could the United States have withstood a foreign invasion during an insurrection, or would the country have simply become two separate nations? These are hypothetical questions, of course, but if Washington truly thought that the Constitution wouldn't last 20 years, he might have done whatever it would have taken to hold the country together—unfortunately, this would have meant keeping slavery intact.

The only definitive answer to the question of what Washington could have done about slavery is that there *is* no answer. Maybe Washington could have been the champion of a truly "free" nation, or maybe he would have destroyed national unity. His role as a personal emancipator and supporter of the enlistment of black soldiers should be acknowledged, even if some criticize him for his silence on an issue that he apparently knew to be in direct conflict with his beloved Constitution. It is naive and unfair to assume that his leadership could have washed away the "original sin" that still haunts us today.

I Cannot Tell a Lie

➤ The following are named for George Washington: a state, the nation's capital, 9 colleges, 33 counties, 121 post offices, and more high schools than D.C. has lobbyists.

➤ In July 1755, as an aide-de-camp to General Edward Braddock, Washington was present at a disastrous engagement in the French and Indian War. Braddock was mortally wounded, but Washington managed to get what men were left to retreat, even though his horse was twice shot out from beneath him.

➤ Washington's only trip outside the United States was when he accompanied his ailing brother Lawrence to Barbados.

➤ According to the notes of Georgia delegate Abraham Baldwin (made public in 1987), Washington said privately that he didn't think the Constitution would last more than 20 years.

➤ George Washington was the only president elected by a unanimous electoral consensus—but only 10 states voted. North Carolina and Rhode Island had not yet ratified the Constitution, and New York was unable to decide in time which electors to send.

➤ Washington was a big theater fan and quoted from Joseph Addison's 1713 drama *Cato* throughout his life. He also attended Shakespeare's works; he saw a modernization of *The Tempest* during the Constitutional Convention and had a children's version of *Julius Caesar* performed at the presidential mansion during his first term.

➤ States 14 to 16 were created during Washington's presidency: Vermont in 1791, Kentucky in 1792, and Tennessee in 1796.

➤ Washington's dentures were made of ivory, not the wood of legend. A New York City dentist, John Greenwood, made several sets for Washington, and none contained any wood. For years, Greenwood also tried to save George's last remaining tooth, the first bicuspid in his left lower jaw.

With a Rebel Yell They Cried More, More, More ... Whiskey in a Jar

The Whiskey Rebellion in 1794 was the first example of the Executive Officer flexing his presidential muscle. In an effort to reduce the national debt (long before anyone heard the name Ross Perot) and to set the country on solid economic footing, in 1791, Washington authorized an *excise tax* on liquor, sponsored by Secretary of the Treasury Alexander Hamilton.

Knowledge Is Power

An **excise tax** is an internal tax levied on the manufacture, sale, or consumption of a commodity within a particular country.

The bulk of the excise tax on whiskey fell on western Pennsylvania, which was the hot spot for hooch production in those days. The grain farmers who converted their corn crops into alcohol to avoid the costs of transporting grain to market were also the distillers. Whiskey was the primary source of their income, and they refused to pay the tax. They thought it was an attack on their right to earn a living, so it didn't take long for organized resistance to take shape—this included the kindly practice of tarring and feathering federal revenue officials. In the spring of 1794, warrants were issued for noncompliant distillers, and a riot broke out in which a federal officer was killed and the home of the revenue collector was torched.

In August, Washington unsuccessfully ordered the insurgents to end their defiant ways. He quickly satisfied the law by securing, from Supreme Court Justice James Wilson, certification verifying that the situation was beyond the control of federal marshals or judicial proceedings, and Washington asked the governors of Pennsylvania, Virginia, New Jersey, and Maryland to mobilize contingents of their militias. Negotiations failed, so Washington ordered 15,000 militia to the area and personally inspected troops in the field. The show of force basically ended the rebellion, but leaders of the rebellion were quickly arrested anyway—all 20 of them. All but two were freed for want of evidence, but Washington pardoned the two convicted of treason because one was thought to be insane and the other mentally incompetent.

Commander in Chief Lore

Pundits often refer to the sensationalism of politics in our tabloid age, but hasn't politics always been sensational? During the Revolution, a low-brow London press claimed that George Washington was rowed across the Hudson each night to carry on with a mistress in New Jersey, and another British publication, *Gentleman's Magazine*, printed forged letters describing an affair between Washington and his washerwoman's daughter.

This was an important moment because it was the first real test of the federal government's ability to enforce the laws and dictate power over the states. It was also the first time the president used his right to call upon the state militias. The Whiskey Rebellion is also interesting because it was set into motion by Hamilton as a way to break up all Democratic-Republican societies, which was where the trouble had started. Hamilton saw the Democratic-Republican societies as a threat to his Federalist party, and he wanted to paint his political enemies as treasonous, even though members of the Democratic societies in Philadelphia and Baltimore were part of the federal force against insurrection. It worked; Federalists gained full control of Congress in the 1794 elections, and the Democratic-Republican societies were kept from the presidency for a few more years.

Legacy

There isn't a lot that hasn't been said about George Washington, but he is 100 percent deserving of the title Father of the Country. Was he a perfect leader? No, but in reality, is there such a thing? His demeanor, humility, and dedication were his greatest strengths, but that is what this experiment called America needed. Washington probably wasn't the intellectual giant that Jefferson was, but he was smart enough to know that the Constitution was the ultimate blueprint and that patience was the ultimate virtue in establishing a new country.

The Least You Need to Know

➤ George Washington's staunch support of a nation based upon the Constitution is as important as any event in America's evolution.

➤ The Whiskey Rebellion led Washington to the first major test of the strength of federal power.

➤ Despite revisionist analysis of his views on slavery or who might have been the better choice, George Washington kept the Union together and deserves to be called the Father of the Country.

Chapter 2

I've Been Thinkin' About Abraham Lincoln

In This Chapter

➤ Why slavery was the sole issue of Lincoln's life and death

➤ From simple lawyer to stately legend

➤ The bearded calm amidst the storms

➤ A great sadness envelopes the United States

In the nearly century and a half since Lee surrendered to Grant at Appomattox, the winds of political change have influenced historians' identification of the underlying reasons for the Civil War. Slavery has always been identified as the primary cause, but now the overwhelming majority of scholars take it as dogma that there wasn't a secondary issue that came remotely close in importance. The issue of federal infringement upon states' sovereignty has always had its subscribers, particularly in the antebellum south, but it is generally accepted that slavery dwarves any others.

One could argue that Abraham Lincoln's personal views on slavery may have had more of an impact on the United States than any belief held by any other of our numerous leaders because only he risked the fate of the country on a moral imperative. So, from what did Lincoln's outlook germinate? Was he always a staunch abolitionist, or were some of his views politically motivated? Above all else, what events in Lincoln's life led him to end the legal practice of slavery in the United States? We'll look at these issues and more in this chapter.

The Man from Illinois Is Defined by Kansas-Nebraska

One of the major legislative measures that satiated both pro- and antislavery groups was the *Missouri Compromise of 1820,* which was undone by the passage of the Kansas-Nebraska Act of 1854.

The Kansas-Nebraska Act repealed the Missouri Compromise and allowed for the individual states to choose whether slavery would be permitted—a concept also known as "popular sovereignty." The sponsor of the bill was Democratic Senator Stephen Douglas of Illinois, who sponsored it in no small part to ensure that Southern senators would vote for a bill that would facilitate the construction of a transcontinental railroad through the northern half of the United States.

After serving in Congress as a member of the Whig party from 1847 to 1849, Abraham Lincoln found that his interest in politics had begun to wane. He did not seek re-election primarily because he had opposed the Mexican War and contended President Polk's declaration that American soldiers had been fired upon by Mexicans on U.S. soil. Although Lincoln voted for every appropriation for the war effort once it began, his goose was cooked back home in Illinois, a staunchly prowar state. (One Democratic paper labeled him a modern Benedict Arnold, and another gave him the moniker "Ranchero Spotty" because he made "spot resolutions" that couldn't be trusted.)

Lincoln returned home to Springfield to practice law with his partner, William H. Herndon. He became one of the most respected lawyers in the area and had a knack for delivering concise, logical points.

Lincoln quickly began touring and denouncing the Kansas-Nebraska Act, which eventually led him into the renowned Lincoln-Douglas debates. Lincoln was basically unknown at the time, but the ensuing arguments catapulted him into the spotlight. He was chosen to reply to Douglas at a state fair in Springfield, and he was so effective that he instantly became the point man of the state's anti–Kansas-Nebraska Act contingent. Lincoln was selected by the newly formed Republican Party to run against Stephen Douglas in the 1858 senatorial election, and he gained national prominence in the ensuing campaign. Even though he

Knowledge Is Power

The **Missouri Compromise of 1820** was a legislative measure enacted by Congress in 1820 that regulated the extension of slavery until the 1850s. Missouri applied for statehood in 1818, which rocked the balanced boat of 11 free and 11 slave states. A bill called the Tallmadge Amendment passed the anti-slave House forbidding the admittance of another slaveholding state, but it was defeated in the pro-slave Senate. Maine applied for statehood in 1819, and a compromise was reached that no Louisiana Purchase areas north of 36° 30' would ever be allowed to own slaves. Maine and Missouri entered the United States within a year of each other to preserve the delicate balance of sectional equality.

lost to Douglas 54 to 46, his eloquent addresses about the importance of preserving the union enhanced his reputation.

The upstart Republican Party was founded by a coalition in 1854 primarily as a party with a platform that staunchly opposed the expansion of slavery into Western territories. The Republican Party consisted of former members of the Free-Soils, Know-Nothings, Whigs, and Northern Democrats.

The two opponents duked it out in the oratorical circle all across what would become the Land of Lincoln. The series of seven debates were hugely significant all across the country, and candidates running for the legislature aligned with either Lincoln or Douglas. The debates were marked by the contrasting views on the morality and spread of slavery, but not, as is often thought, about equality for blacks. Lincoln opposed granting blacks the rights to vote, to sit on juries, to marry whites, or to hold office, and he was committed to white supremacy. He even said:

> I am not, nor ever have been, in favor of bringing about in any way the social or political equality of the white and black races ... there is a physical difference between the white and black races that which, I suppose, will forever forbid the two races living together upon terms of social and political equality.

Still, Lincoln never wavered in his belief that slavery was morally wrong, even if his main concern was preserving the status quo of the Union. The Kansas-Nebraska Act brought Lincoln back into the political fold, and his argumentative prowess made him an up-and-comer in the virgin Republican Party. He and the Republican Party kept rolling along, all the way to his election to the presidency in 1860. By the time Lincoln was inaugurated on March 4, 1861, the Confederate States of America was a reality, and the Civil War loomed. To the Confederacy, Lincoln was a hard-liner, and speaking out in opposition to Stephen Douglas put Lincoln dead center in the potential dissolution of the United States.

Prez Says

"... 'A house divided against itself cannot stand.' I believe this Government cannot endure permanently half slave and half free. I do not expect the Union to be dissolved, I do not expect the house to fall; but I do expect it will cease to be divided. It will become all one thing, or all the other."

—Excerpt from Lincoln's acceptance speech to run for Senator of Illinois, June 1858

There's Sumter Happenin' Here, What It Is Was Exactly Clear

By the time Abraham Lincoln packed and said goodbye to Springfield on February 11, 1861, a major change had marked the beginning of America's sixteenth presidential term. Before Lincoln dealt with the secession issue, Lincoln made a decision that became one of his famous trademarks, by becoming the first president to sport a beard. Perhaps thinking it would add dignity to his self-acknowledged homely appearance, he grew it at the request of Grace Bedell, a little girl who wrote him a letter during the campaign that read, "All the ladies like whiskers and they would tease their husbands to vote for you and then you would be president." On his way to Washington, Lincoln stopped in Westfield, New York, and reportedly invited Grace to visit his train and examine his now legendary black beard. He gave her a kiss as the crowd roared its approval.

Abraham Lincoln, sixteenth president of the United States.

Knowledge Is Power

Jefferson Davis was elected by the Confederate masses and was sworn in for a six-year term in February 1862. (Most Southerners did not own slaves, so the leadership in the Confederacy was actually a dominant minority.)

A Rough Start

There was no grace period for Lincoln upon reaching the White House though, because seven states had seceded from the Union to found their own country. Four more were soon to follow.

South Carolina couldn't even wait for Lincoln to reach Washington. The legislature met on December 20, 1860, as soon as his election was confirmed and unanimously voted to secede. During the next two months, six states followed suit, and lame-duck President James Buchanan declared that the federal government would do nothing to stop them. A week after Lincoln left Springfield, *Jefferson Davis* was elected provisional President of the Confederate States of America. The pieces were now set on the military chessboard for the ugliest match in American history: the Civil War.

Initially, Lincoln spoke of preserving the Union and didn't recognize the Southern secession, but he tactfully placed the onus of dissolution upon the shoulders of he Confederacy. In his inauguration speech, Lincoln said, "In your hands, my dissatisfied fellow-countrymen, and not in mine, is the momentous issue of civil war," and, "You can have no conflict without yourselves being the aggressors." At the same time, he said that the federal government had every right to protect the sacred Union.

Above all else, Lincoln's goal was to preserve the Union, and he was conciliatory to the South, even saying that he offered no threat to the institution of slavery and that the North and South were friends, not enemies. He did not, however, sugarcoat or shrink from his steadfast position that war or peace was up to the Confederacy.

The Question at Hand ...

One question to consider is whether Lincoln assumed that war was inevitable, and thus, framed his speeches to rally Northern support, or whether he believed that the Union could be saved in its former, recognized entirety and wanted nothing more than the status quo, which was by then an impossibility. Furthermore, many historians have noted that Lincoln (and other moderates) believed that a changing economy would eventually destroy the institution of slavery. Even if Lincoln felt slavery could implode, is there anything the ol' "rail-splitter" could have done to stave off the Civil War against a ferociously determined Confederacy?

Lincoln decided to test the Confederate resolve at Fort Sumter, a Union oasis in the Charleston Harbor in South Carolina. Sumter was an unfinished, ungarrisoned, offshore fort that was less vulnerable to land attacks than Fort Moultrie, which was also in the Charleston Harbor and had formerly been a Union post. Most federal forts in the Confederacy had been taken over without a single shot fired, but Major Robert Anderson held firm when Governor Francis Pickens demanded the surrender of Fort Sumter. Lincoln had to decide whether it was worth risking war to have provisions sent to Fort Sumter. He agonized over the decision, but contradictory messages from Anderson helped push the president into sending provisions—but no troops or ammunition—to Fort Sumter. Lincoln contacted Pickens to announce his plans, but Jefferson Davis wouldn't hear of it. He ordered General Pierre Gustave Toutant Beauregard of Louisiana to demand that Anderson abandon the fort.

Anderson said he wouldn't make the decision to evacuate until noon on April 15, when he would receive either supplies or instructions from the Union. The Confederacy didn't wait that long and began firing on Fort Sumter at 4:30 A.M. on April 12. Anderson surrendered 34 hours later, on April 13 at 2:30 P.M. There was no turning back; the Civil War had begun. Ironically, there were no casualties at Fort Sumter until one of the guns burst when Anderson insisted on firing a 100-gun salute as part of his departure.

The day following Anderson's departure from Fort Sumter, the United States sent troops into battle against the Confederacy.

Two days later, President Lincoln issued a statement calling for 75,000 volunteers for three months of service to suppress the rebellion. The spirited rebels stunned the arrogant Unionists at the Battle of Bull Run in July, which ensured that the bloodiest conflict in American history would be a long, horrific affair. More than 600,000 men would die as a result of the Civil War, including the leader who gave the order to send provisions to Fort Sumter.

Facts About Abe, Honest

➤ Lincoln developed a love of books but had no more than a year of formal schooling in all the time he was growing up. The only book the family owned was the Bible, and Lincoln often walked miles to borrow books. One of his favorites was Parson Weem's *The Life of Washington* (no word on whether he believed the legend of the false teeth) .

➤ Abe saw his first city at age 19 when he floated down the Ohio and Mississippi rivers on a flatboat filled with produce to New Orleans. He was horrified at seeing slaves being beaten, whipped, and manacled in chains, and it was here, he said, that his feelings on slavery were formed.

➤ Lincoln suffered from severe bouts of depression throughout his life and frequently slipped into periods of "melancholia." His condition could not have been helped by the death of two of his sons: one in infancy, and Willie Lincoln at the age of 12 (the only child ever to die in the White House). A few years after Lincoln's assassination, Tad Lincoln died at 18, leaving only Robert Todd Lincoln to see his golden years.

➤ As a Congressman, Lincoln introduced a bill to free the slaves in the District of Columbia, but the bill was never brought to a vote.

➤ Lincoln's Secretary of State, William H. Seward, had a plan to preserve the Union by provoking war on a foreign country so that patriotism would sweep across America. And Seward felt that he, not the president, should formulate the policy. Lincoln shot the plan down, but Seward became Lincoln's most trusted aide.

➤ Lincoln was criticized in some circles for the extraordinary measures he took to curb civil liberties during the Civil War—most notably his suspension of writ of habeas corpus, a Constitutional protection against random imprisonment. Although Lincoln led no effort to end antiwar activism, the suspension allowed for the detention of opponents of the Civil War throughout the Union.

➤ The Homestead Act, which granted citizens (or soon-to-be citizens) title to 160 acres of public land after a five-year residence, was passed in Lincoln's first term (1862). The Act sparked the rapid settling of the Great Plains after the Civil War.

Free at First, Free at First ...

To understand Lincoln's strategy in the Civil War and his timing for delivering the Emancipation Proclamation, a little background of the conflict is necessary. The Battle of Bull Run lost the Union nearly 3,000 men, and it changed the complexity of the engagement from a rebellion to a full-scale Civil War. The second Battle of Bull Run, in late August 1862, was another humiliating defeat for the Union. General John Pope managed to get surrounded by Confederate troops—Robert E. Lee's to the south, and Stonewall Jackson's at Pope's rear. The first day was a relative draw, but Pope had to retreat to Washington on the second day after losing roughly 14,500 men.

Confederate morale was sky high, and Lee made the strategic decision to invade Maryland, cut off the North's supply lines, and hopefully get the recognition of a sympathetic country such as France or England. The battle at Antietam Creek was, for all intents and purposes, a stalemate, but it was so violent that the sheer number of casualties took a bigger toll on the Confederacy than it did on the Union. Lincoln visited the Union commanders on the battlefield, and by the time the one-day fighting was finished, the combined number of killed, wounded, and missing soldiers were over 23,000, making it the bloodiest single-day battle in the history of the United States. Lee lost a third of his men, gave up the plan to invade the North, and certainly lost any chance of European assistance.

The European issue is sometimes overlooked, but it played a key role in Lincoln's decision to issue the Emancipation Proclamation, which formally freed the slaves. Lincoln knew that his military tactics weren't working. The only Union success had come at Antietam, and if Lincoln had died at that point, he would be considered a colossal failure today. Lincoln wrote the Emancipation Proclamation knowing that the European stalwarts wouldn't support the Confederacy if slavery were the central issue, because neither France nor England allowed slavery. Lincoln also wanted a new strategy to change the outlook for the war—and because much of the North already viewed the cause of the war as slavery, this was both a logical and a practical executive decision.

Lincoln issued the first Emancipation Proclamation on September 22, 1862, which warned the Confederacy that if it did not rejoin the Union by January 1, 1863, he would issue an order freeing the slaves (but only those in areas not under Union control at the time). The new year dawned, the war continued, and Lincoln fulfilled his promise.

First Family Factuals

A long-standing legend says that Lincoln had to appear before a Congressional committee to defend Mary Todd against treason charges, but that is completely false. Although there was both venomous, vitriolic hatred of Mrs. Lincoln and a large group of abolitionists who believed that she shared her family's support of the Confederacy, she was both a Unionist and an emancipationist. The phony story spread and appeared in print in 1905, but it never happened.

Prez Says

"I do order and declare that all persons held as slaves within said designated States, and parts of States, are, and henceforward shall be free; and that the Executive government of the United States, including the military and naval authorities thereof, will recognize and maintain the freedom of said persons .... And I hereby enjoin upon the people so declared to be free to abstain from all violence, unless in necessary self-defense; and I recommend to them that, in all cases when allowed, they labor faithfully for reasonable wages."

—Excerpt from Lincoln's Emancipation Proclamation

The moral stance behind the Emancipation Proclamation is probably the key to Lincoln's presidency and has been hashed out by historians of all colors. To a small degree, the debate still rages today, but most historians regard the Emancipation Proclamation as one of the greatest state documents ever written. At the time, however, views on the document ran the gamut from an egregious abuse of power to a wishy-washy, legalistic letdown, to a baldly political move, to a courageous attempt to shatter the immoral tradition of slavery and creation of a nation in which men truly are equal. And as the following list makes clear, the Emancipation Proclamation was all those things and then some:

➤ **Abuse of Power.** Lincoln went against what he had always held to the preservation of the Union at all costs. Along with freeing the slaves, in June, 1864, he pushed to add an amendment that would have barred slavery throughout the United States and would have (and did) come to fruition in 1865 with the thirteenth amendment. Except in circles where white hoods are spring's latest fashion trend, it is hard to imagine that issuing a document stating that human beings couldn't be bought and sold could be a radical abuse of power, but that is how the Emancipation Proclamation was seen in the Confederacy.

➤ **Legalistic approach.** Many felt that the Emancipation Proclamation had no soul and thus was a letdown. Staunch abolitionists were hoping for lyrical genius from the bully pulpit, but the proclamation was short and direct. Did that make it any less significant? Some historians say that because Lincoln was a moderate, he wanted only to establish the point of law that the slaves had been freed, but it was a big step toward winning the war and ending slavery once and for all. That's not to mention the fact that, even if he wasn't the hard-line moralist, he was instrumental in solidifying the thirteenth amendment, which ended slavery—and wasn't that the abolitionists' goal in the first place?

➤ **Political approach.** The argument that Lincoln's main goals were political has some merit, but it was too profound a decree to be solely based on political gains. however, Even if the original Emancipation Proclamation allowed for exceptions within the border states and in Southern Union occupation, Lincoln took a risk much bigger than standard political maneuvering and either way, the thirteenth amendment eventually ended slavery everywhere. It is true that only the rebel states fell under the decree, in no small part to undercut their wartime economy, but it was a start. It is also true that Lincoln waited until the victory at Antietam so as not to look desperate. However, more than three million slaves were freed, and many of them became soldiers in the Union army. So, even if the Emancipation Proclamation had been strictly a political move, it helped to end the most violent war in our nation's history.

➤ **Courageous tactic.** What the thought process was behind the issuance of the Emancipation Proclamation is debatable, but the results that followed are not. The document has to be seen in the context of Abraham Lincoln's life, which was defined by his personal abhorrence of slavery. Though his ultimate goal was the preservation of the United States, which he achieved, he reached it by making slavery the central tenant of the Civil War. The Emancipation Proclamation was a courageous document that defined the immorality of the buying and selling of human beings, and the tide of the Civil War turned after Lincoln issued it.

The Only Thing That Mattered

No other president in history has been so intrinsically tied to a single issue in the way that Abraham Lincoln was to slavery. Richard Nixon is remembered for more than Watergate, but other than his assassination, the entirety of Lincoln's political career was wedded with slavery. Lincoln never wavered in his dedication to the Union, and he grew more dedicated to the abolition of slavery while in office. Imagine that: a leader who became more heroic the higher the moral stakes were raised. This was true even after the war, when many Northerners wanted to punish the South for its insurrection.

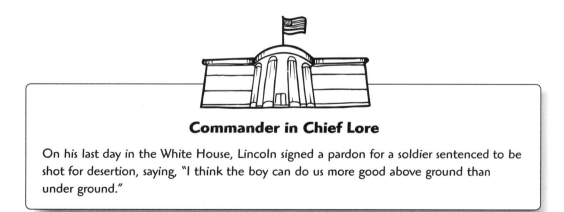

Commander in Chief Lore

On his last day in the White House, Lincoln signed a pardon for a soldier sentenced to be shot for desertion, saying, "I think the boy can do us more good above ground than under ground."

Even if he was misguided at times (he once encouraged a group of black leaders at the White House to consider colonizing somewhere else), Abraham Lincoln was on the right side of an ugly issue. It was an issue that cost more than 600,000 soldiers' lives in the Civil War and an unknown number (estimated in the millions) of lives of slaves over slavery's legal lifetime.

The issue of slavery also cost Abraham Lincoln his own life.

Has Anybody Seen My Old Friend Abraham?

The assassination of Abraham Lincoln on April 14, 1865 was one of the darkest moments in America's history. Lincoln was the first president to be killed while in office. While attending *Our American Cousin* at Ford's Theater, he was shot in the back of the head with a .44 single-shot derringer by John Wilkes Booth, a deranged actor with Southern sympathies. He was officially pronounced dead at 7:22 A.M. on April 15, and most of the nation went into mourning as the tragic news made its way across the country. Ironically, Lincoln may have been the only man with the clout and reserve to bring the South back into the general fold of the United States under the terms of mild reconstruction.

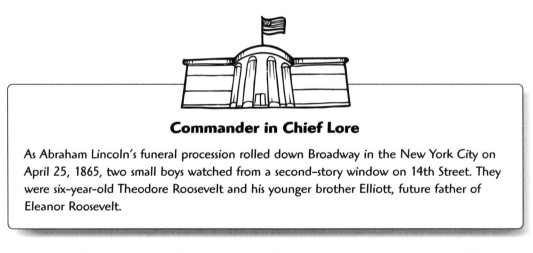

Commander in Chief Lore

As Abraham Lincoln's funeral procession rolled down Broadway in the New York City on April 25, 1865, two small boys watched from a second-story window on 14th Street. They were six-year-old Theodore Roosevelt and his younger brother Elliott, future father of Eleanor Roosevelt.

Lincoln is often regarded as the greatest president this country has ever had. Washington was a great leader, but he (or any other president, for that matter) never faced the crisis of the great experiment in democracy imploding from within. Other than polls commissioned by those who refer to the Civil War as the *War Against Northern Aggression,* Lincoln universally finishes number one in polls that ask historians to identify the greatest president.

Two of the most famous polls were taken by Arthur Schlesinger Sr. in 1948 and 1962. Schlesinger polled 55 notable historians in the first and 75 in the second. Lincoln was the clear choice for the top slot in both polls. In the Sienna Research Institute's

Presidential Ranking Survey, Lincoln finished behind Franklin D. Roosevelt twice (third another time), but this was based on a comprehensive list of questions, many of which were irrelevant to Lincoln's time in office, such as questions about foreign policy or the growth of the economy.

Lincoln was a man of integrity who led the country through its darkest period. His premature death was the first great American tragedy. Perhaps nobody can sum up what Abraham Lincoln meant to America better than Walt Whitman:

> O Captain! my Captain! rise up and hear the bells;
> Rise up—for you the flag is flung—for you the bugle trills
> For you bouquets and ribbon'd wreaths—for you the shores a-crowding
> For you they call, the swaying mass, their eager faces turning;
> Here Captain! dear father!
> This arm beneath your head!
> It is some dream that on the deck,
> You've fallen cold and dead.

—Walt Whitman, 1866

The Least You Need to Know

➤ Abraham Lincoln was out of politics and living the life of a gentleman lawyer until he started speaking out against the Kansas-Nebraska Act.

➤ Although personally against slavery, Lincoln was not a staunch abolitionist at the outset of the Civil War and was more concerned with preserving the Union.

➤ Once Abraham Lincoln defied the South and tried to send supplies to Fort Sumter, he never wavered in his belief that the Confederacy had to be destroyed.

➤ The Emancipation Proclamation has been criticized for not being worded more strongly and morally, but it was the first major step toward the thirteenth amendment, which ended slavery.

Chapter 3

F(our)
D(ecisive)
R(e-elections)

In This Chapter

➤ An aristocrat for the people

➤ Roosevelt faces fear itself

➤ Bringing beer back where it belongs

➤ Why Roosevelt was an innovator, but not a communist

Throughout Franklin Delano Roosevelt's (FDR) long career, the average American citizen was the backbone of his popularity. Even though Roosevelt was an only child raised in a wealthy family on an estate in Hyde Park, New York (less than two hours from Gotham on the train, for all you historical travelers), he championed the little guy. Interestingly enough, he never attended an American public school when he was growing up; he was taught by tutors and governess. But he had a broad education because his family took trips to Europe almost every year.

It is impossible to say exactly where Roosevelt got his compassion for the underclass and his dedication to a *progressive* agenda, but certainly his wife, Eleanor, had a major influence on his world views and never let up on her commitment to the poor and minorities. One of the earliest "dates" she had with Roosevelt as a Harvard student was a walking tour she orchestrated that took him along on her rounds of the filthy tenements in the east-side slums of New York City, where she was a social worker. Roosevelt was reportedly quite moved by the conditions under which immigrants lived, having spent his youth in a privileged, aristocratic style of life.

Rain (Money) on the Scarecrow

Roosevelt hadn't always been sympathetic to the little guy. As a state senator, he had pushed a favorable agenda for upstate farmers, but the tax breaks he advocated then were a far cry from his eventual belief in the power and responsibility of the government to take a major role in curing the country's ailments. In the early stages of his governorship, Roosevelt didn't waver far from the status quo, thinking that relief and aid should be dealt with at a local level and through private means. It was during his time as governor, however, that a key event, the Wall Street Crash of October 1929, helped transform him into an unapologetic activist. Roosevelt was first elected governor of New York in 1928 by the slimmest of margins—25,000 out of 4.25 million votes cast. It didn't take long for his progressive ideals to take shape, and a few of his policy triumphs as governor included tax relief for farmers, easier credit access, and the creation of the Temporary Emergency Relief Administration to help the rising numbers of unemployed workers.

It is a generally held consensus among economic historians that the October 29, 1929, stock market crash didn't cause the conditions that followed over the next decade, it served more like a bullet wound to a diseased body, bringing the infection that would slowly eat its way to the core. Other causes included the unstable world economy after World War I, massive overproduction, rampant bank closures (before FDIC), death of the export market, and a huge rise in unemployment, reaching 15 million workers—almost 25 percent of the able workforce. The crash lowered the country's resistance to combat preexisting problems, which were able to grow, gather speed, and eventually snowball into the oddly titled Great Depression.

Roosevelt became a Depression-era governor at a time when the Depression-era president neither used the government to provide economic assistance nor even tried to improve the economy. President Hoover believed that government intervention would destroy self-reliance, and camps of homeless people sprang up, labeled "Hoovervilles," an acidic jab at President Herbert Hoover. Roosevelt didn't agree with the president and quickly began instituting policies in New York designed to offer practical relief so that those in need could look to their elected officials, not just to overburdened charities.

Knowledge Is Power

A **progressive** is a leader who believes in political change—most often social improvements—through the actions of the government. Progressives are the flip side to conservatives and have included both Democrats such as Franklin Roosevelt and Republicans such as Theodore Roosevelt.

Prez Says

"More and more, those who are victims of dislocations and defects of our social and economic life are beginning to ask ... why government cannot and should not act to protect its citizens from disaster."

—FDR, addressing the 1931 Governors Conference

In 1931, Roosevelt obtained legislation to establish the Temporary Emergency Relief Administration (TERA), which became the model for the New Deal programs. TERA was originally designed to offset spending with tax increases as necessary, but by winter of 1931 and 1932, Roosevelt was borrowing from the state and requesting federal cash. TERA was a success, and almost 10 percent of New York families were given an average of $23 a month at a time when a family could be fed for less than 20¢ a day; thus, mass starvation was averted. The $20 million in aid to the unemployed was the first direct unemployment aid by any state, but FDR's policy would become a common practice across the country.

New Dealer's Choice

By the time of his presidential nomination, Roosevelt had a reputation as an innovator and a man who would break with established traditions if it would help get the country's feet back on the ground. A willingness to experiment was a welcome change from the steadfast adherence to an economic system that wasn't working for the Hoover administration.

At the Democratic convention in Chicago, Roosevelt reiterated the positions that he had set forth, which included the repeal of Prohibition (which probably ruffled a few feathers in Capone's backyard), more federal relief, public works projects, and a refinancing of farm and home mortgages. Roosevelt went on in his speech to say, "I pledge you, I pledge myself, to a new deal for the American people ...," and thus, the New Deal was born, and the federal government became much more directly involved in national affairs.

Riding the crest of an electoral vote victory of 472 to 59, Roosevelt entered the White House and hit the ground running. At his inauguration speech on March 4, 1933, he spoke to the nation with the immortal words "The only thing we have to fear is fear itself," and then he dove into the mammoth task of placating those fears.

Commander in Chief Lore

Roosevelt appointed the first woman to the Cabinet, Secretary of Labor Frances Perkins. Perkins was a key executor of the New Deal program and was instrumental in establishing the Social Security system in 1935 and the passage of the Fair Labor Standards Act in 1938.

Roosevelt felt that the Great Depression went far beyond party politics, and he wanted to be a president for the people of the country, not the president of the Democrats. He gave high-ranking posts to progressive members of both parties, and he continued to consult with his "Brain Trust," a consortium of professors from Columbia and Harvard.

The Banking Crisis

On March 9, Roosevelt called a special session of Congress—he didn't want to wait for the regular session in December. Roosevelt wanted to address the banking crisis posthaste, which was a solid idea considering that the entire banking industry was perilously close to a collapse: Petrified depositors were yanking all their money out at once to put it in safer places, such as Mason jars. More than half the banks in the United States had gone bankrupt or had suspended all withdrawal privileges. Roosevelt declared a nationwide bank "holiday," which closed every single bank until they could be inspected to ensure that they were sound. On March 12, Roosevelt delivered his first "fireside chat" (a format he first used in New York) in which he reassured people across the nation who crowded around their radios that the bank "holiday" was for their benefit.

In one day, Roosevelt introduced, passed, and signed the Emergency Banking Act, giving the federal government sweeping power to handle the banking crisis. It was a significant display of Roosevelt's progressive intentions, which critics have long maintained unconstitutionally strengthened presidential powers. Roosevelt's banking policies of 1933 and 1935 barred banks from dealing in stocks and bonds and established the Federal Deposit Insurance Corporation (FDIC).

Knowledge Is Power

The **gold standard** is a monetary standard under which the basic unit of currency is defined by a stated quantity of gold. This standard usually includes the coinage and circulation of gold, unrestricted conversion of other money into gold, and the use of gold (import or export) for the settlement of international obligations.

Roosevelt issued executive orders that recalled all gold, ended gold exports, and formally took the United States off the *gold standard*. Roosevelt followed the theory endorsed by George F. Warren, an agricultural economist, that gold would rise in value like any other commodity once the United States was off the gold standard. Warren argued that gold would bring up the prices of wheat, grain, cotton, and other staples of an agrarian economy. Going off the gold standard was vintage Roosevelt because it bought what he needed most—time. The dollar dropped 12 percent on international markets, inflation was held at bay, and the prices of farm commodities and metals actually saw modest gains until mid-July.

Lifting the National Spirits

Roosevelt had given the country a much-needed shot of confidence and also had reinvigorated the country's love of liquid courage. The Beer Act raised the level of alcohol considered nonintoxicating from .05 to 3.2 percent, allowing for the sale of low-alcohol ("three-two") beer, which had been illegal under the eighteenth amendment—known as Prohibition to some and as The Dark Ages to others. Shortly thereafter, Roosevelt welcomed the Budweiser Clydesdale team to the White House to receive the first post-Prohibition case of suds.

Franklin Delano Roosevelt, thirty-second president of the United States.

Executive Trial and Error

As Congress dealt with these matters, Roosevelt aggressively pushed his New Deal legislation through Congress. Bills were written by the executive branch so that they would have presidential support as soon as Congress signed them. Roosevelt's determined leadership lead to quick passage of the bulk of his agenda.

Commander in Chief Lore

One of the first policies Roosevelt instituted after becoming president was to demand that if any person in trouble telephoned the White House for help, somebody on his staff would take the call, talk to the caller, and try to figure out some way to offer assistance. After his death, Eleanor received many letters from people who said that they had called the White House during the dark days of the Great Depression and had gotten help.

One common misconception is that the New Deal had an overriding political philosophy or a set of clear, concise, goals. It had neither; it was more a loosely interconnected series of experimental programs designed by Roosevelt and the Brain Trust, which was made up of predominantly Ivy League innovators, but not necessarily dogmatic politicos.

The following sections contain more highlights of the New Deal.

Relief Legislation

➤ **Federal Emergency Relief Administration (1933).** FERA provided financial assistance for the poor, a larger version of TERA.

➤ **Works Progress Administration (1935).** The WPA replaced FERA, basically a dole, to provide jobs and self-respect. The WPA employed nine million people from 1935 to 1943 and employed four million in its part-time sister program, the National Youth Administration. WPA employees constructed 125,000 public buildings, 650,000 miles of road, 75,000 bridges, and numerous docks, roads, and parks. The WPA was also the largest federal subsidy, yet provided for the arts. The Federal Arts Program hired writers, artists, actors, and musicians to perform for the public.

Commander in Chief Lore

Ironically, artistic expression flourished during the Great Depression, particularly "national realism." Murals, folk art, symphonies, operas, an actor-presented "Living Newspapers," and collections of the oral histories of ex-slaves and laboring folks were all created through the Federal Arts and Writers Programs. Roosevelt's former classmate, artist George Biddle, said, "It is strange. Roosevelt has almost no taste or judgment about painting, and I don't think he gets much enjoyment out of it; yet he has done more for painters in this country than anybody else ever did—not only by feeding them when they were down and out; but by establishing the idea that paintings are a good thing to have around and that artists are important."

➤ **Civilian Conservation Corps (1933).** The CCC provided work for unemployed and unmarried young men ages 18 to 25 from poor, mostly urban families. The CCC built roads, planted trees, and worked on flood control and other conservation projects. The young men were stationed in rural camps under the management of military officers and were paid $30 a month—$25 of that was required to be sent back home to families, relatives, and dependents.

Recovery Legislation

➤ **National Industrial Recovery Act (1933).** This was one of the foundations of the early New Deal, and it created both the Public Works Administration (PWA), which greatly expanded the Hoover policy of direct spending on major public construction projects, and the National Recovery Administration (NRA), which was an organization to help business revitalize itself. The PWA took its time distributing money so as to avoid corruption, but after 1937, cautiously developed plans were implemented, and huge damns, buildings, and irrigation projects sprung up across the country. The NRA suspended antitrust laws to foster cooperation with businesses on the road to recovery, and price fixing was no longer illegal. In return, businesses were required to raise wages, improve working conditions, recognize the labor unions, shorten the work week, and halt all child labor. The NRA was a flop; small business owners complained that mammoth corporations were price-fixing them out of the marketplace. A study in 1934 concluded that the NRA was promoting monopolies. The Supreme Court declared the NRA unconstitutional in 1935.

➤ **Agricultural Adjustment Acts (1933, 1938).** The original AAA sought to eliminate the overproduction of basic crops to bring prices in line with the prosperous years of 1909 to 1914 by paying farmers cash subsidies. The funds were raised by a tax on processors of farm products. The AAA plan to restrict production was aided by the Dust Bowl across the Great Plains. The first AAA sizably increased national farm income, but was declared unconstitutional by the Supreme Court in 1936; a voluntary program remained in place. The second AAA loaned money to farmers and stored their surplus (a federal granary, if you will) so that during the rough times, farmers could sell their stored surplus to repay the loans.

Reform Legislation

➤ **National Housing Act (1934).** This bill established the Federal Housing Authority, which helped banks by taking most of the risk of home loans and insuring up to 80 percent of the value of the property, the first direct federal involvement in rebuilding ghettos and constructing low-cost homes. The Great Depression had resulted in many people losing their homes when they couldn't make the mortgage payments, but the banks were often unable to sell or rent out the houses.

➤ **Tennessee Valley Authority (1933).** The TVA was an independent corporation set up to help the depressed region of the Tennessee Valley, which covered 40,000 square miles across seven states. The TVA built a series of dams to harness the waters of the Tennessee River and its tributaries for power production, and it delivered its own hydroelectricity. The TVA also manufactured cheap fertilizers at Muscle Shoals, Alabama, and successfully raised the standard of living for people in the region. Over the next 50 years, the TVA became the nation's largest utility, providing more than $4 billion worth of power annually to 2.9 million consumers.

➤ **Social Security Act (1935).** This act established the Social Security system that provides retirement income for citizens over the age of 65, paid through taxes on employers and employees. It also set up unemployment and disability insurance and provided federal bucks to encourage states to care for dependent children and the blind. (A national health care system or universal health insurance was not added to the bill for fear it wouldn't pass.)

➤ **Wagner Act (1935).** Democratic Senator Robert Wagner sponsored an act that established labor's right to organize and bargain collectively through representatives that they selected. The act also prohibited employees from discriminating against union members or meddling in union affairs.

➤ **Fair Labor Standards Act (1938).** This act set the minimum wage at 25¢ an hour and provided for time-and-a-half after 44 hours, eventually reduced to 40 hours a week in the original law.

FDR fundamentally changed the way the federal government (and particularly the executive branch) operated. Roosevelt wanted to be the nation's problem-solver, and he was successful: The New Deal was the enactment of many measures that are now woven into the fabric of the way we live.

Roosevelt is sometimes cast as some sort of Dr. Frankenstein, toiling away in his laboratory, building a socialist monster to destroy the natural order of the free market system. But the New Deal helped to stabilize the country in the short term, and most of the lasting effects have been positive ones. The Great Depression was one of the two most perilous times our nation has ever faced—and unlike the Civil War, the proper course of action wasn't readily apparent. FDR called upon the Brain Trust to develop programs that could help fix what ailed us, and he was largely successful.

Fireside Facts

➤ Roosevelt was a fourth cousin once removed of Ulysses S. Grant, a fourth cousin three times removed of Zachary Taylor, a fifth cousin once removed of his wife Eleanor, a fifth cousin of Teddy Roosevelt, and a seventh cousin once removed of Winston Churchill.

➤ Roosevelt survived an assassination attempt when a mentally deranged man fired shots at him in Miami, Florida. He was riding with Mayor Anton Cermak of Chicago, who was killed.

➤ The NAACP endorsed FDR in 1936, marking a shift of the African-American vote away from the party of Lincoln and to the Democrats.

➤ Roosevelt had a long affair with Lucy Page Mercer, a woman hired as Eleanor's social secretary after FDR was appointed Assistant Secretary of the Navy in 1913. Eleanor discovered the relationship, and Franklin promised to end it, but didn't keep his vow. Mercer was with the President when he died at Warm Springs, Georgia, but she was quickly escorted away before Eleanor arrived.

➤ In 1921, Roosevelt, 39, was vacationing at the family's summer home on Campobello Island, in Canada, when he suffered an attack of poliomyelitis that crippled both of his legs. He discovered that swimming gave his legs the best exercise, and he began spending his vacation time in Warm Springs, Georgia.

Packing It In

Roosevelt's popularity declined with a recession in 1937 after another stock market crash. The second crash somewhat softened the public's opinion that Roosevelt was a mastermind of economic recovery, but elected him to the top spot again in 1940 and 1944.

An unmitigated failure in Roosevelt's second term was his plan to take on the Supreme Court. The president was often at odds with the Supreme Court over its invalidation of much of the early New Deal programs, and he set out to change the court's standards by putting in sympathetic judges. Roosevelt proposed a bill that would have allowed him to appoint one new justice, up to a maximum of six, for every sitting justice of 70 years of age or older with at least 10 years of service. In doing so, he was breaking with established American standards and traditions. Many supporters quickly deserted Roosevelt, and his plan was dead on arrival to Congress. Even Vice President "Cactus Jack" Garner was against the power play, and he walked through the Capitol holding his nose and giving a thumbs-down sign when asked his opinion of the plan.

Even in his time of failure, however, the Supreme Court reversed its own trend of decisions against the New Deal legislation, so many of his initial ideas were allowed to stand.

The Date That Lives in Infamy

By 1940, Roosevelt's popularity was waning a bit, but his experience in world affairs was vitally important because trouble was brewing across the Atlantic. The aftermath of World War I had fostered a second war to dwarf the first. As the fascist rise of the Axis powers was making significant headway toward taking over Europe, Roosevelt asked for—and got—a billion-dollar appropriation for Naval expansion as early as his second term—interesting, considering that isolationism was the lay of the land in the post–World War I United States.

Building Defenses

Roosevelt loved England and his old friend Winston Churchill, and the president made no secret of his partiality to the Allied countries and his loathing of the Nazi Party. A bill was passed in a special session of Congress following the declaration of war on Germany by the Western powers on September 3, 1939. The bill allowed Americans to sell munitions to nations able to pay in cash and carry them away in ships registered abroad and began the revising of neutrality laws.

Prez Says

"Yesterday, December 7, 1941 ... a date which will live in infamy—the United States of America was suddenly and deliberately attacked by the naval and air forces of the Empire of Japan. No matter how long it may take us to overcome this premeditated invasion, the American people in their righteous might will win through to absolute victory."

—FDR, December 8, 1941

After his reelection in 1940, Roosevelt went full steam ahead with his dual policy of building up U.S. defenses while providing assistance to the Allies. The policy fell under the Lend-Lease Act. Roosevelt ignored the isolationist-leaning America First Committee, which included prominent figures such as Charles Lindbergh and influential Montana Democrat Burton K. Wheeler. The act was put in place for the length of World War II and had an initial appropriation of $7 billion. In June 1941, Churchill welcomed Stalin's USSR as a part of the Allies, and the Lend-Lease Act privileges were extended to the Soviet Union.

Meanwhile, in the Far East ...

On the Asian front, Japan was expanding into China, having invaded in 1937 without declaring war. Roosevelt was as pro-China as he was pro-England, but the combination of geographical limitations and isolationism kept him from offering much in the way of assistance. In 1940, Roosevelt's administration ended the commercial treaty between the two countries. Aid to

China was increased, and an embargo was placed on the export of iron, steel scrap, and, most important, oil to Japan.

In the summer of 1941, the Japanese knew that it was the best time to invade islands across Southeast Asia to commandeer petroleum and other necessities. It appeared as though the Nazis would conquer the Soviet Union, and the United States would not be willing to go to war in the Pacific while Germany was conquering so much of Europe. Japan prepared for war while trying to get the oil embargo lifted, but Roosevelt wanted a withdrawal from China and Indochina, along with a promise that Japan would not force its will on other Asian territories. General Tojo Hideki set November 29 as the deadline for a settlement, but a settlement never materialized.

Commander in Chief Lore

One long-standing presidential conspiracy theory is that Roosevelt knew about the attack on Pearl Harbor but let it take place because he didn't want to be seen as the aggressor in a war with Japan. Roosevelt never considered the unthinkable idea of a raid on Hawaii. He did know that war was coming and that Japan would make a move in the near future, but it *is* ludicrous to think that he deliberately left Pearl Harbor vulnerable. The United States would have gone to war after any attack on Pearl Harbor, regardless of the severity of the aftermath of the raid.

Roosevelt felt that war was imminent, but the attack on Pearl Harbor on December 7, 1941, came as a surprise. The military leadership was lax in its preparations. U.S. intelligence had broken a code regarding the attack, but the transmission was not received until the raid was underway. In less than 2 hours, the Japanese sank or damaged 8 battleships and 13 other naval vessels. The attack was a major success for the Japanese, but it ultimately ensured that the Axis powers would lose World War II because it brought the United States into the war the next day. Germany and Italy declared war on the United States three days after that, on December 11. Admiral Isoroku Yamamoto himself told his officers, "I fear we have only awakened a sleeping giant, and his reaction will be terrible."

Roosevelt implemented the massive buildup of the military, which eventually included some 15 million men in the Armed Forces. He also kept the American people abreast of the war effort and constantly reiterated his calls for their support, although his public appearances were becoming scarcer.

Roosevelt, Stalin, and Churchill at Yalta

Roosevelt attended one key summit in February before his death in April 1945: the Yalta Conference at Crimea with Churchill and Stalin. The Yalta Declaration declared that Nazism would be totally destroyed to "ensure that Germany will never be able again to disturb the peace of the world." Roosevelt also attended Yalta to persuade Stalin to declare war on Japan as soon as Germany was defeated. Roosevelt got what he wanted, but Stalin simply broke all his promises.

During the war, Stalin had been an ally, but after the war he openly broke the free election agreements in Eastern Europe outlined at Yalta. In the 1950s, followers of Senator Joseph McCarthy would use the Yalta Agreement as a basis from which to claim that Roosevelt was enamored with Communism and was thus "soft" on Stalin, allowing for Communism's rampant expansion following World War II. Roosevelt was never a Communist, for if he had been he could have stretched his early policies much more to the left. The charge is ironic and shortsighted, given that during Roosevelt's term, even with all of the New Deal experimentation, America never wavered too far from its capitalist foundation.

Roosevelt died on April 12, 1945, at his retreat at Warm Springs, Georgia. He is regarded by many as the greatest president. Whether he actually was is certainly open for debate, but it is hard to argue that there was a greater twentieth-century president. He steered the United States through its worst economic crisis, and he died knowing that American support in the largest world crisis on record ensured victory against fascism.

The Least You Need to Know

➤ Roosevelt came from a wealthy political family, but his popularity grew out of his desire to help average Americans.

➤ The New Deal was a collection of experimental programs to lift the country out of the Great Depression and fundamentally changed the role of the federal government.

➤ Roosevelt achieved great success keeping the country afloat and created important lasting benefits like Social Security.

➤ Roosevelt took the United States into World War II with full force after the bombing of Pearl Harbor.

Chapter 4

The Renaissance President: Thomas Jefferson

> ### In This Chapter
>
> ➤ The educated everyman
>
> ➤ Jefferson declares America's independence
>
> ➤ The deal of the century

Thomas Jefferson was one of the most distinguished political minds in the brief history of the United States, and his name will always be tied to the phrase "All men are created equal," even if that ideal didn't extend to the slaves he owned.

Thomas Jefferson Moves on Up

Thomas Jefferson was born into a prosperous planter's family on a plantation called Shadwell in Albermarle County, Virginia, in 1743. A well-educated boy, Jefferson began his unending and insatiable quest for knowledge attending private schools and acquiring a strong background in Latin, Greek, history, and natural science. His father, Peter Jefferson, became a political leader in the community but died when Jefferson was 14. In March 1760, Jefferson enrolled at the College of William and Mary in Williamsburg, and came under the tutelage of Dr. William Small, who instructed the young scholar in mathematics, metaphysics, and philosophy. Two years later, Jefferson graduated from the College of William and Mary and began studying law under the leading law scholar in the state, George Wythe.

In 1767, Jefferson was admitted to the Virginia bar, and two years later, he began constructing his famous classical estate, Monticello. He was a moderately successful lawyer, although most of his wealth came from the large tract of land he inherited from his father and the land added by his marriage. Jefferson was certainly not all business, though—he enjoyed attending the theater, hunting, fishing, noting the development of his crops, and throwing and attending parties. He practiced law until 1774, when the courts shut down during the American Revolution.

A Colonial Politico

In 1769, Jefferson was elected to the General Assembly, the lower chamber of the state legislature of the Virginia House of Burgesses. He routinely supported the patriots in the events leading up to the Revolutionary War, and his literary skills were used to write resolutions and papers supporting the patriotic leaders.

In 1773, the Virginia Committee of Correspondence was created to keep in touch with patriots throughout the colonies, and a unified movement against the British began to evolve. Jefferson supported the rebels' activities. After the Boston Tea Party, the Governor of Virginia dissolved the General Assembly, Jefferson was elected to a hastily convened Virginia convention in August 1774.

First Family Factuals

On New Year's Day 1772, Jefferson married a wealthy widow, Martha Wayles Skelton. Martha gave birth to 6 children in the 10 years of their marriage, but only 2 lived past infancy: Martha ("Patsy") and Mary ("Polly"). The births took their toll on Martha, and she died in 1782, leaving Jefferson heart–broken and desolate. He never remarried, and his wife had been dead for 19 years when he reached the White House.

Jefferson penned a harsh pamphlet, *A Summary View of the Rights of British America,* an important contribution to the Revolutionary cause. The pamphlet became known as "Mr. Jefferson's Bill of Rights," and it derided British parliamentary rule over the colonies and accented natural rights. The pamphlet appeared in other colonies after its publication in Philadelphia, and Jefferson's reputation as a superb political philosopher and writer began to grow.

The Declaration of Independence

In 1775, Jefferson was a delegate to the state convention in Richmond, which was assembled to debate the outcomes of the First Continental Congress. It was at this convention that Patrick Henry uttered his stirring proclamation, "Give me liberty or give me death." Jefferson agreed, and Virginia joined the other colonies against Great Britain.

With the battles of Lexington and Concord in 1775, the spirit of a total break with Great Britain was in the air, and Jefferson headed to Philadelphia for the Continental Congress. In the summer of 1776, Jefferson was chosen to draft the Declaration of Independence, partly because of his renowned talents with the quill and partly because of his Southern background.

Jefferson succinctly echoed the revolutionary feelings that permeated the colonies in a stunning opening paragraph that has become as fundamental to American ideology as the Stars and Stripes itself. As brilliant as the Declaration of Independence is, however, all good writers need even better editors.

One of Jefferson's early versions read like this:

> *We hold these truths to be sacred & undeniable; that all men are created equal & independent, that from that equal creation they derive rights inherent & inalienable, among which are the preservation of life, & liberty, & the pursuit of happiness.*

After some judicious pruning by fellow conventioneers Benjamin Franklin and John Adams, which in true writerly fashion irritated the author, it was tightened to read like this:

> *We hold these truths to be self-evident, that all men are created equal, that they are endowed by the Creator with certain inalienable rights, that among these are Life, Liberty and the pursuit of Happiness.*

Jefferson was upset that a section against the institution of slavery was dropped from the Declaration of Independence, but it was probably felt that slavery was too hot an issue and would have overshadowed the problem at hand: freedom from the crown. The Declaration of Independence was influenced by European philosophers such as John Locke, but the rights of man had never been presented in such a crisp, dramatic fashion. The document had an immediate impact and has come to be recognized as a cornerstone of democratic ideals. On July 4, 1776, two days after the original Congressional adoption of an independence resolution, Jefferson's version of the Declaration of Independence was officially adopted, severing all political ties to Great Britain.

Back to Virginia to Add to the Freedoms

In 1776, Jefferson left Congress, returned to Virginia, served in the state legislature, where he began writing bill after bill. He began to establish his basic political philosophy that government is for all citizens and that they should have more say in their own affairs. As the "Man of the People," Jefferson advocated land reform because at the time, only landowners could vote. He was moderately successful in abolishing some of the hereditary restrictions that kept land ownership in the hands of a few. He failed in his attempts to outlaw slavery, but eventually, in 1808, he managed to end the foreign importation of slaves. He also wrote detailed plans for a public school system that wouldn't be adopted until years later.

Jefferson considered his most important achievement of his time in the Virginia state legislature to be the bill that encouraged religious freedom and tolerance and established the separation of church and state with the Virginia Statute for Religious Freedom. Taxes traditionally funded the Church of England in Virginia, and Jefferson was determined to ensure that all citizens could worship how they saw fit and that there would be no national denomination.

Jefferson's *Bill for Establishing Religious Freedom* and the statute upon which it was based were the forerunners to the first amendment of the Constitution of the United States. It also earned him the epithet "blaspheming atheist" and haunted him later in a presidential campaign with the charge that he would confiscate all Bibles and have a huge book-burning. Jefferson spent much of his time during these years at Monticello, and he considered retiring to be with his wife and to study his many fields of interest.

The Unpopular Governor Jefferson

In 1779, Jefferson was persuaded to run for governor of Virginia, and he succeeded Patrick Henry. At the time, the Virginia constitution had put all the power in the hands of the legislature, so there was little for him to do. He didn't sufficiently prepare after warnings that a large British force was headed to Virginia, and he would have had a hard time putting together a strong defense anyway with the restrictions on his office. The British soldiers raided the countryside and the city of Richmond. Jefferson himself had to flee, and his reputation was somewhat discredited. In later campaigns, he was called a coward. His conduct was investigated by the legislature, but he was exonerated.

After a single term as governor, Jefferson returned to Monticello and wrote a natural history book, *Notes on the State of Virginia*. It featured ruminations on slavery, political science, agriculture, Native Americans, religion, and whatever else he saw in his home state. The book was published in the United States and Europe, and it gave rise to his reputation as a thinker, scientist, and scholar.

After Martha's death in 1782, Jefferson spent a few months in seclusion and then emerged to rejoin political life in 1783.

Jefferson spent a year in the Continental Congress and recommended ratification of the Treaty of Paris with Great Britain, which ended the Revolutionary

Prez Says

"Almighty God hath created the free mind. All attempts to influence it by temporal punishments or burthens ... are a departure from the plan of the holy author of our religion .... No man shall be compelled to frequent or support any religious worship or ministry or shall otherwise suffer on account of his religious opinions or belief, but all men shall be free to profess, and by argument to maintain, their opinions in matters of religion."

—From *A Bill for Establishing Religious Freedom*, by Thomas Jefferson

Commander in Chief Lore

Jefferson was a Renaissance man through and through. One of the many hats that he sported was that of an inventor. Among other things, Jefferson invented a letter-copying machine, a pedometer, a swivel chair, a lamp-heater, a machine to make fiber from hemp, the dumbwaiter, the Lazy Susan, and a better moldboard on a plow, for which the French awarded him a medal.

War. He also pushed for the adoption of the decimal system of coinage—thus was born the silver dime and the copper penny. He also wrote a proposal for the organization of the Northwest Territory that would prohibit slavery, which eventually became part of the framework of the Northwest Ordinance of 1787. Jefferson attempted to ban slavery in all future states, but the measure was defeated in a close vote.

French Class

In the spring of 1784, Jefferson was appointed as a diplomat to France and joined his old Continental Congress cohorts Ben Franklin and John Adams in arranging trade treaties with the European community. He replaced Franklin as the U.S. minister to France after his retirement. Jefferson was in France during the writing of the Constitution, but he was supportive because he didn't think that the *Articles of Confederation* were strong enough. He was dismayed to learn that the Constitution didn't feature any guarantees of the freedoms of the citizenry, and he wrote back to James Madison that a bill of rights was needed. Madison proposed the first 10 amendments to the Constitution, also known as the Bill of Rights, and Jefferson was entirely satisfied.

Jefferson was in France during the French Revolution. He supported its basic democratic principles, and grew fond of the French people, although he didn't agree with the violent excesses that would come later.

Knowledge Is Power

The **Articles of Confederation** were the loose articles that made up the first Constitution of the United States. They were effective from 1781 to 1788 and gave the federal government very limited powers. The Articles of Confederation handcuffed the federal government's ability to govern, collect taxes, or oversee trade between the states and provided for a single house of Congress.

Jefferson vs. Hamilton

Jefferson accepted George Washington's appointment as Secretary of State and served in the post from 1790 to 1793. Before long, a rivalry developed between Jefferson and Secretary of the Treasury Alexander Hamilton. The two men were diametrically opposed on almost everything. Jefferson favored a government of the people, alliances with France, agrarian economics, and decentralized power; Hamilton preferred power in the hands of aristocrats, alliances with Great Britain, manufacturing and banking, and a strong central government aligned with business. The division between the two men embodied the differences between the two emerging political parties of the day. Hamilton's supporters formed the Federalist Party, and Jefferson's supporters formed the Republican Party (later to become the Democratic-Republican Party and, later still, the Democratic Party).

The National Bank

Initially, Jefferson and Hamilton were able to make a deal in which Jefferson encouraged Southern congressional representatives to allow the federal government to assume war debts. The South had already paid considerably more than the North, but in exchange, the capital was established in what is now Washington, D.C. However, Jefferson and Hamilton soon had a falling out over the founding of a *national bank*.

Knowledge Is Power

The bank of the United States (a **national bank**) was chartered by the federal government and opened in Philadelphia in 1791. It basically served as the government's banker and issued legal tender that could be exchanged for gold. Although it helped put the country on sound currency footing, it was seen as a tool of the aristocratic power brokers, and its charter wasn't renewed in 1811.

Jefferson hated the idea of centralizing financial interests, while Hamilton felt that it would help strengthen the relationship between business and government.

Jefferson argued a "strict construction" interpretation of the Constitution, which meant that if a power wasn't explicitly mentioned in the document, then the power belonged to the people. The Constitution made no mention of a central bank, so such a governmental creation was unconstitutional, according to Jefferson. Hamilton's liberal interpretation of the Constitution's "implied powers"—that the federal government can broadly interpret the Constitution to build a strong central government and, in turn, a stronger America—won out, and President Washington signed a bill in 1791 setting up the Bank of the United States.

A Frenchman Embarrasses Jefferson

In 1793, France and England went to war, which aggravated Jefferson and Hamilton's allegiances to France and England, respectively. However, Jefferson and

Hamilton were both in agreement with President Washington's desire for American neutrality. That same year, Jefferson was embarrassed by French diplomat Citizen Edmond Charles Genet, who came to Washington, ignoring all manners of diplomacy and U.S. neutrality, in an attempt to enlist support for the French. Jefferson went along with Washington's request that France recall Genet.

Jefferson was growing weary of his position as secretary of state and had been making resignation overtures, but Washington kept persuading him to stay. Finally, at the end of 1793, Jefferson permanently retired to Monticello—or so he assumed.

A Federalist President and His Angry Subordinate

Jefferson kept close tabs on national politics after retiring his post, and he was outraged at the terms of the Jay Treaty, which didn't settle any of the commerce or trade issues between the United States and Great Britain, although it did preserve American neutrality. Jefferson was angry with the Federalists in general and felt that Washington had become one of them by supporting the treaty.

As upset as Jefferson might have been with the political climate, he did little to promote his own presidential nomination in 1796, so he was taken by surprise when he finished a close second to new president John Adams. Jefferson lost by three electoral votes, and under the rules of the day, he became vice president. Jefferson's primary duty was to preside over the Senate, which he handled capably, but he became more partisan as his term wore on.

The division between Federalists and Republicans grew widest when Adams passed the notorious Alien and Sedition Acts. The acts placed restrictions on free speech anti-Federalist citizens and convinced Jefferson that the opposition had no respect for the Bill of Rights. Jefferson then secretly wrote the first Kentucky Resolutions, passed by the Kentucky legislature in 1798, and pronounced the Alien and Sedition Acts both unconstitutional and an infringement upon states' rights. Jefferson made a historic stand for civil liberties in the Kentucky Resolutions, but probably would have been disturbed to learn they were later cited as grounds for nullification and secession from the Union.

At the turn of the nineteenth century, political attitudes around the country shifted away from the aristocratic Federalists, and Thomas Jefferson again ran for president. Jefferson and his running mate, Aaron Burr, each garnered sufficient electoral votes to win the election. The electors, however, didn't indicate which of the two was to be president and which was to be vice president. This was simply a misunderstanding, because it had been clear in the campaign that Jefferson would be president and that was the voter's mandate.

According to the Constitution, anytime a presidential candidate doesn't receive an electoral majority, the election goes to the House of Representatives, and Jefferson and Burr had the same number of votes. (This was changed with the twelfth amendment.) The lame-duck Federalist Congress, however, wasn't going to make it easy. For five days, the election outcome was in doubt, until those Federalists who wanted a smooth transition of power voted with those who feared that Burr was a loose cannon. On the thirty-sixth ballot, the "Sage of Monticello" became President of the United States, the first inaugurated in Washington, D.C., which he had helped to design.

Thomas Jefferson, third president of the United States.

THOMAS JEFFERSON
President of the United States

A New Century, a New Party, a New President

Jefferson's inauguration took place March 4, 1801, and he brought a message of unity, proudly declaring, "We are all Republicans, we are all Federalists." He was conciliatory and noted the tolerant, peaceful transfer of power under the Constitution. His first term was successful and relatively quiet, and he worked well with the members of Congress. However, he was at odds with the judiciary from the beginning.

On John Adams' last night in the White House, open federal circuit court judgeships were filled with what came to be called the "midnight appointments"—a last desperate attempt to leave a Federalist mark on the makeup of the courts. Jefferson succeeded in getting the last-minute circuit judgeships eliminated; ordered his Secretary of State (and future fellow President), James Madison, to withhold the remaining commissions; and repealed the Judiciary Act of 1801.

In the landmark *Marbury* v. *Madison* case, Chief Justice John Marshall established the right of judicial review, which gave the Supreme Court the right to declare acts of Congress unconstitutional. The ruling denied William Marbury's request to have his commission from President Adams filled, and upheld the Supreme Court's right to review legislation. Jefferson overstepped his bounds and tried to replace, through impeachment, federalist judges who were commissioned prior to the midnight appointments. His efforts, however, were a total flop, and he lived with the entrenched judiciary.

Jefferson freed all who had been jailed under the Alien and Sedition Acts, got rid of the excise tax that sparked the Whiskey Rebellion, and reduced the size of the government, the Army, and the Navy. And for all of Jefferson's attacks on Hamilton's financial policies, his administration made few changes. Even the Bank of the United States remained relatively intact.

Prez Says

"If there be any among us who would wish to dissolve this Union or to change its republican form, let them stand undisturbed as monuments of the safety with which error of opinion may be tolerated where reason is left free to combat it."

—From Thomas Jefferson's inaugural address, March 4, 1801

A Great Bargain

Ironically, Jefferson's single biggest achievement as president came about by deliberately going against one of his core political values. In 1802, Jefferson learned that Spain was ceding the immense Louisiana Territory to France. He was concerned that the aggressive Napoleon would cut off the large shipping port at New Orleans, which was vital to American commerce. His allegiances had always been with the French, but it was better for the country if the United States bought the area around New Orleans outright. Jefferson told his representative in France, Robert R. Livingston, to try and negotiate the sale, and he sent James Monroe to help.

What happened next was one of the greatest strokes of luck in American history, because Napoleon wanted to unload the entire Louisiana Territory for the low price of $15 million. Jefferson was conflicted because the Constitution said nothing about such a monumental acquisition. He knew that it would take too long to go through the process of adding a Constitutional Amendment, and he was nervous that the offer might get pulled from the table. Jefferson swallowed his strict-construction interpretation of the Constitution and asked the Senate to ratify the treaty immediately, which they did even though every Federalist voted against it on the grounds of unconstitutionality. In 1803, the Louisiana Purchase was added to the United States, and its 800,000 square miles made up the largest land addition in United States history—and Mardi Gras has never been the same since.

Commander in Chief Lore

Jefferson sent two explorers, Meriwether Lewis and William Clark, out West on a congressionally approved journey. He wanted detailed notes of geography, topography, wildlife, peoples, and climate, no doubt in part because of his own deep fascination with science. Lewis and Clark reached the Pacific Ocean and brought back valuable maps and journals of their expedition to the Northwest.

Another Jefferson Memorial

➤ Thomas Jefferson was a violin player, and one of his major attractions to Martha was that she could play the harpsichord.

➤ Jefferson's daughter Martha ("Patsy") gave birth to the first child born in the White House.

➤ Lewis and Clark brought Jefferson bears from their expedition, which were displayed in cages on the White House lawn.

➤ Jefferson sold more than 6,000 books for around $24,000, much less than their value, to rebuild the Library of Congress after it was burned to the ground by the British in the War of 1812.

Second Term Headaches

Jefferson was easily re-elected in 1804, defeating Charles Cotesworth Pinckney 162 to 14 in the electoral college, but his second term caused a lot more stress. The Federalists were on their last leg, so Jefferson's second-term problems came from within his own party, primarily in Congress.

Aaron Burr, National Troublemaker

Jefferson also had to deal with Aaron Burr, who, for starters, killed Alexander Hamilton in a duel in 1804. Burr bolted to the frontier, where historians have theorized that he wanted to create an empire of his own by either seizing Mexico or building a nation within the Louisiana Purchase and starting a war with the Union. Future President

Andrew Jackson was suckered into the fiendish plot, which was brought to Jefferson's attention by Burr's accomplice, General James Wilkinson. Burr was captured on the Mississippi River and brought to Richmond to stand trial for treason. Jefferson was eager to see Burr convicted, but Chief Justice Marshall again cut him down to size by throwing out much of the evidence that didn't meet the constitutional definition of treason. Jefferson took it as a personal insult when Burr was acquitted.

The Embargo Fiasco

American seamen were being forced by the British Navy to restock its manpower through the forcible impressment of American sailors. The United States still maintained its neutrality in the European wars, but the sovereign rights of the young country were ignored by France and England. In 1807, the U.S. frigate the *Chesapeake* was ordered by the British man-of-war *Leopold* to allow for a search; when the Americans refused, they came under fire. Cries of war were heard, but Jefferson wanted to avoid major conflict and tried to use economic pressures.

Jefferson steered the passage of the Embargo Act through Congress in December 1807. The Embargo Act outlawed all exports to Europe and the sailing of American ships to any foreign ports. The act was a disaster because it virtually shut down the economy, especially in the northeastern manufacturing and shipbuilding regions. Within two years, the national income fell by more than 50 percent.

Another problem with the Embargo Act was that smuggling increased substantially, so the civil liberties that President Jefferson held in such high esteem often had to be ignored to enforce the embargo. Following his strict constructionist views, nothing in the Constitution granted him the power to regulate commerce during a time of peace. Doing so was unpopular, and he finally scrapped it a few days before leaving office in favor of the Non-Intercourse Act, which just banned trade with France and Great Britain. Jefferson turned over the reigns to his successor, James Madison, and chose not to run in 1808 because he didn't want presidents treating the office like a throne.

Prez Says

"Never did a prisoner released from his chains feel such relief as I shall on shaking off the shackles of power. Nature intended for me the tranquil pursuits of science, by rendering them my supreme delight ...."

—Thomas Jefferson

Jefferson's Great Hypocrisy

It is no secret that Jefferson, one of the founding fathers of democracy, the "Man of the People," and the author of the line "All men are created equal," owned slaves. He didn't own just a few slaves either, but several hundred—and a handful of these were purchased while he was President of the United States. This is often excused because "times were different," but there was always an abolitionist movement in the United States. More important, however, Jefferson himself tried to have slavery banned in the new territories. He knew that it was fundamentally wrong for the country, but apparently not wrong enough to forgo ownership of humans at Monticello. It is a sadder legacy for Jefferson than for other colonial slave-owners because he seemed completely aware of the inherent evils of slavery. It is also noteworthy that Jefferson didn't even free his slaves on his deathbed, as did George Washington, pending Martha's death.

Throughout the ages, the most intriguing historical note involving the slaves Jefferson owned has been the relationship between Sally Hemings and him. The story has been told since 1802, when James Callender, a long-labeled "scurrilous" (a description that has recently come under question by some historians) journalist with a grudge against the president, starting spreading the story of Jefferson's slave "concubine" in the *Richmond Recorder*. Federalist opponents picked up the story and used it in an effort to discredit him, but the tale also appeared in 1873 as firsthand testimony from two former Monticello slaves, including Sally's son, Madison. The Hemings story has also been kept alive through African-American oral tradition, but was always strongly refuted by keepers of the Jefferson flame.

Circumstantial evidence has been used to bolster the cases of both sides since the scandal first broke. Believers point to the fact that Jefferson, who frequently traveled, was at Monticello nine months before the birth of every one of Hemings' light-skinned children except one, and the fact that his dead wife Martha's father was regarded as Hemings' sire, making them half-sisters. Nonbelievers pointed to one of Jefferson's nephews, either Peter or Samuel Carr, who were known as Monticello philanderers.

So, who got it right? The human details will always be subject to human interpretation, but using the science that Jefferson so revered, it appears that the hand-me-down stories of a sexual affair between the "Sage of Monticello" and Sally Hemings are accurate. In a 1998 article in the scientific journal *Nature,* DNA tests performed on the supposed descendants of Jefferson and Hemings offer evidence that he did father at least one of her children and possibly more, as has long been speculated. The DNA analysis of the Y chromosome was performed by scientists, including noted retired pathologist Eugene A. Foster.

One Last Masterpiece

Jefferson retired to his mountaintop estate for the final 17 years of his life and spent much of his time refurbishing and repairing Monticello. He kept up his many correspondences and rekindled his old friendship with John Adams. He kept abreast of national affairs and accurately predicted the horrific divisiveness of the Union that slavery would soon bring. Jefferson also continued his study of agriculture and his scientific experiments.

The great masterpiece of his later life was founding the University of Virginia at Charlottesville. He did all the legwork: designing the buildings, outlining the curriculum, hiring the staff, and even serving as the first rector. The school opened the year before he died, and he saw his dream of free public education for students from all economic backgrounds come to life at the university level.

In the epitaph he penned for himself, Jefferson conspicuously ignored his presidency, but his legacy is far greater and more influential than his years in the White House. He expanded the United States geographically, politically, scientifically, and philosophically. Thomas Jefferson had his flaws, but his belief in the power of a government for all people is the foundation of American democracy. Fittingly, the man who wrote "All men are created equal" died on Independence Day, 1826.

The Least You Need to Know

➤ Thomas Jefferson was a scientist, musician, philosopher, naturalist, politician, and scholar all rolled into one.

➤ Jefferson wrote the Declaration of Independence and wanted a government without centralized power.

➤ Jefferson doubled the size of the United States by authorizing the Louisiana Purchase, even though it went against his belief in a strict constructionist interpretation of the Constitution.

➤ Jefferson's equality didn't extend to the hundreds of slaves he owned or to the child that he sired with Sally Hemings.

Part 2

Heavyweights

"You know, the greatest epitaph in the country is here in Arizona. It's in Tombstone, Arizona, and this epitaph says, 'Here lies Jack Williams. He done his damnedest.' I think that is the greatest epitaph a man could have. Whenever a man does the best he can, then that is all he can do; and that is what your president has been trying to do for the last three years for this country."

—From remarks by President Harry S. Truman in Winslow, Arizona, June 15, 1948

Harry gave 'em hell, and he now ranks right up near the top, a notch below the legends, but a fine president of the United States nonetheless. The "heavyweights" also includes the ribald, rowdy, Teddy Roosevelt and Andrew Jackson, and the "forgotten" founders John Adams and James K. Polk.

Chapter 5

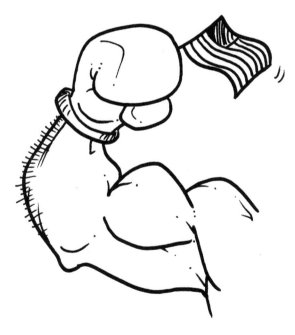

Give 'Em Hell: Harry S. Truman

Historians largely agree on who the best and the worst—or, more accurately, the best and the least effective—presidents have been. Sure, one hears of rankings that place FDR below Harding because of his "activism," say that Thomas Jefferson was overrated due to the slavery issue, or think that Nixon should be on Mount Rushmore after he spent years scrubbing his image, but it is the near-great to the second-rate leaders of the free world over which most heated arguments are waged.

One of the major questions that always stirs debate is whether a president needs to have faced great crises to have achieved greatness. In many ways, that is what separates the near-great from the immortal presidents.

Let's begin with the nasally, unassuming, Missouri farm boy who, after two Puerto Rican nationalists made an attempt on his life, said, "A president has to expect those things."

Born to Believe in Independence

Harry S. Truman was born on May 8, 1884, in Lamar, Missouri, and moved to the small town of Independence in 1890. He was a homebody, as blind as a bat, and a self-described "sissy" who spent his days tickling the ivories and devouring books. He read biographies by the boatload and immersed himself in studying the lives of renowned leaders and the events of military conflicts throughout history.

The Trumans weren't exactly what you would call blue-bloods, and the family's financial difficulties ensured that young Harry would be the last of a dying breed of U.S. presidents: those without a college diploma. Unlike some of his struggling brethren, Truman had such poor eyes that he was ineligible for the service academies.

First Family Factuals

Harry S. Truman met his future wife, Elizabeth "Bess" Wallace, in a Presbyterian Sunday school class when he was all of six years old and she a worldly five. Truman was a shy one, though, and he couldn't muster up the courage to drop a pick-up line until five years later.

Jack-of-Some-Trades

After high school, Truman began a series of jobs, some successful and others that weren't quite as sterling. He basically followed the "anything-for-a-buck" philosophy and changed occupations numerous times. In 1901, he went to work as a timekeeper for the Santa Fe railroad and then relocated to Kansas City to work in local banks—eventually he earned $100 a month as an assistant teller at Union National Bank. In 1906, his parents wanted him to come home and work on the farm—and as with all good sons, the family came first.

For the next 11 years, Truman worked from sunup to sundown plowing, tending to corn and potato crops, and raising hogs—all the efforts that it took to make a living during America's "golden age" of agriculture. He also became active in the community, shedding his reserved nature to follow both his grandfathers into the Masons, and joining Mike Pendergast's Tenth Ward Democratic Club in Kansas City.

One of the Boys of Battery D

Since the death of his father in 1914, Harry Truman had been the primary breadwinner on his family's farm. He had been a member of the National Guard but had been out for six years when, in 1917, Truman enlisted in the United States Army even though he was two years past the age limit set by the Selective Service Act. He wasn't a man who backed down from a challenge, and he saw World War I as both his patriotic duty and the way to make a man out of himself. He memorized the eye chart before his exam and was accepted.

Commander in Chief Lore

Harry Truman may be the most famous failed clothing peddler who ever lived. He and a partner opened the store Truman & Jacobson in November 1919 in Kansas City. At first, the Company D (a.k.a. "Dizzy D") boys repeatedly outfitted themselves in "Captain Harry's" sharp duds, but a depression following World War I hit the heartland hard, and the haberdashery went belly up in 1922. Harry refused to declare bankruptcy and spent the better part of the next two decades strapped for cash as he incrementally paid off his debts.

Once Truman was in the Army, he recruited other Missourians and was elected first lieutenant by the other men of 129th Missouri Field Artillery. In 1918, he set sail for France in command of Battery D and fought in the major battles of Saint-Mihiel and the largest American military action up until that time, the Meuse-Argonne offensive, where he led an artillery battery through the Battle of Argonne. Truman was an effective, popular leader who returned as a major in 1919—making him the only World War I veteran to rise to the presidency—and married the love of his life on a brutally hot day in June at the Trinity Episcopal Church in Independence, Missouri.

The Pros and Cons of the Pendergast

Truman decided to embark on a political career and was quickly assisted by the Pendergast family, who ran the local political organization and dominated Democratic politics. Harry was encouraged by the Pendergasts to run for eastern judge of Jackson County. Their blessing guaranteed votes, so Truman won his first elected office in 1922. The position was administrative rather than judicial, and it dealt primarily with oversight of county road and bridge maintenance.

Correcting an Early Mistake

To curry political favor, Truman initially was advised to join the Ku Klux Klan (KKK), which was growing in popularity in Independence and had thrown its support behind two of his political opponents. He paid his $10 membership, but it was returned after he refused to go along with the KKK's discriminatory policies against blacks, Jews, and Catholics, by saying that he would hire whomever he wanted. Truman wasn't naive, and even to court the Klan was a misstep, especially considering that his battery in France was predominately Catholic, as were the many Irish immigrants loyal to the Pendergasts. But Truman expediently saw the error of his ways and was still able to campaign on his war and farming records.

Truman served the county for a two-year term, but he was voted out of office because the influence of the Klan had grown and their were rumors that he was part Jewish. (The Trumans were blessed in 1924, when their only child, Mary Margaret, was born.) In 1926, Truman was elected to a four-year term as the presiding judge of the entirety of Jackson County, which included more Pendergast supporters than Klans-man in the eastern district. It was a position that gave him much more authority to make decisions regarding the county roads, buildings, expenditures, and collections.

Rage Against the Machine

Truman was always grateful and loyal to the Pendergast machine, but he was never its puppet. In his first four-year term, he cleaned house of those who got their jobs through the spoils system and those who considered kickbacks or lazy days standard protocol. Truman maintained his personal friendship with the Pendergasts, but he told them with typical bluntness that he wanted to hire the best men for local employment.

Truman bucked the system again when he went on a barnstorming tour to raise support for a bond that would raise millions of dollars to build more than 200 miles of roads so that no farmer would be more than 2 miles from one. Truman believed the people would approve the bond as long as they knew that the contracts and internal improvements would be handled fairly and honestly. The bond passed, and within five years the roads were built according to the plans, within the monies raised by the bond, and, as Truman promised, without patronage contracts.

Truman served another four-year term, and in 1934, he assented to Tom Pendergast's request that he run for the U.S. Senate. The combination of the machine's backing, the popularity of his roads, his reputation for integrity, and his endorsement of Roosevelt's New Deal program all helped Truman on to victory and a seat as the Junior Senator from Missouri. Truman was a straight arrow who was a favorite of the Pendergast machine and maintained his ties with the organization. Unbeknownst to him, the machine had become heavily infiltrated by the criminal element and his long-time association cast aspersions on him upon his arrival in Washington.

The Roaring '20s and the days of Prohibition had seen the Pendergast machine become tied to gangsters, who were under a White House investigation. Truman was thought to be a gangster lackey, but he quietly went about his business and eventually earned the respect of influential senators as he supported the New Deal legislation sent by Roosevelt.

Truman was named to both the Interstate Commerce Committee and the Appropriations Committee, and he helped to craft the Civil Aeronautics Act of 1938, which brought uniform standards to the aviation industry and recommended railroad reforms in the Transportation Act of 1940. Even after Tom Pendergast was sent to prison on tax evasion charges, Truman was reelected, although his opponents made sport of his ties to the machine. However, there was never any evidence of malfeasance whatsoever at any point in Truman's career. Still, it was his numerous trips across the state of Missouri and his effective speeches to his constituents that kept him in Congress.

Cleaning Up on the National Stage

Truman became one of the most popular senators among his brethren. He loved the camaraderie and the after-work cocktail and bull sessions. He began to make a name for himself on the national stage after he was named the head of the Senate Special Committee to Investigate the National Defense Program, more commonly called the Truman Committee.

As the country was preparing for World War II, defense contracts were being issued, and Truman had already gotten wind of some of the colossal waste in the defense program. The Truman Committee held hearings, and during a cross-country trip over the course of two years, found that the military was throwing money to contractors in fixed fees. Among all sorts of waste, the committee also uncovered cheaply made raw materials, shabbily built engines, and a secretive project that had $25 million earmarked for military construction in Canada and Alaska. Politicians and the public roundly praised the Truman Committee's work as the greatest congressional investigation in history. Estimates have put the savings in the neighborhood of $15 billion, while the effort cost only $400,000. And there, at the center of the savings, was the vibrant, folksy man who would soon become vice president.

Prez Says

"A politician is a man who is interested in good government .... I would risk my reputation and my fortune with a professional politician sooner than I would with the banker or the businessman or the publisher of a daily paper. More young men and young women should fit themselves for politics and government."

—Harry S. Truman

"From Precinct to President"

FDR was gearing up for his fourth White House campaign as the country endured its third year of involvement in World War II. Prior to the July 1944 convention in Chicago, Roosevelt decided that he needed a new vice president. Roosevelt's failing health necessitated a man who would be popular within the party, and he knew his ardently liberal vice president, Henry Wallace, wouldn't be able to fill those shoes. Truman was a strong supporter of FDR throughout the war, railing against isolationism and calling for a strategic second front in Europe to take the pressure off Russia. Roosevelt cajoled Truman into joining him on the ticket. Truman was not seeking the nomination, but he could not turn Roosevelt down, especially when the President cautioned that the Democratic Party might unravel in the middle of World War II. Truman was nominated on the second ballot, and "the mousy little man from Missouri," as *Time* magazine called him, was sworn in as Vice President on January 20, 1945.

Commander in Chief Lore

During his brief stint as vice president, Truman raised some eyebrows for attending the funeral of Tom Pendergast in Kansas City. Photographs showed the acting Vice President paying his respects to a convicted criminal, but many Americans admired a man who didn't turn his back on his roots.

Only 82 days after he was sworn in as vice president, Harry Truman took a call in House Speaker Sam Rayburn's private Capitol hideaway, a room where Truman had regularly enjoyed drinks with his select Senate peers. The call instructed him to come to the White House right away, where Eleanor Roosevelt greeted Truman, put her arm on his shoulder, and said simply, "Harry, the president is dead." He replied, "Is there anything I can do for you?" To which Mrs. Roosevelt famously answered, "Is there anything we can do for you? For you are the one in trouble now." And on April 12, 1945, at 7:09 P.M., Truman was sworn in as president by Chief Justice Harlan F. Stone.

The Whole World in His Hands

Truman had gone from, in his words, "precinct to president" in a whirlwind, catapulting to the top during a major world crisis. American casualties were averaging more than 900 a day, victory in the Pacific wasn't imminent, he had no relationship with Stalin or Churchill, and he had no experience in foreign relations on a global scale. There was trepidation across the country.

Truman was now walking in the shadow of Franklin Delano Roosevelt, one of the greatest leaders the United States had ever known. Had Roosevelt spent significant time with the new vice president, maybe Truman could have taken over the White House with a measure of confidence—or at least comfort. Unfortunately, Truman and Roosevelt had spoken only twice outside of Cabinet meetings, and important issues were never on the table.

Roosevelt had kept Truman in the dark on his plans, but after a few weeks of briefings from Roosevelt's aides, the new president followed the policies in place. Privately, Truman was frightened by the position he found himself in, but publicly he knew that he needed to give off an air of strength to provide the country with a modicum of security. He didn't waver at all in insisting on unconditional Nazi surrender, and he got it on Victory in Europe Day. (VE-Day coincided with his sixty-first birthday on May 8, 1945.)

Truman requested that the first gathering of the United Nations meet in April in San Francisco, as Roosevelt had scheduled. Later, in June, he addressed the final session and within a week presented the United Nations Charter to Congress for ratification. Isolationism was no longer the central tenant of U.S. foreign policy.

In July 1945, Truman set off for the Potsdam Conference in Germany to decide how to implement the decisions made at Yalta. He met with Joseph Stalin, Winston Churchill, and Clement Attlee (Churchill's successor as Prime Minister), and control of Germany was transferred to French, Soviet, U.S., and British military commanders until a permanent government was instituted. The Potsdam Conference also outlawed the Nazi Party, limited remilitarization, and set the framework for a tribunal to prosecute perpetrators of war crimes. On July 26, Truman issued the Potsdam Declaration, calling for Japan's unconditional surrender and listed terms of peace.

Harry S. Truman, thirty-third president of the United States.

"Little Boy" and "Fat Man"

Harry Truman was briefed about the development of the atomic bomb shortly after taking over the presidency. On Monday, July 16, 1945, the development became a reality when the first nuclear weapon in history exploded at Alamogordo Air Base in the desert of New Mexico. Two days later, Truman was informed of the successful attempt, and after Japan rejected the Postdam Declaration, Truman made the decision to drop the bomb on Japan.

Two atomic bombs were constructed—"Little Boy" and "Fat Man." On August 6, 1945, 9:15 A.M. Tokyo time (August 5, 7:15 P.M. Washington, D.C., time) Little Boy was dropped by a single B-29 on Hiroshima, effectively leveling the city, killing an estimated 80,000 instantly, and killing over 50,000 from radiation and other related injuries over the following months. On August 8, Stalin invaded Manchuria and Korea, joining in the Pacific conflict on the last day of the war. The following day, after Truman received no communications from Japan, the "Fat Man" was dropped on Nagasaki, destroying a third of the city and killing an estimated 70,000.

A number of criticisms have been leveled at Truman for his decision to drop the bomb on Japan. It has been argued that Japan was losing the war and, therefore, the atomic bomb was unnecessary. Truman's military advisers, however, warned that Japan would fight without surrender to the last man (not a single Japanese unit had surrendered throughout the war). Furthermore, they warned, a full year of war could lead to upward of 250,000 to 500,000 American casualties, which definitely would be avoided by dropping the atomic bomb.

There has also been revisionist speculation that the bomb was used largely as a political tool to throw a scare into the Soviet Union. Undoubtedly, Truman and his advisers were aware that the Soviet Union would see the United States' willingness to use the bomb as a threat. However, to make the charge that Truman's decision to use the atomic bomb was motivated largely by considerations other than the war at hand is a far more cynical charge. It also must be noted that there was little opposition to the atom bomb as a means to end World War II at the time and most of the opposition to Truman's decision came later, during the mid-1960s.

On August 14, 1945, Japan surrendered. World War II was over. Harry S. Truman had been blind-sided by fate, thrust onto center stage in a war the likes of which the globe had never seen, and he ended it. For those convinced that Truman made the wrong decision, perhaps it is worth remembering that neither Churchill nor Roosevelt ever expressed a reservation to use atomic weapons if it meant an Allied victory. The use of the atomic bomb certainly had horrific consequences for Japan, but the lives of many American (and Allied) soldiers were saved when they were able to return home.

No Falsehoods About Truman

➤ The "S" in Harry S. Truman was a family compromise between two grandfathers, Anderson Shipp Truman and Solomon Young (and yes, the period is standard).

➤ Truman garnered considerable criticism spending $10,000 to add a balcony behind the pillars of the South Portico of the Blue Room of the White House.

➤ Truman delivered the first address by a president to the NAACP on June 29, 1947. He spoke from the steps of the Lincoln Memorial and called for immediate civil rights for all citizens.

➤ Truman became a hero in Mexico and helped relations with the United States' southern neighbors when he made an unscheduled stop at Stone monument, which bears the names of six teenagers who were killed in the Mexican-American War when U.S. troops stormed Chapultepec Castle in 1847.

➤ Harry Truman gave the first televised State of the Union address in 1947.

From Hero to Goat to Hell-Giving Survivor

When World War II ended, Harry Truman turned his attention to keeping the country's economy humming. Truman thought he would be able to institute additional progressive policies in the style of the New Deal, but the common good that united American citizens during World War II disappeared.

In September 1945, Truman outlined his plan in a message to Congress. In it, he asked for sweeping progressive measures, including a permanent Fair Employment Practices Commission to aid African Americans, an increase in unemployment compensation, an immediate raise in minimum wage, crop insurance for farmers, federal housing money, wage and price controls to stave off inflation, and national health insurance. The coalition of Dixiecrats and Republicans who had stilted FDR in his later stages thought the New Deal was dead. Again, they quickly teamed up to stymie the bulk of Truman's agenda.

Not everything Truman did required the help of Congress. One major achievement of Truman's presidency was the desegregation of the United States' armed forces, which came by Executive Order 9981 after Congress refused to do so. One of the main reasons he demanded it was the disgust he felt that black World War II veterans were being beaten and lynched in the South after having served their country with honor. This was one of the first major civil rights initiatives.

In general, Truman was handcuffed and wasn't able to accomplish much else domestically, especially after the Republicans swept both houses in the 1946 midterm elections. Inflation was rising, and Truman's popularity was sinking faster than a mob snitch in cement shoes, especially as labor unrest led to strike upon strike across the country. In response, and over Truman's veto, Congress passed the Taft-Hartley Act in 1947, which regulated the power of labor unions and allowed court orders to halt strikes that affected national interests.

Meanwhile, Back in Europe ...

As if Harry Truman didn't have enough problems to deal with at home, much of the globe was rapidly turning a menacing shade of red. Joseph Stalin refused to follow the stipulations hammered out at Yalta and Potsdam, and the tentacles of the Communist octopus were beginning to stretch across Eastern Europe. It was the beginning of the Cold War. Tensions grew on each side, and Truman took a "get tough" approach, refusing to send promised reparations from Germany to Stalin's ravaged Soviet Union.

Prez Says

"At the present moment in world history nearly every nation must choose between alternative ways of life. The choice is too often not a free one ....

I believe that it must be the policy of the United States to support free peoples who are resisting attempted subjugation by armed minorities or by outside pressures."

—Harry S. Truman

An early stance against communism took place in the Balkan Peninsula. In 1947, Greece was receiving aid from Great Britain for its civil war against Communist-backed rebels. Prime Minister Attlee told Truman that Britain was having financial difficulties and could no longer assist Greece. Truman proposed two steps, which were outlined in a speech to a joint session of Congress on March 12. The "Truman Doctrine," as it came to be known, called for U.S. aid to Turkey and Greece, and it explained why the United States needed to take the lead role in preventing the spread of communism. It was an early line in the sand against the USSR and a show of support for a sovereign Western Europe.

The official beginning of the Cold War is an oft-debated topic, but the $400 million sent to Greece and Turkey under the auspices of the Truman Doctrine was the beginning of the "containment" of communism. The United States would confront the Soviets whenever they tried to exert their influence and ideology.

Some of Truman's most important work during his first years as president ...

➤ **Marshall Plan.** Truman and Secretary of State George Marshall drew up a plan for reconstructing war-torn Europe, opening markets for trade, and promoting democratic governments. At Harvard University in June 1947, Marshall announced that the United States would fund a cooperative economic rebuilding plan to be drawn up by European nations. Russia was invited to join but balked at working alongside capitalistic countries and instituted its own plan to refurbish the communist states. The Marshall Plan sent almost $13 billion to Europe over the next four years, and it helped to secure a free Western Europe that wouldn't fall to the Soviet Empire. This was one of the great foreign policy achievements in the history of the United States.

➤ **Berlin airlift.** By agreement at the end of World War II, the Soviet Union occupied East Germany, which surrounded Berlin—a part of West Germany—and the Soviets attempted to show up the Allies by implementing a blockade on all rail, water, and highway traffic into the Western city. The food supplies in Berlin would last only a month, and there were American troops stationed there. This was a crucial moment because war over Berlin was a legitimate consideration. Truman instead decided on an around-the-clock airlift of essential supplies that lasted from June 1948 until May 1949, when the blockade was halted. It was a triumph for containment policy and kept the city of Berlin free, until the wall split it in half.

➤ **Recognition of Israel.** Truman sympathized with Jewish survivors of Nazi Germany, and he supported the United Nations partition of Palestine into separate Jewish and Arab states. He officially recognized the state of Israel on May 14, 1948.

By 1948, the economy was skyrocketing, so one might have thought that this would be enough to earn Truman the respect and backing of, at the very least, his own party. No such luck. So, Truman took his message directly to the people and astounded many Americans in what might be the greatest presidential campaign of all time.

Whistle-Stopping to the Top

As the 1948 elections approached, Truman was one of the most unpopular denizens of the White House in terms of the support of his party. He had gotten the ire up of Southern Democrats in February 1948 by asking for broad legislation based on the findings of his Civil Rights Commission. His many program initiatives included antilynching laws, protection of voters' rights throughout the land, elimination of the *poll tax* in the Southern states that still enforced it, and the repeal of *Jim Crow laws.* He also asked Congress to settle claims made by Japanese Americans who had been herded into internment camps during World War II. Truman looked no further than the Constitution

Knowledge Is Power

A **poll tax** was a steep levy upon blacks that had to be paid before they could vote. The **Jim Crow laws** were laws that maintained segregation in the South and kept African Americans from such things as equal ownership of property, voting rights, and job discrimination.

and the Bill of Rights for the basis of attempting to destroy discrimination and the entrenched segregation that permeated the South.

As the 1948 presidential election approached, Truman's party appeared to be in disarray. Northern Democrats meekly tried to add civil rights measures to the party platform, but by then many liberals had jumped ship to align themselves with Henry Wallace's Progressive Party. Southern Senators bolted from the Democratic Party as quickly as one can say "All men are created equal." Led by then Governor of South Carolina Strom Thurmond, they formed the States Rights Democrats, also called the Dixiecrats. Other Democrats were calling for Truman to step down and allow war hero General Eisenhower to run (which probably wouldn't have worked because he was a Republican). And, to top it off, in a nationwide *Newsweek* poll of 50 top political commentators who were asked to predict the outcome of the election, Republican candidate Tom Dewey was favored to win by all 50. By all estimations, the sitting president was a sitting duck.

Truman spoke to the moribund Democratic convention and, through the sheer force of conviction that, by God, they were going to win, brought them to their feet in a great roar. Truman told his constituents that he was calling a special session of Congress in July to give Republicans a chance to fulfill their party platform promises. When no important legislation was passed, Truman had his foil, the "do-nothing" Republican eightieth Congress.

Commander in Chief Lore

In a famous American photograph, Truman is holding up a copy of the *Chicago Daily Tribune* with an enormous smile across his face. Everyone was sure that Harry was a sure bet to lose, so after the polls closed but before the results were tabulated, the paper ran with the headline "Dewey Defeats Truman."

Truman jumped on a train and embarked on a massive whistle-stop campaign across the country, barnstorming from town to town and detailing his record to the working people, the average citizens. Truman was no Roosevelt, but it probably helped him in this case because his appeal was as a down-to-earth, workaday Joe, not as a statesman. He would often fumble through speeches, but when he made a mistake, he started over. There was an utter lack of pretentiousness in this Midwestern boy, and crowds ate it up. He even brought out his wife, Bess, sometimes referring to her as "my boss."

And somewhere early along the line, someone shouted out, "Give 'em Hell, Harry," and the slogan stuck with him across the estimated 25,000 to 30,000 miles he covered by train and in his upward of 350 speeches.

Truman's nonstop whistle-stop campaign led to what is probably the biggest upset in the history of presidential elections. If anything, Truman's victory bolstered his efforts to work for civil rights legislation, and one effective measure he was able to pass was the Housing Act of 1949, which allocated federal money for urban renewal and public housing.

Four More Years, Many More Problems

Truman's inaugural address focused on foreign policy and a "four points" plan basically aimed at the Kremlin. The four points were American support of the United Nations, the continuation of the Marshall Plan, a defense collective of free nations against communism, and a pledge to aid underdeveloped countries, particularly in technological know-how.

The defense alliance was quickly assembled, and the North Atlantic Treaty was signed on April 4, 1949. Western Europe was thrilled to have a solid secure bloc in place because Stalin was tightening the noose in Eastern Europe. The Senate ratified the treaty, and Truman put General Eisenhower in charge of NATO in December 1950.

The Long, Cold "War" in Asia Takes Root

Coming at the heels of the Communist takeover of China by Mao Tse-tung in 1949, Truman's containment policy was given its first major test after Communist North Korea invaded South Korea. The North Korean army was backed and supplied by the Soviet Union. On June 27, 1950, the United Nations Security Council ordered sanctions against North Korea and Truman authorized involvement of air and naval forces. Three days later, Truman authorized the military intervention of American ground troops "police action," as it was called. Later in life, Truman would say that the decision was harder to make than dropping the bomb, because that had ended a world war; he didn't want to open the global can of worms again. A few critics noted that only Congress had the ability to authorize the military action he had ordered, but it was roundly accepted and the constitutionality of his decision was not a major issue.

MacArthur Gets His Walking Papers

As the war in Korea escalated, the Chinese entered the "police action," and the president decided to abandon his plans for a reunified Korea. He settled upon the division at the 38th parallel. The Chinese quickly drove anti-Communist troops back to South Korea. General Douglas MacArthur, commander of the United Nations forces, publicly declared his desire to invade Communist China and then publicly criticized

Truman's policies. The egotistical general had gone too far, and he was relieved of his command on April 11, 1951. The Korean "police action" was successful in its primary goal of containing the spread of communism into South Korea and averting a full-scale war, but the original goal of a unified Korea was too great a risk. Ironically, back home, the Truman Administration was taking a beating in some right-wing circles as being "soft" on communism. The smear campaign was spearheaded by Senator Joseph McCarthy, whom Truman despised.

Commander in Chief Lore

When Wisconsin Senator Joseph McCarthy began his campaign of red-baiting and claimed to have a list of 205 known Communists working in the State Department, Truman said of McCarthy and his followers that they were "chipping away our basic freedoms as insidiously and far more effectively than the Communists have ever been able to do."

Independence Once Again

Harry Truman announced he would not seek the nomination in 1952 and weathered one more storm that April when he seized control of the country's steel mills to avert a walkout threatened by the steelworkers during the Korean War (which wouldn't end until 1953). That summer, the Supreme Court declared the seizure unconstitutional.

As the Republicans took control of the White House, Harry and Bess Truman returned to Independence and moved into the same house at 219 North Delaware Street that had been their residence since they were married. The Trumans traveled extensively, and the ex-president often spoke to college students about life in the American government and civic responsibility. Truman died on December 26, 1972, after slipping into a coma on Christmas morning. He was buried on the grounds of the Truman Library, and his long-life sweetheart, Bess, joined him 10 years later.

At the time Truman left office, he was not regarded very highly, but his stock has risen dramatically in the years since he left office. Had he been able to secure more of his domestic legislation, most of which passed in some form in the following decades, he might stand with the best presidents this country ever had. He faced more serious foreign policy situations than any other president because for the first time man had the nuclear capacity to wipe out cities in seconds and World War II was the largest conflict in the atomic age. He stood up to communism and set the course of the Cold War. Always unassuming and folksy, he took responsibility for his actions and followed his conscience. Of Truman, George Marshall may have nailed it on the head when he said "the full stature of this man will only be proven by history."

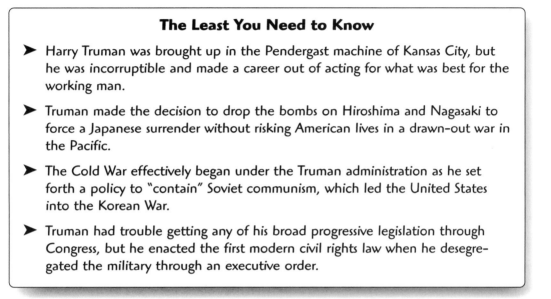

The Least You Need to Know

➤ Harry Truman was brought up in the Pendergast machine of Kansas City, but he was incorruptible and made a career out of acting for what was best for the working man.

➤ Truman made the decision to drop the bombs on Hiroshima and Nagasaki to force a Japanese surrender without risking American lives in a drawn-out war in the Pacific.

➤ The Cold War effectively began under the Truman administration as he set forth a policy to "contain" Soviet communism, which led the United States into the Korean War.

➤ Truman had trouble getting any of his broad progressive legislation through Congress, but he enacted the first modern civil rights law when he desegregated the military through an executive order.

Chapter 6

Teddy Roosevelt: Truly One of a Kind

In This Chapter

➤ A horrific day in February

➤ Who you gonna' call? Trust-buster

➤ Did Teddy save the NFL?

➤ Cutting through the bull with the Bull Moose

The United States of America has truly had only one president of the likes of Theodore Roosevelt. His boundless energy, mammoth interests, and firm belief in getting things done have made him a favorite of historians and the general public alike. There is always debate over who has best served the country in the executive office, but much less over who was the most dynamic.

Start Spreading the News ...

In October, 1858, Theodore Roosevelt became the only president born in New York City. The Roosevelts were wealthy and were able to afford tutors to educate their son and take him on trips to Europe and Egypt. In 1872 and 1873, Theodore Roosevelt lived with a family in Germany to broaden his horizons. He loved books and learning, particularly military history and natural science. He also loved to explore the wilds that, at the time, were still to be found in and around Gotham, and he constantly brought home animals.

Young "Teedie" was a small, sickly child, suffering from asthma and poor eyesight, and he took a strenuous exercise program in the gymnasium his father built on the second floor of their 20th Street brownstone. He partook in boxing, wrestling, hunting, tennis, judo, swimming, and eventually would accept almost any physical challenge put to him. All the traits that would define Theodore Roosevelt as an adult were there in his rambunctious, precocious childhood.

In 1876, Roosevelt entered Harvard College and worked hard to reach the top of his class; the efforts paid off when was elected to membership in Phi Beta Kappa. Roosevelt took numerous science courses and broke with upper-crust tradition by engaging in athletics and taking jaunts into the New England wilderness. After he graduated at 21, he spent the summer on a long hunting trip in the Midwest with his brother, Elliott, before returning to attend law school at Columbia.

Roosevelt found the study of law boring, but it did give him the chance to pen his first scholarly book, *The Naval War of 1812*. He had started researching it while at Harvard, and this was the first of many tomes that Roosevelt would author over the course of his life. Roosevelt always had a big-plate agenda, and besides being an author at a young age he also stated that he "intended to be one of the governing class," and a local Republican club asked if he would be nominee for the state assembly. He accepted on October 28, 1881, and 12 days later he was a 23-year-old New York State assemblyman.

First Family Factuals

In 1880, Theodore Roosevelt married Alice Hathaway Lee, daughter of a Boston blue-blood banker. Roosevelt began courting her when he was 21 years old; "Sunshine," as her friends called her, was only 17.

Upon his arrival in Albany, Roosevelt was mocked for his fancy clothes and his Ivy-League education. It didn't take long for him to make a name for himself, though, because he called for an investigation into the corrupt dealings of railroad bigwig Jay Gould and exposed a crooked judge. He also worked well with the other parties and Democratic Governor Grover Cleveland. Roosevelt became leader of the minority party, but his reform-oriented ideas, didn't sit well with the party leaders. Nevertheless, in 1884, he was made chairman of the New York State delegation to the Republican National Convention in Chicago and campaigned for nominee James Blaine (even though he was initially opposed to him as the candidate).

A Devastating Valentine's Day

On February 13, 1884, Roosevelt was on his way back from Albany to New York City because he had received two telegrams: one joyful, announcing the birth of his daughter, Alice Lee; and one ominous, stating that his wife had become ill after the delivery. Roosevelt got home as quickly as he could and was horrified to find that both his wife and his mother were dying. Alice was stricken with Blight's disease and barely recognized her husband, and his mother had contracted typhoid fever. On the morning of February 14, Roosevelt's mother died—a few hours later, his wife followed suit. Roosevelt was grief-stricken after losing the two most important women in his life, but he managed to complete his term in Albany.

Roosevelt dealt with the deaths of his wife and mother by heading west to try his hand at cattle ranching in the isolation of the Dakota Territory Badlands. Over the next few years, he lived the life of a cowboy and a deputy sheriff, and he even helped capture a group of thieves. He did a lot of writing, including magazine articles and a book titled *Hunting Trips of a Ranchman*. Roosevelt left the ranch and headed back east in 1886, but he continued writing about life in the West—he wrote a monumental four-volume work, *The Winning of the West,* on the subject. His tales of frontier life inspired a lot of affluent Easterner tourism, which led to the creation of "dude ranches."

Roosevelt was heartbroken after Alice's death and wrote a memorial to her while out West, but curiously, after circulating it among the family, he never spoke of her again, even to their daughter. At first, he made note of wanting to remain faithful to Alice forever, but there was still a childhood sweetheart around named Edith Kermit Carow. Roosevelt tried to avoid her for a time, but in 1885, the two ran into one another at his sister Anna's house; it wasn't long before they fell in love again.

On December 2, 1886, Roosevelt married Edith in London, where her mother lived. They then returned to New York to the house he had just built on Sagamore Hill in Oyster Bay, Long Island. The couple had five children—Theodore Jr., Kermit, Ethel, Archibald, and Quentin—and also raised Roosevelt's young Alice. The children would go by the name of the "Roosevelt Gang" during the time they lived in the White House.

Back in the Race ...

Roosevelt spent the better part of the years 1886 through 1889 at Sagamore Hill living, writing, raising his children, and enjoying the life of a sportsman. He ran for mayor of New York City in 1889 but finished a disappointing third, behind a third-party Socialist candidate who siphoned votes off the Democratic winner. Roosevelt's political future outlook wasn't rosy, and for a time he was content to be with his new bride and ever-growing family.

Roosevelt's fortunes changed after 1888, however, when he actively campaigned for Benjamin Harrison and against patronage. Harrison rewarded the energetic Roosevelt by appointing him U.S. Civil Service Commissioner in 1889. His belief in the inherent corruptness of the spoils system led him to make a lot of changes: Examinations were revised, rampant fraud was exposed and rooted out, women were given the same opportunities as men for some positions, and competition for federal jobs was substantially increased. Roosevelt was so effective that an old Democratic co-worker from his Albany days, President Grover Cleveland, reappointed him in 1892.

Roosevelt's reputation as a reformer grew rapidly with the rise of progressive sentiments, and in 1895, he accepted the job of president of New York City's Police Commission. It was a turbulent task because he had to do battle with Tammany Hall and
its illicit ways, as well as big-money interests who wanted to maintain the status quo
and who didn't care for reform. Roosevelt learned firsthand about life in the city's
slums and how alliances between criminals and cops maintained that life. He was
moved by a popular book by Jacob Riis, *How the Other Half Lives,* which detailed the effects of poverty. Roosevelt drew plenty of attention to the problems of police corruption—and to himself—during his two-year stint as the head of New York City's Police Commission.

President William McKinley appointed Roosevelt as Assistant Secretary of the Navy in 1897, even though there was concern that the New Yorker was a bit too prowar. Roosevelt had a romantic image of warfare throughout his life and advocated a strong navy. Before long, he was overshadowing John D. Long, the official Secretary of the Navy.

Prez Says

"No triumph of peace is quite so great as the supreme triumph of war."

—Theodore Roosevelt

Commander in Chief Lore

One of Roosevelt's more flamboyant practices was his nocturnal habit of roaming the
streets of New York City in a black cape and a wide-brimmed hat pulled down over his
face while on the lookout for police officers who were derelict in their duties. The public
initially praised his efforts, but enthusiasm waned when he began to enforce the Sunday
blue laws, which closed beer gardens and saloons on Sunday.

On February 15, 1898, the U.S. battleship *Maine* suffered a mysterious explosion in
the harbor of Havana, Cuba, which was then controlled by Spain. Though the cause
of the explosion was unknown and only years later thought perhaps to have resulted
from spontaneous combustion, Roosevelt privately told friends that President McKinley had "no more backbone than a chocolate èclair" because he wouldn't go to war
with Spain. On April 20, 1898, McKinley approved a congressional resolution calling
for the prompt withdrawal of Cuba by Spain. On April 24, the Spanish government

declared war against the United States, and the next day the United States declared war on Spain. On April 30, the United States attacked the Spanish fleet in Manila Bay, and Roosevelt had the war he was after.

Rough Riders, Mount Up!

Roosevelt was eager to see some action and quickly tired of his administrative duties. He resigned his naval post in May and accepted a commission as lieutenant colonel under Leonard Wood in the Volunteer 1st Cavalry. He quickly recruited an outfit of legendary cowboys and ranch hands from the West, and college graduates and socialites from the East. The group was given the tag "Rough Riders," and Roosevelt maneuvered to get the group on transports to Cuba.

On July 1, 1898, Roosevelt sealed his legendary battlefield status when he led a charge up Kettle Hill (which he referred to as the "San Juan Charge") under heavy enemy fire. Roosevelt lost a quarter of his men, but they were able to take the hill outside the main city of Santiago. The exploits of the Rough Riders—and Roosevelt, in particular—were splashed across newspapers throughout the country; by the time the war ended two weeks later, Roosevelt was a renowned folk hero. He was promoted to colonel, and his popularity shot up again when he worked diligently to get his men home after the Cuban surrender and an outbreak of yellow fever. Years later, Roosevelt would say, "San Juan was the great day of my life."

With Trademark Gusto, Roosevelt Dives Into Politics

Upon his return to New York City from Cuba, Roosevelt was immediately courted to be the Republican nominee for governor. He campaigned tirelessly and was elected, but by a slim margin of fewer than 18,000 votes. His term didn't include any significant reform legislation, and his unpredictable ways alienated him from Republican leaders. Roosevelt supported prolabor initiatives, while simultaneously calling out the National Guard to quell a strike. He took steps to deal with inner-city strife and to outlaw discrimination in the schools, and he devoted himself to conservation issues. Roosevelt had some success as governor, but he lost the support of the Republican Party along the way, particularly when he forced through a tax on corporation franchises.

Prez Says

"There is a widespread conviction in the minds of the American people that the great corporations known as trusts are in certain of their features and tendencies hurtful to the general welfare .... Corporations engaged in interstate commerce should be regulated if they are found to exercise a license working to the public injury. It should be as much the aim of those who seek for social betterment to rid the business world of crimes of cunning as to rid the entire body politic of crimes of violence."

—From Theodore Roosevelt's address to Congress, December, 1901

In early 1900, the Republicans made it clear that they had had enough of the zealous reformer and set out to replace Roosevelt. At the Philadelphia convention in June, the Republican machine decided to nominate him to be McKinley's vice presidential running mate.

At that time a vice presidential spot doomed one to political obscurity, and Roosevelt had mixed feelings about the position. On the one hand, it offered him the chance to be part of the national ticket—but on the other hand, he recognized the severe limitations of the office. His wife, Edith, was against the idea of her husband serving as vice president because she knew that he would be bored presiding over the Senate. The problem was that although Roosevelt had popularity among the masses, he had almost no political base within the Republican Party with which to seek another office, so he took his party's offer. Not everyone was thrilled, though: Republican national chairman Mark Hanna asked, "Don't any of you realize that there's only one life between this madman and the White House?"

Commander in Chief Lore

It was during his time as governor in New York, that Roosevelt told a friend, "I have always been fond of the West African proverb: 'Speak softly and carry a big stick—you will go far.'" Roosevelt used it in a response to Tom Platt, the head of the New York State Republican machine. The proverb became Roosevelt's mantra and is still one of the most famous political platitudes in the history of the United States.

Roosevelt again campaigned nonstop and made hundreds of speeches across the country, while McKinley basically stayed home. They won in a landslide, but six months into his second term, McKinley was shot in Buffalo, New York by an unemployed millworker anarchist named Leon F. Czolgosz who had a self-professed desire to kill a leader. Assured that his boss was going to be fine, Roosevelt went camping with his family in the Adirondack Mountains. A guide was sent to retrieve him, they returned to Buffalo, and at the age of 42, Roosevelt took the oath of office, becoming the youngest President of the United States in history.

A President for the People

Roosevelt was not one to follow the conservative policies of his Republican predecessors, and he aggressively set out to use the presidency for the betterment of society as he saw fit. Initially, he lay low, retaining all of McKinley's Cabinet and saying all the things that big business wanted to hear. He didn't stay low for long, though. In December, he delivered his first address to Congress and made it known that he wasn't going to be Wall Street's puppet.

Roosevelt used the *bully pulpit* of the presidency on a regular basis and was perhaps the greatest sermonizer to ever reside in the White House. He could be self-righteous in his words and foolish in his reckless behavior, but Americans loved his spirit and dedication. Roosevelt was a man who passionately followed an independent course of action, and his handling of the business trusts is one of the best examples.

Coal Miner's Defender

In 1902, a 140,000-man coal strike depleted the national supply. By autumn, hospitals and schools, which relied on coal back then, couldn't open. The workers wanted a wage increase and a nine-hour workday (down from the frequent 12 hours or more), but the owners refused to comply. Roosevelt privately threatened to have the mines taken over if the owners refused arbitration. Such a move wouldn't exactly have been legal, but the threat was effective. The arbiter granted a 10 percent pay increase, half of what the miners were after, and a nine-hour workday, but the owners weren't forced to recognize the United Mine Workers. The country was almost universally behind Roosevelt in the first prolabor intervention, even though he had sizably increased the powers of the presidency.

Knowledge Is Power

Bully pulpit refers to a position of power that provides a forum and opportunity for expounding one's views on a particular issue or topic. It stems from President Theodore Roosevelt's reference to the White House as a "bully pulpit," from which he frequently and persuasively advocated his agenda. Roosevelt often used the word "Bully" to express excitement or joyousness.

Commander in Chief Lore

Early in his term, Roosevelt angered much of the South by having black intellectual Booker T. Washington to the White House for dinner. It was the first time a president ever sat down to dinner with an African American at the White House, and Roosevelt stuck to his guns in the face of criticism from Southern politicians.

Regulating the Railroads

Billionaire and banker J.P. Morgan organized the railroad companies, owned by fellow fat cats such as John D. Rockefeller, under one umbrella called the Northern Securities Company (a *trust*) to control prices and smother competition. Roosevelt felt the merger violated the Sherman Anti-Trust Act, so he had his attorney general prepare an antitrust lawsuit against the company. The Supreme Court eventually upheld the dissolution of the Northern Securities Company on March 14, 1904. In 1903, the Department of Commerce and Labor was created, which utilized federal power to inspect the books of corporations participating in interstate commerce.

Knowledge Is Power

A **trust** is a combination of firms or corporations joined by legal agreement, and often referred to when they reduce or threaten competition. A trustbuster is one who tries to break up the trusts by using antitrust legislation.

The antitrust action made clear that the federal government would tightly follow the Sherman Act, but Roosevelt was content to regulate the trusts, and no string of trust-busting lawsuits followed. Roosevelt was not quite the trust-busting reformer that he is often made out to be, because his goal was regulation of trusts, not dissolution—unless they were severely damaging the country. He wanted a fair balance, not the overhaul that radical progressives wanted.

Commander in Chief Lore

Theodore Roosevelt showed mercy on a tired black bear that had been caught by hounds. He let the animal live—someone else put it out of its misery—and a famous cartoon of the incident led to the rise of the ubiquitous, cuddly "Teddy" bear.

Carrying the Big Stick

Roosevelt's foreign policy was prudent and somewhat reserved, given his earlier proclamations of the blessings of imperialism and the glory of war. His "big stick" theory of international relations was basically control without colonialism—in other words, Roosevelt's idea was to use the threat of war to "encourage" foreign countries (particularly in Latin America) to act in the best interests of the United States and its businesses. He was always ready to use force to protect the interests of the

United States if necessary, but he wasn't as aggressive as some feared he would be upon becoming president.

Roosevelt's Pet Project, the Panama Canal

One of the hallmarks of the Roosevelt administration was the construction of a canal across the Isthmus of Panama. In 1901, the Hay-Pauncefote Treaty had been signed with Britain and the two countries agreed the United States would solely construct and manage the canal. Roosevelt considered it vital to American commerce and military interests, and he wanted to beat other countries to the punch. Six months after taking office, he signed the Spooner Act of 1902, which settled on Panama as the route and authorized treaty negotiations. At the time, Panama was a province of Colombia, which was concerned about giving up sovereign rights unless the United States upped its $10 million offer.

Roosevelt was outraged that Columbia asked for more money and implicitly backed a Panamanian revolt that led to their independence on November 3, 1903. Three days later, Roosevelt enthusiastically gave his support to the new regime and sent ships off both coasts of Panama to keep Colombia from retaliating. A treaty was quickly signed with the new country of Panama, and cash went to Panama in exchange for full sovereignty over a strip 10 miles wide.

Roosevelt knew that the construction of the canal had significant historical ramifications, and he visited it in November 1906, becoming the first president to leave the United States while in office. He paid close attention to every detail of the building of the Panama Canal, which was completed in 1914. (In 1921, Colombia received an indemnity from the United States for aiding in its loss of Panama.)

Theodore Roosevelt (center), twenty-sixth president of the United States.

The Roosevelt Corollary

Roosevelt started off his second term by adding the so-called Roosevelt Corollary to the Monroe Doctrine in 1904. It declared that when any nation of the Western Hemisphere acts wrongly, the United States alone assumes the right to intervene to maintain stability. Roosevelt used the new wrinkle to take over the Santo Domingo (now the Dominican Republic) customs house because the small island wasn't repaying its foreign debts. The majority of the debts were owed to European countries, but Roosevelt didn't want them meddling in the Western Hemisphere so he took control of the situation. U.S. officials took control of tax collection and debt payment in Santo Domingo for two years until its financial picture was squared away.

First Family Factuals

The Roosevelts completely remodeled the White House and designed a new west wing of executive offices, connected by an open colonnade. They also tore up the second-floor offices and added playrooms for the children and private bedrooms for family and guests. Roosevelt capped off the first major renovations in nearly a hundred years by hanging his beloved big-game trophy heads in the State Dining Room. The Roosevelts certainly needed the extra room for their six spirited children and the dogs, cats, snakes, lizards, and other pets that the "Roosevelt Gang" ran around with throughout the Executive Mansion.

Roosevelt's Second Term

Roosevelt's second campaign for the White House offered little drama. He won the Republican nomination in June 1904 and the national election in triumphal fashion in November 1904, winning the electoral vote 336 to 140 over Alton B. Parker. He then made the announcement that he wouldn't seek a third term, which would come back to cause him difficulties in dealing with Congress.

Roosevelt Wins a Big Peace of a Prize

Roosevelt considered the intervention of the United States in international disputes to be a noble necessity. In 1905, he made overtures to be a mediator in the year-old Russo-Japanese War. He was successful in his attempts to bring Japanese and Russian representatives to the bargaining table in Portsmouth, New Hampshire. The Japanese had the upper hand militarily, but they were nearly broke. In 1906, peaceful terms were reached, and for his role in mediating the negotiations that brought about the Treaty of Portsmouth, Roosevelt became the first American to win the Nobel Peace Prize.

Segregation Leads to the "Gentleman's Agreement"

The relationship between Japan and the United States became icy when the San Francisco school board ordered the segregation of all Asian children from public schools. Roosevelt persuaded the school board to reverse its decision in exchange for a limitation of Japanese immigration. The "Gentleman's Agreement" of 1907 allowed Japan to voluntarily limit the number of Japanese laborers immigrating to the United States, and tensions were somewhat steadied. Relations normalized even further when Roosevelt sent the "Great White Fleet," the U.S. Navy, on a world cruise in a show of "big stick" diplomacy and the Japanese warmly greeted the American sailors.

Commander in Chief Lore

Roosevelt's first term was marked by civil rights initiatives such as the appointment of qualified blacks to political jobs in the South and the condemnation of lynching. His second term, however, was a step back as he stood idly by and watched many of his appointments go unfulfilled and said nothing about the horrific Atlanta race riot of 1906 in which numerous blacks were killed, wounded, and disenfranchised. The same year, Roosevelt also discharged 167 black infantrymen without honor who were accused of a trumped-up "silent conspiracy" to protect fellow black soldiers falsely accused of murdering a white man and wounding another in Brownsville, Texas. The 1906 discharge order was reversed in 1972 after a military investigation found the infantrymen innocent.

Cleaning Up Food, Trains, and Forests

Roosevelt's second-term domestic agenda was a mixed bag. Although he was able to pass some important legislation, he was still viewed as a maverick by Republicans. The GOP Congress almost totally snubbed him during his last two years because they knew he wasn't going to run for a third term.

Welcome to The Jungle

A couple successes came in 1906. One was the passage of a bill, the Meat Inspection Act, which mandated federal inspection of meatpacking houses after *muckrakers* exposed their horrible conditions.

Roosevelt had believed a report stating meat was being safely processed, but a commission he sent to Chicago after the publication of *The Jungle* discovered the truth. Roosevelt had a previous beef with rotten meat and at a Senate investigation in 1899, he denounced the diseased food the "Rough Riders" were given to eat. At the time,

Knowledge Is Power

A **muckraker** was a crusader who exposed misconduct by prominent individuals or businesses. The term "muckraker" was derisively coined by Roosevelt as a label for reformers with a socialist bent, although he himself was influenced by the famous Upton Sinclair novel *The Jungle*. Sinclair's book detailed the awful, unsanitary conditions in the meatpacking industry.

Roosevelt announced he would rather have eaten his hat, which would probably have been healthier because the rotten food did more harm than combat. The other was the Pure Food and Drug Act, which extended the regulation of the food industry and banished production of hazardous foods, drugs, medicines, and liquors.

The Hepburn Act

The year 1906 also saw the passage of the Hepburn Act, which was meant to rectify the failures of the Interstate Commerce Act of 1887. Price fixing by the railroads at the expense of average customers had never been successfully addressed. The Hepburn Act granted the federal government increased power to regulate transportation by setting rates and forcing the companies to comply within a month. Roosevelt didn't take the radical step of complete federal takeover of the railroads, but the act set a regulatory precedence that would later be applied to other industries such as pipelines and telephones.

The Life-Long Conservationist

Roosevelt's pet cause was always conservation, and he and his forest chief, Gifford Pinchot, set aside 150 million acres of public lands to keep them from being raped by private interests. Later, another 85 million acres in Alaska and the Pacific Northwest were added.

Roosevelt's love of the land was much greater than any partisan beliefs he held, and he constantly harped on the need to conserve natural resources. In 1902, he supported a Democratic act that authorized numerous irrigation projects, including the construction of the Roosevelt Dam near Phoenix, Arizona. He had some success in encouraging lumber companies to use alternative cutting procedures, and he doubled the number of national parks and established many federal wildlife refuges. Roosevelt even convened a "Congress of Governors" with all the states to discuss national conservation policies.

The Knickerbocker Bank Panics

Roosevelt was out on a bear hunt when the Panic of 1907 hit Wall Street, after the fall of the powerful Knickerbocker Bank in New York City. Stock prices dropped like a concrete balloon, and many smaller investment firms went bankrupt because of the lack of currency at the big bank. At the time, banks were wholeheartedly dependent on their own currency resources and any fiscal mismanagement, wild speculation, or even simple rumors could affect the financial status. A depression set in, and the Knickerbocker Bank had to be bailed out by a consortium of financiers led by J.P. Morgan. Roosevelt lectured the country on the evils of playing the stock market and the corrupt practices of big business. However, economics wasn't his bag, and Roosevelt took no steps to examine the root causes of the panic or to keep a similar crisis from happening again. A provisional measure, the Aldrich-Vreeland Act of 1908 propped up unstable banks with federal funds, but it didn't address the fundamental banking issues that crippled the nation 21 years later.

Commander in Chief Lore

Roosevelt enjoyed football while in college, and he considered it a fine way for young men to build strength of body and character. Ten of his "Rough Riders" engaged in pigskin battles. Unfortunately, in 1905, 18 young men died in separate incidents while playing an extremely vicious form of the Sunday afternoon game, and its popularity began to decline rapidly. Roosevelt called representatives of Harvard, Yale, and Princeton to the White House and, with fire and brimstone, persuaded them to make the game safer. A committee was formed, and the following year changes were made that included the forward pass, elimination of wholesale gang tackling, and the creation of a 10-yard first down, instead of five yards.

Gone Hunting, but Not for a Third Term

Roosevelt stayed true to his word and didn't seek a third term, even though the citizenry still loved him. He assumed that his chosen successor, William Howard Taft, would uphold his policies and continue to steward the country in the same fashion as he had. He campaigned for Taft's winning campaign and then headed off to Africa with his son Kermit for a big-game hunt.

After amassing hundreds of animals that included lions, elephants, and rhinoceroses, Roosevelt and his family went on an extended tour of Europe, where they were wooed by the leaders and cheered by the masses. While there, he got word that Taft was following a much more conservative course, and Pinchot went abroad to tell him that his beloved conservation policies were on the back burner.

Roosevelt Relived

➤ Theodore Roosevelt was the first president to fly. In 1910, he was a passenger for a four-minute flight in a biplane in St. Louis.

➤ In 1902, Roosevelt was the first president to ride in an automobile when he cruised in a Columbia Electric Victoria.

➤ While on vacation in Europe with his wife in 1882, Roosevelt scaled the Matterhorn in Switzerland.

➤ Roosevelt attempted to have the phrase "In God We Trust" banished from U.S. coinage because he saw it as sacrilegious and unconstitutional.

➤ In 1904, Roosevelt lost sight in one eye in a boxing match with a professional fighter at the White House.

➤ During World War I, Roosevelt tried to persuade President Wilson to let him raise a volunteer division to fight the allies, but he was rebuked because of his advancing age of 58.

➤ Upon Roosevelt's death, his son Archie cabled his brothers fighting in Europe with the message: "The lion is dead."

Do That to Me One More Time

Roosevelt returned to a hero's welcome in the United States and went on a speaking tour to promote "New Nationalism," which encouraged the improvement of national welfare over personal or regional gains. He called for more regulatory programs and an extension of the progressive ideals of his last term in office. In 1912, he declared, "My hat is in the ring," in case the Republicans wanted to nominate him for the presidency.

Taft had alienated Roosevelt by filing an antitrust lawsuit against U.S. Steel, which had been acquired by J.P. Morgan, for a deal that had been approved by Roosevelt as a way to combat the Panic of 1807. Taft's managers were aligned with the Republican machine, which dominated the convention in Chicago. The machine refused to allow the seating of pro-Roosevelt delegates at the convention. After that, supporters encouraged Roosevelt to form an independent third party, and he zealously followed their advice.

Roosevelt's supporters reconvened in Chicago on August 5 and nominated him as the candidate of the Progressive Party, or the Bull Moose Party, as it came to be known. They laid out a platform calling for social reforms that included women's suffrage. It was a typically energetic Roosevelt campaign, and the Bull Moose ticket had a surprisingly successful showing for a third party. Roosevelt came in second to Woodrow Wilson, and he got revenge against Taft and the Republican machine by beating the establishment candidate. Roosevelt proudly took 27 percent of the popular vote and won six states with a party that had been created only a few months earlier.

In 1916, the Bull Moose Party again asked Roosevelt to run for president, but he declined and threw his support behind Republican candidate Charles Evans Hughes.

Commander in Chief Lore

In Milwaukee on October 14, 1912, a would-be assassin wounded Theodore Roosevelt with a shot that hit him in the chest. Fortunately, the large text in front of him provided a shield, a "bulletproof speech" if you will. Roosevelt refused treatment until he finished his address (he spoke for nearly an hour), and as blood stained his vest, he said, "It takes more than that to kill a Bull Moose." After he finished, he collapsed and was taken to the hospital, but two weeks later he was able to speak to the throngs at Madison Square Garden. The failed assassin said, "Any man looking for a third term ought to be shot."

Another Tragedy Befalls Roosevelt

Roosevelt spent the years 1912 through 1914 writing his autobiography and touring South America. He and Kermit explored the River of Doubt (now the Roosevelt River) in Brazil; Roosevelt said of the expedition, "It was my last chance to be a boy." His exploits were told in the bestseller *Through the Brazilian Wilderness,* but his time in Brazil also gave him a tropical fever. Roosevelt returned to the United States and became the leader of the loyal opposition to Wilson's efforts regarding World War I. He was never much of a believer in peace through neutrality and was known to say, "Fear God and take your own part."

Another tragedy deeply affected Roosevelt when his son Quentin was killed in air combat in France. Although his son's death was devastating, Roosevelt didn't withdraw and probably would have been the Republican nominee in 1920, but he died in his sleep at Sagamore Hill early on the morning of January 6, 1919.

The Least You Need to Know

➤ Theodore Roosevelt made a national name for himself when he lead the Rough Riders in the "San Juan charge" up Kettle Hill during the Spanish-American War.

➤ Roosevelt became president after McKinley was assassinated, and he led a series of business reforms, including a precedent-setting antitrust suit.

➤ Roosevelt became the first American to win the Nobel Peace prize for mediating the treaty that ended the Russo-Japanese War.

➤ Roosevelt ran as a third-party candidate for president as the nominee of the Progressive, or Bull Moose Party; he finished second.

Chapter 7

The Staunchly Sometimes Progressive: Woodrow Wilson

In This Chapter

➤ The big man on campus after campus

➤ America moves to a leading role in world affairs

➤ Fourteen points and what did he get?

➤ The progressive segregationist

Woodrow Wilson occupies a unique position among the presidents: He was our only president with a doctoral degree—a Ph.D. from Johns Hopkins University. Interestingly, his dissertation was entitled *Congressional Government,* which was critical of the congressional powers within American democracy during times of weak leadership. But although Wilson was a relative newcomer to politics, one thing he was not was weak.

Despite his significant shortcomings, Wilson was a dedicated public servant and was committed to his ideas, if not to compromise. He could be bull-headed, but he had a vision for the United States that far exceeded many of his predecessors', and that certainly elevated the country to the premier international standing we hold today.

The Son of a Preacher Man

Woodrow Wilson was born in Stanton, Virginia, the son of a preacher. At a very early age, Wilson moved with his family to Augusta, where his father, Dr. Joseph Ruggles Wilson, became pastor of the First Presbyterian Church.

Wilson's love of learning came from his brilliant father, who also was a chaplain in the Confederate Army and a strong sympathizer, a trait Woodrow Wilson would carry all the way to the White House. Wilson was a young boy during the Civil War, but the images of the walking wounded in his father's church, a temporary hospital, were indelible.

When Wilson was 13, his family relocated to Columbia, South Carolina, where Dr. Wilson had accepted a professorship at Columbia Theological Seminary. In 1874, they packed up again and this time headed to Wilmington, North Carolina.

Joe College

Wilson's combination of schooling and religion became the central tenet of his life. He was always a diligent student. He began his collegiate career at Davidson College, a small Presbyterian school in North Carolina, ostensibly to follow in his father's footsteps and join the ministry. In 1875, after taking time off to recover from an illness, he switched to the Presbyterian College of New Jersey at Princeton (now called Princeton University), where he abandoned the idea of life as a cleric. He was a mid-level student, but he was active on campus, serving as editor of the campus newspaper in his senior year and founding the Liberal Debating Club.

Wilson made up his mind that he was going to become a statesman, so he enrolled in statesman school, the law school at the University of West Virginia. He then became ill again and had to finish his studies at home, but he went on to found a law firm in Atlanta. He stayed with the firm for an entire year before entering the graduate school at Johns Hopkins to study history.

Wilson's next move was to teach at Bryn Mawr, a women's college, but he wasn't thrilled with this job because he wasn't tolerant of the intellectual abilities of females. He later jumped at the chance to teach "a class of men" at Wesleyan University in Connecticut.

Commander in Chief Lore

Woodrow Wilson was the man-about-campus at Wesleyan. He was a faculty leader and a popular lecturer, and he wrote a lengthy work of comparative political and social analysis, *The State*. He even found time to coach the football team to a victorious season.

In 1890, Wilson became Professor of Jurisprudence and History at Princeton University. He became a leading academic voice and published writings on a variety of topics, including *More Literature and Other Essays, George Washington,* and *History of the American People,* which was a mammoth five-volume work. When the president of Princeton resigned in 1902 after a dispute with the trustees, Wilson was unanimously selected, the first layman ever chosen to the presidency of the university.

Wilson took the bull by the horns at the elite New Jersey college and restructured a variety of programs. He raised the level of scholarship, and although enrollment dipped, academic standards were improved. In 1905, he introduced the preceptoral plan, which added 50 teachers who lived in the student dormitories and provided personal tutorials. His overall aim was to create communities of students.

Wilson tried to do away with the upper-class eating clubs and to substitute common dining halls, but the alumni revolted. There had been rumblings all along about Wilson's democratization efforts, and the alumni yearned for a return to the old aristocratic ways. The trustees withdrew their support, but this enhanced Wilson's reputation across the state as a champion of the average Joe, and the Democrats came calling.

What Exit You from, Governor, Joisey?

Wilson made his name as a progressive, reform-oriented governor in New Jersey, which had been a conservative state. He instituted direct primaries to rid the back-room, ballot-stuffing shenanigans of *political machines;* pushed for and got workmen's compensation; regulated the public utilities to fix rates; reorganized the school system; and pushed for and got a corrupt practices act that diminished the powers of huge corporations within the state.

Wilson was elected as the gubernatorial candidate after Democratic machine leader James "Sugar Jim" Smith handpicked him because of his scholarly background and fresh face. However, Wilson was not a puppet. He was a progressive, at a time when a new spirit of activist politics was taking hold across the state of New Jersey, as well as the rest of the country. He showed "Sugar Jim" little loyalty by campaigning for the opposition candidate running for the Senate, and the Democratic candidate lost. From 1911 on, Wilson openly pined for and actively sought the Democratic nomination for the White House.

Knowledge Is Power

Political machines are organized local partisan political organizations that can mobilize large numbers of voters. In the United States, machines were dominant from the period after the Civil War to the outbreak of World War II. Machines usually mobilized votes in exchange for favors, kickbacks, or even to cover for its criminal activity. Some machines were led by a single "boss" such as Kansas City's Thomas J. Pendergast, and others had a collective committee such as New York's notorious Tammany Hall.

The GOP Split Is Wilson's Gain

Wilson was chosen as the Democratic nominee on the 46th ballot as he slowly built momentum at the 1912 Democratic convention after three-time presidential loser William Jennings Bryan put his weight behind Wilson on the 14th ballot. He vigorously campaigned on a platform of the "New Freedom," which called for breaking up monopolies to help small business owners.

Meanwhile, Teddy Roosevelt accepted the nomination of the new Progressive Party (a.k.a. the Bull Moose Party), an action that split the Republican vote in half. William Howard Taft, the Republican nominee and current president, knew that the election had become a lost cause and did little to change the situation. The divided Republican vote enabled Wilson to win both the popular and the electoral vote. The final tally was 435 electoral votes for Wilson, 88 for Roosevelt, and 8 for Taft.

Mexican War Revisited?

A series of revolutions in Mexico worried American business owners, who began to pressure Wilson to intervene to keep the money in their mining interests flowing. In February 1913, Victoriano Huerta, head of the Mexican Army, illegally seized power, and Wilson refused to acknowledge his regime because it came about after the arranged murder of President Francisco Madero. Wilson backed the opponent Venustiano Carranza and his supporters, but Huerta controlled the power in Mexico City.

In April 1914, American sailors were arrested by a Huerta officer. Even though the sailors were released, Wilson ordered the Navy to occupy Veracruz. A conflict broke out, killing more than 300 Mexicans and 90 Americans, but war was averted when mediation came from Argentina, Brazil, and Chile. By this time, Carranza had replaced Huerta, and he refused to accept the findings of the mediators.

Wilson then backed the Mexican peasant and bandit leader "Pancho" Villa, but Villa wasn't interested in diplomacy. He crossed into New Mexico, killed citizens, and burned a local town. In response, Wilson sent more than 6,000 troops, under Brigadier General John J. Pershing, to Mexico. Villa outfoxed the American troops and drew them across the Rio Grande.

A full-scale war became a real threat but was averted when Carranza called for a constitutional convention, which met in Querétaro in 1917 to draft a new constitution. Delegates from Mexico met to discuss political and social reforms, which was good enough for Wilson to start recalling the troops. The turmoil in Mexico continued and Carranza was killed in a revolt, but Wilson's focus was across the Atlantic as World War I loomed.

That War Is None of Our Business

The causes of World War I were numerous and dated back many years, but the catalyst of the Great War was the assassination of Archduke Francis Ferdinand, heir to the

Austrian and Hungarian thrones, and his wife, the Grand Duchess Sophie, on June 28, 1914, in Sarajevo. The assassination led to the immediate conflict between Austria-Hungary and Serbia, but within a few months it was a massive global war that would enlist the service of 32 countries and leave 37 million casualties in its wake. Most Americans, the president included, wanted to stay out of the conflict though because it seemed irrelevant and remote to national interests and international loyalties were divided among the citizenry.

Wilson Tries to Remain Neutral

Between August 4 and November 6th, 1914, Wilson issued 10 Neutrality Proclamations, laying out the details that would keep the United States out of the war. The prevailing mood across the country was to avoid participation, and Wilson encouraged citizens to remain impartial in thought and action. But although Wilson tried to preserve American neutrality, neither Germany nor the Allies seemed to recognize it. Germany, however, violated Belgium's neutrality and declared that the seas were a war zone and that all vessels could come under the attack of German submarines (U-boats). For Wilson, who had always sympathized with the Allies, particularly Great Britain, that tipped the scales because the Germans had threatened neutral citizens.

Woodrow Wilson, twenty-eighth president of the United States.

Sinking Ships

On May 7, 1915, German U-boats sank the British liner the *Lusitania,* killing more than 1,100 passengers and crew, including more than 120 Americans. Wilson warned that if Germany continued, war would be inevitable. With that, the vast majority of Americans sentiment was on the side of the Allies. After torpedoing the *Arabic* in

August 1915 and sinking the *Sussex* in March 1916, the German government gave its pledge to follow conventional tactics when attacking Allied merchant ships. Wilson's primary goal remained one of peace, but in January 1916, he spoke for the first time of increasing the armed forces as a means of preparedness.

Wilson began his second term still hoping to mediate a peace settlement overseas. In January 1917, he appealed to the European nations to accept "peace without victory," but his dream faded fast. Germany announced on January 31 that it would sink any ship, neutral or not, that traded with the Allies. On February 3, Wilson broke off diplomatic relations with Germany.

Commander in Chief Lore

In 1916, Democrats campaigned for Wilson with the slogan, "He kept us out of war," as a reminder that Teddy Roosevelt demanded intervention in World War I. Both Wilson and his opponent, Charles Evans Hughes, were reform-oriented candidates, and it was a very close race. Wilson's mix of progressivism and promise of continued neutrality gave him enough votes in the South and the West to win the election 277 to 254 in the electoral college. (California's 13 electoral votes would have changed the outcome, which Wilson won by less than 2,000 popular votes.)

Of Course You Realize, This Means War

Even with relations severed, Wilson and many Americans still hoped to stay out of the war, but the last straw was broken when the British presented Wilson with the Zimmerman note. This was a message that had been intercepted and decoded by British intelligence between Germany and Mexico that promised Mexico states in the southwestern United States if the country joined in a Mexico-Germany alliance against the United States. On April 2, Wilson asked Congress for a declaration of war to help make the world safe for democracy; on April 6, 1917, it was adopted.

Wilson went straight to work, and his determined leadership effectively mobilized the United States' resources. He brought progressives on board to man the Committee on Public Information, which was designed to explain the war goals to the public and to get leftists on his side, many of whom were still skeptical. There was a vocal opposition made up of pacifists, German-Americans, socialists, isolationists, and other dissenters who often clashed with citizens who followed Wilson's calls for dedicated patriotism. The wartime mobilization was relatively unimpeded, partially because Wilson gave the men in charge—including Herbert Hoover and Bernard Baruch—full, supported authority. Wilson was never afraid of swift, decisive action, such as taking over the railroads in December to keep the mobilization wheels greased.

That's Bolshevik

The Bolshevik Revolution broke out in Russia in October 1917 when Vladimir Lenin and Leon Trotsky became the leaders of a new Communist government after seizing power in a bloodless up-rising. The new Communist regime was bent on pulling out of World War I, and leaders quickly signed an armistice with Germany. They also published secret treaties among France, Britain, and the old Czarist Russian government. The documents revealed that the Allied war goals were no more altruistic or idealistic than the German Empire's, but Wilson assured the country that the United States' goals were to establish democracy in Europe, whether Europe wanted it or not.

Prez Says

"The right is more precious than peace, and we shall fight for the things which we have always carried nearest our hearts—for democracy, for the right of those who submit to authority to have a voice in their own governments, for the rights and liberties of small nations, for a universal dominion of right by such a concert of free peoples as shall bring peace and safety to all nations and make the world itself at last free."

—From Woodrow Wilson's address to Congress on April 2, 1917

Fourteen Points Is Enough for Victory

Wilson had drawn up an extensive plan for peace called the "Fourteen Points," which included open instead of covert treaties, return of Alsace-Lorraine to France, Poland's sovereignty and independence, freedom of the seas, disarmament, and, his most cherished idea, "a general association of nations." This was to become the League of Nations.

American troops, weaponry, and supplies flooded Europe. The Allied troops were revitalized against Germany, and the tide of war shifted in the fall of 1918. Wilson's Fourteen Points played a major part in ending the Great War because they included a face-saving provision for Germany. Under the terms of the settlement rooted in the Fourteen Points, Germany never had to admit defeat. Wilson and the Allies signed the armistice on November 11, and the brutal fighting of the Great War was over (for at least 30 years, anyway).

A League of Their Own

Woodrow Wilson urged his citizenry to vote early, often, and Democratic so that he could have a veritable carte blanche to implement his plans. Unfortunately for

Wilson, the 1918 midterm elections gave control of both the House and the Senate to the Republicans.

The First Sitting President Visits Europe

Wilson wanted to be sure that his Fourteen Points were the basis for the political settlements in Europe, and he surprised many Americans when he set sail for France in December 1918. No sitting president had ever been to Europe during his administration, and this raised some eyebrows around the country, especially when he didn't include any members of the Senate or Republican representatives in his peace commission. Wilson was by and large received triumphantly as the Allied savior, but he found that not all the European nations were as committed to the League of Nations as he was.

The Peace Conference began in Paris on January 18, 1919. Wilson addressed the opening of the conference and called for the creation of a permanent peacekeeping body. By the time the Treaty of Versailles was signed with Germany in June, Wilson's Fourteen Points had been watered down, and he made numerous concessions to keep his beloved League of Nations alive, but there were successes, including the establishment of an independent Poland. However, Wilson's most egregious concession ran counter to the spirit of the armistice agreement. Germany was stuck with a huge debt for reparations and saw its army gutted (which sparked a nationalist movement led by Hitler that would come back to shake the world to its foundations).

First Family Factuals

Woodrow Wilson's first wife, Ellen Louise Axson, whom he met and married after he accepted a position as an associate professor at a women's college in Bryn Mawr, Pennsylvania, died in August 1914. Wilson was terribly distraught, and his own health wasn't strong. He dived into work, played golf, wrote heartfelt letters, and gradually came out of his depression. He then met a 43-year-old widow, Edith Bolling Galt, began courting her, and finally married her on December 18, 1915.

A League of Nations Without the United States

In July 1919, Wilson returned to the United States confident that the Treaty of Versailles would be roundly supported and that the League of Nations would become the standard-bearer for worldwide democracy. Unfortunately, for the dogged president, his time in Europe (not the entire conference, for the record) had given the Republican opposition plenty of time to put together a coalition to defeat his treaty. The key sticking point was the commitment to collective security in the League of Nations constitution. The collective security measure was an assurance that the members of the league would protect the territorial independence of other members against aggression, a united defense against the threat of war.

Wilson did what all greatly confused Americans do: He took a road trip. The president traveled 8,000 miles (sources vary; some say 9,500 miles) explaining to folks why the Treaty of Versailles was needed, but he was never able to whip the public into a ratification frenzy. In late September 1919, he collapsed from exhaustion after speaking at Pueblo, Colorado. On October 2, back home in Washington, he became paralyzed on his left side after a stroke. At the time when Wilson absolutely had to explain and sell the reasons for U.S. participation in the League of Nations if it were to pass, he was incapacitated.

The Treaty of Versailles was defeated in the Senate twice, in November 1919 and March 1920. Republicans wanted to add reservations to the treaty to diminish the United States' responsibility in the League of Nations, but Wilson told Democrats not to accept the new version, which he saw as a nullification of his high-minded ideals. Even though most senators probably wanted the treaty in some form, the stubbornness of both Republican leaders and Wilson kept the United States out of the League of Nations. Wilson refused to consider any alternative, and it cost him.

First Family Factuals

First Lady Edith Wilson would not allow vice president Thomas Riley Marshall to assume the top spot, even though she had no legal or constitutional authority to follow her chosen course of action. She said that Wilson would fight the good fight in order to get back to his day job, and because the public was unaware of the president's condition, there would be no harm. Marshall went along with the plan, and Wilson was sitting in cabinet meetings seven months after his stroke.

A Nobel Effort to No Effect

Wilson was not asked to run by the Democrats in 1920, but he encouraged them to make the treaty ratification the central issue. James Cox, the Democratic candidate, was soundly defeated by Warren G. Harding, who signed a separate peace agreement with Germany and made it crystal clear that the United States would not be joining the League of Nations or accepting any of the responsibilities outlined in the Treaty of Versailles. Wilson's "my way or the highway" demeanor had alienated him from many fellow politicians who could have picked up the League of Nations torch.

Ironically, Wilson received the Nobel Peace Prize in 1920 for the creation of an organization that his own country rejected. He retired to a house on S Street in Washington, D.C., where he lived out his days in relative seclusion, believing that history would prove him right and prove that the League of Nations would be the world's saving grace. He died in his sleep on February 3, 1924.

The World of Woodrow Wilson

➤ Woodrow Wilson was known as the "Schoolmaster in Politics."

➤ Ellen Wilson planted the first rose garden in a seventeenth-century Italian garden style.

➤ Ellen Wilson once took a group of Congressmen on a tour of Washington ghettos, which led to the sponsoring of a bill that ensured suitable housing.

➤ Wilson is the only president buried in Washington, D.C. (at the National Cathedral).

The League of Nations didn't save the world because it did little to oppose Axis aggression, and World War II was the result. However, the idea of a league of some sort never died, and the United Nations was formed in 1945 after World War II. This time, the United States joined, but the question of what role the world's sole superpower should play in international diplomacy hasn't changed since the Wilson Administration.

Although World War I and the ensuing League of Nations crusade dominated Wilson's time in the White House, there were other noteworthy initiatives. The following are a few examples of domestic doings under Woodrow Wilson's watch:

➤ **Tariff reform.** To give consumers the chance to get out from under the thumb of protected monopolies, the Underwood Bill was introduced to slash taxes on imported goods, completely remove tariffs on some goods (including iron and sugar), and provided for the first graduated federal income tax under the new sixteenth amendment. Tariffs had not been reduced since prior to the Civil War.

The bill passed quickly in the House, but the Senate dragged its feet. Wilson took his case to the streets: He appealed to the working class across the country to help pass the bill, which was opposed by big business. Senators were snowed under in letters, and the Underwood Bill was signed on October 3, 1913. However, World War I limited the effectiveness of tariff reform.

➤ **Seventeenth, eighteenth, and nineteenth amendments.** During Wilson's time in office, three major amendments to the Constitution were added. In 1913, the seventeenth amendment ensured that the people, not state senators, would directly elect United States senators. (This helped to tame the frequently corrupt political machines of the day.) The eighteenth amendment, which outlawed the manufacture, sale, and distribution of booze (which Wilson apparently believed pertained to only the ground floor of his home on S Street, as drinking was permitted upstairs). The nineteenth amendment, which gave women the right to vote, was only lukewarmly supported by Wilson because he didn't think that women had the ability to be part of the political process and actually had suffragists arrested.

➤ **Banking reform.** Wilson introduced an agency to run the nation's banking system. The Federal Reserve Act of 1913 created 12 central Federal Reserve banks, a new currency, and a board of presidential appointees to control and oversee the national banking system.

Commander in Chief Lore

There have always been rumors of Woodrow Wilson's dalliance with a woman named Mary Peck, giving gossip-mongers the opportunity to label him "Peck's Bad Boy." However, there doesn't seem to be any truth to the matter. Wilson definitely enjoyed the company of Miss Peck, but so did his first wife, Ellen.

➤ **Federal Trade Commission.** In 1914, the FTC was conjured to keep monopolies from taking over a single industry. It was the dawn of a more regulatory style of governing because the White House could prevent unfair business practices if it saw fit.

➤ **Clayton Anti-Trust Law.** The Clayton Act weakened big business's ability to use the Sherman Act against labor and ensured the right of unions to strike. (The Clayton Act wasn't interpreted in the courts to labor's advantage.)

➤ **Other progressive policies.** Wilson asked Congress for legislation to grant workers an eight-hour work day. Legislation also was passed under Wilson's "New Freedom" agenda that granted loans to farmers, improved safety for sailors, and gave unemployment compensation for federal employees. Wilson also pushed for a bill to ban child labor, but that bill was declared unconstitutional by the Supreme Court.

Backward Thinking

Besides Wilson's unprogressive view of women's suffrage, he excluded African Americans from his "New Freedom." His Southern upbringing may have shaped his thinking, because he was both an educated man and an outspoken racist who set back whatever civil rights advances had been made since the Civil War. His administration introduced legislation designed to undercut advances for African Americans

Prez Says

"It is as far as possible from being a movement against the negroes. I sincerely believe it to be in their interest."

—Woodrow Wilson, regarding his administration's segregation policy, 1913

but it failed to get through Congress. His most egregious bigotry came when he segregated the federal government, the first time since the days of Reconstruction. Wilson even vetoed a clause that would have called for racial equality in the Covenant of the League of Nations. Black leaders across the country, including Booker T. Washington, were disgusted that the president allowed segregation of federal agencies and were appalled at his insistence that it was in their "best interests."

During the Wilson years, the KKK grew in power across the country, partially because of the notoriously racist, pro-Klan, D.W. Griffith film *Birth of a Nation*, which had been screened at the White House and admired by Wilson.

The Least You Need to Know

➤ Woodrow Wilson was the most educated President, receiving a Ph.D. from Johns Hopkins and eventually becoming president of Princeton University.

➤ Mirroring popular sentiment, Woodrow Wilson did everything in his power to keep the United States out of World War I, but Germany's aggressive tactics made neutrality impossible.

➤ Wilson designed a "Fourteen Points" plan for rebuilding Europe and maintaining peace through a League of Nations. However, the Treaty of Versailles, which contained the Fourteen Points, was never ratified in the United States, and his beloved league was created without the United States.

➤ Wilson was a progressive, activist president who introduced legislative measures to curb big business and help the working class, but he was also a racist who segregated the federal government and a sexist who only supported suffrage for political gain.

Chapter 8

You Couldn't Make Up a Character Quite Like Andrew Jackson

In This Chapter

➤ Jackson's 1812 overture

➤ Settling scores the old-fashioned way—duels

➤ An inaugural saturnalia

➤ An examination of nullification

In our age of consternation over the indiscretions of presidential candidates, it's interesting to look back on a beloved, immensely popular leader who was a horse-betting, Indian-killing, wife-stealing, associate-murdering, party-throwing, hot-tempered, modestly educated man of the people who made no apologies for his actions and who steered the young country through one of its key fundamental shifts in development. Meet the living embodiment of the greatest protagonist that fiction could hope to create: Andrew Jackson, seventh president of the United States.

"Old Hickory" in the Big Easy

Let's begin with the event that made Jackson a folk hero and that propelled him on to Washington, D.C. Like so many other presidents, Jackson became a potential candidate after victory on the battlefield. Jackson had been elected major general of the Tennessee militia in 1802, and he offered to lead an attack on Canada at the outbreak of the War of 1812. President James Madison ignored his requests, however, because of Jackson's previous association with Aaron Burr.

Jackson and his Tennessee militia were ordered to Natchez, Mississippi, by Governor Willie Blount. After a long march in the winter of 1813, Jackson received an order from the War Department to disband his troops. They were without food and supplies, but instead of leaving every man for himself, Jackson marched back to Tennessee with the troops. He walked the entire way so that the soldiers who had fallen ill could ride on the horses. Jackson's rise to fame began with this march. The soldiers said Jackson was as tough as hickory, and he would come to be known by the famous handle "Old Hickory."

Prez Says

"One man with courage makes a majority."

—Attributed to Andrew Jackson

Commander in Chief Lore

Andrew Jackson was a Jeffersonian but was at odds with Thomas Jefferson over his association with Aaron Burr, who suckered him into his bizarre, mysterious, plan to seize a large tract of land in the Louisiana Purchase and get the United States involved in a war. While traveling out West, Burr stayed with Jackson and convinced him that he had the support of President Jefferson to lead an armed invasion of Spanish territory. Jackson built Burr some riverboats but got out of the scheme when he got wind that it was an independent plot. Jackson, however, was not called to testify after he made it clear he respected Burr more than the president.

In September 1813, Jackson called his militia together and headed south to battle with Creek Indians, allies of the British who had massacred 250 settlers at Fort Mims in the Mississippi Territory. Jackson's soldiers were undertrained and undernourished, and supplies never reached the (now) Alabama wilds. Jackson led his men to victory in a series of engagements that came to a head with the Battle of Horseshoe Bend in March 1814. After allowing the Indian women and children to get to safety, Jackson decimated the tribe. Chief Red Eagle surrendered, and the war with the Creek Indians was over. They eventually signed a treaty with Jackson that ceded 23 million acres to the United States. President Madison rewarded Old Hickory with an appointment as a major general in the regular army.

Andrew Jackson, seventh president of the United States.

Jackson was sent to New Orleans to defend against a British attack, but he detoured to march on a British military base at Pensacola, along the Gulf Coast in Spanish Florida. In November 1814, he ran a quick raid on Pensacola, captured the city, and headed west to New Orleans. The city was defenseless, so he quickly organized a makeshift army of loyal Tennessee and Kentucky sharpshooters, pirates, blacks, Creoles, and local militiamen. He learned of a British sneak attack that was to take place that afternoon, and he launched a counteroffensive that stopped their advance. He then set up a defense position behind a dry canal just outside the city. On January 8, 1815, the British attacked in force with veteran soldiers. Jackson's men were waiting, and their relentless rifle and cannon fire cut down the British to the tune of more than 2,000 dead and injured; the Americans recorded single-digit deaths and fewer than 20 wounded in the *Battle of New Orleans*.

The War of 1812 is often remembered as an American victory solely on the basis of the Battle of New Orleans, but that battle was minor at best. Heavy

Knowledge Is Power

The **Battle of New Orleans** actually came after the signing of the Treaty of Ghent by Great Britain and the United States on Christmas Eve, 1814. The treaty set terms for the end of the war, but it didn't officially take effect until both governments ratified it in early 1815.

losses and major defeats, including the burning of the Capitol and the White House, were sustained at the hands of the British. What's more, the Treaty of Ghent, which ended the war, dealt with almost none of the causes of the war. One great victory, however, was the personal acclaim for Jackson. Old Hickory became a household name as stories of his war heroics made their way across the country. Jackson instantly became a pillar of American strength, and it wouldn't take long for him to become a favored choice for President of the United States.

First Family Factuals

Jackson became the only president to ever have been a prisoner of war. He and his brother were captured in 1781 and sent to a British prison at Camden, South Carolina. A British soldier ordered Jackson to shine his boots; upon refusal, he was slashed about the hands and face with a saber, leaving permanent scars. The boys were released to their mother when smallpox broke out in the prison, and the disease killed Robert (some accounts claim it was untreated wounds). His mother went to Charleston, South Carolina and helped nurse other American prisoners, and she, too, died of a disease, possibly smallpox or cholera.

Old Hickory as a Young Bud

Andrew Jackson was the first future president to be born in a log cabin on March 15, 1767, at the settlement of Waxhaw on the border between North and South Carolina. His father died a few days before he was born, and Jackson and his two brothers were raised by their mother in the home of a nearby relative. Jackson was educated in frontier schools and had a distinct advantage over many of the adults in the community: He knew how to read. Jackson was one of the children who took a turn as a public reader to the community. Later in life, he recounted the thrill of reading aloud the Declaration of Independence when a newspaper reporting the developments in Philadelphia reached Waxhaw in the summer of 1776. At age 13, Jackson joined the South Carolina militia as a courier and served in the Revolutionary War. Jackson's older brother, Hugh, died in the war in 1779.

Jackson was 14 and had no immediate family. He received an inheritance from his grandfather, but he blew it living the high life in Charleston, South Carolina. He eventually decided to take up the study of law with an attorney in Salisbury, North Carolina, and passed the bar at age 20.

Married with Troubles

Jackson practiced law from 1787 to 1788 until Cumberland Road opened a mountain pathway. At that time, he crossed over to the frontier village of Nashville, which was in North Carolina's Western District. He had been appointed public prosecutor of the area, and made his mark going after debtors, for which he often was paid in land and slaves. He also met the love of his life, Rachel Donelson Robards, who would also become the great tragedy of his life.

In Nashville, Jackson boarded at the home of Rachel's mother and fell hard for Rachel, who was estranged from her cruel, insanely jealous husband, Lewis Robards. In 1791, they were married after hearing—and believing—that Robards had gotten a divorce from Rachel on the grounds of adultery (which was probable because they had gone to Jackson's land in Natchez together).

The Jacksons moved into a farm in Nashville and were living happily ever after when the sky fell: Robards had never gotten a divorce, and the two were living in sin in an illegal union. The Robards marriage wasn't dissolved until 1793, and the Jacksons quickly remarried in 1794. Jackson was upset that the claims of adultery were validated. This would be used against him by his political opponents, to the ultimate demise of his beloved Rachel.

Commander in Chief Lore

Besmirching Rachel's name was a sure way to invite the wrath of Andrew Jackson which meant that a duel was sure to come. Jackson never backed down from a fight, and he was involved in numerous duels. Two famous incidents left Old Hickory with new wounds. The first was in 1806 against a Nashville attorney, Charles Dickerson, who insulted his wife's past. Dueling with pistols, Dickerson got off the first shot and hit Jackson in the chest, leaving a bullet close to his heart for the remainder of his life. Jackson retaliated by killing Dickerson before he collapsed.

The second legendary melee was with future Missouri Senator Thomas Hart Benton and his brother Jesse in 1813, which shattered Jackson's left arm and left a bullet in it for 19 years. By the time the bullet was removed, Benton was a Jacksonian, and they were closely aligned.

The couple never had any children of their own, but they watched over a large clan. The Jacksons formally adopted Rachel's young nephew, Andrew Jr., and took care of other children they were related to and a Indian boy whose parents had been killed in the war with the Creek Indians.

Early Political Life

Jackson was a delegate at the Tennessee Constitutional Congress in 1796, called to shape the newest state in the Union. He was elected without opposition as the first representative to Congress and aligned with the Jeffersonians. He was disappointed when John Adams was elected president: Jackson was strongly anti-Great Britain and felt that the Jay Treaty wasn't good for the United States.

Jackson was elected to fill in for Senator (and future Governor) Willie Blount after Blount was expelled, but Jackson served in the Senate for only a brief time: He retired in 1798 to try to improve his personal financial picture. He was appointed as judge of the Tennessee Superior Court in 1798 and served until 1804.

In 1804, Jackson enjoyed retired life by developing his plantation, Hermitage, a few miles outside Nashville. The cotton industry wasn't good to Jackson or his many slaves, but the thoroughbred industry was. He borrowed money, bought a racehorse, and won thousands, which allowed him to buy more racehorses and thoroughly improve his bottom line. Jackson never grew tired of the sport of kings and kept racehorses in the stables at the White House.

A Volunteer Politician

After the War of 1812, Jackson could do no wrong, and he soon bolstered his reputation as a man of uncommon battlefield valor. In 1815, Jackson was named commander of the South District Army and was ordered to put down the Seminole Indian uprising in Florida two years later. The Seminoles were crossing into the United States from Florida at the Georgia border and were raiding and sacking settlements. They would retreat into the safe haven of Florida, which was still under Spanish control. Jackson was told to use all means necessary, and he chased the Seminoles all the way into Florida, where he commandeered a military post at St. Marks and executed two British subjects for encouraging the insurrection.

Jackson followed up by capturing the military fort at Pensacola, but an international incident ensued. Spain and Great Britain were furious, Monroe denied giving the orders, and many members of Congress wanted to take action against the renegade soldier—this included Secretary of War John C. Calhoun, who called for his arrest. John Quincy Adams stepped in, staunchly defended Jackson, and urged Monroe not to apologize to the European countries. Spain decided that cession of the territory was the best course of action, in part because Jackson was a big hero in the South and the West, and Adams sealed the deal. In 1821, Monroe appointed Jackson as the first governor of Florida, but he stayed for only a few months before returning to Tennessee.

In 1822, Jackson was encouraged by a group of influential friends—most notably Senator John H. Eaton—to consider a run for the 1824 presidency. He was promptly elected to the U.S. Senate by the Tennessee legislature in October 1823. He followed the standard Western line and voted for high tariffs, import taxes, and internal improvements. He made a run for the White House in 1824 after he was endorsed by political conventions in a number of states.

The "Stolen Election" of 1824

The year 1824 was still a time when candidates didn't do any politicking for themselves. There was only one party of note, so the election came down to personalities. Jackson won both the popular and the electoral vote count, but the final electoral tally didn't produce a majority. Jackson received 99 votes, Secretary of State John Quincy Adams got 84, Secretary of the Treasury William Crawford earned 41, and Speaker of the House Henry Clay pulled in 37. The election was sent to the House of Representatives. The rules stipulated that each state got one vote, and only the top three candidates qualified. Clay helped engineer a shift in his Western votes to Adams, which gave the country the first son of a former president to follow suit.

Initially Jackson accepted the outcome as fair, but when Clay was appointed secretary of state, he and his followers believed they had been duped by a "corrupt bargain." Although Clay certainly lobbied for Adams, there was no evidence of any sort of deal. Still, it was seen as a stolen election—taken from the common man, who supported Jackson, and given to the corrupt political aristocracy. The stolen rights of the common man became the central creed of Jacksonian Democracy, and Jackson dedicated himself to winning the 1828 election.

Did Negative Ads Kill a First Lady?

The 1828 campaign was particularly vicious in the annals of American presidential elections. Jackson was labeled a drunk, a gambler, a murderer, and an adulterer (all true, to a degree), and a pamphlet circulated listing all of his altercations. Worse, Adams's followers went after Rachel, and the ugly business from her previous marriage was trumpeted in the newspapers. Rachel was apprehensive about Jackson becoming president, and the campaign affected her health. In December, she saw a pamphlet in Nashville that renounced all the rumors about her, but she had no idea how low the mudslinging had sunk. She broke down instantly and died of a heart attack. Jackson was convinced that it was brought on by the treacherous behavior of his opponents, and he remained bitter throughout his life.

The Jacksonian supporters were highly organized (as were their mudslinging attacks), and they covered a wide cross-section of citizens who were opposed to the Eastern elite. Jackson helped his cause by making one of his campaign stops at the site of his greatest victory, New Orleans. He cruised to an easy electoral victory over Adams 178 to 83, and John C. Calhoun was elected as his vice president.

Knowledge Is Power

The **spoils system** was the standard practice of awarding political jobs and public appointments to family and party affiliates instead of on merit. The spoils system flourished from the colonial days through the end of the nineteenth century but has never been totally eliminated and is still practiced to a much smaller degree today.

Jackson repaid those who were personally loyal to him, including Martin Van Buren, who became his secretary of state, and Senator John Eaton, who was named secretary of war. He relied more on a small group of unofficial and informal advisers known as the kitchen cabinet, who also kept his spirits up after Rachel's death. Two thousand of his supporters were given jobs through what would become known as the *spoils system.*

First Four Years: Sexual Affairs and Southern Nullification

Jackson didn't set the White House on fire during the first years of his administration, and the biggest issues centered on personality clashes. John C. Calhoun and Martin Van Buren were at odds over who would be the president's successor, and the dispute coalesced over a sex scandal involving Margaret Eaton (Peggy O'Neill or another version, O'Neale), wife of longtime Jackson friend John Eaton. Eaton and Jackson had resided at the boardinghouse owned by Margaret's mother, and he and Mrs. O'Neill, married to a naval officer, were rumored to be having an affair. When Mr. O'Neill died at sea, Margaret and John Eaton were quickly married. Once Eaton became secretary of war, the wives of the other Cabinet members, including Mrs. Calhoun, snubbed her and spread gossip about her immoral behavior. Jackson saw parallels to Rachel's situation, and Van Buren's refusal to ostracize Mrs. Eaton helped make him Jackson's protégé.

Commander in Chief Lore

Jackson's inaugural reception was a wild, raucous affair attended by thousands of his closest hard-drinking friends. They ran through the executive mansion like it was a frat house on homecoming weekend, breaking glass and china, knocking over trays of food, tracking mud on the furniture, spilling whiskey, and spitting chewing tobacco everywhere. Throngs of folks tried to get a glimpse of Old Hickory, who finally escaped out a back door. The crowds were disbursed by placing the refreshments on the lawn and locking the doors behind them.

Calhoun also supported South Carolina's attempts at nullification, which argued that a state could rightfully deny any federal legislation if it wasn't in the state's best interests. Calhoun's home state was becoming much more antiprotectionist, and he felt that the 1828 "Tariff of Abominations" was unconstitutional and called for the doctrine of nullification. Jackson's supporters waited to hear his repudiation of Calhoun. At a Jefferson birthday dinner in 1830, Jackson looked at Calhoun and said, "Our Federal Union, it must be preserved." To which Calhoun replied, "The Union—next to our liberty, the most dear!" (As a senator, Calhoun would later defend South Carolina's nullification ordinance against the tariff, which raised Jackson's ire, even though he, too, was a states' rights proponent.)

After there were rumblings of secession from the Union, Jackson put the military on notice and spread the word that Calhoun would hang if South Carolina bolted from the Union. A compromise tariff passed in 1833, but the incident foreshadowed the divisions between the North and South that would lead to the Civil War.

In light of the Eaton affair, the kitchen cabinet informed Jackson that Calhoun had called for his arrest during the Seminole War. In 1831, Eaton and Van Buren resigned from the Cabinet to give Jackson more leeway in a wholesale change. All the Calhoun supporters were sent packing, and Jackson was able to appoint his own men.

Driving Native Americans from Their Home

Jackson may have been billed as a "man of the people," but not to the Indian people. Jackson was always reported to be a benevolent slave owner, and he allowed women and children to escape during the Seminole War, but the personal decency he exhibited was far overshadowed by the complete disregard of Indian peoples on a national level.

Jackson may have offered the olive branch at his inauguration, but he coldly turned his back on their concerns. In Georgia, the Cherokee nation was being driven from its native land, and Jackson stated that he wouldn't interfere with the sovereignty of individual states (except, of course, when it came to abiding by the tariff). The Cherokee peoples appealed to the Supreme Court, and Chief Justice John Marshall ruled that the federal government had full jurisdiction over Indian lands, which should be protected. The renowned Native American-killer Jackson is said to have responded, "John Marshall has made his decision. Now let him enforce it."

The removal of the Cherokee nation continued unabated until all the tribes were marched to their new territory in present-day Oklahoma. Jackson's horrible record in dealing with Native Americans began with the Indian Removal Act of 1830 and

Prez Says

"It will be my sincere and constant desire to observe toward the Indian tribes within our limits a just and liberal policy, and to give that humane and considerate attention to their rights and their wants which is consistent with the habits of our Government and the feelings of our people."

—From Andrew Jackson's inaugural speech, March 4, 1829

led to an estimated quarter of the peoples dying on the "Trail of Tears." Although there was criticism of Jackson's policies regarding Native Americans, he was certainly not alone in his exploitative frontier attitude.

Taking on the Bank

In 1832, one of Jackson's major concerns was his opposition to the re-chartering of the Second Bank of the United States, which expired in 1836. The bank had been established to oversee the nation's monetary system in a cooperation between private and public interests. Jackson wanted to revoke the bank's charter when it expired because he felt that it favored the creditors and aristocrats and didn't benefit the working classes in an economy that was still agrarian. Although the Bank of the United States certainly favored the privileged, it also provided stability for American business, which Jackson disregarded. Jackson didn't want the bulk of the country's wealth concentrated in the hands of the few.

Commander in Chief Lore

The 1832 presidential race was the first to have national party conventions. Jackson was nominated in Baltimore by the Jacksonians, a group that evolved into the Democratic Party.

In the summer of 1832, Henry Clay steered legislation through Congress that renewed the charter, which Jackson promptly vetoed. Clay brought the issue to the table four years early because he wanted to make it the central issue of the fall presidential election, hoping that so many people would owe the bank a big chunk of money that they wouldn't want to see it close. Clay's plan worked: This became the central issue, but it backfired because he was trounced 219 to 49 in electoral votes.

Knowledge Is Power

Pet banks were smaller state banks that received a portion of federal funds distributed after the National Bank was dissolved.

In 1833, Jackson set out to destroy the Bank of the United States and took steps to transfer federal funds to selected *pet banks,* or state banks, throughout the country. The Senate voted to censure Jackson for his unconstitutional actions, but the House passed resolutions pledging support of the president. The president of the bank, Nicholas Biddle, dug his heels in and began calling in loans and limiting credit. In 1834, the country slipped into a depression, and Jackson laid the blame at the feet of Biddle. The public rallied around Old Hickory as Biddle's entrenchment gave credence to the belief that concentrated wealth was a detriment to the public at large. The Bank of the United States disappeared into the winds of fiscal ghosthood when its charter expired in 1836.

Wildcat Woes

Jackson was able to do something no other president has been able to do: He lived up to his inaugural pledge and totally wiped out the national debt in January 1835. The country was rapidly expanding westward, and sale of public lands raised a large federal surplus.

A brief period of prosperity followed, but problems soon arose because Jackson distributed extra funds to the pet banks. They began overextending credit in paper notes called specie that exceeded the silver and gold in their holdings. "Wildcat" banks sprang up throughout the West and were about as fiscally responsible as the banker in a game of Monopoly at the Department of Defense. Inflation set in, and the value of specie plummeted, leaving the federal government with worthless paper money. In 1836, Jackson issued the Specie Circular, ordering all payments for federal land to be made in gold or silver. After he left office, Jackson's opponents blamed his measures as the root cause of the Panic of 1837.

That's the Facts, Jackson

➤ In 1835, Andrew Jackson survived the first presidential assassination attempt. While attending a funeral, a man drew pistols, but they misfired.

➤ Jackson's White House parties were always open to the public and heavily attended, the guests once ate a 1,400-pound cheese wheel in two short hours.

➤ Jackson was the first sitting president to ride a train, taking the Baltimore and Ohio in Maryland from Ellicott's Mills to Baltimore on June 6, 1833. John Quincy Adams had ridden the same route after leaving office.

➤ Jackson appointed Roger Taney as Chief Justice of the Supreme Court, and later Taney denied the right of a slave to sue for freedom in the landmark Dred Scott Case of 1857.

➤ On his last day in office, Jackson formally recognized the independence of Texas, paving the way for future annexation.

French Toast

The greatest achievement in Jackson's foreign policy was standing up to the French and demanding reparations for damages rendered upon a neutral U.S. ship during the Napoleonic Wars. France agreed to payments in 1831, but three years later, Jackson hadn't seen a single dime. Jackson asked Congress to allow him to seize French holdings in the United States, and he alerted the military. France broke off diplomatic relations but thought better than to test the military legend of Jackson and the upstart new nation. France made four past-due installments in 1836, which renewed friendly relations.

A Jackson in Winter

By 1836, Jackson was suffering from tuberculosis and didn't entertain any precedent-setting ideas of seeking a third term. However, he ensured that his handpicked successor, Martin Van Buren, was the nominee. At Van Buren's inauguration, thousands of common folk went wild for their departing president. (The two men would later have a falling out when Van Buren didn't back the annexation of Texas, so Jackson supported James K. Polk for president in 1844.)

He spent the last eight years of his life at Hermitage following national affairs and tending to his plantation. He had suffered throughout his adult life from the bullets stuck in his body and from consistent hemorrhaging and dysentery. On June 8, 1845, Andrew Jackson died in his bed, long after bullets, arrows, tomahawks, sabers, swords, and fists had given him all that he could handle. He was buried beside his great departed love, Rachel.

Jackson was certainly one of the most unique men to ever grace the office of president of the United States. He used the presidential veto as his personal prerogative, breaking standard tradition that it should be used only for unconstitutional matters and strengthening the executive branch. He was also the leader during a great shift westward, and Jacksonian Democracy truly included the working class in the political process for the first time. Unfortunately, he didn't extend the same rights to Native Americans.

Jackson's frontier spirit has become part of the internal fabric of the United States, and breaking out on one's own away from the constraints of federal power is as relevant today as it ever was. For better or worse, Andrew Jackson was a wild man, an amazing character in a life greater than a work of fiction.

The Least You Need to Know

➤ Andrew Jackson was a tough war hero who made his name by dominating the British at the Battle of New Orleans.

➤ Jackson was the first populist president, and his working-class Jacksonian supporters evolved into the Democratic Party.

➤ Jackson abolished the Bank of the United States because he felt that it concentrated wealth in the hands of the few.

➤ Jackson may have been a man of the people, but that didn't include Native Americans.

Chapter 9

The Formidable Forgotten: James K. Polk

In This Chapter

➤ Why isn't Polk better known?

➤ "Young Hickory," Jacksonian to the core

➤ Stretching the states from sea to shining sea

➤ What's this? Campaign promises actually fulfilled?

An informal ranking of the eight greatest presidents by Harry Truman was discovered after his death. Next to one name he had written, "This may surprise some people," and the inclusion of James Knox Polk probably did. But, maybe it shouldn't have; maybe Polk should be renowned as the Jacksonian protégé who saw fit to follow through and accomplish everything he set out to do. Yes, that's right—we once had a leader who made good on all his campaign promises.

Rocky Top Rearing

James Polk was born on a farm on the North Carolina frontier in 1795, but his family moved to central Tennessee during his youth. His father became a leading landowner, and James Polk became a sickly and lonely child. He suffered from severe abdominal pains, and the resulting inactivity forced him to spend most of his time in solitary confines. Life inside a weakened body made him determined to have a sharp mind, but it would be tough because he could barely read or write until his formal education began at the age of 18.

Commander in Chief Lore

In 1812, Polk's father took him to Kentucky to see the famous surgeon Dr. Ephraim McDowell, who diagnosed James with gallstones that needed to be removed immediately. Medical standards did not yet include anesthesia or antiseptics, so James Polk was strapped to the table, and the operation commenced with only alcohol to dull the pain. Surgery itself was a common killer in those days, but McDowell's handiwork was a success. Polk enjoyed much better health following the procedure.

In 1813, at age 18, Polk began his formal schooling at a Presbyterian school near his home and dedicated himself to making up for lost time. Within a year, he knew Greek, Latin, and proper English grammar, and in five short years he graduated with first honors in mathematics and the classics from the University of North Carolina. Polk was also introduced to the world of politics—particularly the politics of Thomas Jefferson—and, more importantly, to Tennessee's favorite son Andrew Jackson. Old Hickory had far and away the most influence on Polk's political life.

"Napoleon of the Stump"

Polk studied law under Congressman Felix Grundy. During his studies, the Panic of 1819 hit the country, especially in the agricultural communities of the West. Polk and Grundy were out on the judicial circuit, and Polk saw firsthand the suffering of the lower class and the resulting unrest. The tour reinforced Polk's adherence to a Jacksonian democracy and made him distrustful of banks, creditors, and paper currency. Grundy became an advocate for the causes of those in need, and Polk learned from his mentor.

Polk was admitted to the bar at the age of 24 and practiced law in Columbia, Tennessee, but his heart was in politics. He served in the state legislature until he was elected to Andrew Jackson's seat in the House of Representatives. He was known by his early supporters as "Napoleon of the Stump" because of his small stature, but he was an effective campaigner and speaker.

On New Year's Day, 1824, Polk married Sarah Childress, daughter of a leading family in Murfreesboro, the home of the legislature. James and Sarah Polk never had any children, but they had a happy marriage and shared a close relationship. She was completely devoted to his political career and would go on to become a popular First

Lady dedicated to her husband, who was not very well-liked because of his detached, suspicious, cold, and humorless personality.

Polk made a name for himself in the state legislature by championing the debtor class and pushing issues such as free public education. Polk entered the House of Representatives in 1825 just after the House passed over Jackson in favor of John Quincy Adams, even though Jackson had won the plurality of the popular and electoral votes. Jackson didn't hold a majority, though, and when Henry Clay, who was in fourth place, shifted his votes, Adams was the man in the White House. Polk would get his revenge against Clay later, but he was incensed at what happened to Jackson. In his debut speech, he called for an end to the electoral college and encouraged a constitutional amendment to give the people the chance to elect the president by direct popular vote.

First Family Factuals

It has been said that Sarah accepted Polk's marriage proposal on the condition that he run for the state legislature before they were wed. James was taken aback, but he agreed to the terms and ended up with a wife and an office.

Polk moved up the ranks quickly, serving as chairman of the Ways and Means Committee and making a name for himself as Old Hickory's right-hand man. Polk worked both behind the scenes and in the forefront to help get Jackson elected in 1828. He then helped steer the administration's legislation through the House of Representatives.

Polk believed in Jacksonian Democratic ideals, which aimed at helping create an agrarian society. Polk also was against high protective tariffs, a national bank, and the use of federal financing to build up the infrastructure—improving roads, bridges, etc.—even when it was a benefit to his constituents. Like his mentor Jackson, Polk adhered to a strict interpretation of the Constitution and to the importance of state's rights. He loathed the idea of consolidating power at the federal level, and he said that the power of money at the top will "control your election of president, of your senators, and of your representatives."

The Sole Speaker of the House

Dropping *Republican* from the Democratic-Republican Party and becoming simply the Democrats, the Jacksonians elected Polk to be Speaker of the House for the last two years of the Jackson administration and the first two years of the Van Buren era. (Interestingly, Polk is the only man to ever serve as both *Speaker of the House* and president.)

Polk was thrown into the soup with the hottest issue of the day—what else but slavery. The abolitionist movement was beginning to gather steam with a more hard-line agenda, and Polk had never known the intensities and passions surrounding the issue

Knowledge Is Power

The **Speaker of the House** is the presiding officer of the House of Representatives. After the vice president, the speaker is next in line for the presidency. The speaker is nominated by a caucus of the majority party members of the House and is elected by the House. The speaker appoints all select committees and has the right to vote, but usually exercises only the right to break a tie.

James K. Polk, eleventh president of the United States.

of slavery. Polk had grown up in a family of slave owners and had owned them himself on his plantation, viewing slavery as a necessary evil. He was wary of the motivations of the abolitionist movement, but he was not a militant supporter of slavery.

The Whig delegation in Congress had grown in size, and Polk was a constant target of their abuse. He resigned from Congress in 1839, and after 14 years in Congress, "Young Hickory" headed back to Tennessee to run for governor. In 1835, the Jacksonian Democrats had lost the governorship for the first time and he was considered the only man who could win it back now that Jackson was retired. The Panic of 1837 had provoked some criticism of Jackson's fiscal policies, but Polk was able to win the election by a narrow margin over the incumbent. He was able to rally the Democratic Party, but he failed to institute banking reforms. Polk lost the gubernatorial race in both 1841 and 1843, so his political outlook was not as rosy as he had once hoped.

Right Place, Right Time

In 1844, Martin Van Buren went into the Democratic convention in Baltimore as the front-runner, but he didn't support the annexation of the republic of Texas, so he wasn't very popular in the South or the West. James K. Polk was still considered a worthy candidate for the Democratic vice presidential nomination because he hadn't alienated the pro- and anti-Van Buren factions, which had split the party down the middle. After several ballots, it was obvious that the anti-Van Buren crowd was going to keep the vote deadlocked, and no candidate would emerge.

Polk's people started pressing the flesh and promoting him as both the perfect compromise candidate and Andrew Jackson's personal choice. On the ninth ballot, the delegates turned to Polk, and he was unanimously selected as the Democratic presidential nominee. Young Hickory was the first *dark horse* presidential candidate of a major party.

Knowledge Is Power

In a political arena, the term **dark horse** refers to a little known candidate who is unexpectedly nominated for higher office, usually as a compromise between differing factions within a single party.

Commander in Chief Lore

Polk's nomination was flashed from Baltimore to Washington, D.C., by the relatively new invention of Samuel F.B. Morse, the telegraph. This was the first political use of the communication device. Many of those in the nation's capital who got the message, however, thought that the gadget didn't work because they believed that the news it had relayed had to be wrong.

"54–40 or Fight!"

James Polk butted heads in the 1844 campaign with his old adversary, Henry Clay, the Whig candidate who had shifted his votes from Jackson to Adams a few years back. Clay played it coy and asked, "Who is James K. Polk?" when he learned who was to be his opponent. The question became the theme of Clay's campaign. But it didn't work. Polk was successfully able to use the same wedge issue that had separated him from Martin Van Buren: Western expansion.

Clay waffled on the Texas annexation, while Polk stood firm on his desire to acquire the Lone Star and Oregon territories from Mexico and Great Britain, respectively.

Knowledge Is Power

The **Liberty Party,** formed in 1839, was the first antislavery party in the United States. Birney was its candidate in both 1840 and 1844, and unfortunately for the cause, the 60,000–plus votes he received in New York ensured that the proslavery Polk would defeat the antislavery Clay.

Polk's catchy campaign ditty was "54–40 or Fight!" The slogan implied that Polk was willing to challenge Britain's possession of Oregon up to the 54 40 parallel, which would have made Alaska part of today's continental United States. Manifest destiny was all the rage out West, so Polk carried every Western state except for Ohio and, ironically, Tennessee.

Andrew Jackson intervened and wielded his influence to get President Tyler to withdraw as an independent candidate, which helped Polk's cause. More importantly, a candidate from the *Liberty Party,* John G. Birney, took away enough votes from Clay in New York to allow Polk to carry the state, making the difference in the nip-and-tuck election.

The final results were very tight. The popular vote was 1,338,464 to 1,300,097 (although some estimates have differed slightly), and the electoral vote was 170 to 105. The 36 votes in New York were the deciding factor, and a mere 5,000 separated Polk and Clay.

Other Forgotten Presidential Types

James Polk is generally considered to be the best president that time forgot, but here are some other presidential names that have been lost as well. Most likely because you never heard of them in the first place.

➤ **David Rice Atchison.** As the United States' only president for a day, he served in the 24 hours between the official end of Polk's presidency on March 3, 1849, and the swearing in of Zachary Taylor on March 5. "Old Rough and Ready" was a staunch Episcopalian and refused to be sworn in on a Sunday. As president pro tempore of the Senate, Atchison was in charge and took advantage of his power by going to bed.

➤ **Rev. Channing Emery Phillips.** This man from Washington, D.C., was the first black candidate ever endorsed by a major party—the Democrats at the Chicago convention in 1968. (Frederick Douglass was the first candidate ever to receive a nominating vote, a complimentary token on the fourth ballot at the Republican convention, again in the Second City, this time in 1888.)

➤ **Charles O'Conor.** At the Democratic convention in Louisville in 1872, O'Conor, from New York, was the first Catholic ever nominated for president. O'Conor declined the nomination but still garnered 30,000 votes.

➤ **Victoria Claflin Woodhull.** She was the first female presidential candidate, nominated by the Equal Rights Party at a meeting in 1872 at Apollo Hall, in New York City. (Frederick Douglass was the vice presidential nominee, although he wasn't present and didn't find out until later.) Margaret Chase Smith of Maine was the first woman nominated by a major party, in 1964 at the Republican National Convention in San Francisco.

➤ **John Hanson.** This man actually was the first president of the United States. Yes, Hanson was the first president to serve a full term after the full ratification of the Articles of Confederation. He was chosen unanimously by Congress (which included George Washington) to be their president and served a one-year term, which included ordering the removal of foreign troops from American soil, establishing the first Treasury Department, and decreeing that Thanksgiving would fall on the fourth Thursday of every November. Seven other men served one-year terms before Washington was elected under the Constitution and became the "first" President of the United States.

Sticking to the Game Plan

James Polk entered the White House with clear objectives on the table. He wanted to settle the Oregon boundary issue with Great Britain, reduce the tariff to a revenue level and eliminate the protective principle, and establish an independent treasury as an alternative to a strong central bank. And, he added that he would like to acquire California.

Deep in the Heart of Texas

Three days prior to Polk's inauguration, President Tyler signed a bill annexing Texas to the United States. By the fourth month of Polk's administration, the annexation was complete. Mexico cut off relations with the United States because Texas had originally agreed to remain an independent nation. In 1845, Polk sent diplomat John Slidell to Mexico to try to purchase New Mexico and California for around $40 million, but relations were beyond repair. Polk was preparing for war when word came on May 9, 1846, that Mexican troops had crossed the Rio Grande and fired on American troops. It was a disputed territory between the Rio Grande and Nueces and there has long been speculation that U.S. troops instigated the fighting to have a concrete reason for going to war. The exact details will never be known, but whatever happened in the disputed region, on May 11, Polk charged that Mexico "invaded our territory and shed American blood."

On May 13, Congress declared war on the United States' neighbor to the south. Abolitionists opposed the war with Mexico, and many saw it as a conspiracy to enlarge proslavery territory. A young man in the House of Representatives named Abraham Lincoln called the president on the carpet for starting the conflict, but the war was popular with Westerners and most Southerners, the bulk of Polk's constituents. In February 1847, Zachary Taylor led his troops to an astounding victory at the Battle of Buena Vista, and Americans captured Mexico City that September.

There was a large outcry in 1847 for Polk to annex all of Mexico, but he showed fairly remarkable restraint for the days of Manifest Destiny and added only New Mexico and California to U.S. holdings. A peace treaty was signed in February 1848, and Mexico was given $15 million for more than 500,000 square miles and a set border at the Rio Grande.

The war was important for reasons other than land acquisition. It was the first time that a president had his feet to the fire as commander in chief. Polk showed the world that a president (and one without military experience, no less) could indeed manage a war. It also sent a message to the monarchs of Europe that this new republic was not as weak as many of them assumed.

Oregon Ducks Another Battle

American settlers had been moving into the Oregon Territory in great numbers, and the United States claimed all land north of the Columbia River to the 54 40 parallel. Both Great Britain and the United States claimed the territory, and Polk had used the land as the centerpiece of his campaign.

Polk negotiated a compromise with Britain at the 49th parallel, which came off smoothly because the British had moved their fur trading operations north to Vancouver Island. Thus, the boundary was set at the 49th parallel, giving the United States its first Pacific beachfront property, and establishing the border that stands today. Some felt Polk was willing to fight to expand slave territory in the Southwest, but not in the antislavery Northwest. However, he took the Senate's advice and decided that "54–40 or Fight!" was a better campaign slogan than a policy.

Treasury Island

The Independent Treasury System, which had been put into place by President Van Buren in 1840, had been repealed in 1841 during the Tyler years. Polk was fortunate enough in the first two years of his term to be blessed with Democratic control of both houses of Congress, which basically gave him *carte blanche* to pass whatever legislation he saw fit. One of Polk's early acts was to reinstate the Independent Treasury System, which controlled the nation's nickels and dimes until the Federal Reserve System was put into place in 1913.

Walker, Tariff Ranger

Democrats had always been opposed to tariffs because they favored the Northern manufacturing base, not the cotton growing regions in the South. In 1846, Polk and his secretary of the treasury, Robert J. Walker, concocted a new tariff act that substantially lowered import duties on essential materials, such as coal and steel, and left higher rates remaining on luxury items. Polk pushed for more free trade with Great Britain, selling the program in the West by arguing that lower tariffs would allow for the sale of surplus grain overseas, which is exactly what happened.

Everybody Polk-A!

➤ The Polks banned drinking, dancing, and gambling from the White House, in part because both the First Couple were workaholics.

➤ During Polk's administration, the U.S. Naval Academy in Annapolis, Maryland was founded.

➤ As crucial as Polk's leadership was in helping establish Texas as a state in 1845, Young Hickory never set foot in the Lone Star State.

➤ Polk vowed to serve only one term, and he held true to his word.

➤ As president, Polk kept a thorough diary, which was originally published in four volumes in 1910 and has been abridged and reprinted in later years. It is considered one of the greatest insights into the day-to-day operations of life inside the White House during the times of expansion.

All Work and No Play Makes the Polks

Polk and his wife, Sarah, found outside activities frivolous, and if the parties they threw ran late, they would cut back on sleep to catch up on the work they missed. They never took vacations; he said, "No president who performs his duties faithfully and conscientiously has any leisure."

Polk constantly worked 12-hour days, and it probably contributed to his death, although he also had lifelong digestive problems. After leaving office in March 1849, he and Sarah planned a trip to Europe, but his health gave out. He died from

Prez Says

"Peace, plenty, and contentment reign throughout our borders, and our beloved country presents a sublime moral spectacle to the world."

—From James K. Polk's final State of the Union address

cholera within three months, but not before he was baptized a Methodist the week prior to his passing away. Sarah lived for another 40 years and turned their mansion into a museum of Polk's presidency.

From Sea to Shining Sea

Without a doubt, James K. Polk made the United States what it is today. Under the guise of Manifest Destiny, he added Texas, New Mexico, California, and Oregon, and gave the young country the Pacific border that ensured there would be no foreign settlements to impede the fledgling republic's westward drive. For that, James K. Polk deserves to be recognized as the most important and successful president between Jackson and Lincoln.

One theory as to why James Polk isn't a household name is because his personal demeanor was stiff, cold, a bit paranoid, and devoid of magnetism or charm. His greatest flaw, however, was probably sitting idly by as the Democratic Party was taken over by the proslavery faction. Still, he was a president who laid his plans on the table and saw them through, creating the continental United States we know today.

The Least You Need to Know

➤ James K. Polk is the best of the "forgotten" presidents.

➤ Polk was a Jacksonian Democrat through and through, and he was an integral cog in the party's shift to an agricultural working-class constituency.

➤ Polk oversaw the greatest expansion of the United States since the Louisiana Purchase by adding California, Texas, Oregon, and New Mexico.

➤ Polk's humorless demeanor contributed to his second-tier historical reputation, but his accomplishments were substantial.

Chapter 10

John Adams, Second-Chair Founding Father

In This Chapter

➤ Stamping out an unjust tax

➤ Taking on the case for a massacre

➤ Franklin, Adams, and the Treaty of Paris

➤ Now I know my XYZs

➤ Grumpy old men, Adams and Jefferson

If there is a "forgotten" founding father, a lesser-known framer of the United States of America as we know it, it would have to be John Adams. Although his name is instantly recognizable, his fascinating career and undue influence aren't as generally renowned as those of George Washington, Benjamin Franklin, and his political enemy, Alexander Hamilton.

But John Adams was one of only two presidents of the United States to sign the Declaration of Independence (Jefferson was the other). His signature on the hallowed document is a prime example of his crucial role in the country' struggle for freedom. Though his curse is always to be overshadowed by a fellow forefather such as the esteemed Thomas Jefferson, Adams deserves recognition for helping to champion—as lawyer, foreign minister, vice president, and president—the ideals of a young nation.

The Great Brain from Braintree

John Adams was raised in Braintree, Massachusetts, now known as Quincy, on the family farm in 1735. His family was well established within the community, and his father, John, served as an officer in the local militia. Adams entered Harvard College at the age of 16. After graduating in 1755, he took a job teaching school in Worcester for a year. He had ditched his original plans to join the clergy, but he didn't find education much to his liking, either. Like the majority of future presidents, he decided that a career in law would be the best choice.

James Putnam was the leading lawyer in Worcester, and Adams became his apprentice after giving up the schoolhouse. In 1758, Adams was admitted to the bar and returned to Braintree to practice law, hoping to use family connections to become a lawyer in the big city of Boston.

Unfair Paper-Stamping Unites the Colonialists

Adams began making regular trips to Boston for his practice and began taking an active role (along with distant cousin, Samuel Adams) in opposing the Stamp Act. The Stamp Act, passed in 1765, was a revenue-raising law imposed upon the colonies by the British Parliament. It required that all documents—from contracts to newspapers, to pamphlets, to pretty much any piece of paper floating around the colonies—had to be stamped in order to be legal. Of course, you had to pay a tax to get the stamp. Colonists hated the Stamp Act because they were being assessed a monetary penalty without having a voice in Parliament, and Adams began drawing up resolutions opposing it.

Adams argued that colonists had the same rights as British subjects under English law, and they weren't obliged to adhere to the Stamp Act because they had no voice in Parliament to give consent. Adams also argued that "no free man can be separated from his property but by his own act or fault," and he quickly became a prominent figure throughout the colonies. Great Britain repealed the Stamp Act in 1766, but a nationalist feeling had been born, and it was a slippery slope to the American Revolution.

In 1768, Adams moved his family and law practice to Boston. His patriotic reputation continued to grow as he gave legal assistance to residents who didn't kowtow to British authorities. Adams also drafted a letter, which made its way through the colonies, opposing

First Family Factuals

Traveling to and from Plymouth, Adams would stop in Weymouth to visit Abigail, daughter of the Reverend Mr. William Smith. Although she was 10 years younger than the 29-year-old Adams, they were married on October 25, 1764. They shared a heartfelt love and respect that is clearly portrayed in the letters they sent during 1774 to 1784, when Adams was in Europe representing the new nation. John and Abigail Adams are one of the great couples in United States history.

the 1767 Townsend Acts, unpopular British laws that included forced import taxes on glass, tea, paper, lead, and other commonly used goods.

John Adams, second president of the United States.

Liberty Trumps Violent Patriotism

A case could be made that Adams was the leading legal mind of colonial America, but such scholarship wasn't blinded by patriotism. Adams supported resistance to the English crown and was dedicated to liberty, but his independent spirit was also dedicated to justice. In 1770, he defended the British soldiers accused of murder in the *Boston Massacre* despite a great public indignation against the soldiers.

Over the denouncements of his cousin Samuel and other patriots, Adams and Josiah Quincy successfully got acquittals for all but two of the soldiers, who were convicted on the lesser charge of manslaughter. Although he was rebuked in many circles for taking the case, he was praised by many for his dedication to the ideals of liberty, and his patriotic reputation stayed intact.

Here Comes the Continental Congress

John Adams served in the Massachusetts legislature for a few months in 1770. He grew ill and moved back to Braintree, but soon he was back in Boston writing letters opposing British policies. Adams had always believed in what was based in law; he had never been opposed to reconciliation with Britain, but he fully embraced the rebellious act of the Boston Tea Party on December 16, 1773. Samuel had helped organize the protest of the British tea tax and unfair trade restrictions. Great Britain retaliated by shutting down the port of Boston, and from then on, Adams was aligned with the radical protesters.

Knowledge Is Power

The **Boston Massacre** resulted in the deaths of five Bostonians, shot by British soldiers on March 5, 1770. Colonists had been protesting the Townsend Acts since they were imposed, and one unruly mob incited British troops to fire on a crowd. Samuel Adams used the Boston Massacre to unite colonists and stir up resentment against Great Britain. This was another crucial event along the road to the American Revolution.

Prez Says

"A government of laws and not of men."

—From the *Novanglus Papers*, by John Adams

John and Sam in Philly

In 1774, John and Samuel Adams were both delegates to the First Continental Congress in Philadelphia, Pennsylvania. The First Continental Congress was convened primarily to deal with the Intolerable Acts, British laws that included the closing of the port of Boston, the requirement that colonists lodge English soldiers, and the revocation of Massachusetts' charter. Opinions varied as to what action should be taken, but a total separation from Great Britain wasn't on the table. The Adams cousins, however, were adamant about taking a hard line against the injustices being foisted upon the colonies.

Ultimately, the strongest measure was a call to form an association that would boycott trade with Great Britain. Adams returned to Massachusetts and wrote articles for the *Boston Gazette* under the pseudonym Novanglus, detailing the principles of liberty and law that characterized the patriot position.

By the time the Second Continental Congress convened in Philadelphia in 1775, the American Revolution had already begun with the shot heard 'round the world and the battles of Lexington and Concord. Adams was zealous for action against Great Britain. Other delegates were wary of uniting the colonies and preparing for war. Adams saw the potential for a split between the eager New Englanders and the cautious South, so he nominated Virginia militia colonel George Washington as commanding general of the new Continental Army. The troops consisted primarily of Northern militiamen, and Adams thought that a Southern leader would help establish a national army. Adams also successfully lobbied for the institution of a naval force to challenge Britain's oceanic dominance; in May 1776, he saw the passage of his proposal that urged all colonies to create independent governments.

Today Is Our Independence Day

Adams worked diligently to get Congress to formally declare the colonies' freedom from Great Britain. His wish was fulfilled in June 1776 when a committee was formed to put the sentiments into an official document. Adams had a reputation as a fine writer, but he deferred to Thomas Jefferson. The reasons, noted in the *Diary and Autobiography of John Adams,* were that Jefferson was a Virginian, a Southern man, and "I had been so obnoxious from my early and constant Zeal in promoting the Measure, that any draught of mine would undergo a more severe Scrutiny and Criticism in Congress than one of his composition."

Adams was the spokesman for the Declaration of Independence to Congress; a series of arguments ensued because there was still hope for reconciliation with Britain in some delegations. Adams stepped up and led the independence cause, and on July 4, 1776, Congress (with New York abstaining) approved the Declaration of Independence.

Commander in Chief Lore

Adams called the day Congress voted for independence "the most memorable epoch in the history of America" and said, "I am apt to believe that it will be celebrated by succeeding generations as the great Anniversary Festival." Of course he was speaking of—July 2? Adams wrote these lines to Abigail on the day Congress adopted Virginia delegate Richard Henry Lee's resolution that said, "These United Colonies are, and of right ought to be, free and independent States"—July 2. But Jefferson's Declaration of Independence wasn't accepted until two days later. Perhaps we should all take July 2 through 4 off to celebrate our freedom and call it even—but only in deference to President Adams, of course.

Adams was ecstatic that the colonies had pronounced themselves free of British rule. He wrote his beloved Abigail from Philadelphia that the event "ought to be solemnized with pomp and parade, with shows, games, sports, guns, bells, bonfires, and illuminations, from one end of this continent to the other, from this time forward, forevermore" (and firecracker wholesalers have been grateful ever since).

John Adams: The European Years

Now a hot patriot property, Adams was elected to go to Europe as commissioner to France to help negotiate a military and commercial coalition and sign treaties of friendship with the European power that recognized the United States. Unfortunately, by the time he got to Paris in 1778, Benjamin Franklin had taken care of business. There was nothing for Adams to do except wait for his Congressional commission, so he and his son (and future president) John Quincy took in the sights and studied European politics. Adams returned to Braintree in 1779 and took an active role in the Massachusetts constitutional convention. He wrote most of the state constitution, which became the model for many other states across the country and still hasn't been fundamentally altered.

Prez Says

"The rich, the well-born, and the able, acquire an influence among the people that will soon be too much for simple honesty and plain sense, in a house of representatives. The most illustrious of them must, therefore, be separated from the mass, and placed by themselves in a senate; this is, to all honest and useful intents, an ostracism."

—John Adams, from *A Defence of the Constitutions of the Government of the United States of America*

Adams was sent back to Paris in 1780 with full power to negotiate a peace treaty to end the Revolutionary War with Great Britain. As was his nature, he grew impatient with the delay caused by Britain's refusal to sign a treaty recognizing the United States' independence. Furthermore, France wanted the United States to defer to its interests. Adams flew the coop to the Netherlands and convinced the Dutch to fork over a $2 million loan, recognize the new United States, and sign a treaty of friendship and commerce. His treaty with the Dutch was a shot in the arm for Americans because the Dutch weren't known to dole out money lightly.

Commander in Chief Lore

While traveling during the American Revolution, John Adams and Benjamin Franklin followed the custom of the day and shared a bed. There is an oft-told anecdote that the two stubborn men argued deep into the night over whether the window should stay open or closed.

Adams returned to France in October 1782 and joined John Jay and Benjamin Franklin in discussions with Great Britain. They decided to completely ignore their instructions to allow French oversight of the peace agreement and negotiated the Treaty of Paris, which officially ended the American Revolution on September 3, 1783. Ignoring their intervention was important because the French were willing to accept the Appalachian Mountains as the western boundary of the United States. Adams added two other key provisions to the treaty. He insisted on the rights for Americans to fish off the Canadian coast in the North Atlantic and expanded the young country's western boundary as far as he could, to the Mississippi River. Benjamin Franklin has long gotten most of the credit for the Treaty of Paris, but Adams and Jay deserve equal acclamation for their efforts in securing the sovereignty of the United States of America.

Adams stayed in Europe, becoming the United States' first minister to Great Britain in 1785. It was a relatively fruitless endeavor; his efforts to establish a commercial trade treaty were rebuffed at every turn, and the two countries weren't able to lay the groundwork of friendly relations. During this time, Adams penned *A Defence of the Constitutions of Government of the United States of America,* which would be cited at the Constitutional Convention in 1787. He also became close friends with Thomas Jefferson, who was living in Paris at the time. They toured the home of William Shakespeare together and frequently corresponded. Adams grew restless and frustrated over the lack of progress with Great Britain and returned to Braintree in February 1788.

Knowledge Is Power

The elections of George Washington and John Adams were carried out by members of the **electoral college,** who were chosen by each individual state. The two differences between the system then and the system now were that each elector got two votes and that the second highest recipient automatically became vice president. Before 1804, even if a candidate ran in good faith as the vice president, if he received enough electoral votes, he could become president or at least throw a wrench in the works (see the election of 1800). The twelfth amendment to the Constitution, ratified in 1804, changed the election process of the vice president to mirror the election of the president. Electors voted for each office separately from then on.

The No. 1 No. 2

By the time Adams returned to the shores of the infant nation, the Constitution had been written and individual state ratification was underway. A new system for electing a President of the United States had been created, called the *electoral college.* In the first presidential election, all 69 votes went to the beloved American war hero George Washington. Washington's next-in-line wasn't selected with the same ringing endorsement, but the respected diplomat John Adams garnered the second highest vote total, 34, and became the first vice president in American history.

Adams Dwells Within the "Most Insignificant Office"

Adams didn't care much for the job of vice president; he was a lively man who courted numerous responsibilities and duties. He called the vice presidency the "most insignificant office that ever the invention of man contrived or his imagination conceived." (This spirited endorsement for the position was probably outdone only by Franklin Roosevelt's vice president, John Nance "Cactus Jack" Garner, who said that the office wasn't "worth a bucket of spit.")

Adams did cast some important tie-breaking votes in the newly invented Senate, consistently supporting his boss George Washington and measures that strengthened the powers of the executive office. Adams also tried to follow Washington's example and remain above partisan politics, but this stance worked against him. Adams endorsed a strong central government, one of the tenets of the Federalist Party, but his efforts to remain nonpartisan enabled Alexander Hamilton to become the Federalists' leader.

Prez Says

"It has been said that it is extremely difficult to preserve liberty .... It is so difficult that the very appearance of it is lost over the whole earth, excepting one island and North America."

—From *Discourses on Davila*, by John Adams

Opposed to the Federalists was the Republican Party (soon to be known as the Democratic-Republican Party, and ultimately the Democratic Party of today), led by Secretary of State Thomas Jefferson. The Republicans favored putting the power in the hands of the individual states and, ostensibly, the people. Jefferson didn't agree with Adams's articles, entitled *Discourses on Davila,* which came out against the civil disobedience and governmental configuration of the French Revolution. Jefferson was a firm believer in the cause of the French Revolutionists, but Adams didn't share Jefferson's faith in human nature; he feared that domination by the people was just as likely as domination by the monarchy. The violence and chaos of the French Revolution strengthened Adams's belief that Great Britain was the only European country getting it right.

Although Adams generally supported the Federalist Party, he and the other high-profile party member, Alexander Hamilton, had basic differences. Hamilton envisioned a government run by a select cadre of aristocrats, whereas Adams favored a government run by career politicians and wanted life-long terms for the Senate so that they couldn't be voted out on the whim of the masses. Hamilton would have preferred that someone besides Adams be the primary Federalist Party representative, but he failed to rally enough support for his favored candidate Thomas Pinckney. Adams's reputation grew in the eyes of moderate politicians when he stayed out of the dispute over the pro-England Jay Treaty with Great Britain in 1794, which, among other provisions, ended the seizing of neutral American ships by England. The Jay Treaty was generally unpopular outside of the staunch Federalists because it was viewed as too favorable for the British, and it was hated by the pro-French Republicans. This led to partisan bickering in the newspapers, and since Adams' more moderate disapproval of the Jay Treaty mirrored many politicians, it helped his political standing. Adams also had the backing of almost all of his native New England and the endorsement of the nation's beloved leader George Washington, which included all the federal workers who had their jobs because of him. Adams now clearly had the best chance to win the presidential election of 1796, but it would turn out to be very close.

Adams and Jefferson Square Off in the First Two-Man Contest

George Washington declined to run for a third presidential term, which made his choice, Adams, the de facto Federalist candidate. For the first time in American history, there would be a contested election for the highest office in the land, against Republican candidate Thomas Jefferson. Hamilton still supported Pinckney, but this was before parties nominated a single candidate and there was no official nomination (born in the West Indies, Hamilton was ineligible for the highest office). Neither actively campaigned, but their supporters did a fine job of setting the precedent for future mud-slinging in national elections. Jefferson's backers claimed that Adams's ultimate goal was to establish a monarchy for his offspring; Adams's backers said that Jefferson wanted to overthrow the Constitution and start a revolution like the one in France.

Commander in Chief Lore

The 1796 election of Federalist President John Adams and Republican Vice President Thomas Jefferson is the only time in the history of the United States that the top two leaders came from different political parties.

Alexander Hamilton almost lost the election for the Federalists by encouraging southern electors to vote for Thomas Pinckney as vice president, which, coupled with his presumed northern support for Adams and Pinckney, would give his man the majority of electoral votes. Hamilton wanted Pinckney because he would be able to wield much greater control and influence, but many New Englanders left Pinckney off their ballot when they learned of the plan. Adams was elected the second president of the

United States by the slimmest of electoral margins, 71 to 68 (Pinckney grabbed 59), and the election standards of the day made Jefferson his vice president.

Adams was inaugurated at Federal Hall in Philadelphia, still the nation's capital, on March 4, 1797. He noted in his address that the world had just witnessed the peaceful exchange in the executive office in the new republic and called for an end to the constant partisanship (sound familiar?). Huge cheers went up; unfortunately for President Adams, they were mostly for the outgoing President Washington. Adams was no sooner in office than he was confronted with the prospect of war with France.

First Family Factuals

In 1800, John and Abigail Adams moved from Philadelphia to the new executive mansion in Washington, D.C., becoming the first residents of the White House while the paint was still drying. Abigail became the first to preside over the "President's House" and found the yet-to-be completed mansion and surroundings to her liking. Abigail was perturbed, however, that she couldn't seem to get anyone to go into the woods and chop and bring firewood for the Adams' Family fires.

The ABCs of XYZ

The Jay Treaty with Great Britain had so enraged France that it began plundering American vessels in the high seas in early 1797. Relations with France had deteriorated throughout the pro-British Washington administration. They had wanted American support in their war against Great Britain and felt the Jay Treaty aided British shipping concerns, which wasn't the stated American neutral stance. By summer, the French had commandeered some 300 ships, announced that they would hang any American caught on British crafts, and sent U.S. diplomats to France back home.

Adams advocated neutrality, but it was rapidly becoming an impossible stance to maintain. The political rift was right down the middle; Federalists backed Hamilton and his calls for war, but Republicans followed Jefferson's lead and pledged their loyalty to the French. Adams called a special session of Congress and proposed a compromise: to prepare the national defense while a three-man diplomatic envoy tried to work things out with France.

Gaulish Graft

The commissioners Adams sent to France were met with an unexpected proposal by agents from the office of French foreign minister Charles Talleyrand. The agents proposed that the United States pay Talleyrand a substantial sum of money and finance a large loan to the French government. In other words, they were asking for an old-fashioned bribe.

The diplomats rejected the shady "proposal" and reported back to an anxious Adams. Adams considered calling for a declaration of war, but he decided to keep the information secret and concoct a new course of action. Republicans, thinking that Adams was suppressing information that would help their pro-French cause, demanded that he reveal what had happened. Adams allowed the details to be published intact, altering only the names of the French agents to X, Y, and Z. The XYZ Affair gave rise to a higher degree of anti-French sentiment in the United States.

Commander in Chief Lore

As anti-French feelings grew throughout the country, a national call of "Millions for defense, but not one cent for tribute" was used to voice sentiment for what Adams's policy should be.

In the Navy

In January 1798, Adams suggested the formation of a navy department and asked for funding to ensure preparedness if war became inevitable. Adams recruited George Washington as the supreme head of the new U.S. Army (Hamilton was appointed second in command), Benjamin Stoddert was named Secretary of the Navy, and three frigates were built.

Adams was still searching for a way to avoid war with France, but popular sentiment favored engagement. Hamilton maneuvered behind the scenes to get the United States into war. Out of respect to Washington, and because no protocol had been established, Adams made a crucial mistake by keeping the entire Cabinet intact. The Cabinet was exceedingly Hamiltonian and often consulted Hamilton behind the president's back, which certainly hindered his presidency.

On February 18, 1799, Adams made a bold, independent move by announcing a new attempt to open diplomatic relations with France. He dispatched William Vans Murray with full treaty powers. When congressional Federalists refused to back the plan, Adams simply told them that he would retire and leave the presidency in the hands of their hated rival, Thomas Jefferson. In another unexpected wrinkle, Adams ordered the commissioners (it had grown to three: Patrick Henry and Chief Justice Oliver Ellsworth would join Murray) to set sail ASAP.

Alienating Free Speech

In 1798, the threat of war reached its fever pitch, and the Federalist Congress passed the Alien and Sedition Acts. The acts were created to limit criticism of Federalist policies in Jeffersonian newspapers and among political opponents, and gave the federal government the power to throw said offenders into jail. The acts, which were in direct violation of the Bill of Rights and severely crippled free speech, were signed into law by Adams, although he never applied or enforced them very stringently. The Alien and Sedition Acts did open the floodgates of protest against the Federalist Party and built support for the Republicans, which made sense, because they were the most egregious assault on American free speech in history.

Negotiations with France were slow, but a treaty was signed on September 30, 1800. Adams kept the United States out of a war with France, which would have been lead by the glory-seeking hawk Alexander Hamilton because Washington, leader of the armed forces, had died in December 1799. It isn't a stretch to say that Adams's ability to keep the young republic out of another major war with a European power was one of the top achievements of the early days of the United States.

Would You Believe, It's John Adams?

➤ John Adams was often called the "Atlas of Independence."

➤ In 1796, Adams spearheaded (with Franklin and Jefferson) the addition of *E Pluribus Unum,* meaning "Out of Many, One," to American coinage.

➤ Adams was the great-great-paternal-grandson of John and Priscilla Alden, Puritan pilgrims who landed at Plymouth Rock in 1620.

➤ Adams was the first president of the United States to establish and review the U.S. Marine band, the country's oldest professional musical organization.

➤ Adams didn't attend Jefferson's inauguration, but it isn't known whether that was because he was bitter over the election, whether he was still grieving over the death of his son, or whether he was simply uninvited.

➤ Adams lived longer than any president—90 years and 247 days.

A Federalist Split Sends Adams Packing

Hamilton helped see to it that Adams didn't get re-elected in 1800. Hamilton was furious that Adams had bluntly forced the resignations of two cabinet members, Secretary of State Timothy Pickering and Secretary of War James McHenry, who were disloyal to the president and often followed Hamilton's orders. He engineered the subversion of Adams's chances by circulating nasty Cabinet gossip and innuendo against the president and by rallying support for Thomas Pinckney. Hamilton had finally triumphed over Adams, but the victory was a hollow one: The presidency went to the complete anti-Federalist Thomas Jefferson.

In 1801, Jefferson and Adams had a falling out over Adams's last-minute "midnight" appointments of Federalist judges and court officials. Jefferson considered some of the appointees political enemies and felt that the sitting president had acted in bad faith to spite the new president after the election had taken place. Adams's reasons are his alone, but he did leave early the next morning for Massachusetts, bitter that he had been abandoned by his own party.

Adams never served in another public office. He did become president of the Massachusetts Society of Arts and Sciences, however, and he continued to write. He took great pleasure in living to see his son John Quincy Adams elected as president in 1824. He and his rival Thomas Jefferson eventually reconciled as well and began a lively correspondence that lasted the rest of their lives.

John Adams will always be a character actor compared to leading men like Washington, Franklin, Hamilton, and Jefferson, but perhaps he shouldn't be. Adams was an equally important founding father who kept a young country out of a war it may not have been ready to fight.

Commander in Chief Lore

In one of those bizarre coincidences that would seem completely phony if it were made up, John Adams and Thomas Jefferson died on the same day, within a few hours of each other. Adams's last words were, "Jefferson still survives," which wasn't the case because Jefferson had died a few hours prior. And what day did the only two presidents to sign the Declaration of Independence die on? July 4, 1826, the fiftieth anniversary of the independence of the United States of America.

The Least You Need to Know

➤ John Adams was a leading colonial lawyer who showed himself to be on the side of law and liberty: He crusaded against the unjust policies of England, yet he defended the British soldiers in the Boston Massacre.

➤ Adams played a key role in both sessions of the Continental Congress and in the presentation of the Declaration of Independence.

➤ Adams played a key role in the negotiations of the Treaty of Paris because he expanded the western border of the United States to the Mississippi River.

➤ Adams kept the United States out of a major conflict with France, despite the fact that the XYZ Affair brought the country to the brink of war and that his own Federalist Cabinet was against him.

➤ Adams was hung out to dry by Alexander Hamilton and the Federalist Party, but his influence on the founding of the United States is undeniable.

Part 3

Middleweights

"And still the question, 'What shall be done with our ex-Presidents?' is not laid at rest; and I sometimes think Watterson's solution of it, 'Take them out and shoot them,' is worthy of attention."

—From a letter written by Grover Cleveland to William F. Vilas, April 19, 1889

Don't be so harsh on yourself, President Cleveland—had the citizenry followed your recommendation after your initial administration, you wouldn't be the answer to the trivia question, "Who is the only president to have served two nonconsecutive terms?" The "Middleweights" are a group of men, like Dwight Eisenhower and William McKinley, who ably served in the executive office, but who didn't have quite the impact on the office as the leaders in the first two sections. This section also incorporates presidents such as Ronald Reagan and Lyndon Johnson, who made huge gains but also faced major setbacks.

Chapter 11

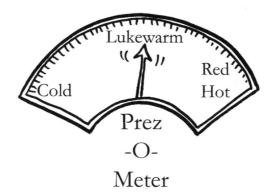

Cleveland Rocks the White House: Grover Cleveland

Mention Grover Cleveland to most folks, and one nugget of presidential trivia instantly comes to mind: He was the only man to call the White House home for two nonconsecutive terms. Even Grandpa Simpson recalled this fact when he told young Bart and Lisa that discipline used to be handed down from above and that he was "spanked by Grover Cleveland on two nonconsecutive occasions."

It is one of those bits of wisdom that everybody seems to recall from their grade school civics class, a *Jeopardy* question we can all buzz in on. Is this Cleveland's only contribution to the annals of presidential history? Of course not, but it will probably be the only thing you remember a year after reading this *Complete Idiot's Guide*. It might take a little effort, but remember also that Cleveland is regarded as a man who showed true character in a time of corruption and backroom deals, to the point that he alienated many of those who voted for him in the first place.

New York State of Mind

Stephen Grover Cleveland was the fifth of nine children born to a Presbyterian minister in Caldwell, New Jersey, in 1837. Times were tough in the Garden State back then (the strip mall had yet to be invented), so the family packed up and headed west—all the way to Fayetteville, New York. Cleveland attended the local academy, but his father died in 1853 and college became a financial impossibility. He then headed off to Gotham and spent a year teaching at the state institution for the blind in New York City.

Cleveland went on to live with his uncle, Lewis F. Allen, near Buffalo and began working in Allen's lucrative cattle-breeding business. Allen was well known and was able to get Cleveland a nonpaying job in one of the top law firms in Buffalo. Cleveland studied law intensely and was soon given a modest salary. In 1859, at the age of 22, he was licensed to practice law.

After Millard Fillmore, Allen was the most prominent man in Buffalo, and he organized Erie County's Republican Party. But his nephew eschewed his political affiliation, revealing an independent streak that would become his trademark. Cleveland preferred the Democrats because they believed in "solid" and "conservative" thought, and he didn't much care for the Republican presidential nominee John Charles Freemont.

Commander in Chief Lore

When the Civil War broke out, Grover Cleveland exercised his legal right, under the Federal Conscription Act, to hire a substitute (for $150) to take his place in the Union Army. Two of his brothers volunteered, but Cleveland defended his actions on the grounds that he had to earn enough money to take care of his mother and five sisters.

Cleveland worked in local Democratic wards and was appointed assistant district attorney of Erie County in 1863. He served until 1865, spent six years in private practice and became sheriff in 1871. His reputation as a hard-working man of integrity grew, and the Democrats of Buffalo nominated Cleveland for mayor in 1881, a political office that had been ripe with corruption and inefficiency for many a moon.

Cleveland won by a comfortable margin, garnering votes from all walks of citizens looking for an honest mayor. He became known as the "veto mayor" because he vetoed so many shady bills put forth by Buffalo aldermen and thwarted a scheme to bilk the city out of $200,000 in a cleaning contract.

Cleveland's stint as mayor was short-lived, however, because he was nominated for governor in 1882.

Everything's Coming Up Cleveland

If the old adage that luck is the intersection of hard work and opportunity has any truth to it, it could be found in the remarkably rapid rise of Grover Cleveland. The 1882 gubernatorial election in New York pitted two lackluster candidates for the Democratic nomination at a time when a large number of reformers clamored for a man who wasn't aligned with Tammany Hall. Democratic leaders read the tea leaves and selected Cleveland as a new candidate who would appeal to a broad spectrum of party members and voters. Cleveland was elected in a landslide.

Cleveland's stint as governor was also short-lived and marked by his disregard for the spoils system. He was not inclined to give jobs away as payment for political loyalty and tried to appoint people to office based on their personal merit. Cleveland was by no means a liberal or a progressive; he took the conservative viewpoint that government should stay out of business, and he believed, in accordance with his "law and order" reputation, that its primary function was to keep the peace.

Cleveland brought his love of the veto to the governor's mansion, sending bill after bill back unsigned. He famously vetoed the Five-Cent Fare bill, which would have gone against the transit company charter and reduced fares for elevated railway riders in New York City. Cleveland was consistent in going his own way, though, and he broke with Tammany Hall on more than one occasion.

The Blaine from Maine and the Nasty Campaign

In 1884, the Republicans nominated James G. Blaine, a Congressman from Maine who had been accused of pocketing bribes in the railroad graft of the scandal-ridden Grant administration. Reformers were furious, and a large group of Republican *"mugwumps"* bailed and pledged to back Cleveland.

At the convention in Chicago, Tammany Hall loyalists rallied to rid the ticket of Cleveland, but he was selected as the nominee on the second ballot. The Mugwumps were staunch supporters of Cleveland, and he would need their support in an ugly campaign of personal attacks.

Knowledge Is Power

Mugwumps was a dismissive term that came from the Algonquian word for "chiefs." It was given to the reform Republicans who backed Democrat Cleveland in 1884, and it has come to be used for any group of independent party members who are a threat to jump ship.

Digging through presidential skeleton closets may be considered a modern phenomenon, but it isn't. Republican newspapers and pro-party orators found out that Grover Cleveland had fathered an illegitimate son with a widow, Maria Halpin (a campaign dig at Cleveland was "Ma, Ma, where's my Pa? Gone to the White House, Ha, Ha, Ha!"). Cleveland wasn't a "deadbeat dad"—he financially supported the child—but it was still quite a shocker when he acknowledged that he was indeed the father; no room for denying sexual relations in this instance. Meanwhile, Democrats kept the heat on Blaine's shady connection to the railroads. It was a close race, but Cleveland defeated Blaine in the electoral contest 219 to 182—his home state of New York provided the difference.

Cleveland was inaugurated on March 4, 1885, breaking the 24-year stranglehold the Republicans held on the White House. He was the first Democrat elected to the top spot since James Buchanan.

Commander in Chief Lore

Cleveland received a major unsolicited boost in the state of New York when a Blaine supporter put his foot squarely into his mouth. Reverend Samuel D. Burchard said that the Democrats were the party of "rum, Romanism, and rebellion," which managed to offend the Irish, Roman Catholics, and the South in a single breath. This clever caveat was never rebuked by Blaine and it cost him any chance he had of carrying New York City, and thus the state—and, in turn, the 36 electoral votes that gave Cleveland the presidency.

First Time Around—Clean House (and Senate)

Cleveland never wavered in his commitment to follow his own course of action, a course designed to weed out corruption and patronage and not use the government as a tool for progressive activism.

From the beginning, he attempted to ignore the spoils system and follow the Pendleton Act of 1883, which set regulatory standards for civil service positions. Cleveland initially resisted the pleas of the hungry Democrats, eager for jobs after all those years of Republican leadership. Eventually, though, party pressure led to capitulation, and he replaced some Republicans with loyal Democrats.

In 1887, Cleveland strengthened the office of the president during his first term by fighting for the repeal of the Tenure of Office Act. The Congress was seen as the most important branch of government during those days, and the president was generally expected to answer to Congress. Cleveland wanted the power to be able to remove incompetent officeholders, but his hands were tied. He appealed directly to the American people to grant him the power to remove whomever he saw fit without giving full disclosure to Congress. In 1887, Congress repealed the Tenure of Office Act and restored some of the power to the presidency that had been lost during the years following the Civil War.

Cleveland brought his vetoing stick with him to the White House and stamped a big fat "no" on hundreds of fraudulent private pension bills from Civil War veterans. There had been a hefty raid on the treasury since the war, and many of the claims were without merit. Although Cleveland signed more pension bills than any previous president, he was the first president to deny claims. Veterans groups were infuriated and were quick to remind folks that Cleveland had paid his way out of the war.

Congress responded to the powerful Unions' Veterans group, the Grand Army of the Republic, by drafting a bill that would have granted pensions to all disabled veterans, no questions asked. Cleveland vetoed that bill as well, and it came back to haunt him in the 1888 election. Cleveland also called for a reduction in the tariff, but he was never able to secure legislation because he didn't even have the backing of much of the Democratic Party. The tariff reduction became the wedge issue Republicans were looking for, and without the support of New York Democrats (Tammany Hall), Cleveland lost the electoral total to Republican Benjamin Harrison 233 to 168, although he received 100,000 more popular votes.

First Family Factuals

Grover Cleveland became the only President of the United States to get married in the White House itself. In June 1886, at the age of 49, he wed Frances Folsom, the 21-year-old daughter of his former law partner. He had known her since her infancy, and many years down the road Frances would become the first presidential widow to remarry.

First Family Factuals

Frances and Grover had their first child, Ruth, in New York City in 1891. The New York newspapers—and the general public—fell in love with the little girl and she was the inspiration for the birth of a new candy bar. The *Baby Ruth* brought chocolate, nougat, and Americans together.

Cleveland's Midterm Break

➤ As sheriff of Erie County, Grover Cleveland served as hangman twice, the first time executing a criminal who killed his mother and the second time executing a criminal who shot a man over a card game.

➤ In his first term, the Interstate Commerce Act of 1887 was passed. This act was the first attempt at federal regulation of the railroads and said that charges must be "reasonable and just."

➤ Upon leaving the White House after Cleveland's first term, Frances told the staffers to take good care of the furniture because they would be back in four years.

➤ Cleveland dedicated the Statue of Liberty in New York Harbor on October 28, 1886.

➤ Cleveland's favorite pastime was fishing, especially in the Adirondacks, but exercise was an afterthought, as he went 5-foot, 11 inches, 250 pounds.

➤ In 1893, the Clevelands welcomed the only baby, Esther, born in the White House.

Cleveland spent the next four years practicing law with a New York City firm on Wall Street. He found Harrison's monetary policies irresponsible, but he rarely spoke out against them because he didn't think it was proper.

Prez Says

"Under our scheme of government the waste of public money is a crime against the citizen, and the contempt of our people for economy and frugality in their personal affairs deplorably saps the strength and sturdiness of our national character."

—From Grover Cleveland's Second Inaugural Speech, March 4, 1893

Just a Four-Year Intermission

Two of the main issues of the 1892 election were the free coinage of silver and the omnipresent tariff. Cleveland was firmly against the unlimited minting of silver, which was popular in the South and the West because it would increase the amount of money in circulation and help people pay off creditors sooner. Cleveland stuck to his guns against his fellow free-silver Democrats, and he was attacked as a tool of Northern business interests.

Cleveland was still selected on the first ballot at the Democratic convention. His conservative fiscal policies helped bring enough Republicans into the fold to defeat Harrison 277 to 145 in the electoral college.

Major Depression

Grover Cleveland had the misfortune to return to the White House just when a major depression (Panic of 1893) hit the United States. The panic was brought on by railroads that had overextended themselves and expanded too quickly. The ripple effect from the companies that went belly up led to bank closures, farm foreclosures, and the unemployment of some four million citizens. Other contributing economic conditions were falling agricultural prices and slim crop harvests, the overexpansion of banks and other industries, and a financial slump in Europe.

Grover Cleveland, twenty-second and twenty-fourth president of the United States.

The depression following the Panic of 1893 was the worst financial crisis up until that point, but Cleveland was not about to start using the government as a tool of fiscal or social engineering. There would be no attempts to combat the financial woes, other than to persuade Congress to repeal the Sherman Silver-Purchase Act of 1890, which Cleveland had thought foolhardy since its passage.

The repeal of the act had a negligible effect on the economy. Cleveland angered many citizens by asking Wall Street bankers to float bond issues (*gold bonds*) to supply the needed gold to maintain the gold standard.

The deal with the Wall Street bankers gave the impression to many outside of the Northeast corridor that firms such as J.P. Morgan were buying the country out from under them.

The tariff reduction Cleveland sought was part of the House's Wilson-Gorman Tariff Act, which lowered the rate from 48 to 41 percent, but a coalition of Republican and

145

Eastern Democrat senators raised duties in a variety of categories. Although he was opposed to the act, Cleveland knew the Treasury needed money and chose not to veto, so it became law without his signature in 1894. His seven-year ordeal to lower the tariff ended with a watered-down whimper.

Knowledge Is Power

Gold bonds were sold to the financiers at a discount, and they, in turn, procured gold from overseas so that there wouldn't be anymore withdrawals from the dwindling U.S. reserves. Later, the bonds were offered to the public at a higher price, which raised American holdings and lined the bankers' pockets.

Prez Says

"If it takes the entire army and navy of the United States to deliver a post card in Chicago, that card will be delivered."

—Grover Cleveland

Losing Liberals and Labor

Cleveland was rapidly losing control of the Democratic Party, and two events in his second term hurt his credibility among the working class.

First, in the spring of 1894, he dismissed the concerns of "Coxey's Army," a group of 500 unemployed men, and a smattering of women, and children who marched on Washington, D.C., demanding relief. They were led by Jacob Coxey, a self-made Ohio businessman who wanted the federal government to fund a large public works project to provide employment.

Second, Cleveland also caused an uproar when he sent federal troops into Chicago to break up the Pullman railroad strike. The American Railway Union, led by labor organizer Eugene V. Debs, had come to the aid of the workers and refused to move any trains that included Pullman cars. Cleveland used the army on the basis that the strike had interrupted the delivery of the U.S. mail.

Debs and other union leaders were thrown into jail for violating a federal injunction, but it was a blanket court decision that didn't include any type of trial, jury or otherwise, and that didn't sit well with many citizens. Some business leaders and antilabor groups praised Cleveland's hard-line stance, but many liberals, union members, and states' rights supporters thought he went too far. Criticism of Cleveland became widespread and vociferous.

Grover Is No Imperial Wizard

Much in keeping with his steadfast belief in the gold standard and a reduced tariff, Grover Cleveland adhered to the dogma of the Monroe Doctrine and did not believe in *imperialism*.

Cleveland managed to regain some of his lost popularity by standing tall to England when it refused to allow the United States to mediate a long-standing boundary dispute between Venezuela and British Guiana. Venezuela requested U.S. assistance, but Britain repeatedly refused to allow the country's arbitration.

In 1895, Cleveland sent a letter that had been written with Secretary of State Richard Olney to Congress asking to establish a commission to resolve the boundary matter. The "Olney Corollary" strongly advised Great Britain not to take aggressive action on the western side of the globe. Britain agreed to international arbitration. Cleveland's support of the Monroe Doctrine, even in a boundary dispute, was widely praised.

Cleveland's anti-imperialist beliefs remained steadfast throughout his administration and afterward. In 1893, he withdrew from the Senate a treaty calling for the annexation of Hawaii after he was told that the Hawaiian people were against it. In 1895, Spain exerted its power over Cuba after an uprising on the small island. Cubans were herded into disease-ridden confinement camps, and thousands died. There was sympathy in the United States for the Cuban people, but Cleveland remained neutral and stood firm in his anti-imperialist beliefs, taking no chances in getting into a war. After he left office, he became a member of the Anti-Imperialist League, which opposed the annexation of the Philippines in 1898.

Knowledge Is Power

Imperialism is the practice, policy, or advocacy by which nations or peoples seek to extend their power or dominion over weaker nations or peoples. This can be through direct territorial acquisition or indirect control over the political or economic life of another area. The British conquest of India in the nineteenth century is an example of imperialist control.

Commander in Chief Lore

One of the odder presidential exhibits you might want to check out if you happen to be in Philadelphia is at the Mütter Museum, at the College of Physicians of Philadelphia, on 19 South 22nd Street between Chestnut and Market. See the "Secret Tumor of Grover Cleveland," a growth he had clandestinely removed from his jaw while serving the nation as president. *Anybody* can go see Independence Hall or the Liberty Bell, but this is the tour stop that all Grover Cleveland Groupies can't afford to miss.

Reformist First, Nonconsecutive Guy Second

The Democrats didn't ask Grover Cleveland to run for a third term in the 1896 elections, instead choosing free-silver candidate William Jennings Bryan, who was soundly beaten by William McKinley. The Clevelands returned to a large home they had purchased in Princeton, New Jersey. In 1904, Cleveland authored the book *Presidential Problems* to defend his policies. He served as a trustee of Princeton University and died in 1908 at his Princeton home. His last words were, "I have tried so hard to do right!"

The Least You Need to Know

➤ Grover Cleveland rapidly moved up the political ranks because he was incorruptible and didn't adhere to the spoils system.

➤ Cleveland was a staunch anti-imperialist, believed in the gold standard, and tried unsuccessfully for years to reduce the tariff.

➤ Cleveland didn't think that the government should interfere with the economy, and his popularity consequently dropped during the depression of the mid-1890s.

➤ Cleveland was the only president to serve two nonconsecutive terms, from 1884 to 1888 and from 1892 to 1896.

Chapter 12

Like Forefather, Like Son: John Quincy Adams

In This Chapter

➤ A French toast to the talented prodigy

➤ Indoctrinating Monroe

➤ The House of "Corrupt Bargains"

➤ Can't keep a good man down

With all due respect to the Kennedys, the Harrisons, and possibly not long after this book is published, the Bushes, the executive office has been best served by none other than the Adams family.

John Adams had a distinguished career, but his son, John Quincy Adams, was no slouch, either. Although his presidency wasn't a rousing hit, John Quincy Adams was a dedicated public servant who served the United States for 50 years and made his mark as a diplomat, statesman, independent thinker, Congressman, and man-about-the-world. The influence of the Adamses cannot be understated, and although the son's career was marred by a consistent unpopularity, his handiwork helped shape and expand the United States exponentially.

Just Another Trial of the Century

The life of John Quincy Adams can be encapsulated in a single trial late in his days. The *Amistad* trial of 1839 gave Adams a chance to argue his antislavery views in front of the Supreme Court at a time when the abolitionist movement was still in its infancy. Fifty-three African slaves were captured and shipped to Havana, Cuba, and the sale violated international law. The slaves were being shipped to a plantation in the schooner the *Amistad* and along the way, the slaves revolted, killing two crewmen in the process. The rebels ordered the owners to send the ship back to Africa, but it was intercepted off the Atlantic Coast by an American ship, and the Africans were sent to a prison in Connecticut.

Adams successfully defended the Africans, led by Cinque, from their return to the Spanish plantation bosses who claimed ownership. Adams successfully argued that any persons who escape from illegal bondage should be considered free men. The court found in favor of the Africans, abolitionists raised money for their return trip, and the remaining Africans (estimated to be between 32 to 35) lived to see their homeland of Sierra Leone. It was vintage John Quincy Adams, using his independence and intelligence to further a cause that he believed was the right course of action for his country.

Prez Says

"The Constitution of the United States recognizes the slaves, held within some of the States of the Union, only in their capacity of persons .... The Constitution no where recognizes them as property. The words *slave* and *slavery* are studiously excluded from the Constitution. Circumlocutions are the fig-leaves under which these parts of the body politic are decently concealed. ... Slaves, therefore, in the Constitution of the United States are recognized only as persons, enjoying rights and held to the performance of duties."

—John Quincy Adams before the Supreme Court, on February 24 and March 1, 1841

Commander in Chief Lore

Beginning in 1783, John Quincy Adams began keeping a diary that would eventually cover more than 60 years of his remarkable life. His son, Charles Francis Adams, published historical portions of the diary later in life in the massive *Memoirs of John Quincy Adams*.

Wunderkind

John Quincy Adams was born on July 11, 1767, in Braintree, Massachusetts (which is now named Quincy), the eldest son of John and Abigail Smith Adams. His parents educated him early on—primarily his mother, because his father was often busy with the burgeoning revolution. As a boy, Adams watched the *Battle of Bunker Hill* from the summit of Penn's Hill above the family farm.

At the ripe old age of 10, John Quincy Adams went to France with his father, who was trying to get assistance for the American Revolutionists. He learned French and studied at the University of Leiden. Overall, he spent eight years studying in Europe, and his knowledge played a defining role throughout his life. In 1782 and 1783, at the age of 14, he was appointed to be secretary and interpreter of French to Francis Dana, United States envoy to Russia. Adams spent two years in St. Petersburg and then returned to the Hague in the Netherlands to pick up his schooling. In 1783, he met up with his father in Paris and witnessed the signing of the treaty ending the American Revolution. Adams was quite the scholar by the time he returned to Harvard in 1785 to complete his formal education.

Adams studied law and started his own practice, but he found the profession slow and bland. It didn't take long before he found himself in a life-long career serving the public.

Knowledge Is Power

The **Battle of Bunker Hill** was the first large-scale conflict of the Revolutionary War. It was fought on June 17, 1775, in Charlestown, Massachusetts, which is now in the city of Boston. The heavy casualties inflicted upon the Brits gave confidence to the quickly formed green militias and helped spread and cement the rebellious spirit throughout the 13 colonies.

Not That Deep a Throat

In 1793, a war erupted between Great Britain and France, and loyalties were divided down the middle back in the states. Jeffersonian disciples primarily supported France, while the Federalists backed England. In the middle was President George Washington, who wanted the United States to remain neutral. He was criticized in many circles, but an unknown columnist writing under the pseudonym Publicola in the Boston newspapers was an adamant supporter of Washington's decision to stay out of the quagmire. Washington found out that the author of the articles was none other than John Quincy Adams, and Washington appointed the wily wordsmith to be U.S. minister to the Netherlands.

A New England Yankee in European Courts

From 1794 to 1797, Adams sat in at the Hague, reporting back to the United States during a time of great European upheaval. He was eminently qualified for the position because, in addition to French, he spoke fluent Dutch and knew international law and European politics. Adams' primary thesis was that Washington was right: The United States should stay out of European affairs. The continent was dealing with the wide-ranging consequences of the French Revolution, and Adams reiterated the importance of American neutrality.

Adams followed up his time in the Netherlands by becoming the Minister to Prussia (1797–1801). The new president, John Adams, who was encouraged by Washington to use the diplomatic talents of his offspring, promoted him.

Mr. Adams Goes to Washington

John Quincy Adams was called back to the United States after his father lost the election to Thomas Jefferson. He returned to Boston and tried his hand at law once again, but it wasn't his calling. In 1802, the Federalist Party in Massachusetts elected Adams to the state senate based on his diplomatic record and family name. The following year, they elected him to the United States Senate, but the love affair didn't last long.

Adams refusal to toe the line for the New England Federalists cost him his job before his time was up. One of the major points of contention was Adams's vote for Thomas Jefferson's treaty buying the big chunk of land known as the Louisiana Purchase. Adams was the only Federalist to cast an affirmative vote. He knew that it would diminish the power of New England, but Adams also recognized that the expansion of the United States would be good for the country on the whole.

In 1807, Adams broke ranks with the Northeast corridor and voted for Jefferson's Embargo Act, which prohibited all trade with Europe. It was meant to be a show of United States force, dictating that the European powers would respect the new country's rights on the seas, but all it did was cripple American shipping and commerce. The shipping magnates in Massachusetts took it on the chin, and the Federalists voted Adams out of office before the end of his term.

First Family Factuals

While working in the Netherlands, John Quincy Adams married Louisa Catherine Johnson, daughter of Joshua Johnson the U.S. consul in London.

Back Across the Atlantic

Adams's time out of politics was brief. President James Monroe appointed him to be the U.S. Minister to Russia, where he served from 1809 to 1814. Adam's wife, Louisa, didn't like the bitter cold she dealt with while living in the Russian capital of St. Petersburg, but her husband held a position of extreme importance. The Embargo Act left Russia as the United States' lone outlet for trade. John Quincy Adams witnessed and reported back about Napoleon's invasion of Moscow, Russia, and the retreat a month later, which united the rest of the countries against the French emperor and led to his downfall shortly thereafter.

During Adams's tenure, the War of 1812 broke out between the United States and Great Britain. Adams's friend Czar Alexander I offered to mediate, and Adams relayed the message to Madison. The British, however, decided that they would rather deal directly with the United States.

In 1814, Adams went to the peace commission at Ghent, Belgium, and led the negotiations with the British. The Treaty of Ghent was signed after months of haggling, and diplomatic relations were reopened between the United States and Great Britain. Adams spent the next two years as the minister to Britain. Although the Treaty of Ghent didn't solve any of the issues related to the embargo and resulting blockades, it gave Americans the sense that they had won the War of 1812.

Later, Adams was able to secure treaties opening trade routes to British colonies, and he worked on establishing the border between the United States and Canada.

Prez Says

"Nothing was adjusted, nothing was settled—nothing in substance but an indefinite suspension of hostilities we agreed to."

—John Quincy Adams

The Man Behind Monroe

In 1817, John Quincy Adams settled back in the United States when President Monroe summoned him to be secretary of state, a cabinet post he would hold until becoming president. It was an interesting period in American foreign policy because it was the first time there was relative peace in the United States and no European problems on the horizon.

Adams's first major task was to resolve the shaky situation in the Spanish colony of Florida. The Spanish troops stayed primarily behind their fortified garrisons and didn't adhere to their treaty-mandated responsibility to keep the Seminole Indians from rampaging across the U.S. border. Violent clashes led to the outbreak of the First Seminole War, under the direction of Andrew Jackson. Jackson drove the natives back, occupied settlements, and had two British agitators executed. Both Spain and Great Britain filed protests, and John Quincy Adams was the only member of Monroe's Cabinet to stand up and support "Old Hickory." Adams placed the blame squarely on Spain's shoulders and convinced Monroe that Florida had to be governed effectively or turned over to the United States.

Acting in complete autonomy, Adams convinced Spain that the land should stretch to the Pacific Ocean. The frontier line ran from the Gulf of Mexico, at the mouth of the Sabine River, to the Rocky Mountains and along the 42nd parallel. Spain capitulated, and the Adams-Onis Treaty was signed on February 22, 1819 and ratified on

February 22, 1821. The treaty ceded Florida to the United States and cemented the western boundary of the Louisiana Purchase. Adams was an integral part in the United States' stretch from the Atlantic to the Pacific.

Adams crafted one of the two basic principles of the Monroe Doctrine the year prior to 1823, when President James Monroe announced "his" doctrine. Adams also kept the British from reclaiming the northeastern frontier and held the line of 49° in the Oregon country. On more than one occasion, John Quincy Adams has been placed at the top of the short list of great secretaries of state.

The Two-Time Loser Is the Big Winner

John Quincy Adams hit a snag in his brilliant political career, and unfortunately, it came during his time as president. It started with the election of 1824, which featured four candidates—Adams, General Andrew Jackson, Secretary of the Treasury William H. Crawford, and Speaker of the House Henry Clay. None of the candidates received a majority of the electoral votes, and Adams trailed Jackson 99 to 84. Jackson, a popular war hero, carried most of the West and had the majority of the popular vote. Adams was supported by his New England constituency and New York.

The twelfth amendment to the Constitution of the United States declares that if no candidate receives a majority of electoral votes, the House of Representatives must decide from the top three electoral vote-getters. Henry Clay was in fourth place, so he was eliminated. However, he was also the Speaker of the House, and he was directly involved in the process. Clay threw his support and 37 electoral votes to Adams, clandestinely meeting with Adams shortly before the final balloting. In February 1825, Adams accepted the presidency after stating that he would throw it open to a popular election, which would have been unconstitutional.

Shortly thereafter, Adams appointed Clay to be his secretary of state, and the already suspicious Jackson supporters howled that there had been a "corrupt bargain" in place. It was a claim that haunted his presidency as Jacksonians tried to yank the presidency away from him. Historians generally agree that Clay would have gone along with Adams because they had the most similar ideology. There is also agreement that there was no absolute corruption but that the two probably had an understanding. The messy affair doomed his White House years and led to his defeat in the particularly shameless and vulgar campaign of 1828.

Chip Off the Old Block

➤ John Quincy Adams read four or five Bible chapters every morning in the hour immediately after rising from bed.

➤ Adams was the first president to be photographed, the first to be married abroad, and the first to marry a woman born outside the states.

➤ Adams translated Christoph Martin Wieland's book *Oberon: A Poetical Romance in Twelve Books* from German to English.

➤ The construction of steam engine railways began during Adams administration.

John Quincy Adams, sixth president of the United States.

Adams Part II: The Undistinguished Term

Upon entering the executive office, Adams alienated some of his Federalist supporters by filling out his Cabinet with a cross-section of party politicians. He believed in hiring people based on merit and was trying to calm the waters after the election controversy. However, he was so free of partisanship that it seemed as though his party affiliation ceased to matter, and he wasn't able to build a network of influence. On top of that, Adams was a surly, aloof man who loathed small talk and had a quick temper. With all that and the large Jacksonian element trying to wrest the White House away, the circumstances of Adams's presidency were not a recipe for success.

Still, Adams had big ideas, and his first annual address to Congress included large national works projects that would have been much more in tune with the times of Teddy or Franklin Roosevelt. He called for federal funding of infrastructure improvements such as new canals, railways, highways, and harbor refurbishment. He wanted a strong national Bank of the United States as the fiscal epicenter and national administration of the settlement of public lands. Adams called for a stronger, unified army and navy, and educational direction from the federal level, including a national university. He went against the grain and promoted national protection of the Indian tribes and their lands.

Some of the strongest criticism was leveled at his pitch for the federal development of the arts and sciences, which would incorporate geographical research, the construction of observatories, and financing expeditions. Adams was ahead of his time for how he thought the federal government could be used; his was still the heyday of the states rights movement. Southern politicians were always wary that Northern abolitionists were out to end slavery, so there was an unending stream of complaints that Adams's ideas were unconstitutional.

In 1828, Adams signed the first substantial tariff, the "Tariff of Abominations," into law and drove the final nail into his reelection coffin. The tariff was passed by Northern congressmen and placed high duties on imports to ensure that their profits were not hurt by cheap foreign goods and raw materials.

As you will notice throughout this book, the tariff issue was the second hottest issue in the nineteenth century following slavery, and this is where it had its genesis. Adams didn't agree with the tariff because it adversely affected the South, which relied on imports to keep the cotton trade flowing. But the presidential veto was not yet commonly utilized; it was reserved for bills thought to be unconstitutional. Adams reluctantly signed the "Tariff of Abominations" into law, and Andrew Jackson used it as a rallying cry in the campaign of 1828.

First Family Factuals

John Quincy Adams's prickly personality didn't just grate on the nerves of Congressmen and politicos—he and his wife suffered on occasion as well. Louisa was a gentle woman, and his moodiness put undue strain on their marriage, which couldn't have helped the migraine headaches that plagued her throughout her life.

One Ugly Election

Andrew Jackson championed himself as a man of the people, and Adams never had a very secure political base to begin with. Jacksonians attacked the stately Adams as a tool of the wealthy who aspired to be an American monarch. They went on to accuse him of having sex with Louisa before they were married, installing gambling tables in the White House (billiards, actually), skipping mass, and, best of all, pimping for Czar

Alexander I by securing young American hotties for the Russian leader. Adams's followers, in turn, said that Andrew Jackson engaged in theft, bigamy, drunkenness, and murder, and called his mother a garden-variety whore. In the end, the seediness of the campaign didn't matter much—Adams lost the electoral vote, 178 to 83, carrying only a few states in the Northeast. John Quincy Adams was so bitter after the 1828 election that he followed in his father's footsteps and boycotted his successor's inauguration.

Heeeeeere's Johnny

Disgusted with the corruption charges leveled at him during the campaign, John Quincy Adams retired from politics and returned to Massachusetts to mind the family farm and continue his writing. In November 1830, the voters of the Plymouth District elected him to the House of Representatives, where he would capably serve for the next 17 years.

"Old Man Eloquent" returned to Washington and proudly followed his tradition of voting independently for what he thought would best suit the nation as a whole. He unsuccessfully lobbied against Jackson's removal of funds from a national bank to smaller state banks on the grounds that it would lead to a depression, which it helped to do in 1837. He also helped craft a compromise tariff that angered both the North and the South (probably right where Adams wanted it), and in 1836 he voted against the annexation of Texas, fearing that it would become a slave state, and thus staving off the Lone Star statehood until 1845. Adams was also instrumental in seeing that the $500,000 gift from British chemist James Smithson established a center of learning, the new Smithsonian Institute.

Commander in Chief Lore

John Quincy Adams regularly swam the Potomac River in his birthday suit, all the way up until the age of 79. Adams had repeatedly snubbed journalist Anne Royall, so she showed up one morning on the bank of the Potomac and sat on his clothes. John Quincy Adams relented and gave the first presidential interview to a woman.

One of Adams's great triumphs later in life was the repeal of the "gag rule," which he spent eight years, using every trick in the book trying to eliminate. The gag rule had been passed in 1836 to stop the stream of petitions to Congress calling for the end of slavery. It stipulated that the House automatically had to table all abolishment petitions, many of which were presented by Adams, including a resolution that nobody born in the United States after 1845 could be a slave. This resolution went nowhere obviously, but Adams and his supporters were able to get the gag rule lifted in 1844 on the grounds of unconstitutionality.

On February 23, 1848, John Quincy Adams responded to the roll call in the House of Representatives he so brilliantly served, and then he suffered his second stroke. He died in the Capitol two days later.

When speaking of the great thinkers and idea men who have graced our elected offices, John Quincy Adams belongs right up there, even if his greatest successes came in the Cabinet, the Congress, and overseas rather than in the White House.

Prez Says

"This is the last of earth! I am content."

—The final words of John Quincy Adams

The Least You Need to Know

➤ John Quincy Adams, son of John Adams, was a respected diplomat who served American interests in a variety of European countries, but firmly believed in the neutrality of the United States.

➤ Adams was an outstanding secretary of state under President James Monroe and helped to shape the ideology behind the Monroe Doctrine.

➤ Adams presidency was undermined by hostile Jacksonian congressmen.

➤ Adams rebounded by brilliantly serving his constituents in the House of Representatives for 17 years after he left the White House and worked to end slavery, which he felt was unconstitutional.

Chapter 13

Win Two Terms for the Gipper: Ronald Reagan

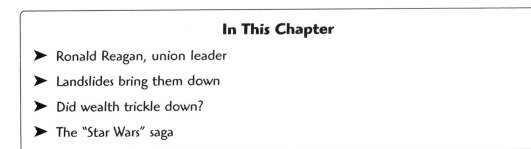

In This Chapter

➤ Ronald Reagan, union leader

➤ Landslides bring them down

➤ Did wealth trickle down?

➤ The "Star Wars" saga

One thing was true about Ronald Reagan: He sure knew how to win people over, and his love affair with the American people continues unabated. Reagan became the living embodiment of a friendly grandfather, quick with a story or a joke but not always fully aware of what the kids were up to. Not surprisingly, the former actor had media savvy and clearly communicated his positions, whether they were upper-class tax cuts or the end of communism. He certainly has his detractors, and the United States has barely made a dent in the deficit he left behind, but as a man, he generally remains one of the most beloved figures of the late twentieth century.

Hooray for Hollywood

Ronald Wilson Reagan was born in Tampico, Illinois, on February 6, 1911, and the family moved to Dixon, Illinois, when he was nine. Reagan's father was an alcoholic, a victim of the "Irish disease," as Reagan later called it, but in Dixon he was able to borrow enough capital to become a part owner of a store. Reagan's Middle America upbringing was important because even though he grew up relatively poor, his ardent optimistic outlook and belief that all politics are local were shaped in his small-town roots. In high school he was a football player, president of the student council, and a lifeguard during the summer. He called his upbringing in Dixon "the happiest times of my life." The Reagan family referred to him as Dutch and called his older brother John, Moon.

Reagan attended Eureka College from 1928 to 1932 during the Great Depression and took to the stage at the small Disciples of Christ Presbyterian school outside of Peoria. As president of the freshman class, he assisted in formulating a student strike against curriculum cutbacks, and the president of the college resigned as a result. After graduating in 1932, Reagan hitchhiked around the Midwest looking for a job as a radio broadcaster. He became sportscaster for WHO in Des Moines, Iowa, calling the action of a variety of local sports, including Big Ten football and basketball, prize fights, and track meets.

Commander in Chief Lore

Ronald Reagan did most of his play-by-play live, but he often gave simulated game descriptions of Chicago Cubs baseball outings based on Western Union telegraph accounts of games in progress. In one game, the wire went down as a Cubs batter was at the plate at a big moment, and Dutch spent more than five minutes fouling off pitch after imaginary pitch until the wire kicked in and he could get back to calling the actual action.

Reagan became one of the most recognized voices in the Midwest, and a friend arranged for a screen test at Warner Brothers in 1937 when Reagan accompanied the Cubs to Catalina Island, the home of their spring training. The test went well, and he was instantly signed to a standard seven-year, $200-a-week, contract. Reagan's debut was in the movie *Love Is on the Air,* and appropriately enough, he played a radio announcer. He would go on to star in more than 50 films, making his last movie appearance in 1964.

Commander in Chief Lore

Two of Reagan's more memorable roles were in the films *Knute Rockne—All-American* and *King's Row*. In the former he played George Gipp, a dying football player who challenges Rockne to "win one for the Gipper." In the latter, which is generally regarded as Reagan's best performance, he played Drake McHugh, a man stunned to find that his legs have been amputated by a vengeful, sadistic, surgeon. McHugh replies, "Where's the rest of me?"—which Reagan used as the title of his 1965 autobiography.

In 1940, Reagan married actress Jane Wyman. In 1942, he took a hiatus from his film career and served in the United States Army. He had enlisted in the reserves while working as a sportscaster in Iowa, and was called to active duty after the attack on Pearl Harbor. His poor sight kept him from being eligible for combat duty, so he used his craft for the cause and made training films, rising to the rank of captain.

Reagan returned to Hollywood and served as president of the Screen Actors Guild (SAG), the union for film actors, from 1947 to 1952 and from 1959 to 1960. In those days, Reagan was a Democrat who campaigned for Harry Truman in 1948, but as president of SAG he began a shift from an advocate of the New Deal to a staunch conservative. He was concerned with "communist infiltration in American society," especially in labor organizations such as the actors guild. He appeared before the House Un-American Activities Committee in 1947 and committed himself to keeping communists from gaining a foothold in the film industry. In 1948, his marriage to Wyman dissolved, in part because she was tiring of his political activism, and they got a divorce that caused him great pain.

Reagan's film career started to dwindle, so he got a job in television that became an important moment in his political development. In 1954,

First Family Factuals

In 1952, Reagan remarried, this time to an actress named Nancy Davis who had first contacted him because her name was wrongly being circulated on a list of suspected Communist sympathizers, and she didn't want the phony rumors to affect her career. Legendary actor William Holden was best man at the Reagan matrimonial ceremony. The couple has enjoyed a long, happy union and even had the thrill of starring in *Hellcats of the Navy* together in 1957.

General Electric hired him to be host of the weekly series *General Electric Theater*. In addition to hosting and occasionally acting in the dramatic offerings, Reagan was required to travel around the country as a public relations spokesman for General Electric. He was shifting to a conservative ideology and found that he identified with worker's complaints about an overburdening tax system. Reagan also realized that he had a natural gift for making speeches, and increasingly his speeches focused on the inequities of big government and the virtues of the business world. In 1962, Reagan changed his party affiliation from Democrat to Republican and became a leading conservative spokesman.

Striking Gold with Goldwater

October 27, 1964, was a major turning point in the establishment of Reagan's political career. He gave a speech on national television in support of right-wing presidential candidate Barry Goldwater, a senator from Arizona. Reagan attacked big govern- ment as the major obstacle to individual success, and hundreds of thousands of dollars came pouring in for the Goldwater campaign. Conservative California businessmen quickly suggested to Reagan that he consider a run for governor. It didn't take long for Reagan to become the leading candidate, and he defeated incumbent Democratic Governor Edmund G. (Pat) Brown (father of Governor "Moonbeam" Jerry Brown) by nearly a million votes—the largest victory that had been won over a sitting governor in American history.

Reagan campaigned against the student demonstrations, the "Great Society," and of course, big government but in the folksy manner of a populist. He was a hit with the moderate middle-class voters—a trait he would maintain throughout his career—and as governor of California in the late 1960s and early 1970s, he was thrust into the national spotlight. Reagan's popularity among Americans who totally disagreed with the counterculture of the 1960s and 1970s rose after he took on the protesters of the "free speech movement" at the University of California at Berkeley. Reagan's simple slogan to the demonstrators and their sit-ins was "observe the rules or get out."

Reagan was re-elected in 1970, and his eight years as governor of California are tough to assess. For six of the years, he butted heads with an uncooperative Democratic legislature, so his record of accomplishment and failure is in proportion to his dealings with the political opposition. In his first campaign, Reagan said that taxes had to be lowered and state spending slashed, but the budget more than doubled during his two terms, and he had to raise taxes by a billion dollars during his first year of office. He said it was an absolute necessity to balance a state budget that was headed toward bankruptcy. In 1971, he compromised with the Democrats and produced a major welfare overhaul. More than 300,000 names were dropped from the welfare rolls, while benefits for those who still qualified were increased. And Reagan had promised to reduce the number of state employees, but more than 40,000 people went to work for California.

Just a Warm-Up

At the end of his second gubernatorial term in 1974, Reagan was urged to run again, but he had his eyes on the prize. In 1968, he had made a last-minute effort to secure the Republican nomination, but it was futile. In 1976, Reagan took his first shot at the White House, running against incumbent Gerald Ford. Ford was somewhat vulnerable, having lost a great deal of American support after his pardon of Richard Nixon. Reagan lost the first Republican *primary* in New Hampshire by a close margin on February 24.

Reagan didn't fare well in the next few primaries, so he broke with Republican tradition and went on the offensive, attacking Ford's more moderate policies. He scored an unexpected victory in the North Carolina primary and followed that up by winning others in the South. At the 1976 convention in Kansas City, Missouri, Ford received the nomination by only 57 delegates.

Reagan spent the next four years at his ranch in Santa Barbara living a life of luxury from prosperous real estate investments made in the 1950s and from speaking engagements. He also spent time raising money for his bid to win the White House in 1980.

Knowledge Is Power

A **primary** is an election held prior to the general election in which qualified voters (usually registered party members) select a candidate for political office. The first presidential primary of any election year is held in New Hampshire. The United States is one of the few countries to have primary elections, and these elections came out of the Progressive Era reforms early in the twentieth century as a way to diminish the control of political machines.

Ronald Reagan Realities

➤ Ronald Reagan claimed that his father would not allow his brother Moon and him to see the D.W. Griffith film *Birth of a Nation* because of its racial stereotypes.

➤ Reagan was the oldest president of the United States ever to take the oath of office.

➤ Reagan signed a bill from his hospital bed the day after the assassination attempt on his life.

➤ Reagan appointed the first woman, Sandra Day O'Connor, to the Supreme Court.

➤ Reagan submitted the first $1,000,000,000 (that's one trillion) budget to Congress.

Reagan's Resounding Victory

Reagan had spent the better part of 12 years making connections and preparing himself for his big push to the presidency. In 1980, he breezed to the nomination with victories in almost all the primaries. At the Republican convention in Detroit, Reagan garnered 1,939 votes—only 55 votes went to the rest of the field. Gerald Ford was mentioned as a dream ticket running mate, but he reportedly wanted more power than Reagan was willing to cede, so George Bush was chosen.

The 1980 campaign was closer than people probably assume, with most public opinion polls saying that the contest between Reagan and Jimmy Carter was too close to call shortly before the election. Reagan got a boost during the debate a week prior to the election when he stressed the shortcomings of the current economy and asked the voters to consider the question, "Are you better off than you were four years ago?" Still, most observers thought that the election was going to be neck and neck, a possible photo finish, if you will. They weren't even close. Reagan won the electoral election by a count of 489 to 49, carrying all but six states and the District of Columbia.

Commander in Chief Lore

The Reagan landslide tradition continued in 1984 when he and Bush whitewashed Democratic challenger Walter Mondale and Geraldine Ferraro, the first female vice-presidential nominee of a major American party. The final electoral count was 525 to 13, the highest amount ever amassed by a victorious candidate. Mondale carried only his home state of Minnesota and the District of Columbia, even though Ronald Reagan did not participate in a formal news conference from July to November. His domination was such that Reagan's political advertisements didn't even mention Mondale, focusing instead on patriotic "Morning in America" imagery.

Part of Reagan's great success came from his ability to unite varying groups, from the white, blue-collar voters known as the "Reagan Democrats" to the ultraconservative, antiabortion folks of the religious right to the wealthy who were looking for upper-class tax cuts and less governmental business regulation, to the Cold War zealots who thought that the USSR was hell-bent on world domination. Groups who had little in common and who cared about entirely different issues came under the Reagan umbrella because he was the "great communicator" who endeared himself to people through charm, optimism, and a belief that opportunity abounded for any American who wanted it. Critics often charged that he was shallow and relied on anecdotes instead of evidence, but it was a message that resonated. He went from having never held a political office to being governor of the largest state in the union to being president of the United States in a relatively short time.

Reagan's inauguration was a lavish extravaganza, and he topped off his inaugural address by announcing that the 444-day hostage ordeal in Iran was over and that the 52 Americans held captive at the United States embassy in Iran were flying to freedom.

On March 30, 1981, Reagan was wounded in the chest in an attempted assassination by John Hinckley Jr., a loner trying to impress Jodie Foster, star of *Taxi Driver*. Hinckley was later found not guilty by reason of insanity and was committed to a mental hospital. Reagan quickly recovered, and his self-deprecating wit throughout the affair raised his esteem in the eyes of the public. His popularity soared. One of his famous quips to the doctors was, "I just hope you're Republicans." To which one of the doctors replied, "Today, Mr. President, we're all Republicans."

Prez Says

"We have every right to dream heroic dreams. Those who say that we are in a time when there are no heroes just don't know where to look .... There are entrepreneurs with faith in themselves and faith in an idea who create new jobs, new wealth and opportunity. They are individuals and families whose taxes support the Government and whose voluntary gifts support church, charity, culture, art, and education. Their patriotism is quiet but deep. Their values sustain our national life."

—From Ronald Reagan's Inaugural Address, January 20, 1981

Ronald Reagan, fortieth president of the United States.

Domestic Years: Reaganomics Takes Shape

Reagan entered office in the midst of an economic recession that only got worse during his first two years. By the fall of 1982, the unemployment level was hovering around 11 percent, interest rates were way up, and the country was in the throws of an economy that hadn't been seen since the Great Depression. From the beginning, Reagan pushed an economic policy of cutting taxes while reducing government, which became known as "Reaganomics." Reagan blamed the recession on federal growth by previous administrations and continually harped that economic recovery was on its way.

Part of Reagan's initial economic stimulus package was an across the board cut of 30 percent in income taxes (enacted at 10 percent a year for three years), an expansion of tax write-offs, and a reduction in government spending in all areas except for defense. The economy did experience a turn around, and Wall Street boomed, even though the federal deficit was then skyrocketing, primarily because of the record defense spending and forced compromises with the Democratic Congress.

The benefits of Reaganomics were much greater for the rich than for the poor, and the disparity between the upper and lower classes increased. Reagan believed that stimulating growth at the top would cause wealth to trickle down to all levels of society, but the conditions in American inner cities worsened throughout the 1980s just as social services were slashed.

Commander in Chief Lore

One memorable event early in the Reagan administration was the firing of roughly 12,000 (some have put it as high as 13,000) air traffic controllers who went on strike in August 1981 over demands for higher pay, greater benefits, and extended safety measures like a shorter work week. The controllers hoped to shut down the country's major airports, but federal law prohibited their actions, so Reagan canned them and decertified their union. He brought in military personnel until new air traffic controllers could be brought in and trained, and he refused to hire back the strikers even after labor leaders pleaded on their behalf. Union organizers staged a massive demonstration in Washington, D.C., in September of the same year.

To this day, Reaganomics has strong supporters who site the 20 million new jobs, an unemployment rate of around 5.5 percent in 1988, and the increase in international trade as proof of Reagan's success. However, there are equally strong critics who point to the disappearance of the country's manufacturing base and the higher-paying blue-collar jobs along with it (leaving primarily newly created jobs in the low-paying service industries), the large increase in families living below the poverty line, and a $3 trillion legacy of debt that would have to be paid off down the line.

Reaganomics came under fire on October 19, 1987, as the stock market fell by more than 500 points. The five-year bullish run had seen a wave of billion-dollar mergers, takeovers, and leveraged buyouts as the stock market surged, but after the crash critics called into question the fiscal wisdom of Reagan's policies. However, the market recovered relatively smoothly.

The 1980's saw the rise of the AIDS epidemic as well. The epidemic was all but ignored by the Reagan administration, until his friend Rock Hudson went public with his revelation that he had the disease.

First Family Factuals

Nancy Reagan was heavily criticized in the early years for caring mainly about her elegant lifestyle, which included acquiring a new set of $200,000 china that was paid for by private funds. Her popularity rose after she began to address public causes, and her antidrug "Just Say No" program was a ubiquitous mid-1980s phrase. "Just Say No to Drugs" clubs sprouted up around the country, and Nancy even went on the television show *Different Strokes* to spread the message.

Foreign Affairs: Facing Down the "Evil Empire"

Reagan was ardently opposed to communism, referring to the Soviet Union as an "evil empire" in a 1983 address. The détente (uneasy coexistence with the Russians) policies of previous administrations were put on the back burner, and a show of strength was placed on the front. Reagan wholeheartedly believed that the Soviets could never match a dramatic increase in American defense spending and that they would eventually concede the Cold War. Peace through strength would lead to the elimination of nuclear weapons. There was no thaw in American-Soviet relations in Reagan's first term as the military buildup went forward unabated.

In March 1983, Reagan announced his Strategic Defense Initiative (SDI), popularly called "Star Wars," which was a security system designed to intercept and destroy enemy missiles in flight, and he ordered research to get underway. Detractors decried the massive potential costs, the possibility of an even larger arms race with Russia, and the fact that there was a good chance it was technologically impossible.

Early in his second term, Reagan met with reform-oriented Soviet leader Mikhail Gorbachev in Geneva. Gorbachev was strongly opposed to the SDI and protested it throughout the course of their continued summits in 1985, 1986, 1987, and 1988. The two men were able to sign the first treaties in history to reduce the nuclear arsenals of both nations. In Washington, D.C., in 1987, Gorbachev and Reagan put their names on a historic treaty, the Intermediate Range Nuclear Forces (INF) Treaty, which provided for the elimination of intermediate-range nuclear forces and stringent procedures to keep the banned missiles from being produced in the future. Reagan stood tough on the research and development of his beloved SDI, and Gorbachev didn't let it stand in the way. May 29 through June 1, 1988, President and Mrs. Reagan made a reciprocal visit when he attended a friendly summit meeting in Moscow as the Cold War started to come to an end.

Trouble Spots Span the Globe

During Reagan's eight years in office, the United States steered clear of any major wars, but numerous little situations involved American intervention. Here are a few examples to consider with an atlas in hand.

➤ **Afghanistan and Angola.** The Reagan administration sent large amounts of cash and military equipment such as Stinger missiles to the Muslim guerrillas fighting the Marxist government of Afghanistan, which was backed by the Soviet Union. The Reagan administration joined with South Africa and supported rebels in Angola against the Popular Movement for the Liberation of Angola, which was also supported by the USSR and assisted by Cuban troops.

➤ **Nicaragua.** Right after taking his first oath of office, Reagan suspended aid to Nicaragua and wholeheartedly pronounced his support for anti-Sandinista Contra rebels trying to overthrow the recently established Marxist regime. In 1982, Nicaragua signed a pact with the Soviet Union, and Reagan used the CIA to clandestinely provide monetary and military support and training. He also worked on a public campaign to get momentum for an overthrow of the Sandinistas. In 1984, in response to questionable CIA tactics, Congress passed the Boland Amendment, that prohibited direct or indirect aid to the Contras. A cease-fire was ultimately signed in 1988 between the Contras and the Sandinistas, so Reagan's goal of overthrowing the Marxist government was never realized.

➤ **Grenada.** Grenada is a small, independent, Caribbean island group that had a coup d'ètat, leading to in-fighting between communist factions. The Reagan administration invaded the island on October 25, 1983, ostensibly to protect Americans students, but also it was thought Grenada might have become a dangerous Soviet outpost. The U.S. troops rapidly defeated a Marxist Cuban division and arrested the communist heads of the Grenada government and all military personnel were out by the end of the year. A noncommunist regime was voted into office in 1984, and the last American technical advisers left.

➤ **Lebanon.** The invasion of Grenada came just days after 241 America Marines (and 58 French military personnel) were killed by a terrorist attack upon their headquarters in Beirut. Reagan had vowed that the United States would never deal with terrorist organizations, and the attack in Beirut was perpetrated by a terrorist Arab organization opposed to Western intervention in assisting Israel with the expulsion of the Palestine Liberation Organization (PLO) from Beirut. Reagan withdrew the remaining Marines in early 1984, only to watch the kidnapping and torturing at the hands of Muslim extremists of a handful of American citizens who had remained in Lebanon. A rebel sect of the PLO also hijacked the Italian cruise ship the *Achille Lauro* in 1985 and singled out Americans for brutality, including the murder of an invalid American whose body was thrown overboard. Egypt allowed the hijackers to fly to Tunisia aboard one of its commercial airlines, but Reagan sent Navy jet fighters to intercept the flight and force a landing in Italy. The terrorists later stood trial in Germany, and Reagan sent the message to all rogue groups that "you can run, but you can't hide."

➤ **Libya.** In June 1985, TWA flight 847 was hijacked after departing from Athens and was forcibly sent to Beirut and Algiers. The 17-day ordeal frustrated the Reagan administration, and staffers were horrified to watch as the body of a U.S. Navy man murdered on 847 was thrown onto the runway. The murder, combined with the harsh treatment of the other remaining 39 passengers aboard spurred more decisive action against the Libyan terrorists and their leader, Muammar al-Qaddafi. Tensions had been growing since 1981, when two Libyan jets were downed by U.S. planes during military training in the Gulf of Sidra. In December 1985, the ticket counters of the Israel; airlines in Rome and Vienna were bombed, killing 13, including American citizens. Evidence surfaced that Libya was involved in the attacks, and Reagan suspended all official ties with the country. Again, shots were fired in the Gulf of Sidra, but the conflict didn't escalate until a bomb in a West German nightclub killed an American soldier and wounded over 130 others. Intelligence reports pointed to Libya, so Reagan ordered an attack on the capital city of Tripoli in April 1986. The invasion was carried live on television in the United States, Qaddafi's headquarters was hit, and his 15-month-old daughter was killed.

Scandal Breaks, Reagan Escapes

The last two years of Reagan's presidency was marred by the Iran-Contra scandal, which broke in late 1986 after foreign newspapers uncovered that the federal government had been secretly selling arms to Iran and diverting the funds to the Contras, in direct violation of the Boland Amendment. Congress demanded an investigation to explain what took place and why it hadn't been informed of the covert operation. For months, Reagan denied that the trading of arms with Iranian enemies was to secure the release of American hostages in Lebanon, and that he had broken his pledge not to negotiate with terrorists.

Later, the administration admitted that it had been selling arms to Iran, but Reagan said that he had absolutely no knowledge of the diversion of funds to the guerrillas in Nicaragua. Blame was placed squarely on the shoulders of National Security Adviser John Poindexter and his deputy, Lt. Colonel Oliver North. The scandal took on greater proportions when North revealed that he had shredded official White House documents. Reagan appointed a special committee, and hearings were held in the summer of 1987.

Both Poindexter and North were later indicted, and in 1989 a document was released that suggested that both Reagan and Bush were aware of the operation. The question of whether the Reagan administration violated the Boland Amendment was never answered, and North became the scapegoat even though he testified that he had not acted on his own. In eight hours of sworn video testimony, Reagan repeatedly said, "I don't recall," and there was never any further investigation into the financing of the Contras, which has long been alleged to be tied to drug money.

The Iran-Contra Affair was embarrassing to the Reagan administration on two accounts, first because of the potential illegalities committed by staff members, but second because it appeared that a "shadow government" was operating and that Reagan was unaware of what his underlings were doing. He had always been a hands-off leader, and the scandal proved to his critics that he was little more than a figurehead, bolstered by reports that he often fell asleep in Cabinet meetings.

Still, the numerous scandals of Reagan's subordinates never hurt his popularity, and he left office with the highest approval ratings of any modern president. His influence on today's Republican Party far exceeds any other conservative, and he has become the icon of the GOP.

Dutch's Sadly Ironic Final Days

After leaving the White House and retiring to a $2.5-million Bel Air estate, Reagan wrote his second autobiography, *An American Life,* in 1990. He was in huge demand as a speaker and presided over the dedication of the Ronald Reagan Library in Simi Valley in 1991.

In November 1994, Ronald and Nancy Reagan revealed to the world what his doctors and close friends had suspected for quite awhile. He was suffering from the memory-destroying neurological illness known as Alzheimer's disease, and the "Great Communicator" was unable to access the stories he loved to tell. The Reagans established an institute for the study and treatment of Alzheimer's disease. Even though he is in seclusion in a time of personal struggle, Ronald Reagan continues to endear himself to the American people and remains the most popular ex-president the country has known in a long time.

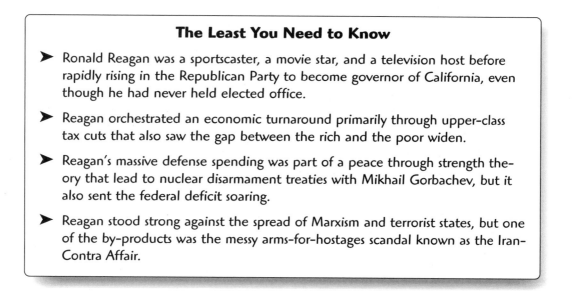

The Least You Need to Know

➤ Ronald Reagan was a sportscaster, a movie star, and a television host before rapidly rising in the Republican Party to become governor of California, even though he had never held elected office.

➤ Reagan orchestrated an economic turnaround primarily through upper-class tax cuts that also saw the gap between the rich and the poor widen.

➤ Reagan's massive defense spending was part of a peace through strength theory that lead to nuclear disarmament treaties with Mikhail Gorbachev, but it also sent the federal deficit soaring.

➤ Reagan stood strong against the spread of Marxism and terrorist states, but one of the by-products was the messy arms-for-hostages scandal known as the Iran-Contra Affair.

Chapter 14

The Bigger They Are, the Harder They Fall: Lyndon Johnson

In This Chapter

➤ The young politico from the Lone Star State

➤ Legendary legislative leader

➤ How great was the "Great Society"?

➤ The Vietnam War brings down the president

Lyndon Baines Johnson (LBJ) assumed the presidency during one of the saddest times of twentieth-century America and walked away from it during one of the angriest. Johnson was a man of prodigious appetites for food, booze, women, companionship, legislative accomplishment, and, ultimately, for proving that the United States could win the Vietnam War. His four years in the White House were an incredible Shakespearean drama of amazing highs and devastating lows.

Deep in the Heart of Texas

Johnson was born on a farm near Johnson City in southwestern Texas in 1908. The Johnson clan had let family roots grow deep into the Texas soil, but the ground didn't reciprocate in abundance. The Johnsons were far from bluebloods, but that didn't keep Samuel Ealy Johnson Jr. from taking part in politics. He served five terms in the Texas legislature and instilled a passion for politics in his eldest son, Lyndon.

Commander in Chief Lore

After his high school graduation, Johnson took part in the most red-blooded American adolescent activities and drifted aimlessly. He and his boys bought some wheels and headed out to have some fun in that warm California sun. Johnson worked a series of menial jobs and eventually hitchhiked back to Texas and took a job workin' on the highway.

Lyndon Johnson was a public school product, graduating from Johnson City High School in 1924. In 1927, Johnson enrolled at Southwest Texas State Teachers College in San Marcos. He took a hiatus from his studies to teach in a school for Mexican children in Cotulla. Johnson empathized and understood what it meant to be raised in poverty, and later in life he recalled the Mexican children, saying "I was determined to spark something inside them, to fill their souls with ambition and interest and belief in the future." It was the beginning of a long career dedicated to helping uplift the least fortunate Americans, a dedication that continued through the "Great Society" of the 1960s. He returned to college, graduated in 1930, and began teaching public speaking and debate at Sam Houston High School in Houston, Texas; but it wasn't long before he was bitten by the bittersweet bug of politics.

In 1931, Johnson was appointed secretary to Congressman Richard M. Kleberg. Johnson reached Washington, D.C., as President Hoover was exiting and the champion of government-initiated works projects, Franklin Delano Roosevelt, was entering. Johnson was a shrewd, hard-working, young man who asked questions, learned how the federal government machinery operated, and befriended the right people, including the legendary 25-consecutive-term Texas Representative Sam Rayburn. When he returned, Johnson continued to build important political friendships in Texas. In 1935 he became Texas administrator of the National Youth Administration, a post that

First Family Factuals

On the afternoon of November 17, 1934, Johnson and Lady Bird were about to be married at St. Mark's Episcopal Church. The conscientious bride asked her husband whether he had a wedding ring, which he had forgotten. LBJ sent a friend over to Sears to purchase another ring, and he brought back a tray of low-priced samples. Lady Bird chose a temporary $2.50 gold band for the ceremony. On their way out of the church the minister said, "I hope this marriage lasts"—it did, for more than 38 years.

enabled him to follow the workings of the New Deal and to use the powers of government to find educational and employment opportunities for young Texans.

Along the way, Johnson met a young graduate of the University of Texas named Claudia Alta Taylor. Johnson married "Lady Bird" in 1934 after a whirlwind courtship.

A New Dealers Debut

An unexpected death opened up the Representative seat in the 10th district of central Texas, and Johnson entered the special election. Bringing together his ever-growing network of friends and supporters, and with a small loan from his wife, Johnson ran as a consummate believer in Roosevelt and the New Deal. He easily outdistanced his opponents, and the 28-year-old Johnson became a member of the House of Representatives. The relationships he had cultivated from his earlier days in Washington—particularly his friendship with Mr. Rayburn—quickly paid off. Johnson was appointed to the important Naval Affairs Committee, and he pushed for the increased development of naval prowess.

Johnson earned a reputation as a tireless worker for his constituents. His support of the New Deal was noted by President Roosevelt, who gave the young congressman the access of a seasoned veteran. Johnson brought public electricity to the Lone Star State through the Rural Electrification Administration and managed to bolster the Texas coffers for infrastructure improvements, such as roads, dams, federal buildings, and naval training facilities that were bustling with activity during the World War II years. In 1941, Johnson ran unsuccessfully for the Senate. He announced his candidacy from the steps of the White House and was wholly endorsed by Roosevelt, but he lost a very tight race to an anti-Roosevelt Democrat.

Commander in Chief Lore

In 1940, Johnson signed up with the naval reserves and served as a lieutenant commander in World War II from December 1941 to July 1942. Johnson was one of the first congressmen to join the armed forces and was sent on an observation mission to Australia and New Guinea. On an observation tour in the South Pacific, his bomber was shot down by the Japanese. For this mission, Johnson was awarded the Silver Star for gallantry from General Douglas MacArthur. Johnson was also aboard a plane that had a near fatal crash-landing in Australia, but one thing he never lost was his seat in the House.

Roosevelt ordered all congressmen on active duty to return to Washington and the business of the nation. Johnson worked on a subcommittee that helped modernize the navy, and he continued the development of the armed forces. Later, Johnson was deeply saddened by the loss of his mentor and the man he considered a second father, Franklin Roosevelt.

Taking a Step to the Right

After the war, Lyndon Johnson shifted to the right and became somewhat more conservative. He didn't support the call by liberals to expand the New Deal, and he voted for the Taft-Hartley Act of 1947, which greatly reduced the power of organized labor. He even went so far as to override President Truman's veto of Taft-Hartley, but he supported the "containment" of communism and a stronger military. In 1948, Texans felt that he was more in tune with their concerns, and he was elected to the Senate. The election was tight; Johnson triumphed in the Democratic runoff by a scant 87 votes, which led to a failed court challenge and the cheeky nickname "Landslide Lyndon." Johnson wouldn't leave the political arena of Washington, D.C., until his stunning announcement of March 31, 1968.

Instantly Influential

Johnson continued to reap the benefits of the relationships he had made and was named to the Senate Armed Services Committee. Johnson supported Truman's decision to intervene in Korea and maintained a strong anti-Communist position. He chaired the Preparedness Investigating Subcommittee, an heir to Truman's investigating committee during World War II, and Johnson's committee, too, saved money by fleshing out military waste. By 1951, Johnson had moved into a position of solid Congressional power: Democratic whip, an office in which his primary duty was to bring fellow party members to the floor of the Senate chamber for crucial votes. In 1953, the Democrats lost the executive office and the Congress, but they elected Johnson to be their minority leader.

As minority leader, Johnson followed the principle that Democrats shouldn't play the role of perpetual obstructionists and shouldn't kow-tow to the Northern liberal wing of the party, which wanted to fight the Eisenhower administration at every turn. One congressional tradition Johnson tweaked was to convince a number of the senior members of his party to give up at least one prime committee assignment so that each incoming freshman senator would be able to have a plum slot. The freshmen class was understandably thrilled and thankful, including a young senator from Massachusetts who went by the name of John F. Kennedy.

In 1954, the Democrats gained control of both houses of Congress, and the popular Johnson became Senate majority leader, working in tandem with his old pal, Speaker of the House Sam Rayburn. Ironically, President Eisenhower had more legislative success with the middle-of-the-road Democrats than with the stridently conservative

Republicans. Johnson was never one to give away the farm, but he believed in working with the president, and he let it be known to his colleagues that nobody benefited from wholesale attacks on Eisenhower.

Commander in Chief Lore

The workaholic Lyndon Johnson suffered a massive heart attack on July 2, 1955, during a ride to a friend's Virginia estate intended to be a much-needed relaxing break over the July 4 weekend. He spent six weeks recovering in the Bethesda, Maryland, Naval Hospital followed by a recuperation period at his ranch in Texas, until Congress opened up shop in 1956. Johnson's weight had ballooned to 225 pounds, and he was forced to quit his three-pack-a-day cigarette habit cold turkey; jokingly, he asked doctors if he had to stop smoking as he entered the hospital.

Johnson did, however, criticize the president for military cutbacks and for not making space exploration a top priority. After the Soviets successfully launched the Sputnik 1 satellite into outer space in October 1957, Johnson personally led the charge to speed up the American space program.

Civil Action

Johnson had voted against Truman's civil rights program in 1948, but he was able to unify his divisive party and pass two civil rights acts in 1957 and 1960. Johnson knew that the Democrats were on the verge of losing the black—and even some of the liberal—votes in the North because the Republican Eisenhower administration had placed a civil rights proposal on the table. Johnson narrowed the focus of the bill to the issues of voting rights and a shift to jury trials for those accused of interfering with the voting rights of American citizens. It was the first civil rights law since the days of Reconstruction, and in 1960, he steered another civil rights law that dealt with voting rights through Congress.

Prez Says

"I am a free man, an American, a United States Senator, and a Democrat, in that order. I am also a liberal, a conservative, a Texan, a taxpayer, a rancher, a businessman, a consumer, a parent, a voter, and not as young as I used to be nor as old as I expect to be—and I am all these things in no fixed order."

—From 1958's *My Political Philosophy* by Lyndon Johnson

Johnson was quite possibly the most effective legislator the United States has ever known. He had a knack for bringing together opposing viewpoints on a particular proposal and finding common ground upon which to build a foundation. Johnson was in a position of power, so he was often able to trade favors, a vote here or the promise of support there might ensure a certain Senator that the pet bill he or she has been salivating over would get moved along through the legislative process. His powers of persuasion are the stuff of legend and his staple platitude, "Let us reason together," kept the legislative process humming along and he made darn sure that laws were passed. His years in Congress were remarkably successful on many levels, but they have long been overshadowed by the triumphant and tumultuous eight years as president.

Lyndon Baines Johnson, thirty-sixth president of the United States.

(Photo by Cecil Stoughton, courtesy of the LBJ Library)

Get to Know LBJ

➤ The town where LBJ grew up, Johnson City, Texas, was named for his grandfather.

➤ Johnson was the first legislator in Washington, D.C., with a car phone.

➤ In 1953, Lyndon Johnson became the youngest man ever elected Senate minority leader in history, at the age of 44. At the age of 46, he repeated the impressive accomplishment as the youngest man ever elected as majority leader of the Senate.

➤ The first black Supreme Court Justice, Thurgood Marshall, was appointed by Johnson in 1967.

➤ Legislation was enacted by Johnson that established the National Endowment for the Arts and the Humanities.

➤ Lady Bird Johnson's pet cause was the cleaning up of the country, and Congress passed a Highway Beautification Act in 1965 that was designed to limit billboards on federal highways.

➤ Johnson made increasingly fewer public appearances throughout 1967 and 1968 because of the constant protests and heckling and the numerous threats on his life.

America's Tragedy Begets Johnson's Presidency

In 1960, Lyndon Johnson had his eye on the White House and hoped to be the Democratic nominee, but didn't enter the primaries out of deference to his senatorial colleagues John Kennedy, Hubert Humphrey of Minnesota, and Stuart Symington of Missouri. He didn't declare his candidacy until July because he and his advisers, led by Sam Rayburn, assumed that there would be a deadlock at the convention in Los Angeles and that his reputation and connections could easily lead to a groundswell of support as the second choice of the delegates. Once his name started to circulate, Johnson figured, he would be the perfect choice to break the deadlock. It was a fine plan, except for the fact that the young, good-looking Catholic Senator from Massachusetts was a tactful campaigner who sewed up the Democratic nomination on the first ballot.

Kennedy surprised just about everyone, Johnson included, when he asked him to be his vice president. Johnson, in turn, surprised many political observers by accepting. The convention delegates nominated Johnson, and he campaigned hard for Kennedy, helping to ease the suspicions of his fellow Southerners. Many Protestants still cast a wary eye toward a Catholic candidate and his ties to the Pope—not to mention a general Southern congressional trepidation toward a Northerner from liberal Massachusetts—but Johnson helped Kennedy carry the states of Texas, Louisiana, New Mexico, and Nevada, which had voted Republican in 1956. Kennedy and Johnson won a close election over Richard Nixon and Henry Cabot Lodge Jr.

Many wondered how the maniacally energetic workaholic Lyndon Johnson would survive in an office that called upon its inhabitants to be as omnipresent as a dinosaur, but nobody needed to worry about the big ol' Texan fading into the background. Kennedy and Johnson got along quite well, and the president gave him more responsibility than any vice president had ever been accorded, even though it probably wasn't enough for a man of his temperament. Johnson was a regular at Cabinet meetings; served as chairman of the National Aeronautics and Space Council, moving its headquarters to Houston; and chairman of the President's Committee on Equal Employment Opportunities, which helped blacks find jobs. He also was called upon by Kennedy for advice, and the president kept Johnson abreast of his plans well in advance.

Johnson always thought that his ties and skills at handling Congress could have been used more effectively, and he didn't get along with the White House staff, who seemed to turn up their nose at the blunt, folksy Texan. However, Johnson did take goodwill trips on behalf of the Kennedy administration—a standard vice presidential function these days. Johnson visited 33 countries, including West Germany after the erection of the Wall, and South Vietnam, where he pledged continued U.S. support. Johnson wholeheartedly backed Kennedy's increase in the buildup of the military and the commitment of military advisers to Vietnam.

Commander in Chief Lore

Lyndon Johnson was sworn in as the new president of the United States aboard Air Force One, which was parked at Dallas' Love Field about 112 minutes after Kennedy's assassination. He was the first president to receive the oath of office from a woman, Judge Sarah Hughes, and his first executive order was to get airborne. He returned to Washington, D.C., with Jackie Kennedy and the body of her deceased husband. Johnson's first words to the American people after Air Force One landed were, "I will do my best. That is all I can do. I ask your help, and God's."

On November 21, 1963, President and Mrs. Kennedy flew to Dallas, Texas, to try to bridge the gap that had opened between liberal and conservative Democrats and that had allowed Republicans to make inroads in the Lone Star State. The following day, the Johnsons weren't far behind the Kennedys when bullets from the gun of Lee Harvey Oswald struck the president.

Getting Down to Business

Johnson stayed out of the spotlight during the funeral services, but in a special address to a joint session of Congress on November 27, he made it clear that he wanted continuity. He appealed to the senators and representatives to honor their slain leader's memory by pushing forward on his agenda.

Johnson asked all of Kennedy's Cabinet and staff to remain and immediately set out to see that passage of the civil rights and tax revision measures would come to fruition. In his State of the Union address, he called for his famous "war on poverty" and met with Dr. Martin Luther King Jr. and other black leaders to discuss what could be done to combat poverty. He also began working with his former congressional brethren to secure his bills. President Kennedy started the tradition of calling key legislators to make sure he had their vote, but Johnson expanded it to include visits to Capital Hill, personal correspondence with just about every member of Congress, and dinners at the White House. Johnson came of age in Congress, and behind-the-scenes maneuvering was what he knew best, except now he had the power of the executive office behind him.

Johnson's methods were effective. In 1964, Congress passed the Tax Reduction Act, a tax cut that lowered the governmental revenue by $11.5 billion, money that would be made up by economic growth. Congress also passed the sweeping Civil Rights Act of 1964 that banned discrimination based on color in the work place; in public accommodations and facilities; by employers, unions, or on federally funded projects; and in education. Johnson was aided by a national mood that wanted to see Kennedy's legislative legacy enacted, but his steady, thorough leadership and focus were equally important.

Prez Says

"Let us here highly resolve that John Fitzgerald Kennedy did not live—or die—in vain."

—Lyndon Johnson to Congress, November 27, 1963

"Landslide Lyndon" Lives Up to His Name

In 1964, Lyndon Johnson was overwhelmingly selected by *acclamation* to run again. He selected liberal Minnesota Senator Hubert Humphrey as his running mate, and the delegates also nominated him through acclamation.

Johnson ran as a consensus candidate for all of America, which wasn't hard to manage against the Republican nominee, the ultraconservative Arizona Senator Barry Goldwater. Johnson supporters used friendly buzzwords such as "peace" and "unity," while Goldwater himself took a hard right and uttered, "Extremism in the defense of liberty is no vice! ... Moderation in the pursuit of justice is no virtue!"

Knowledge Is Power

Acclamation is a boisterous, eager, affirmative vote—in this case, for the Democratic nominees for president and vice president—expressed through yelling, cheering, and applauding rather than balloting.

Commander in Chief Lore

Johnson's campaign staff ushered in the age of negative television advertising with the famous "Daisy Fields" spot. In it, a little girl picks petals off a daisy in a field of flowers as a man's voice counts down from 10 to 1. A worried look comes across her face, and a close-up of her eye morphs into a nuclear explosion. Over the image of a mushroom cloud, narration intimated that children everywhere would die if Johnson isn't elected president and said, "The stakes are too high for you to stay home." The infamous ad ran only once, but it (and others of the same ilk) was effective in portraying Goldwater as a radical hawk.

Johnson coasted to a huge victory, defeating Goldwater by an electoral margin of 486 to 52. Johnson lost only Goldwater's home state of Arizona, and a handful of Southern states adamantly opposed to the civil rights initiatives. He had managed to build the large consensus that he yearned for, including Republicans wary of extremism and the almost unanimous support of black voters.

Four Unbelievable Years

Johnson returned to the White House with a Democratic majority in both the House and the Senate that included a much larger liberal bloc than ever before and what amounted to a mandate by the American people, who had given him more than 60 percent of the popular vote. It was a heady time for the Democrats and their leader, Lyndon Johnson, and no one could have predicted that his administration would unravel over an Asian country that half of Americans couldn't have found on a map.

The Great Society

Johnson defined his administrative plans in a speech at the University of Michigan on May 22, 1964. He took a phrase he had used occasionally, the "Great Society," and used it as the label for his plans to build a better American mousetrap. Before the parties held their conventions and Johnson received the nomination—let alone won the election—he had put together 14 individual task forces to study various facets of American society. The average group size was nine and included both scholars and governmental authorities who looked at issues such as economics, international relations, and education. Proposals were drawn up after the recommendations were analyzed, and congressional experts were consulted on how to best attack the legislative process. Johnson touched on his large-scale activism in his inaugural address of January 20, 1965.

Many of the proposals from the "Great Society" initiative were approved by the 89th Congress and became laws, including the following:

➤ **The Elementary and Secondary Education Act of 1965.** This first large federal aid to education program was a multibillion-dollar school improvement package that helped schools obtain supplies, start special education classes, and refurbish libraries.

➤ **The Higher Education Act of 1965.** This act gave more federal dollars to universities, added low-interest student loans, and expanded the availability of scholarships.

➤ **The Medical Care Act of 1965.** This act expanded the social security system to create Medicare, which provides medical care and health insurance for the elderly and Medicaid for the needy.

➤ **The Voting Rights Act of 1965.** This act eliminated literacy tests or other "qualification" obstacles that were used to keep blacks and other minorities from exercising their constitutional right to vote—or, in some cases, even to register. It also reinforced the Civil Rights Act of 1964 by allowing federal examiners to look into problem areas. Within three years of the act, a million more blacks registered to vote.

Johnson also added two new federal Cabinets: the Housing and Urban Development Department in 1966, and the Transportation Department in 1967. Federal funding also was made available to improve housing and recreation in urban areas, the expansion of food stamps and increased unemployment compensation, youth employment initiatives, and further advances in the space program. In the waning days of his presidency, Johnson was able to congratulate the three astronauts of *Apollo 8,* William A. Anders, Frank Borman, and James A. Lovell Jr., who orbited the moon 10 times.

Unfortunately, whatever domestic successes Johnson had, they were all outdone by the Vietnam War.

Prez Says

"We believe that all men are created equal, yet many are denied equal treatment. We believe all men have certain unalienable rights, yet many Americans do not enjoy those rights. We believe all men are entitled to the blessings of liberty, yet millions are being deprived of those blessings, not because of their own failures, but because of the color of their skin."

—Lyndon Johnson following the signing of the Civil Rights Act of 1964

The Vietnam War Cripples Johnson at Home and Abroad

The conflict in Vietnam had been steadily growing since President Eisenhower first sent supplies to South Vietnam and vowed to help it maintain its sovereignty against the Communists. On the Cold War front, Johnson was able to maintain relatively friendly relations with the Soviet Union. He and Premiere Aleksey Kosygin signed a treaty that banned nuclear weapons from space, kept the Six-Day War in the Middle East from becoming a bigger deal even though Americans and Soviets backed opposing sides, and opened direct flights to and from Moscow and New York City. It made little difference, though, because the situation in Vietnam became an all-encompassing nightmare.

Johnson completely supported the containment of the North Vietnamese Communists from day one and fully intended to honor the United States commitments. President Kennedy may have considered a withdrawal from Vietnam, because he mentioned the potential recall of 1,000 advisers, but Johnson was determined to show that the United States would stand up to Communist aggression in Vietnam. By the summer of 1964, he had increased the number of Americans in Vietnam (still officially there as advisers to the South Vietnamese) to more than 25,000. Earlier that year, Johnson had approved covert CIA raids into North Vietnamese territory and had allowed the Navy to run electronic surveillance missions along the coast. On August 2, the USS *Maddox* was fired upon after crossing the boundary in the Gulf of Tonkin. More ships were sent, and two days later, the USS *Turner Joy* reported being fired upon. Johnson then asked Congress for a resolution to do whatever he needed to do "to prevent further aggression."

Johnson quickly increased the aid to South Vietnam and launched a major retaliatory air strike against North Vietnam. Starting in February 1965, after Communist guerrillas attacked U.S. bases, a massive bombing of North Vietnam began. Starting in the summer, American ground troops were rapidly expanded. By the end of 1965, nearly 200,000 U.S. troops were fighting in Vietnam. Johnson didn't want the world to see the Communists take control of Southeast Asia as the United States stood by idly, so he planned to escalate the involvement of the United States until the North Vietnamese could be brought to the bargaining table. He halted the bombing raids in May and December of 1965 to try to bring about a settlement, but both times he came up empty. By now North Vietnam was receiving military assistance from China and the Soviet Union and saw little value in ending the war.

In 1966, Johnson upped the ante and began bombing Hanoi, the capital of North Vietnam, but it was to no avail. American casualty and death figures were starting to rise in a guerrilla war in the jungles of Vietnam. A peace movement was starting to take shape in the United States, young men were fleeing the country to avoid the draft, and support for the war by American citizens was dropping, as was their faith in Lyndon Johnson. The president was caught between the "doves" who wanted an immediate end to the war effort and the "hawks" who wanted to increase military power and go for a decisive victory.

The Vietnam War led to violence in the streets, the protest chant of "Hey, hey, LBJ, how many kids did you kill today?" a rise in inflation, and no new domestic Great Society initiatives to deal with the rioting that broke out in urban areas such as Watts in 1965 and Detroit and Newark in 1967. The *Tet Offensive* wiped out much of Johnson's remaining support, and even members of his own party, Eugene McCarthy and Robert F. Kennedy, both opposed to the Vietnam War, decided to run against him for the 1968 Democratic nomination.

Johnson Drops a Final Bomb

On March 31, 1968, Johnson went on national television and announced that he was calling for a partial halt to the bombing to show that America was serious about ending the Vietnam War, which would be his main priority. He also stunned the nation by announcing that he would not run for the office of President of the United States in 1968.

Peace negotiations began in Paris between American and North Vietnamese emissaries, but little progress was made before Johnson left office in January 1969. He also watched his hopes for a summit meeting with Russia, to discuss arms reduction, go out the window when the Soviets invaded Czechoslovakia in August 1968. That year also saw the assassinations of two men Johnson had worked with: Dr. Martin Luther King Jr. and Robert F. Kennedy. Finally, Hubert Humphrey lost the 1968 election to Richard Nixon, and Johnson turned over the White House to the Republicans.

Lyndon and Lady Bird Johnson returned to their ranch near Johnson City, Texas, and he wrote his presidential memoirs, *The Vantage Point: Perspectives of the Presidency, 1963–1969*. The Johnson library was dedicated at the University of Texas in May 1971. On January 22, 1973, Lyndon Baines Johnson died of a heart attack, five days before an agreement was reached in Paris ending the fighting in Vietnam. (President Nixon had informed Johnson of the truce over the telephone.) Johnson was a solid president when it came to domestic legislative ingenuity and loved to roll up his sleeves to

Knowledge Is Power

On January 30, 1968, the Viet Cong launched the **Tet Offensive,** named for the Vietnamese festival of the lunar new year. It was an all-out, coordinated attack on over 100 targets in South Vietnam. Although the campaign was technically not a military success because of the large number of enemy casualties, the three-week attack firmly cemented the idea in the heads of many Americans that this war would never be won.

Prez Says

"I shall not seek and I will not accept the nomination of my party for another term as your President."

—Lyndon Johnson, March 31, 1968

work as a public servant, but he tried to dictate the outcome of the Vietnam War through escalation, which crippled his presidency and his legacy.

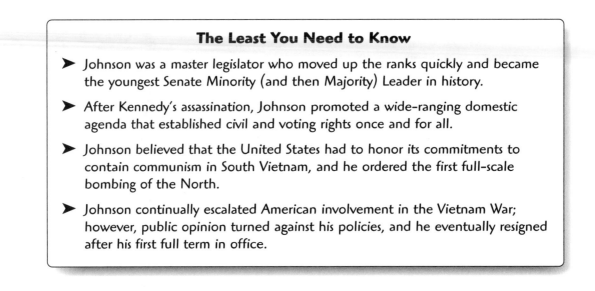

The Least You Need to Know

➤ Johnson was a master legislator who moved up the ranks quickly and became the youngest Senate Minority (and then Majority) Leader in history.

➤ After Kennedy's assassination, Johnson promoted a wide-ranging domestic agenda that established civil and voting rights once and for all.

➤ Johnson believed that the United States had to honor its commitments to contain communism in South Vietnam, and he ordered the first full-scale bombing of the North.

➤ Johnson continually escalated American involvement in the Vietnam War; however, public opinion turned against his policies, and he eventually resigned after his first full term in office.

Chapter 15

Any Which Way to the White House: Rutherford B. Hayes

In This Chapter

➤ Crooked election, honest man

➤ Deconstruction of reconstruction

➤ Morning prayers, the Hayes "Happy Hour"

➤ Old-old-school liberal?

Rutherford B. Hayes was at the heart of a beautiful American paradox; one of the most corrupt elections in presidential history gave the nation one of its most honest leaders. The Hayes presidency is not particularly notable for its major accomplishments, but more by the solid (opponents would say Puritanical) character of the White House residents. Hayes's great attempt at reconciling the rift between the North and the South went a long way toward healing the Civil War wounds, even if it left a system in place that would dominate segregationist Southern politics for decades to come. Hayes was not in love with the presidency. His proudest moments came on the battlefield, possibly because of the inauspicious beginning of his term.

One—That's the Magic Number

The watershed mark of the Rutherford B. Hayes presidency was the election itself, which differentiates him from any other man voted to the highest office. Truman's victory over Dewey was remarkable, but it isn't the centerpiece of Truman's legacy. Hayes, on the other hand, has come to be primarily recognized for the disputed election.

In 1876, the leading contender for the Republican nomination was Speaker of the House James G. Blaine of Maine. Like many in the Ulysses Grant years, however, Blaine had recently been charged by a congressional committee with corruption, using his political influence to reward a railroad company. Hayes was selected on the seventh ballot at the National Convention in Cincinnati, primarily because of his reputation as a teetotaler and a man above the scandals that had become routine.

Hayes's Democratic opponent was Samuel J. Tilden, the governor of New York, who had gained a national reputation as a reformer because he had broken up the Tweed Ring, a notoriously corrupt faction of Tammany Society led by William Tweed that had cheated New York City out of millions (some estimates are as high as 200) of dollars. The campaign was bitter and hotly contested—both sides were calling for reform and two reformers were at the center of it all. The morning after the election, Hayes was not shocked to see headlines declaring Tilden the victor. Hayes and Tilden had pulled out all the stops right up until the election, but once the returns began to come in, the former governor of Ohio knew that the writing was on the wall.

Sometimes the Numbers Do Lie

The popular vote showed 4,284,020 for Tilden and 4,036,572 for Hayes, and the electoral votes stood 203 to 166, but not for long. A Democratic Chairman wanted to confirm the electoral college vote, so he contacted the editorial department at *The New York Times*. His query was received by a Republican, editor John Reid. The chairman asked how many secured votes Tilden had, which got Reid to thinking about how to get his man Hayes into the White House.

Reid contacted the party bosses, and the Republican election officials refused to accredit Tilden's returns in South Carolina, Louisiana, and Florida (and a single disputed electoral vote from Oregon) claiming that blacks had been kept from the polls. This made the actual secured number of electoral votes 184 to 166, so Hayes needed only 19 votes (Tilden only one) for a majority. Hayes got the southern votes, leaving a tie at 184 apiece. And Republicans used more than one underhanded technique to secure their votes: Money and other bonuses were handed out to election workers as they took care of correcting the results.

The Senate at the time was Republican, and the House was Democratic, so the prospect for deadlock seemed inevitable. For three months, the leaders of the two major parties met in secret to hammer out a solution to the two "official" election outcomes. The Electoral Commission of 1877 was appointed, consisting of five men each from the House, the Senate, and the Supreme Court. It was intended to be a nonpartisan collection, with the impartial justices providing the buffer between an equal number of Republicans and Democrats. The justices were supposed to select the fifteenth member, and it was expected that they would choose Justice David Davis, a man with no clear affiliation. Before the vote, however, Davis was appointed a U.S. Senator by the Illinois State Legislature, and he resigned from the Supreme Court. The commission instead chose a Republican, Justice John Bradley, so the count for every state ran eight to seven in favor of Hayes. The final electoral count was 185 to 184, so Hayes defeated Tilden.

The Tainted Victor

Many people across the country were outraged because the voting had gone along strict party lines. During the months of crisis, the country was up in arms over the issue—and at least one citizen actually took up arms and fired a bullet into Hayes's house as he ate dinner. The Democrats may have lost the White House, but they got an assurance from the House that Hayes would withdraw federal troops from the South and push appropriations for rebuilding Confederate areas. The deal left governments in the South in the hands of local whites, which had major implications in the decades to come. Ironically, Hayes had nothing to do with the deal; it was made through party bigwigs.

After all that, Hayes was formally declared the victor, only 56 hours before the scheduled inauguration. To avoid exacerbating the controversy, Hayes was secretly sworn in on March 4, 1877, in the Red Room of the White House.

The aftermath of the Civil War still hung in the air, and Hayes was not the type of man to rock the American apple cart. Hayes was a moderate, virtuous, deeply religious man whose presidency was relatively lackluster. However, it was lackluster because his hands were tied somewhat by the election arrangement and also because the Democrats controlled the House during the first two years of his term and the Senate after the midterm elections. Passing legislation was no more than a passing fancy for the meritorious Ohioan. The Democrats had boycotted his inaugural address

Prez Says

"The president of the United States of necessity owes his election to office to the suffrage and zealous labors of a political party, the members of which cherish with ardor and regard as of essential importance the principles of their party organization; but he should strive to be always mindful of the fact that he serves his party best who serves the country best."

—From Rutherford B. Hayes's Inaugural Address

and had no desire to share their legislative powers with the Republican who had "stolen" the 1876 election. Hayes garnered the unflattering nicknames "His Fraudulency," "Rutherfraud B. Hayes," "the Usurper," and (in kinder, gentler, circles) "Dark Horse President."

Rutherford B. Hayes, nineteenth president of the United States.

The Hayes Code: Conciliatory Politics

Hayes took an interesting approach to filling out his Cabinet, one that mirrored his desire to serve the country first and the party second. He appointed David M. Key of Tennessee, a Democrat and former Confederate colonel, to be Postmaster General, a position that gave him power to appoint other former Confederates pending Hayes's approval. This striking appointment was called for in the bargain with the South, but it was also a conciliatory step toward unity.

Hayes hoped that he could help build a Republican base in the South, with visions of a national party such as the Whigs, but it never came to fruition. The Democrats would dominate Southern politics for years to come. Hayes also appointed Carl Schurz, the reformer who had been on the forefront of the Liberal Republican mutiny against Ulysses S. Grant four years earlier, and William M. Evarts was his secretary of state. Evarts had provided legal defense for Andrew Johnson during his impeachment trial, which ironically, Hayes had supported. It was Hayes's desire to be above the spoils system and to build a diverse forward-thinking inner-circle that would be representative of the nation as a whole.

Hayes also made good on the promise to remove federal troops from the South, and the remaining Union soldiers said goodbye to South Carolina and Louisiana. By the end of April, all the army units were gone. Reconstruction already had been dismantled in the Northern part of the South, and Hayes just supplied the finishing touch. Unfortunately, the deep South was where blacks had made their most substantial progress, including holding a black Republican majority in the statehouse in South Carolina. Republican influence in the South vanished into the Dixie air, and the Democrats formed a tight-knit bond known as the *Solid South*.

Hayes was a progressive in many ways, and he probably would have detested the segregationist Democratic policies in the South. During his presidency, Hayes won a significant battle with Congress over riders that he had fastened to appropriation bills that were intended to safeguard blacks' right to vote, guaranteed by the fifteenth Amendment to the Constitution.

Rutherford B. Hayes was a president who tried to do the right thing, but he was also a man of self-awareness, who knew that his accomplishments would not rank with the giants of the presidency, and he was never enamored of his time in the White House.

Knowledge Is Power

The **Solid South** was a collection of Democratic members of Congress that usually voted as a bloc in the best Southern interests, which was marked by that which favored white landowners. Democratic victory lead to a massive rollback of Reconstruction's formidable accomplishments. Laws were soon enacted to keep blacks subordinate and to ensure a segregated society through such nefarious means as the poll tax, literacy tests, and whites-only primaries. The "Solid South" would maintain substantial power until the latter half of the twentieth century and would stay loyal to the Democratic Party until it became a bastion for Northern Democrat support of minority groups and labor unions.

Prez Says

"I am more gratified by friendly references to my war record than by any other flattery. I know that my place was a very humble one—a place utterly unknown in history. But I also am glad to know that I was one of the good colonels."

—Rutherford B. Hayes

First Family Factuals

The Hayeses were the first First Couple to celebrate their silver anniversary at 1600 Pennsylvania Avenue. On December 31, 1877, the Rev. Dr. Lorenzo Dow McCabe of Ohio Wesleyan University performed the ceremony on the big twenty-fifth. He was familiar with the protocol because he had united the couple in marriage on December 30, 1852.

Four Wounds and No Funeral

Hayes grew up in Delaware, Ohio, and became a banner student at Norwalk Academy in Ohio and then at a private school in Middletown, Connecticut. Hayes moved on to Kenyon College at Gambier, Ohio, and was valedictorian of his class in 1842. He proceeded to Harvard Law School and became a practicing attorney in 1845. In December 1852, Rutherford married Lucy Ware Webb, a woman he first met at the age of 16 but really got to know when she attended Wesleyan Female College. The two shared a love for the arts and high culture and a disdain for the devil's drink, alcohol. Their long, joyous union produced a daughter and seven sons, three of whom died during childhood.

As the Civil War broke out, Hayes joined the Union effort, even though he initially had hoped that an agreement could be reached between the North and the South. Hayes offered his services to the state of Ohio. Governor William Dennison appointed him to the rank of major in the 23rd Ohio Volunteer Infantry. His regiment quickly saw action in West Virginia, and before long Hayes was promoted to lieutenant colonel.

Hayes was a distinguished soldier, and time on the battlefield brought out the best in the young Ohioan. He was severely wounded on September 14, 1862, at the Battle of South Mountain, Maryland, as he continued to lead his men on a charge up the mountain. Despite the fact that a third of his unit was dead or wounded and that his arm had been torn apart by a bullet, Hayes held his ground. He was promoted to colonel, and he sustained two more injuries. He continued to impress, and during the Battle of Winchester, Virginia, 1864, his unit's flags were the first to enter the town. Hayes got his fourth nonfatal wound at the Battle of Cedar Creek.

The Battle-Tested Buckeye Enters Politics

Hayes was a true Union hero in the Civil War who had four horses shot out from underneath him. He received a battlefield promotion to brigadier general in October 1864, and to brevet major general in March 1865. Hayes always looked back on his years in the military as the best years of his life, and his numerous admirers back in Ohio nominated him for Congress in 1864. Hayes responded to a friend who wanted him to return and campaign with this gem, "Thanks. I have other business just now. Any man who would leave the army at this time to electioneer for Congress ought to be scalped." His proud patriotic platitude was instrumental in getting him elected, and he took his seat in December 1865.

It was a short-lived time in Congress, although Hayes was reelected in 1866. He voted in step with the *Radical Republicans* and went along with the tough reconstruction measures for the defeated South. He also sponsored an unsuccessful effort to include in the fourteenth amendment an educational test for all voters, black or white.

In August 1867, Ohio Republicans nominated Hayes for the governorship, and he resigned from Congress and ran a vigorous campaign. He pressed for a controversial amendment to the state constitution to open the vote to all adult males, blacks included. It was a risky stance to take, but he was popular enough to win the election by 3,000 votes.

Prez Says

"His whole nature seemed to change when in battle …. He was, when the battle was once on … intense and ferocious."

—Future President William McKinley, who served under Rutherford B. Hayes

Knowledge Is Power

The **Radical Republicans** were a group of Northern Republicans who were against Andrew Johnson's Reconstruction policies. They were strongly opposed to the Black Codes, which were individual state laws in the South that severely limited the civil rights and economic freedoms of African Americans, and the reentry into politics of former Confederate leaders. The Radical Republicans wanted to abolish slavery and, in lesser terms, to reshape the power structure in the South.

Oh! B. Hayes

➤ In Cincinnati, Hayes was volunteer consul for the Underground Railroad and worked to ensure that fugitive slaves gained their freedom.

➤ As a Congressman, Hayes was instrumental in establishing the U.S. Botanical Gardens in Washington, D.C., and served as the chairman of the Joint Committee of the Library of Congress, adding an important scientific compilation.

➤ Lucy Hayes was the original White House wife with a college degree, from Wesleyan Female College in Cincinnati. She was also the original "First Lady," a term used in an article criticizing her for not taking a more active role in advancing women's issues.

➤ A law passed in 1876 to forbid the use of the Capitol grounds as a playground after kids tore up the grounds prompted the Hayeses to hold the first Easter Egg roll on the South lawn of the White House. The Easter Monday tradition is still around today.

➤ As president, Hayes used the bully pulpit to get the completion of the Washington Monument back on track. Construction was begun in 1848 and stopped in 1860 when the money ran out. President Grant had authorized federal funding for the memorial in 1876, and in 1878 the U.S. Army Corps of Engineers resumed construction, which was completed in 1884.

➤ Alexander Graham Bell installed the first telephone in the White House during Hayes's term.

'Ello Guv'nuh

Hayes's time as governor was particularly notable for its lack of corruption and his efforts at progressive reform. In his first term, he butted heads with the Democratic legislature, but in his second term, he had a Republican majority and was able to pass more of his agenda. Buckeye fans spanning the globe surely remember the founding of Ohio Agricultural and Mechanical College (now Ohio State University), and he prided himself on the passage of the fifteenth amendment, giving blacks the right to vote. He also addressed reform in the prisons, schools, mental hospitals, and relief for the poor.

After inheriting Spiegel Grove, a large estate in Fremont, Ohio, from an uncle, Hayes retired to the life of a gentleman farmer. However, it didn't take long for the politics in his blood to start flowing again, and he bowed to Republican wishes to run for a third term as governor in 1875. He campaigned mainly on the issue of *sound money* and defeated the popular Democratic Governor William Allen, a *greenback advocate,* by a mere 5,500 votes. The triumph made Hayes a national figure, popular because of his war record and reputation for integrity. The following year, he was nominated for the presidency.

These Are Hayes to Remember

Once in Washington, President Rutherford B. Hayes did little to distinguish himself as a memorable leader. Of course, there were interesting moments during his term. The following are a few of these days to remember:

Knowledge Is Power

The **sound money** principle is rooted in the idea that paper money should have an individual, stable standard of value, and that standard is usually gold.

Greenback advocates wanted a monetary system based on bimetallism (usually gold and silver) and unlimited federal issuance of paper currency. (The actual paper currency known as the greenback was so called because the reverse side was printed in green ink.)

➤ **The Specie Redemption Act of 1875.** As part of his long-standing adherence to the sound money principle, Hayes supported the passage of the act, which would make greenback paper money redeemable in gold starting in 1879. Congress wanted to pass legislation to issue "cheap" silver dollars, but Hayes wanted to back the paper currency and bonds from the Civil War primarily with gold. He felt that making the greenbacks payable in gold would decrease the total supply of money and head off inflation. In 1877, Congress passed bills repealing the Specie Resumption Act and requiring the unlimited coinage of silver—which were vetoed by Hayes, but his veto was, overridden as the Bland-Allison Act. Hayes's ideas generally won out however, because an amendment was added to allow the secretary of the treasury to decide how much silver was an acceptable monthly purchase.

➤ **Civil service reform.** Hayes was instrumental in bringing about the beginning of the end of the spoils system. In June 1877, Hayes issued an executive order that forbade federal workers from taking an active role in politics. A civil service investigation into the practices of the New York Custom House found many employees shirking their duties to work for the Republican Party. In an early test of the strength of the reform effort, Hayes unseated two fellow GOP members— Alonzo B. Cornell, and the port collector, future President Chester A. Arthur, who, ironically, would back major civil service reform legislation in the wake of Garfield's assassination.

➤ **Foreign affairs.** Hayes insisted on American control of a proposed canal to be built across Central America (and his policy eventually led to the construction of the Panama Canal). After Congress passed a bill limiting the number of arriving Chinese immigrants to 15 per ship, the president vetoed it as exclusionary and in violation of a treaty with China. He then sent envoys to the Far East to negotiate a new treaty, which regulated the immigration of Chinese laborers. However, this was very unpopular because of the anti-Chinese wave spreading throughout the West.

Lucy in the Dry with Lemons

One of the legendary legacies of the Hayes White House was a strict adherence to temperance. Lucy was thought to be the brains behind the operation, earning the nickname "Lemonade Lucy" because lemonade was the strongest drink she would serve in the executive mansion. However, Rutherford took credit for the rules (which also banned tobacco, profanity, and, apparently, fun). Early on in the administration, wine was served at a dinner with two Russian Grand Dukes, but no bouquet was ever poured again. Shockingly, this policy rankled many of the congressional guests, and a sympathetic steward was said to have put rum into the oranges served at official banquets during the "Life-Saving Station" part of dinner. Hayes, however, claimed that the oranges were cleverly seasoned with rum flavor.

A Hayes-ey Shade of Liberal

Rutherford B. Hayes was not asked by the Republican Party to run for a second term, because he had alienated too many party loyalists with his independent stances. It wouldn't have mattered either way, though, because he made it clear when he accepted the nomination that he would serve a single term. In his inaugural address, he proposed adding a constitutional amendment that would have limited the president to one six-year term with no possibility for re-election. In his final address to Congress, he called for appropriations to secure free education and drew attention to the oppression of freed slaves in the South.

Rutherford and Lucy retired for good to Spiegel Grove, where he continued to press for his progressive pet projects such as prison reform and education. He died at his estate after an attack of angina on January 7, 1893, and was buried next to his beloved wife, Lucy, who had died of a stroke in June 1889. The last words of Rutherford B. Hayes were: "I know I am going where Lucy is."

Prez Says

"The paramount question still is as to the enjoyment of the right by every American citizen who has the requisite qualifications to freely cast his vote and have it honestly counted."

—From Rutherford B. Hayes' final address to Congress in December 1880

The Hayes presidency wasn't a particularly remarkable one, but he was a man of integrity. His dedication to the human rights abuses in the South was quite noble. Unlike so many of his day—Republicans included—he was against slavery on moral grounds. After he retired, he worked for aid and manual training for blacks, free public education (with an emphasis on the South), help for veterans to acquire their pensions, and the maintenance of a myriad of universities, particularly the one in his Buckeye backyard, Ohio State.

Hayes was an early advocate for civil rights legislation and had a progressive liberal streak at a time when it wasn't all too popular.

The Least You Need to Know

➤ Rutherford B. Hayes was a battlefield legend during the Civil War.

➤ Through outside party maneuvering, Hayes was elected after a corrupt electoral compromise that granted him the White House he didn't originally win in exchange for the withdrawal of federal troops from the South and putting local governments in the hands of Southern whites.

➤ Hayes ended the last remaining decade-old policies of Reconstruction by pulling the troops out of South Carolina and Louisiana.

➤ Rutherford and "Lemonade Lucy" allowed liquor only once during their time as First Family.

Chapter 16

If I Could Be Like Ike: Dwight David Eisenhower

In This Chapter

➤ The mastermind of D-Day

➤ U-2 can get shot out of Russian skies

➤ Crazy Joe and his Pinko Paranoia

➤ The genesis of our interstate love affair

The 1950s are often fondly recalled as a time of "Happy Days": bobby soxers, Elvis Presley, new suburban developments, prosperity, peace, growth, and the expansion of America's highway system. On the other hand, it is naïve to label the decade that saw the first Cold War police action and the reactionary violence to the modern civil rights movement as a time when everything was "perfectamundo." A better description of the 1950s might be the cool, calm decade—at least, that is how Dwight Eisenhower's years in the oval office are often remembered.

The Only Way Out: Football

Dwight David (Ike) Eisenhower was born in Denison, Texas, in 1890, but his family returned to Abilene, Kansas, the following year. His father was a mechanic at a local creamery, and the Eisenhowers barely had enough to make ends meet. It was a tough upbringing for the future commander in chief. Dwight and his six brothers (a seventh brother died in infancy) worked from the time they were very young, growing vegetables in the large family garden and taking odd jobs as soon as they were old enough. It was a religious household—the Eisenhowers were members of River Brethren, a fundamentalist Protestant sect—but religion never became central to Eisenhower's life. He never joined a church and rarely attended services in his adult life.

The one arena that Eisenhower relished and excelled in was sports. He was an average student whose only strong subject was history, and he thoroughly enjoyed the biographies of military heroes. On the athletic fields, however, he was a star, playing in the outfield during baseball season and in the trenches as a lineman when the leaves changed and the pigskin started flying. He took his prowess with him to West Point.

Commander in Chief Lore

As a boy, Eisenhower's brilliant military career almost came to an end before it ever existed. At 15, he developed blood poisoning after scraping his knee, and the family doctor wanted to amputate his leg. With the collaboration of his brothers, Eisenhower went against the advice of the doctor, and his leg healed itself. He probably was thrilled just to be able to hit the baseball diamond or gridiron again, but had he lost his leg, the ramifications would have been much greater.

Eisenhower started working in the town creamery where his father worked after high school because his family couldn't afford to send him to college. He and his brother Edgar agreed to attend school on an alternate-year schedule to be funded by the sibling in the workforce. Eisenhower discovered that an appointment to the U.S. Naval Academy offered the chance for a free education and the chance to strap on a leather helmet and cleats again. He went to Topeka for the test and found that the exam was being given for both Annapolis (but by age 20, he was too old for the admissions exam for the Naval Academy) and West Point; in 1911, he headed off to the United States Military Academy.

Eisenhower fell back on a familiar pattern of mediocre grades combined with stellar athletic performance. A devastating knee injury forced him to quit the team, so he joined the cheerleading squad and coached the junior varsity football team. After that, his enthusiasm for secondary education waned, and he contemplated quitting school. However, A roommate convinced him otherwise, and he graduated sixty-first in a class of 164 cadets.

Makings of a Military Man

As a second lieutenant, Eisenhower was assigned to the 19th Infantry at Fort Sam Houston in San Antonio, Texas, even though he had hoped to serve in the cavalry corps. Two weeks later, he met Marie "Mamie" Geneva Doud and was smitten instantly. Eisenhower was "dating up"; Miss Doud came from a wealthy Denver family, reared in a life of luxury. Her father was wary of his daughter marrying an army man because of the unsettled existence, but they were married on July 1, 1916, a banner day on which Eisenhower also was promoted to first lieutenant. (The old softy proposed on Valentine's Day.) The Eisenhowers went on to celebrate 52 anniversaries.

World War I

At the outbreak of World War I, Eisenhower was made a captain and became a training instructor at different military camps. He yearned to go to France, but his application to go overseas to fight was not as important to the military brass as his ability to organize and prepare young soldiers. He moved from station to station, from Fort Sam Houston to Fort Oglethorpe in Georgia, to Fort Leavenworth in Kansas, to Fort Meade in Maryland. He then wound up in command of Camp Colt at Gettysburg, Pennsylvania, where one of the first army tank corps was formed. Eisenhower trained his troops in the ways of operating tanks and learned how to effectively turn civilians into soldiers.

First Family Factuals

Dwight and Mamie Eisenhower had two sons, Doud Dwight ("Icky") and John Sheldon Doud. Icky died in January 1921, just after Christmas, at the age of three from scarlet fever. The Eisenhowers were deeply scarred, blaming themselves and not discussing their personal devastation for years to come. John was born in 1922 and eventually graduated from the Military Academy on the same day his father embarked upon the invasion of Europe.

Ike Learns from the Military Masters

On October 14, 1918, Eisenhower celebrated his twenty-eighth birthday with the news that he had an order to assume command of an armored troop in France the following month—but, darn the bad luck, they signed that pesky armistice. Eisenhower received the Distinguished Service Medal, but he was disappointed that he never saw any action.

The isolationist fervor that swept through the country after World War I reduced the army exponentially. Promotions were few and far between, so Eisenhower remained at the rank of major for 16 years. He did all he could to learn the ways of the masters in military know-how, including a stint as an instructor at Infantry Tank School at

Camp Meade with his mentor, Colonel George S. Patton. The two men remained life-long friends.

In 1922, Eisenhower was sent to the Panama Canal Zone and served under Brigadier General Fox Conner, who tutored the future president in military history and the impact of war upon societies throughout the ages. Unlike his college days, Eisenhower became an excellent student, and Conner helped him get into the Army's Command and General Staff School at Fort Leavenworth, Kansas. It was a highly competitive institution, but Eisenhower finished number one in a class of 275.

Eisenhower went on to the War College in Washington, D.C., and his reputation as a solidly capable staff officer continued to blossom. He followed that by making the trip to France he had once coveted and produced a guidebook to the European battlefields of the Great War.

Eisenhower was then chosen by General Douglas MacArthur to be one of his aides and went to the Philippines to shore up the island defenses against any possible attack. There he helped to build an army of native Filipinos. MacArthur made Eisenhower his chief of staff, and Eisenhower stayed in the region until 1939, when the powerful National Socialist German Workers' Party invaded Poland and the World War sequel was underway.

The Big Gun in the Big One

Eisenhower returned to the United States as the country began to rapidly replenish its dwindling military ranks, ultimately instituting a draft in 1940. In June 1941, he was appointed chief of staff under General Walter Krueger of the Third Army and followed the circle of life to his old stomping grounds, Fort Sam Houston. Eisenhower further distinguished himself in the maneuvers held in Louisiana by the Second and Third armies and was promoted to brigadier general in September 1941.

A few days after the Japanese attack on Pearl Harbor, Eisenhower received orders from Chief of Staff General George C. Marshall and was put in charge of the War Plans Division. His experience in the Philippines was essential to developing a game plan in the Pacific, and he accurately predicted that Japan would quickly crush Filipino defenses. He recommended constructing a base in Australia but also adhered to a policy of "Europe first," which meant focusing on defeating the German forces before turning Allied attention to the Far East. Marshall made Eisenhower commander of the European theater of operations. The respected general had yet to spend a minute in combat, but he arrived in England in June 1942 eager to begin his mammoth assignment.

Eisenhower was put in charge of Operation Torch, after Winston Churchill convinced Marshall that the Allied forces weren't ready for a cross-Channel invasion of Europe. Instead, Eisenhower led 60,000 soldiers into French North Africa. The troops suffered a major setback in Tunisia, where they attempted to capture General Erwin Rommel but met up with ugly winter weather. Eisenhower was able to make the technical adjustments and, seven months later, drove the Germans back and headed north into Italy in the summer of 1943, liberating the island of Sicily along the way.

Supreme Allied Commander

In December 1943, Franklin Delano Roosevelt appointed Eisenhower supreme commander of all Allied forces in Europe. His primary task was to head *Operation Overlord*. The gravity of the situation was not lost on Eisenhower—he told the combined chiefs of staff, "We cannot afford to fail."

Eisenhower worked 20-hour days, diligently training his troops for the surprise attack on Normandy. A key component to the success of the invasion was the "Transportation Plan," which called for Allied bombers to wipe out French railway systems and keep the Nazis from having quick access to the refortification of their divisions. He also ordered the majority of the bombs dropped to be outside the projected invasion area to throw off the Germans and keep them from shifting their troops.

Knowledge Is Power

Operation Overlord was the code name for the largest amphibious landing in history, a tactical maneuver of mind-boggling complexity. The invading force, an integration of more than 150,000 Allied troops of every stripe, crossed the English Channel, landed in France, and charged on into Germany. On June 6, 1944, Eisenhower's dramatic organization and orchestration of the D-Day invasion of the beaches of Normandy was the hard-fought victory that led to the liberation of France—and, ultimately, Europe.

D-Day

Airborne troops started dropping shortly after midnight on June 6, 1944, and the ground forces came ashore at dawn. A beachhead was fortified, but it took seven weeks to drive forward.

Eisenhower has been criticized by a small but vocal number of historians for his slow advance, which was compounded by his refusal to fire the cautious British commander Sir Bernard Montgomery. Eisenhower also has been criticized for the slow-moving, broad-front offensive with Patton leading the troops in the south and the British in the north. The argument is that concentrated Allied forces could have quickly dominated the Nazis in the chaos following D-Day, but it is impossible to know what would have happened. Eisenhower believed in a patient, methodical, complete success, and that is what he delivered.

Now a five-star general, Eisenhower led his troops in battle against a massive German counterattack in the Ardennes region of Belgium, the *Battle of the Bulge*.

Knowledge Is Power

The **Battle of the Bulge** got its name because the Germans advanced 32 miles into Belgium and Luxembourg after staging a counteroffensive trying to recapture the seaport of Antwerp. The Nazis initial success caused a "bulge" in the Allied defense, but it wasn't enough. They were soon stopped, and the massive Nazi casualties served as a contributing factor in their collapse in the spring of 1945.

World War II Comes to an End

Initially, the Allies had to retreat, but Eisenhower quickly regrouped and plugged the gaps in the lines. The broad front along the Rhine wiped out most of the Nazi forces in a campaign that devastated the Germans.

One question remained: Which way should the advancing Allied troops take? Churchill and Montgomery wanted to mount an offensive in Berlin and keep the city in the western sector, at least until the Soviet Union made concessions on Poland. The Allies had divided Germany into occupation zones, and Berlin was divided into sectors, part of which fell within the Russian zone. Eisenhower was not willing to risk American lives against a major resistance in order to take Berlin, which they would have to turn over to the Russians anyway, per their agreement.

The Russians took Berlin and lost more than 100,000 men. Eisenhower sent troops into southern Germany and continued his broad-front attack. Europe was wrestled from under Hitler's thumb, and the Germans signed the unconditional surrender document at Eisenhower's headquarters in Reims, France, on May 7, 1945.

Marshall sent a cable to Eisenhower, calling his successful mission "the greatest victory in the history of warfare." The war in Europe was over, but his decision regarding Berlin became controversial, and the United States began a 40-plus year tête-à-tête with the Communists who dwelled behind the Iron Curtain.

A Hero Returns

After heading the occupation in Europe for six more months and promoting democratic ideals, Eisenhower returned to the United States as a hero of the first rank. Besides his military sagacity and personal moxie, and besides the five stars he accrued while leading the Allies to victory over the Nazis in World War II, he also happened to be a down-to-earth, friendly man who deplored the pompous attitudes of the "glory-hoppers" in the army. Both parties wanted him to run for the presidential nomination in 1948, but he repeatedly said that he had no interest in politics and wouldn't reveal whether he was a Democrat or a Republican.

Eisenhower replaced Marshall as President Truman's Chief of Staff of the U.S. Army from 1945 to 1948. He oversaw a major demobilization and shrinking of the American Army by more than seven million men and women. He also worked with Truman to try to unite the armed forces under a single command, the National Military Establishment, which ultimately became the Department of Defense. In 1947, he wrote *Crusade in Europe,* a memoir of his World War II experiences, which became a bestseller.

In 1948, Eisenhower retired from active duty to serve two years as president of Columbia University. In 1950, he answered Truman's call and returned to active duty as supreme commander of the newly created North Atlantic Treaty Organization (NATO). He became the first man to lead a multinational peacetime force, and he tried to build a Western army that could take on Communist troops if the situation arose.

The Call of the White House

Eisenhower was finally sucked into the race for the presidency in 1952 when Governor Thomas E. Dewey of New York publicly threw his support behind the beloved war hero. Eisenhower had only recently even aligned himself with a party, the Republicans, whom he felt were less inclined to put faith in a centralized government over individual liberty. At the time, the Republicans hadn't served in the oval office for 20 years, and their party had shifted to the conservative candidacy of an isolationist, Robert A. Taft of Ohio. As a more centrist Republican, Eisenhower found Truman's domestic agenda to be too liberal for his taste. He decided it was his duty to run because, as he saw it, either the Democrats would win again, or Taft would win and take the United States out of NATO.

Prez Says

"The same day [April 12, 1945] I saw my first horror camp. It was near the town of Gotha. I have never felt able to describe my emotional reactions when I first came face to face with indisputable evidence of Nazi brutality and ruthless disregard of every shred of decency. Up to that time I had known about it only generally or through secondary sources. I am certain, however, that I have never at any other time experienced an equal sense of shock."

—From *Crusade in Europe,* by Dwight Eisenhower

The nomination was a tough battle. Taft's supporters were many of the delegates who voted in the caucuses. At the Republican convention in Chicago, the junior senator from California, Richard Nixon, helped secure the nomination for Eisenhower by delivering a majority of the state's delegates. In turn, Nixon was selected as Eisenhower's running mate, which appeased many of the more conservative party members. As early as 1949, Truman had decided not to run and his announcement in March 1952 left Adlai Stevenson to get walloped in the electoral voting 42 to 89. Republicans also won control of both houses of Congress, partially because Southern Democrats (Dixiecrats) were defecting to the GOP because of their objection to Truman's civil rights program.

First Family Factuals

There have always been rumors that Dwight Eisenhower had an affair with one of his jeep drivers in World War II, Kay Summersby, but he always denied it. A 1976 updated memoir by Summersby, penned with a ghostwriter and titled *Past Forgetting: My Love Affair with Dwight D. Eisenhower,* recalled a tryst that had been absent from her 1948 book, *Eisenhower Was My Boss.* Mamie Eisenhower never doubted her husband's word or the loving correspondences he sent during WW II.

The campaign was relatively benign, with the catchy slogan "I Like Ike" melding nicely with Eisenhower's plainspoken manner, bright smile, and choice television appearances. Eisenhower deftly added that he would personally go to Korea if he had to, which enabled hawks to envision an activist military willing to take on Communist China. Those who wanted to give peace a chance could take the words to mean that Eisenhower was searching for an end to the conflict.

In December 1952, during the interim period before his inauguration, Eisenhower visited Korea. It wasn't long into his administration, however, that it became obvious that he wanted to end the conflict. A cease-fire was negotiated, after making clear to Communist Chinese in no uncertain terms that the United States wouldn't be "constrained" in the use of nuclear weapons. A truce was signed on July 27, 1953, and North and South Korea remained split along their previous boundary.

The Relative Calm of the Eisenhower Era

As president, Eisenhower relied on a solid chain of command and the proper delegation of authority, building consensus instead of pushing original, activist programs. He toed a pragmatic conservative line and thought that issues should be dealt with on a local level, not through federal initiatives. He had a sharp analytical mind and relied on his advisers to lay out all possible alternatives of a particular problem. However, he was not about to tackle tough issues unless they reached the boiling point. Eisenhower preferred working behind the scenes and was not one for partisan confrontations.

Foreign Policy Focus: Containment

Eisenhower went in to Washington speaking out against Truman's "containment policy," but he wound up following its basic tenets and didn't attempt to roll back Soviet acquisitions. The hawks in Congress may have wanted a hard-line stance taken against the Communists, but Eisenhower thought that the threat of nuclear war was a much greater concern. For this reason, he refused to intervene in Hungary as Russian tanks crushed the brief rebellion in 1956. A war with Nikita Khrushchev and the Soviet Union was too great a risk now that nuclear technology had been added to the fold.

Dwight David Eisenhower, thirty-fourth president of the United States.

In 1954, Secretary of State John Foster Dulles urged President Eisenhower to intervene in Vietnam, where French colonial forces were surrounded by the Vietminh Communists forces. Eisenhower abstained at first, but after Vietnam was divided in half, he eventually sent American advisers and military equipment, the beginnings of the rumble in the jungle that would haunt future presidents. His rationale was that if South Vietnam fell, other countries would fall like dominoes. The "domino theory" became the philosophy behind escalation in Vietnam.

Eisenhower chose his own course of action in 1956 when the British, French, and Israelis invaded Egypt in an attempt to recapture the Suez Canal, which had been nationalized by Gamal Abdel Nasser, who was also supported by the Soviet Union. The United States and the Soviet Union condemned the action, and the invaders were stunned that Eisenhower wouldn't assist American allies. Eisenhower saw the invasion of Egypt as "gunboat diplomacy," which went against the essence of NATO. It was the United States' first venture into Middle Eastern politics.

The sweeping stranglehold of Communism crept closer in 1959 when Fidel Castro came to power 90 miles off the coast of Florida in Cuba. The president asked the CIA to draw plans to invade Cuba.

Prez Says

"Our most realistic policy is holding the line until the Soviets manage to educate their people. By doing so, they will sow the seeds of their own destruction."

—Dwight Eisenhower

One of the last official acts of Eisenhower's administration was to break off diplomatic relations with Cuba. Castro had the last laugh, though, because the Old Man in the Beard has outlasted nine American presidents and is still sitting pretty today.

In 1957, Congress approved the "Eisenhower Doctrine," which was to provide American military assistance to any country that was facing armed aggression by Communist infiltrators and that requested it. In 1958, Eisenhower deployed the U.S. Marines to Lebanon after a left-wing uprising in Iraq, and he sent the U.S. Navy to provide protection for Chinese nationalist ships providing aid to islands in the Formosa Straits in their struggle against the Red Chinese.

Rockets and High-Flying Spies

An embarrassing blow to the U.S. ego was delivered on October 4, 1957, when Russia launched its manmade satellite Sputnik. Americans were dumbfounded by the Soviet success, and the debate over a missile gap grew more vociferous. And because Sputnik was a technological achievement requiring educational resources, the question of whether America's educational system was a match for its communist counterpart also sparked debate.

In 1959, Eisenhower and Khrushchev held a summit in the United States, and there was guarded optimism that a test ban treaty could be reached at a summit in Paris in 1960. But hopes were dashed, because shortly before the Paris meeting of the United States, Britain, France, and the Soviet Union, an American U-2 spy plane was shot down over Russia. Eisenhower admitted that the high-flying reconnaissance spy plane had been flying missions since 1956 to take photographs of Soviet military installations, which up until then could always be denied because it was thought that Russia didn't have the weapons needed to shoot down the U-2 plane. Eisenhower had allowed for one final flight on May 1 to be piloted by Francis Gary Powers. Hours later, Eisenhower got word that the plane was missing, but he responded to Khrushchev's announcement that they had shot down an American plane with a blanket denial. He said that it was possible that a weather plane had been shot down, but days later, he was shocked to find that the Soviets had both the plane and Powers.

Khrushchev abandoned the Paris summit when Eisenhower refused to apologize. Eisenhower stated that he had no choice because it was essential to American interests to find out whether the Soviet Union was preparing for a first-strike nuclear attack, and the Soviet Union was conducting its military affairs in secrecy. Khrushchev stormed out, no treaty was signed, and the Cold War continued. Eisenhower knew that his term was coming to an end and thought the fallout from Paris was a major setback to U.S.-Soviet diplomacy.

The McCarthy Era

Eisenhower entered the White House at the height of Cold War paranoia, fueled by the reprehensible behavior of everybody's favorite Commie-baiter, Senator Joseph McCarthy of Wisconsin. In 1950, McCarthy made his infamous claim that he had a list of 205 Communist employees working in the State Department, which was never substantiated, but by then the *Red Scare* was in full effect.

Eisenhower personally deplored McCarthy's tactics, but he didn't want any public mud slinging for fear that it would just increase McCarthy's reputation. He backed down from denouncing McCarthy at a stop on the campaign trail in Wisconsin in 1952 after he had attacked his mentor and friend, General George Marshall. Eisenhower opted to follow the course of political advantage and not risk rocking the boat and losing the votes of the good people of Wisconsin. But forgoing the condemnation of McCarthy and defense of Marshall was a decision he later regretted (although documents were declassified that seem to suggest he worked behind-the-scenes to rid the country of McCarthy).

Eventually, McCarthy went too far and Eisenhower's plan to ignore him proved successful. McCarthy set out to expose Communists in the U.S. Army, of which he had no concrete evidence. He called for documents to be turned over detailing the meetings between the Eisenhower administration and the military brass, but the president simply invoked executive privilege on the grounds that to do so could breach national security. Without an inquisition to conduct based on the documents, McCarthy's hearings became a series of unfounded, paranoid attacks, and he lost momentum and national support. Eisenhower encouraged Republican senators to censure McCarthy, which they did in December 1954.

Knowledge Is Power

The **Red Scare** was the belief during the Cold War that Communists had infiltrated American society. In 1947, the House Committee on Un-American Activities (HUAC), began holding hearings about supposed Communist infiltration throughout the entertainment industry. Some people who were called as "friendly" witnesses listed the names of alleged sympathizers, and a secret blacklist developed in Hollywood, destroying the careers of hundreds of people even though they had never done anything illegal. The scare reached its height later with Senator Joseph McCarthy, who claimed he had evidence of subversive Communist activity within the State and Defense Departments. He became chairman of an investigative committee in the Senate.

Four Firsts for the Father of the 1950s

➤ Born David Dwight Eisenhower, his father David called him by his middle name to avoid confusion, and by the time he reached West Point he was signing his name Dwight David.

➤ Eisenhower was the first president to fly in a helicopter. He purchased two UH-13Js in March 1957.

➤ He was the first president to install a putting green on the White House lawn.

➤ Eisenhower was the only president to serve in both World Wars.

➤ He held the first televised press conference.

Ike Eisenhower vs. Orval Faubus

African Americans returning from World War II quickly realized that they were still second-class citizens and weren't getting their slice of the vast economic pie of the 1950s. In the *Brown* v. *the Board of Education* case of 1954, the Supreme Court—under Eisenhower's appointee Chief Justice Earl Warren—declared that the policy of "separate but equal" (segregated) public schools was unconstitutional. The Supreme Court ordered the South to integrate its schools.

Enforcing desegregation was not a top priority for Eisenhower's Justice Department because Eisenhower preferred that local governments handle their own affairs, and he didn't view the White House as an agent for social change. He was also wary about alienating Southern segregationists because the white power structure of the South was shifting away from the Democrats to the Republicans. Eisenhower never publicly commented on the Supreme Court decision, but he made it clear that he would uphold the Constitution.

The Supreme Court decision was viewed by some whites as a violation of states' rights, and violent protests swept the South. In 1957, tensions came to a head at Central High School in Little Rock, Arkansas, when nine black teenagers tried to enroll. Governor Orval Faubus called in the state National Guard to keep the students from receiving their constitutionally mandated education.

Eisenhower met with Faubus and was confident that the governor understood that he would lose in a showdown with the federal government, but he underestimated the power of the segregationist system. Faubus returned to Little Rock but wouldn't allow the students into the school. A federal judge ordered him to stop interfering, so he dismissed the National Guard and left the students with only local police protection against the raucous, angry mob, which numbered in the thousands.

In late September, Eisenhower sent 1,000 members of the 101st Airborne Division to Arkansas to accompany the students and to disperse the riotous throng. Many white

Southerners viewed his actions as an act of aggression, while many other Americans around the country thought he waited too long to take action and let the situation spiral out of control.

A Second Term and a Booming Economy

Eisenhower suffered a heart attack in 1955 and wanted to retire. However, doctors assured him that he was fit to serve, and Republicans didn't want to run the risk of losing the election. Eisenhower ran again, defeating Stevenson by more than 9.5 million popular votes and inflicting an electoral whitewashing of 457 to 73. It was a time of prosperity for the United States, and voters were anxious to reward their beloved president, even if there were critics who felt that he wasn't doing much of anything except playing golf (a bumper sticker read "Ben Hogan for President. If We're Going to Have a Golfer, Let's Have a Good One").

Eisenhower was far from a hands-on president, but he also didn't dismantle the majority of the New Deal programs. The United States became the richest nation in the world and enjoyed a run of economic success. The GNP more than doubled between 1945 and 1960, and personal savings, per capita income, and capital investments all rose during Eisenhower's administration. Eisenhower expanded Social Security to include about seven million farmers, and he raised the minimum wage to $1 an hour. And in 1956, the Interstate Highway system, the largest construction project in American history, got underway, which eventually added 42,000 miles of highways.

Like most second-term presidents, however, Eisenhower didn't have the opportunity for much innovation, in part because the Republicans lost both houses of Congress in 1954, and partly because innovation wasn't his style. Critics have maintained that Eisenhower could have done a lot more in terms of civil rights, but even a modest proposal to study racial discrimination was killed by Southern Democrats.

Retirement in Gettysburg

After his second term, Eisenhower retired to his farm in Gettsyburg and, despite his stumbles, was still an extremely popular leader. He was upset that Kennedy had been elected, but he conferred with the young president during the Bay of Pigs Invasion of Cuba.

Prez Says

"In the councils of government, we must guard against the acquisition of unwarranted influence, whether sought or unsought, by the military-industrial complex. The potential for the disastrous rise of misplaced power exists and will persist."

—Dwight Eisenhower, in his farewell address, January 17, 1961

On his farm, Eisenhower wrote two volumes of memoirs of his presidential years, *Mandate for Change* and *Waging Peace,* but his health was failing. He had three heart attacks between 1965 and 1969, and he died at the age of 78 of congestive heart failure at Walter Reed Army Medical Center in Washington, D.C. His proudest accomplishment was that "the United States never lost a soldier or a foot of ground in my administration. We kept the peace. People asked how it happened—by God, it didn't just happen, I'll tell you that." Eisenhower's greatest successes were more on the battlefield than in the White House, but keeping us out of conflict during the height of the Cold War was not too shabby.

The Least You Need to Know

➤ Dwight David Eisenhower was a brilliant military strategist who oversaw the organization and implementation of the invasion at Normandy.

➤ Eisenhower was an extremely popular president whose middle-ground conservatism guided the country as it enjoyed the economic boom of the 1950s.

➤ Eisenhower's Cold War diplomacy kept us out of war, but the U–2 spy plane incident set U.S.-Soviet relations back.

➤ With *Brown* v. *the Board of Education,* Eisenhower had to send federal troops into Arkansas to ensure that nine black students could attend high school.

Chapter 17

Has Anyone Seen My Old Friend William (McKinley)?

In This Chapter

➤ The friendly chap of the GOP

➤ The tariff is near! The tariff is near!

➤ The strain with Spain is plainly from the *Maine*

➤ Anarchy in the United States

One of the strange paradoxes of the assassination of an American president is that he instantly becomes a martyr to freedom. An assassination of a president is an abomination on the democratic process, robbing the people of their vote. The four presidential assassinations have become benchmark in the respective legacies of the four men who have been killed by a man with a gun, and such is the case with William McKinley.

The Nice Guy Finishes First

In the years since William McKinley's death, his stature among historians has never been near the top , but it is always noted that he was a fine individual. It has been said that any adversary could enter his office and leave a friend, even if McKinley didn't do a blessed thing for his or her cause.

McKinley was the seventh child in a family of nine children, born in Niles, Ohio, on January 29, 1843. His childhood was marked by his studious nature and his love of oratory. He was a fine public speaker at Union Seminary private school in Poland, Ohio, and he became president of a local debating society. McKinley was 18 when the Civil War broke out, and he wanted to follow the family tradition of service during wartime. He enlisted in the 23rd Ohio Volunteer Infantry in June 1861.

Curiously, McKinley's superior officer was Major Rutherford B. Hayes, a fellow Ohio native who became the nineteenth president of the United States in 1877. The regiment was sent to Virginia, and McKinley was made a commissary sergeant after Hayes noted his bravery during a year of fighting against small Confederate units. McKinley distinguished himself at the Battle of Antietam in 1862, as he rode a team of mules through heavy fire to deliver food to the Union soldiers at the front. He continued to move up, and by the end of the war he left the army as a major.

McKinley followed the novel presidential route of becoming a lawyer back home and then running for public office. He studied law in the office of county Judge Charles E. Glidden of Youngstown, and then he spent a year studying at law school in Albany, New York. He joined a practice in Canton and quickly immersed himself in the local Republican Party. McKinley became a popular man about town and spent a lot of time involved in civic affairs. His career as a lawyer, however, was never very lucrative.

First Family Factuals

When William McKinley was the governor of Ohio, he ate with Ida and then waved to her every morning before he entered the State Capitol across the street. At three o'clock in the afternoon, he always stopped what he was doing, opened the window in his office, and waved a white handkerchief toward Ida until she responded.

McKinley was married during his time in Canton to Ida Saxton, daughter of a leading local banker and businessman. Unfortunately, it was a marriage that would resemble Franklin Pierce's, dominated by sadness and tragedy. Their first daughter, Katie, died at the age of four of typhoid fever, which had been preceded by the death of an infant daughter after only five months. Ida developed phlebitis, which left her partially crippled, and she suffered a mental breakdown after the baby's death. Throughout her life, she suffered from epileptic seizures and chronic fits of depression, and would spend her life as a semi-invalid. McKinley's devotion and affection to Ida was always mentioned as proof of his dignity and won him sympathy throughout his years in office.

McKinley quickly shot up the ranks, serving in Congress from 1877 to 1891 and missing only one term. His primary platform issue was his unbending support of high protective tariffs. His family had owned a small iron foundry, and his father had ingrained in his son the importance of protective tariffs for American industries.

William McKinley, twenty-fifth president of the United States.

McKinley penned the McKinley Tariff Act in 1890, which raised tariffs to an all-time high. The tariffs were favorable to the manufacturing, banking, and industrial base in the Northeast because they spurred domestic spending, but they were nowhere near as popular in places in the West and the South, areas that purchased cheaper imported goods. It is ironic that McKinley was regarded as a conservative Republican in his day because tariffs are an anathema to most of today's global industries that make up one of the core constituencies of the Grand Old Party. McKinley's rhetoric is more in line with populist themes, but like many an elected official, McKinley completely abandoned this belief later in life. He voted for the Sherman Silver Purchase Act of 1890, a compromise between adherents to the gold standard and those who wanted bimetallism, which used both gold and silver as legal tender, in exchange for votes on his beloved tariff.

McKinley's popularity in Ohio, based in no small part in his support of the tariff, helped him to the governorship. During the depression of 1893, McKinley sent cars all across the state with provisions for the unemployed.

McKinley befriended Cleveland millionaire Mark Hanna, who was instrumental in helping him get to the White House. Hanna and others paid for a 10,000-mile trip through 17 states, where McKinley delivered more than 370 speeches. A majority of Democrats rejected their sitting president Grover Cleveland in favor of William Jennings Bryan, and the race took on an entirely different tone.

Bryan was an ardent believer in unlimited silver coinage and believed that economic reform was necessary to curb the abuses of wealth. His Populist ideas were a hit in the West, where farm commodity prices had fallen, but Bryan's ideas were totally dismissed by big business.

215

McKinley came out on the side of the gold standard, and raised piles of campaign money with Hanna—more than $3 million, a record for the time. McKinley was able to raise the huge sum by frightening bankers, manufacturers, and businessmen with the idea that inflation would cripple business and lead to more federal controls. The $3 million was used to hire touring speakers on McKinley's behalf, while he stayed at home and received delegates in a "front porch" campaign and to flood the nation with favorable pro-McKinley campaign literature. He won the electoral votes 271 to 176 and appointed Senator John Sherman as secretary of state, which allowed his old friend Hanna to become a senator from Ohio.

Before the Newspapers' War, Business as Usual

Throughout the turbulent history of mankind, wars have been valiantly and tragically fought for a number of reasons: land, property, religion, love, insanity, philosophy, boredom, and, of course, the never-ending human yearning to raise the circulation of newspapers.

The early stages of McKinley's presidency were relatively positive. Spurred on by his election, big business was reinvigorated, and prosperity returned. He pushed the Dingley Tariff Act through Congress, which levied even higher taxes, but he had the magic touch with all his old friends in Congress. The United States went solely on the gold standard in 1900, and McKinley basically allowed big business to have its way, even ignoring regulations that were already in place. McKinley has been regarded as a puppet to his big business masters because he made no attempts to reform the monopolistic industries that had a stranglehold on American business in the late nineteenth century.

No False "Idol of Ohio"

➤ One of McKinley's favorite tricks to appease those men he disagreed with was to take the red carnation that he frequently wore in his lapel and give it to the man as a gift for his wife. This became the flower of his home state of Ohio.

➤ McKinley's political future was almost undercut by a friend whose bank notes he had endorsed. The friend and financial partner went bankrupt and left McKinley with more than $100,000 in debts. Wealthy friends started a fund that covered his monetary behind.

➤ McKinley was the first president to use a telephone for campaigning, calling 38 of his campaign managers from Canton before the 1896 election.

➤ Millions of mourners lined the railroad tracks as McKinley's funeral train took his coffin from Buffalo to Washington for a state funeral and then on to Canton for burial.

Our *Maine* Man Takes Us into the Spanish-American War

McKinley's service during the Civil War had tempered his lust for conflict, but the United States entered an imperialistic period in which isolationism fell by the wayside and expansionism returned. In 1895, in Cuba, a revolution broke out under the leadership of Jose Marti against brutal Spanish rule. The Spanish government sent more than 100,000 troops to the island, and members of the peasantry were rounded up and thrown into disease-ridden concentration camps. In the United States, popular sympathy was firmly on the side of the Cuban rebels, but McKinley was cautious about entering the conflict. President Cleveland had managed to keep the United States out of the conflict, and McKinley was hoping for a peaceful term in office.

In an effort to boost circulation, the competing New York papers *The New York Journal,* published by William Randolph Hearst, and the *New York World,* published by Joseph Pulitzer used the atrocities by the Spanish government against the Cuban people as perpetual front-page news. The sensationalistic headlines and stories sent back from reporters sparked indignation against the Spanish, and the outcry contributed greatly to U.S. involvement. The nonobjective, populist, tabloid techniques of the dailies became known as *yellow journalism,* named for Hearst's inclusion of a color comic strip called *The Yellow Kid.*

American imperialism was fueled by the newspapers, and on February 15, 1898, the catalyst for rushing into the Spanish-American War splashed across the country's front-pages with all the force of a William Taft cannonball off a high-dive. The U.S. *Maine* mysteriously exploded and sank in the Havana harbor, and all 266 officers and men were killed. The sinking of the battleship sparked an eruption of populist reaction against the Spaniards, even though there was no official explanation as to why and how the explosion occurred.

Prez Says

"We want no wars of conquest; we must avoid the temptation of territorial aggression. War should never be entered upon until every agency of peace has failed; peace is preferable to war in almost every contingency."

—From William McKinley's first inaugural speech in 1897

Commander in Chief Lore

After the explosion of the *Maine*, an American commission investigated the circumstances as McKinley discreetly asked Congress to pass a $50 million defense appropriation, which became law on March 9, 1898. In 1976, however, a Naval study was published theorizing that spontaneous combustion in the ship's coal bunkers was the cause.

"Remember the *Maine!*" rang throughout the United States, and McKinley followed the directive. On April 10, the American ambassador in Spain sent word that an armistice was on the way, but McKinley sent a message asking Congress that he be given the power to use the U.S. Army and Navy in Cuba. On April 19, a joint resolution of the Houses gave him the authority to intervene, but with an amendment preventing the annexation of Cuba. The declaration of war against Spain, which followed on April 25, was a mere formality.

American Domination

Right away, the United States showed its force when Commander George Dewey destroyed a Spanish fleet in Manila Harbor on May 1. The Spanish-American War was stretched to the Philippines because the U.S. Navy game plan was to form a blockade to the island of Cuba in the Caribbean Sea. To do so, it was decided that the Spanish Navy must be eliminated, so the Spanish fleet's base in the Philippines was attacked. Eventually the Philippine Islands themselves were conquered.

The Battle of Manila Bay was one of total American domination. Dewey's famous command to his captain, "You may fire when ready, Gridley," was the beginning of an aquatic thrashing in which America saw only eight of its own men wounded, no American deaths, and no serious damage to any of its own ships, while the Spanish fleet, on the other hand, was eviscerated.

The Spanish fleet in the Caribbean didn't fare any better. It was demolished at Santiago, Cuba, on June 10 under the command of Admiral William Sampson. Spanish power in the Americas was waning, and American troops easily took Puerto Rico after landing on July 25.

U.S. troops began to arrive at Manila on July 17, and there were some 8,500 troops within a couple of weeks. On August 15, the Spanish-American War ended with the unconditional surrender of the Philippines.

The Spoils and Violent Aftermath

Spain ceded Puerto Rico, Guam, and the Philippines to the United States. It was the end of the great Spanish colonial power and the beginning of the United States as a world force to be reckoned with, a force that was quickly criticized from outside and within for its annexation of the Philippines, which was seen by many as an affront to democracy. A two-year war broke out on the Philippines between U.S. soldiers and Filipino guerrillas, which took somewhere between 200,000 and 600,000 Filipino lives.

McKinley's role in all of this was rather simple: He watched as we won, even though it came at a price that could have been avoided. In all, 298 soldiers died in combat, but thousands more died of diseases brought about by woefully inadequate food, medical care, and sanitary conditions. The president continued the imperialistic fervor by signing the congressional resolution that granted the annexation of Hawaii on July 7, 1898. He also oversaw the acquisition of the island of Tutuila, in what is now American Samoa.

McKinley's efforts were popular, and the imperialism issue never became much of a sticking point. Today, many historians feel that McKinley meekly stood by as the United States was driven into the Spanish-American War by Hearst and Pulitzer, especially considering that McKinley was opposed to a war with Spain over Cuba, in part because he was always sensitive to popular opinion about him and sentiment was on the side of aggressive expansion. However, the Spanish-American War wasn't a disaster, by any means. Although McKinley allowed outside influences to shape his agenda, the acquisitions of the war came in handy in the Pacific Theater during World War II.

Open Door Expansionism

McKinley announced an Open Door Policy with China, stating that every country should have equal access to China's markets. A Chinese revolutionary society, the I-ho T'uan (regularly called the Boxers in the West because of their pugilistic approach to readying for war) started a rebellion in 1900, with the intent of ridding Beijing of all foreigners. McKinley ordered U.S. Marines to join an international relief expedition and help to hunt those responsible and to restore order to the Chinese capital.

McKinley Gets Buffalo Winged

McKinley cruised into his second term as president, again beating William Jennings Bryan. The Democrats tried to peg McKinley as both a stooge for big business and an imperialist, but it didn't make any difference. He carried 28 states and 292 electoral votes. The first few months of his second term went by peacefully, but an ill-fated trip to the Pan-American Exposition in Buffalo, New York, on August 4, 1901, cost him his life.

McKinley was looking forward to speaking on the importance of world trade, a far cry from his protectionist stance of years before. In his last address, he made note of the leading role the United States was beginning to play in the world and said, "Isolation is no longer possible or desirable."

On September 6, McKinley was participating in one of the mammoth handshaking sessions he was known for at the Temple of Music. A young anarchist, Leon F. Czolgosz, stepped up with a revolver hidden under a handkerchief and shot McKinley twice—one bullet grazed his ribs, and the second penetrated his abdomen. A crowd starting beating Czolgosz bloody, but McKinley ordered them not to hurt the man. McKinley also asked his friends to be careful when telling his wife.

McKinley was taken to a local hospital for immediate medical attention, but gangrene (incurable at the time) set in, and he died on September 14. Ida remained strong, visiting him every day with a determination to bolster his spirits. Czolgosz was tried and electrocuted the following month in Auburn, New York.

Assassination Under God

➤ On November 9, 1863, President Lincoln watched an actor named John Wilkes Booth play Raphael in *The Marble Heart* at Ford's Theater. Lincoln sat in the same box in which he would be murdered by Booth in 1865.

➤ Booth was hiding in a barn in Virginia. Union soldiers surrounded it and set it ablaze to bring him out. Against orders, Boston Corbett shot Booth through the neck and he had to be dragged from the fire. Barely able to speak, Booth asked the soldiers to "tell Mother I died for my country."

➤ After Charles Julius Guiteau shot James Garfield, a railroad police officer named Patrick Kearney arrested him. Kearney was so excited about apprehending Guiteau that he failed to take the assassin's gun off his person until after they arrived at the police station.

➤ Guiteau was sentenced to hang on January 23, 1862. Always trying to cash in on his delusions of celebrity, he tried to sell the suit he had been wearing when he shot Garfield for $100, and he peddled his autograph and picture through local newspaper ads.

➤ On August 4, 1901, Leon F. Czolgosz was grabbed by a guard as he made his way toward President McKinley. The guard thought he was getting too close. Czolgosz started to run, and the guard knocked him to the ground but didn't search his pockets, where he would have found the six-shot .32 Johnson revolver that was used two days later.

➤ At his trial, Leon F. Czolgosz said, "I am an anarchist, a disciple of Emma Goldman." (Emma Goldman was a leader of the U.S. anarchist movement.) He also said that he was proud of accomplishing his goal of killing a ruler.

➤ Lee Harvey Oswald defected to the USSR in 1959, but was unable to secure citizenship. He returned to the United States with his Soviet wife, Marina, in 1962.

➤ The Warren Commission concluded that Lee Harvey Oswald also attempted to kill Major General Edwin A. Walker on April 10, 1963, in Dallas, Texas. Their finding was based on a detailed note Oswald left for his wife Marina, photographs of Walker's home found in his possession taken from the rear position where a single shot was fired, and firsthand testimony from his wife.

William McKinley is generally not considered one of the great American presidents because of his political weakness to allow other outside sources to dictate his policies. On a personal level, though, he will always be remembered as a decent, respectable man who lovingly cared for his wife through years of pain and suffering—and there is something to be said for that.

The Least You Need to Know

➤ William McKinley's early career was defined by his allegiance to promoting higher American tariffs.

➤ McKinley was renowned for being a good guy, devoted to his sickly wife, always cheerful and friendly, even toward his political opponents.

➤ McKinley was easily influenced by outside sources, and he took us into the Spanish-American War in no small part because of Hearst and Pulitzer's lurid and sensational yellow journalism.

➤ McKinley was very popular at the time of his assassination by an anarchist named Leon F. Czolgosz.

Part 4
Club Fighters

"If you have not chosen me by secret ballot, neither have I gained office by any secret promises. I have not campaigned either for the presidency or the vice presidency. I have not subscribed to any partisan platform. I am indebted to no man, and to only one woman—my dear wife—as I begin this very difficult job."

—From Gerald Ford's remarks upon taking the oath of office, August 9, 1974

The difficulty of the job cannot be overstated: It is an occupation in which half the people see you as damned if you do, and the other half see you as damned if you don't. There is always the chance that the president will come face to face with a crisis that has the potential to cripple the United States, and credit for anything is often grudgingly acknowledged, if at all. It is no wonder that some of those who have called the White House home seemed ill-prepared, such as Jimmy Carter and Millard Fillmore, or just happy to be there, including William Howard Taft and Martin Van Buren. The "Club Fighter" section is dedicated to the executive officers who gave it their all but just fell short.

Chapter 18

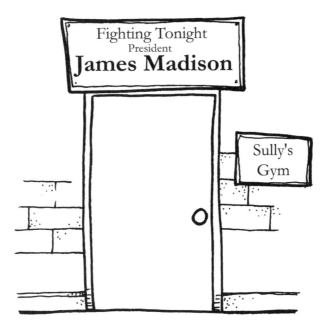

That Ole' Virginia Dynasty: James Madison and James Monroe

James Madison and James Monroe were part of the Virginia Dynasty that began with George Washington and dominated politics from the Constitutional Convention until well into the nineteenth century, winning two terms in the presidency in four of the first five elections. From the first term of Jefferson, the Democratic-Republicans were in power at a time when the Federalists were more or less finished and oversaw the country as young men went West and opened up the land for wagon trains, home-steaders, pioneers, and outlaws.

Madison Makes a Name for Himself

James Madison was born in the home of his grandparents' in Port Conway, Virginia, in 1751. Shortly after his christening, Madison went with his mother to his father's Orange County estate, Montpelier, where he lived for the rest of his long life. Madison was educated at home until he went to a preparatory school during his adolescence.

He enrolled in the College of New Jersey (now Princeton University) in 1769 and graduated two years later after studying philosophy, theology, history, Latin, Greek, and politics. He considered a career in the ministry, but he had a thin voice and, after six months of postgraduate study, returned home to Montpelier. From 1772 to 1775, Madison was ill and spent most of his time reading inside the family estate. He was sickly and weak from the time of his youth (which fostered a nervous, shy, tentative personality), but it has been suggested that his illnesses were exacerbated by a psychosomatic condition that led to seizures and symptoms of a non-existent disease. During his long isolation, a deep interest in public policy and governmental systems took root, and he decided to enter the local political mix, a fortuitous decision because he did not die at a young age like he assumed he would.

In 1776, Madison served as a delegate to the Virginia constitutional convention, which declared the state's independence from Great Britain. Madison helped draft the state constitution and worked with Thomas Jefferson, who became a lifelong friend and mentor. Madison was a great champion of individual liberties—he helped modify and secure passage of the religious freedom statute and advocated the separation of church and state. When the Virginia constitution went into effect, Madison became a member of the state legislature.

Commander in Chief Lore

Because he didn't keep with tradition and refused to indulge the electorate by providing free whiskey in exchange for votes, Madison wasn't re-elected by his Orange County constituents after only one term in the state legislature.

He served on the governor's council and worked with the government on problems brought about by the Revolutionary War. He then was elected to the Continental Congress at age 29 and took his seat with the Virginia delegates as the youngest man in Congress. After the American Revolution, Madison advocated a strong central government. He left Philadelphia in April 1783 with a reputation as a fine legislator and was renowned for having a sharp mind.

In the spring of 1784, Madison was elected to the Virginia assembly and spent the next three years in the state legislature continuing to work toward strengthening the federal government. He supported Jefferson's religious liberty bill and steered its passage, and the separation of church and state became law in 1786. He also helped defeat a tax on Virginians for state support of the Anglican Church and engineered passage of a bill that decriminalized heresy and eliminated the religious test that was required to hold public office.

Madison was concerned with interstate commerce as well, and organized a conference between Virginia and Maryland to debate the rules and regulations on the Potomac River. The conference was a flop, however, because not all states were present, so Madison and his supporters proposed an all-state convention in Annapolis—that convention, too, suffered from lack of interest. Fortunately, Madison and Alexander Hamilton were able to convince those in attendance to convene for a major conference in Philadelphia to revise the Articles of Confederation.

Madison recognized that the Articles of Confederation had too many weaknesses: The document didn't allow for a strong defense, and Madison recognized that sectional differences had the potential to dissolve the unified country. He also believed that a strong federal government provided the only effective way to monitor and regulate commercial interests between states.

Father of the Constitution

Madison was one of the initial delegates to reach Philadelphia in 1787, and he played a phenomenal role in the development of the United States. Madison took it upon himself to keep a detailed journal of the Constitutional Convention proceedings, and his notes on the debates, published posthumously, provide the only complete record.

JAMES MADISON.
President of the United States.

James Madison, fourth president of the United States.

227

He also wrote the comprehensive Virginia Plan, which laid the groundwork for the Constitution. In this plan, Madison proposed a strong central government with a judiciary and an elected executive. Madison encouraged a two-house Congress and representation within each chamber decided by the population of each individual state. A compromise was reached that made all representation equal in the Senate and determined by size in the House of Representatives. Although Madison didn't completely agree with the compromise, a federal government under a system of checks and balances was his vision, and that came to fruition in the drafting of the Constitution. He also helped to speed the process of getting the Constitution to the states for ratification instead of allowing it to get bogged down with amendments.

James Madison, Alexander Hamilton, and John Jay decided to wage a nifty little public relations campaign for the new document and began writing a series of articles explaining and defending its brilliance. The *Federalist* papers were a series of 85 essays refuting the arguments of the press attacks on the Constitution. Most of the essays originally appeared in the New York City newspaper *The Independent Journal* between October 1787 and spring 1788. The *Federalist* tracts went a long way in gaining support and momentum for the Constitution and still are considered an unparalleled explanation of the strengths of the American political system. Madison is generally credited with having authored at least 26 of the tracts, but the pseudonym was first "A Citizen of New York" and, later, "Publius."

Prez Says

"If men were angels, no government would be necessary. If angels were to govern men, neither external nor internal controls on government would be necessary."

—From the *Federalist*, #51, by James Madison

Back in Virginia, opposition to the Constitution had grown, and George Washington and other supporters asked Madison to run for the state ratification convention, which he did, even though he originally was not going to participate. Madison debated Patrick Henry, skillfully outlining all the precise arguments for the Constitution found in the *Federalist* papers and picking apart the opposing viewpoints. The delegates ratified the Constitution by the count of 89 to 79, but Henry used his substantial pull to keep Madison from becoming a U.S. Senator in 1788. The following year, Madison ran against and prevailed over fellow future president James Monroe in the battle for one of Virginia's seats in the House of Representatives.

Four Terms in the Formative Years

As a state representative, Madison grew to be a major figure in the early development of the United States under the Constitution. Although he started out on the side of Federalists such as Alexander Hamilton, as time went on, he began to view their policies that favored industrial-North policies as anathema and became a leader in Jefferson's Democratic-Republican Party. While in Congress, Madison introduced its first piece of business, a tax to help pay off the national debt. He also secured legislation that gave the president responsibility for the executive branch and sponsored the first 10 amendments to the Constitution. The Bill of Rights included fundamental American ideas such as the freedom of speech, the right to a jury trial, protection against unlawful search and seizure, and the often debated topic of the right of the people to keep and bear arms.

Madison continued to clash with Hamilton. Among Madison's points of opposition was a Federalist proposal that the federal government assume the states' war debts—he rejected the proposal because Virginia had already paid more than other states and thus would assume more of the burden. However, the bill passed after a deal was engineered with Southern leaders to establish the nation's capital in Washington, D.C. Madison also led the charge against Hamilton's proposal for the charter of a national bank and a substantial tariff. Instead, Madison aligned himself with Thomas Jefferson and belief in a republic for the people, not the privileged. Madison and Jefferson became a Democratic-Republican tag-team, working and collaborating together for the rest of their days.

Commander in Chief Lore

Madison had his hands in every aspect of the new Constitutional American way of life, even going so far as to write George Washington's inaugural address (albeit, the speech consisted of ideas that Washington had included in another manuscript). Madison then wrote the House of Representatives' warm, congratulatory reply to the address, and he followed that up by penning Washington's response to the House's warm, congratulatory reply.

Madison didn't support John Adams for the vice presidency in 1792, and the rift between the Federalists and him became permanent. Madison and Jefferson's party was sympathetic to the French, the Federalists were loyal to Great Britain, and President Washington wanted to leave well enough alone and remain neutral in the ongoing wars between the two European powers. Madison penned a series of letters under the name of Helvidius, excoriating Hamilton's defense of neutrality because it implicitly favored England. Madison also angrily opposed the signing of the Jay Treaty because it didn't change the old trade regulations and gave Great Britain the upper hand in dealings with the young America. After John Adams was elected president, Madison called it quits, returning home with the intention of making a life as a gentleman farmer.

Well, Hello Dolley

James Madison was 43 when he met and married a young Quaker widow, 17 years his junior, named Dolley Payne Todd. Dolley Madison became one of the most charming, vivacious First Ladies the country has ever known. Though the couple was childless, they raised her son from a previous marriage.

Madison was transformed by his wife. After meeting her, he reportedly became more comfortable in public, and his disposition was much friendlier and he had more confidence.

You Must Be Mad-ison

➤ James Madison is large in stature, but he was short in reality, standing only 5 feet, 4 inches and weighing less than 100 lbs.

➤ Madison was the first president to wear cutting-edge fashions; he donned pants instead of knee breeches.

➤ Dolley Madison sent the first personal message by the Morse telegraph, conveying her love from the Capitol to a friend in Baltimore.

➤ A famous story has it that James met Dolley in Philadelphia after she slipped on ice and fell into his arms, but alas, it is an American myth.

➤ Madison was the last of the founding fathers—the last signer of the Constitution and the last survivor of the Constitutional Congress when he died at the hearty age of 85.

A Leading Light of the Virginia Dynasty

Madison toyed with the idea of staying in Montpelier for good, but unconstitutional Federalist policy brought him back into the limelight. He wrote the Virginia Resolutions in response to the assault on civil liberties from John Adams's Alien and Sedition Acts. Madison and Jefferson assailed the abuse of federal power and asserted the protection of states' rights. Madison again served in the state legislature and campaigned vigorously for Thomas Jefferson in 1800. Madison was dutifully repaid with an appointment as Jefferson's secretary of state.

The two men worked very closely during the next eight years, and in some ways it was more of a fruitful partnership. Jefferson certainly had his own ideas, but he always consulted and analyzed issues with Madison. Madison assisted in the negotiations for the Louisiana Purchase and helped preserve American neutrality during the hostilities between France and Great Britain.

Picking a Fight

American sailing vessels were constantly being raided and confiscated by the British navy, which was forcibly impressing American sailors into active duty. Madison wrote protest letters to French and British authorities, but nothing came of them. Madison then promoted the Embargo Act of 1807, which abolished trade with Europe, but it didn't phase the belligerents.

As Jefferson's handpicked successor, Madison defeated the Federalist challenger Charles Coatesworth Pinckney in the presidential election of 1808. He entered the executive office at a time of great peril as foreign interference threatened the sovereignty of the United States.

War was not out of the question, but both France and Great Britain were trampling American rights. The United States was regionally split over which country was the enemy.

Both of Madison's terms were dominated by the international crisis, and he wasn't always equipped with the demeanor to handle the volatile situations. Although he was a brilliant political thinker, he didn't have a clear idea of how to ease tensions without going to war.

Neither France nor Britain gave the United States much respect because the country was divided over whom to support and had little in terms of national defense. In 1810, Madison was suckered into believing that the French would leave American vessels alone. Secretary of State James Monroe negotiated with Great Britain, but the country refused to drop its restrictions on American shipping. War became imminent.

A Bright Light During Times of Crisis

Dolley had frequently served as official hostess in the executive mansion for the widowed Thomas Jefferson, and her parties were the highlight of the social circuit. She radiated good will, and her loving union with her husband certainly helped his political life. Although she basically stayed out of her husband's political affairs, Dolley changed the role of the First Lady, actively supporting her husband and making a name for herself socially, independent of President Madison. Her fashion trends also were copied by women everywhere. When she sported a silk cloth wrapped like a Turkish headdress, it became a fashion statement in both the United States and Europe. Dolley Madison was a warm, sprightly, woman who became a truly beloved First Lady.

The War Hawks Get Their Wish in 1812

The War of 1812 also had its roots in the Western expansionist movements of the times. A congressional group led by Henry Clay and John Calhoun, known as the "war hawks," wanted to stretch U.S. territory into British-held lands in the West,

Canada, and Spanish-held Florida. The war hawks blamed a major Indian revolt on the British, which led to the crushing Indian defeat by William Henry Harrison at the Battle of Tippecanoe in November 1811. Madison had not authorized the use of troops, but it enabled him to work with Congress to ready the military. A declaration of war against Great Britain was passed by a count of 18 to 13 in the Senate, and 79 to 49 in the House in June 1812. On June 18, Madison signed the declaration, and the War of 1812 was on. Ironically, Great Britain had revoked the blockade restrictions on American shipping, but word didn't reach the United States until the war was in full swing.

First Family Factuals

British troops captured Washington, D.C., on August 24, 1814. Madison had asked Dolley to flee to Virginia, but she insisted on waiting until she knew that her husband was safe. She had to make tracks as the British quickly moved in, but she first loaded up a wagon with items, including her husband's papers and a famous Gilbert Stuart portrait of George Washington, which is still in existence. The troops ate the still hot food in the Executive Mansion before burning it to the ground along with other public buildings and the Capitol. The Madisons returned three days later and the reconstruction of the Executive Mansion was overseen by the original architect James Hoban, who made the call to paint the charred sandstone exterior walls white, making it the *White House*.

The War's Pluses and Minuses

The Vietnam War is often regarded as the first war that the United States didn't win, but a case could be made that the War of 1812 was, at best, a draw. Madison didn't have the military experience to build an effective war apparatus, and enthusiasm was mistaken for readiness. The U.S. Army had barely 10,000 troops, and the U.S. Navy had a pittance of ships.

Madison's attempts to bolster the military were often openly mocked. The country was spilt, and the New England states balked at supporting "Mr. Madison's War." The Federalists went so far as to organize the Hartford Convention of 1814 and 1815, which seriously debated signing its own agreement with Great Britain. The U.S. suffered a couple of humiliating defeats: An army of 2,000 surrendered at Detroit without firing a shot, and New York militiamen refused to enter Canada to back up their countrymen, leading to a loss on the opposite side of the Niagara River and an outright retreat from forces entering from Montreal. Still, amid strong criticism of the war, Madison was re-elected over Federalist candidate De Witt Clinton by an electoral count of 128 to 89.

The War of 1812 did have American successes, including heroic sea victories by the USS *Constitution* (a.k.a. "Old Ironsides") and the defeat of the British on Lake Erie, prompting the famous quote by Commander Oliver Hazard Perry, "We have met the enemy and they are ours." General Harrison forced the British back into Canada, and after American troops defended Fort McHenry in Baltimore, a spectator named Francis Scott Key wrote an inspired poem (which quickly became a song and eventually the national anthem), "The Star Spangled Banner." Finally, Andrew Jackson's victory at the Battle of New Orleans ended the fighting on a major high note for the United States.

The Treaty of Ghent was signed on December 24, 1814, and each side restored prewar boundaries. However, the primary issues of neutral shipping rights and impressment of American sailors were ignored. Madison was honored for the unity of the new country, and more Americans began to view themselves as one entity. The War of 1812—particularly the Battle of New Orleans—also gave Americans the sense that they no longer had to worry about Great Britain dominating their former colonies, and a national character began to emerge.

Back to Montpelier

Madison's last two years in office were a time of economic growth and great expansion westward. A more nationalist feeling in the country led him to reconsider and support a few of the Federalist policies he previously disdained, including signing the 20-year charter of a United States Bank and a higher tariff act. This was the first time of peace and prosperity under the Constitution, and Madison was celebrated by the continuation of the Virginia Dynasty with the election of his designated successor, James Monroe.

After his presidency, Madison returned to Montpelier and lived a relatively quiet life. He helped Jefferson found the University of Virginia and served as co-chairman of a state convention in 1829 that revised the Virginia constitution that he had been instrumental in writing 50 years earlier. He also spoke out against nullification when his Virginia Resolution was used as a basis for ignoring the federal government.

His later years were beset by chronic illness, and he died June 28, 1836, at 85, having lived to see the country's growth from a colonial burg to a 25-state union stretching to the Mississippi River.

Another Leader from "Old Dominion"

James Monroe, the fourth link in the quarter-century domination of the Virginia Dynasty, followed the same Jeffersonian course as Madison and was at the center of the ideological development of the Democratic-Republican (ultimately, Democratic) Party.

Monroe was born in 1758 into a rural planter's family in Westmoreland County, Virginia. He trekked several miles through the wilderness to attend school, and at the age of 16, he entered The College of William and Mary. He bolted from his studies at the outbreak of the Revolutionary War, however, enlisting in the Third Virginia Regiment of the Continental Army.

Monroe was commissioned a lieutenant at age 18, and his regiment joined Washington's troops outside New York City and saw action at Harlem Heights and

White Plains. Monroe led the advance at Trenton after his captain was wounded, and he took a shot to the shoulder, causing severe damage. Washington promoted him to captain, and Monroe then saw action in the battles of Germantown, Monmouth, and Brandywine, and he spent the famous winter of 1777 to 1778 at Valley Forge. In 1779, he returned to Virginia to build up a regiment of recruits, but he was unable to find the manpower and took to studying law under Thomas Jefferson.

Monroe was elected to the Virginia state legislature in 1782, and the following year he and Jefferson were elected to the Continental Congress that ratified the Treaty of Paris and secured recognition of American independence by Great Britain and ended the Revolutionary War. Monroe also chaired two committees, one that pushed for free navigation of the Mississippi River and another that dealt with the issue of governing Western land, which he wanted to open to veterans of the Revolution. He also proposed for federal regulation of interstate and foreign commerce.

Monroe served three years in Congress. During a recess in 1784, he took a trip to the Ohio Valley, which constituted the Western frontier at that time. Always interested in championing Western rights, the trip led him to take an active part in crafting the territorial government expressed in the Northwest Ordinance that was passed by Congress in 1787.

Monroe returned to Virginia, began a law practice in Fredericksburg, and built an estate called Ash Lawn, not far from Monticello. Monroe supported a strong central government in Congress, but he opposed the ratification of the Constitution while serving as a delegate at the state convention. He felt that the document went too far in establishing federal power, but he was placated by assurances that the Bill of Rights would quickly be added. He still voted against ratification, but he accepted the outcome with little complaint.

Monroe lost to Madison in a race for a seat in the House of Representatives, but he was elected to a vacated Senate seat in 1790 and again to his own term in 1791.

Monroe joined Madison in opposing the Federalist faction. He was a major French sympathizer and constantly butted heads with Alexander Hamilton over the centralization of the governmental and financial power base.

First Family Factuals

Monroe met Elizabeth Kortright while serving in the Continental Congress in New York City, and the two were married in 1786. Elizabeth seemed cold and formal in public, and she only occasionally entertained at the White House—this was a far cry from Dolley Madison and her lively gatherings. Unbeknownst to Washingtonians, however, Elizabeth suffered from an unnamed illness throughout her husband's administration.

Plenty of Posts Prior to the Presidency

Monroe served in a variety of public service occupations between his resignation from the Senate in 1794 and his election as president in 1816. In chronological order, they were as follows:

➤ **Minister to France, 1794 to 1796.** George Washington appointed Monroe to be his minister to France for two reasons: Monroe's advocacy and support of the French Revolution was well known, and Washington wanted to maintain relations with both France and Great Britain, where John Jay was in negotiations. Monroe sat in with the legislature and received a reprimand from the U.S. secretary of state for his overwhelming approbation of the French. He didn't strongly support the Jay Treaty (although he didn't state his political objections publicly or to French officials either) and thus was recalled by Washington in 1796. Monroe returned to the United States and wrote *A View of the Conduct of the Executive,* a 500-page book attacking the Washington administration's foreign policy, which damaged relations with America's former ally, France.

➤ **Governor of Virginia, 1799 to 1802.** Monroe returned to serve as governor of Virginia during a relatively uneventful three years. His relationship with Jefferson and Madison deepened during these years, as the Democratic-Republican Party blossomed and its main men ascended to the White House.

➤ **Envoy to France, 1803.** Jefferson sent Monroe to France as an envoy to Minister Robert R. Livingston on an "extraordinary mission." Negotiations had been underway between Livingston and Napoleon; when Monroe got there, he was pleasantly surprised to learn that the territory for sale had been expanded from an area in and around New Orleans to the entire Louisiana territory. Although the Americans had no authorization to make a purchase of this magnitude, Monroe took the responsibility for negotiating the treaty that doubled the size of the United States with the Louisiana Purchase at the low, low price of $15 million.

➤ **Minister to Britain, 1803 to 1807.** Monroe headed across the English Channel to try to sign a treaty to end the chaos over American shipping. He made little progress with Great Britain—he signed (with co-envoy William

First Family Factuals

James and Elizabeth Monroe enjoyed living in France, and they decorated the White House with furniture and silverware bought at an auction. Who was the previous owner of the items? None other than Marie Antoinette, the former queen who was executed by guillotine for treason in 1793.

Pinkney) a treaty that didn't address the issue of impressment, and Jefferson never sent it to the Senate. Monroe's jaunt over to Spain to try to secure the sale of Florida was equally futile.

➤ **Secretary of State, 1811 to 1817.** Monroe returned to the United States, and some momentum built for a run at the presidency, which alienated him from Madison, whom he blamed for the rejection of his treaty with Great Britain. The strain between the men may have kept him from an initial cabinet post in Madison's administration. Monroe served in the state assembly in 1810 to 1811 and was then elected governor on January 1, 1811. By then, however, relations between he, Madison, and Jefferson were fine. Madison appointed him secretary of state, and Monroe helped in dealings with Congress during the War of 1812. Monroe was given a second cabinet post, secretary of war, after the sacking of Washington, D.C. Monroe went a long way in restoring military morale, adding recruits, and securing loans.

James Monroe, fifth president of the United States.

JAMES MONROE L.L.D.

The Next Logical Step

Monroe was Madison's choice for president, and because the country was on a prosperous high, he became the Democratic-Republican nominee. Monroe defeated Federalist Rufus King, carrying the electoral votes of all but three states and winning 183 to 34. He followed much of the same agenda as Madison and Jefferson, but he also saw the need for a stable military. He helped settle sectional difficulties by assembling an outstanding cabinet made up of such luminaries as Secretary of State John Quincy Adams, of Massachusetts, and Secretary of the Treasury William H. Crawford, of Georgia. Monroe also embarked on a tour of the New England states and made conciliatory overtures to his Federalist critics. He was a big hit, and a Boston newspaper declared it the "Era of Good Feelings," which didn't even outlast Monroe himself.

During Monroe's tenure, expansionist fever took hold as Americans headed westward. Monroe listened to Adams in his support of Andrew Jackson's efforts in Florida, and as a result, the Adams-Onis Treaty was signed ceding Florida to the United States.

Domestically, Monroe was hands-off when it came to leading Congress, and little substantive legislation was passed. A minor panic hit in 1819, but because Monroe was a devotee of limited government, he took limited measures. He reduced construction of coastal protections and his Secretary of the Treasury William H. Crawford offered alleviated land mortgage payment terms. Later, he refused federal financing for internal improvements because it wasn't covered in the Constitution. Although he agreed that the country needed roads and waterways, he used his only veto in 1822 to thwart a measure that would have used federal funding to build toll booths to raise money for westward expansion of the nineteenth-century highway known as Cumberland Road.

One monumental decision that came about during Monroe's presidency was the Missouri Compromise in 1820. Missouri applied for statehood in 1818 and Maine followed suit in 1819, the former as a free state and the latter as a slave state. Northerners and abolitionists were concerned that Missouri's admittance would open the entire Louisiana Purchase to slave-owning states. Monroe stayed out of the bitter sectional debates in Congress and signed the Missouri Compromise into law. The Missouri Compromise admitted Maine as a free state and also admitted Missouri without slavery restrictions, but it did mandate that slavery was barred above 36°30' north latitude.

Commander in Chief Lore

Monroe ran virtually unopposed in the 1820 election, and his popularity was at an all-time high. The "Era of Good Feelings," coupled with the death of the Federalist Party, made him an unequivocal shoe-in. He received all but one lone electoral vote—one New Hampshire elector voted for John Quincy Adams, reportedly to ensure that George Washington kept the distinction of being the only unanimously elected president of the United States.

Prez Says

"This difference proceeds from that which exists in their respective Governments; and to the defense of our own .... We owe it, therefore, to candor and to the amicable relations existing between the United States and those powers to declare that we should consider any attempt on their part to extend their system to any portion of this hemisphere as dangerous to our peace and safety."

—From the "Monroe Doctrine" address to Congress by James Monroe on December 2, 1823

Although the divisions over slavery were beginning to tear the country apart, Monroe's second term was relatively quiet. His biggest triumphs were again in foreign policy, starting with the famous doctrine that bears his name. On December 2, 1823, Monroe addressed Congress and proclaimed a new policy to keep the affairs of American states free of European interference. This came about after a variety of Latin American countries won their independence from Spain and Portugal, and there was concern that a European alliance of Russia, Austria, Prussia, and France would invade the former Spanish colonies. Great Britain agreed and wanted to issue a joint statement, but Adams convinced Monroe that the United States should take a strong, independent stance. The two main tenants of the doctrine were that the United States opposed any further colonization in the Western hemisphere, and that any interference in U.S. business would be considered an unfriendly act.

Although Adams put together much of the policy, and although the ideas had been bantered about for years, it was Monroe who expressed the doctrine as basic American policy. The aptly named Monroe Doctrine became the cornerstone of U.S. foreign policy, and Monroe deserves credit for being the first president to concisely deliver the sovereign message.

Died on the Fourth of July

Monroe left office with his cabinet embroiled in malice and division. Had he taken the reigns and sought unity, it is possible that the splintering of the Democratic-Republicans might have been avoided. Instead, he stayed aloof until his retirement, in no small part because he didn't want to offend any of his underlings by handpicking a successor.

Monroe returned to a mansion, Oak Hill, near Leesburg, Virginia. Public service wasn't lucrative, and Monroe quickly fell into financial disrepair. He tried to collect on old, unsettled accounts with the government, but President Jackson considered his claims outrageous. Monroe finally received half his request, $30,000, but it wasn't enough money to keep Ash Lawn. After Elizabeth died in 1830, he sold Oak Hill and moved to New York City to live with his daughter and her husband. James Monroe died on July 4, 1831, and was buried in New York City, although he was reinterred in Richmond, Virginia, in 1858.

Tell Me More About Monroe

➤ James Monroe helped get Thomas Paine released from a French prison in 1794.

➤ Monroe was the first president to have an outdoor inauguration, and the first to have it held on March 5th because the 4th was a Sunday.

➤ Monroe earned the nickname "The Last Cocked Hat" because he wore Revolutionary-era outfits.

➤ The U.S. Marine band played first at his inauguration—and has played at every one since.

➤ Monroe supported the colonization of freed slaves outside the United States, and his private support of the efforts of the American Colonization Society in Liberia earned him the honor of being the only president with a foreign capital bearing his name, Monrovia.

Both Madison and Monroe served the country ably, although not without significant drawbacks. Madison took the country into a war that it wasn't prepared for and for which it got only modest returns. Monroe's two terms were peaceful, but he didn't address the divisions starting to come about over slavery, even if they may have been unavoidable. The entire public service careers of Madison and Monroe are quite impressive, however, and both men were instrumental in the expansion and unification of the newly sovereign United States.

The Least You Need to Know

➤ James Madison and James Monroe were the third and fourth presidents in the Virginia Dynasty that included Thomas Jefferson and George Washington.

➤ Madison lead an underprepared United States into the War of 1812, which saw the British burn Washington, D.C., to the ground but involved a major American victory at the Battle of New Orleans.

➤ James Monroe presented a doctrine that established the policy of American sovereignty in the Western hemisphere.

➤ Monroe was a hands-off president during the "Era of Good Feelings," but he sat by idly as political turmoil within his administration developed after the Missouri Compromise.

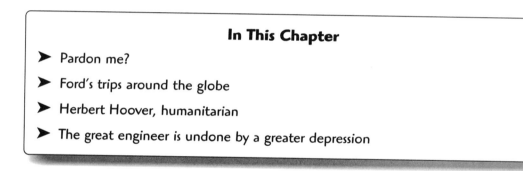

Chapter 19

Single Days Doom Their Terms: Gerald Ford and Herbert Hoover

In This Chapter

➤ Pardon me?

➤ Ford's trips around the globe

➤ Herbert Hoover, humanitarian

➤ The great engineer is undone by a greater depression

Like most presidents, Gerald Ford and Herbert Hoover steered the country over the course of a few years, but their respective terms are often defined by a single day. Ford entered the White House and tried to put the ugly past behind the country, only to have the country pass him by. Herbert Hoover tried to use the government to avert financial disaster, but it all came crashing down around him.

The Pinch Hitter

It is fair to say that no man was ever handed a more odious oval office, and no man ever inhabited the White House with less of an opportunity to make his mark than the old Eagle Scout himself, Gerald Rudolph Ford. Ford was the quintessential fall guy, the right man in the wrong place at the wrong time. Any discussion of the two and a half years Ford served as president hinges upon his controversial decision to grant a pardon to Richard Milhouse Nixon. However, before we look at the ramifications of the pardon, let's look at how he ended up in the nation's highest office in the first place.

Spending a Long Time in the House

Gerald Ford was elected to the House of Representatives from Michigan's Fifth District in his hometown of Grand Rapids in 1948. That was a big year for Ford, because he also married Betty Bloomer Warren, a divorced former Martha Graham dancer. However, the marriage was kept quiet for the brief remainder of the campaign because of the anti-divorce stance of many of the Dutch Calvinists in the district.

Prez Says

"I have come to a decision which I felt I should tell you and all of my fellow American citizens as soon as I was certain in my own mind and in my conscience that it is the right thing to do .... Now, therefore, I, Gerald R. Ford, president of the United States, pursuant to the pardon power conferred upon me by Article II, Section 2, of the Constitution, have granted and by the presents do grant a full, free and absolute pardon unto Richard Nixon for all offenses against the United States which he, Richard Nixon, has committed or may have committed or taken part of during the period from January 20, 1969, through August 9, 1974."

—From the pardon of Richard Nixon issued by Gerald Ford

Ford went on to serve for a quarter of a century in the House—he was re-elected a dozen times at 60 percent of the vote or higher each time. He gained a reputation for his loyalty to the district and to a centrist Republican platform. He slowly worked his way up the federal food chain, serving on the House Appropriations Committee, chairing the House Republican Caucus, and spending the years from 1965 to 1973 as the House Minority Leader.

Ford had always hoped to become Speaker of the House, but in 1973 he couldn't foresee the Democrats losing control of the House any time soon and decided to run for one more term before retiring to a private law practice in 1976. Ford was a well-respected member of the House with moderate conservative credentials, and broad-based support. He also was considered by most to be honest and forthright, but every step he made would be filtered through the Watergate lens.

One incident that came back to bite him was his attempt to impeach liberal Supreme Court Justice William O. Douglas. Ford charged Douglas with accepting money from a private organization with alleged ties to organized crime, defending the civil disobedience of the Vietnam War protesters, and supporting the publication of pornography. Ford said, "An impeachable offense is whatever the majority of the House of Representatives considers it to be at a given moment in history." Under normal circumstances, this type of partisan remark can be overlooked and forgotten, but it was repeated during discussions of the potential impeachment of Nixon.

Commander in Chief Lore

Lyndon Johnson appointed Ford to serve as one of two House members on the President's Commission on the Assassination of President Kennedy, the Warren Commission. Ford hired his old college buddy and original campaign manager, Jack Stiles, to be a part of his staff. The report totaled almost 300,000 words and featured over 500 interviews. After the Warren Commission reported its findings that Lee Harvey Oswald was "acting alone and without advice or assistance," Ford and Stiles co-authored the book *Portrait of the Assassin.*

Ford was criticized for backpedaling from his broad definition of an impeachable offense when he refused to apply the same standard to Nixon, arguing that the impeachment of the president should have more concrete, conclusive evidence of wrongdoing. The line was quoted throughout the impeachment hearing, but it wasn't the last time that Ford would be haunted by his attempts at reconciliation with the ghosts of Nixon.

Getting Caught in the Tangled Web Dick Weaved

The long, cold shadow of Watergate influenced Ford's brief White House tenure until it ended with the 1976 election of Jimmy Carter. Ford was selected by Nixon to replace the disgraced Vice President Spiro Agnew, who resigned in 1973 in lieu of bribery charges after pleading no contest to charges of tax evasion. Nixon selected Ford because he had a squeaky-clean reputation and because leaders of both parties told Nixon that Ford was the only Republican with a real chance for a quick confirmation by Democrats in both houses of Congress. On December 6, the confirmation vote was 92 to 3 in the Senate and 387 to 35 in the House, and Ford was sworn into the office of the vice president an hour later under the twenty-fifth amendment to the Constitution, which provides for the nomination by the sitting president of a vice president to fill a vacancy.

Commander in Chief Lore

Ford refused to fire any of Nixon's appointees in an effort to keep things running smoothly, but it may have hindered his efforts to establish his agenda. Within two years, all the heads of the executive departments were gone mostly through resignations, with the exception of Secretary of State Henry Kissinger and Secretary of the Treasury William E. Simon.

Ford was in a precarious position right off the bat because the Watergate scandal reached its apex during his eight-month stint as vice president. Ford remained loyal to Nixon, even though each new revelation helped to shatter the nation's collective conscience. Nixon's resignation surprised Ford, who believed his professions of innocence, and it has long been reported that he felt betrayed by Nixon. Ford was sworn in as President of the United States on August 9, 1974, becoming the only man to serve unelected in both the nations' highest offices. He issued the famous statement, "Our long national nightmare is over."

Initially, Ford was welcomed with open arms by the American people as a down-to-earth, middle-class antidote to the poisoned well of Watergate. Betty Ford was very popular, and the family came across as regular folks—Ford's daughter, Susan, refused to abandon her blue jeans even though White House staffers found them gauche. It would quickly come to a head, though, on the quiet Sunday morning of September 8.

The Pardon

Ford dropped a bombshell that effectively ruined his chances to craft his own presidency. He pardoned Richard Nixon after consultation with only a handful of political leaders and the pardon went against the tide of public opinion. Ford's press secretary, J.H. terHorst, resigned immediately, an hour before the telecast. Within a week, Ford's Gallup poll numbers plummeted from a favorable rating of 71 percent to a bleaker 49 percent.

What is often overlooked and should have been explained better in the speech is that a pardon does not absolve the recipient of wrongdoing—it was not an acquittal. Ford addressed the fallout from his speech in his book *A Time to Heal,* and he wrote, "Compassion for Nixon as an individual hadn't prompted my decision at all. And I have to confess that my televised talk failed to emphasize adequately that I wanted to give my full attention to grave economic and foreign policy matters. Nor did I explain as fully as I should have the strong judicial underpinnings, in particular, the Supreme Court's ruling that acceptance of a pardon means admission of guilt."

Gerald Ford wanted to cleanse the nation's palate, but the country wanted Nixon to face the music. What is interesting to consider, however, is that the accepted legality of a pardon includes an admission of guilt, so Ford cemented Nixon's place in history. Ford noted in his pardon that it would take one or two years before Nixon could be guaranteed a fair trial, and it would cause further division in this country over the possible fate of a man who paid the penalty of having to resign from the highest office in the land.

The ugly fallout doomed Ford's time in the White House. Conspiracy rumors quickly spread that Ford and Nixon had devised a secret deal that had helped him secure the presidency. In truth, Chief of Staff Alexander Haig had visited vice president Ford on behalf of Nixon to propose a deal for a pardon. Ford considered it for a day, rejected the plan, and ultimately the pardon was his and his alone. As president, on October 17, 1974, Ford even appeared before a House Judiciary Subcommittee investigating the pardon. He assured the country that there was no deal, and it was the first time a sitting president had ever given up his right to executive privilege for a congressional inquiry.

Playing Out the Back Nine

Ford never recovered after the pardon, but he also suffered from having to deal with Nixon's failing economic policies. Inflation was taking hold of the country, and prices were higher than at any other time in the post-World War II era. Government spending during the Vietnam years on both foreign and domestic policies, coupled with a huge spike in world oil prices, had raised national prices.

To combat inflation, Ford had encouraged Americans to "whip inflation now" (WIN). Some American consumers began purchasing less, but it was another kick to the weakened manufacturing base, emblematic of which were the automobile plant closures and worker layoffs. Ford tried to combat the hike in oil prices by OPEC with deregulation of the price of domestic oil, but he was stifled by Congress and ended up calling on citizens to voluntarily reduce their energy consumption. By 1975, unemployment crept up to 9 percent, the highest level since the Great Depression. The WIN campaign became a joke and it was abandoned as the recession worsened.

The press hammered Ford for everything after the pardon and made great sport of his supposed clumsiness. Ford had tripped and tumbled down the stairs of his plane onto the tarmac in Salzburg, Austria, and a feeding frenzy took hold. On more than one occasion, he was caught eating snow while skiing, and he quickly gained a reputation as an oaf. On television, it became a comic staple for Chevy Chase to walk out on the stage of *Saturday Night Live* and do his Ford impression, which consisted of falling down every few seconds and knocking over things like the White House Christmas tree. The most ironic aspect to the gag was that Ford was the most athletic president since Theodore Roosevelt—he loved to ski, swim, play tennis, and of course, play golf.

Amnesty

Eight days after the Nixon pardon, Ford offered conditional amnesty to the young men who had avoided the Vietnam War by evading the draft or deserting the armed forces. Draft dodgers could successfully fulfill a two-year commitment of alternative service for amnesty, and deserters could spend two years in the branch of the military in which they had served. They would receive a clemency discharge, but they wouldn't have access to standard VA benefits. Too lenient for conservatives who wanted prison terms, and too harsh for liberals who wanted general amnesty, the program was a flop. Only a fifth of the estimated 100,000 draft evaders applied for the amnesty.

The Mayaguez *Incident*

On May 12, 1975, two weeks after the fall of South Vietnam, Cambodian Communists seized an American freighter, the *Mayaguez,* in the Gulf of Siam and took 39 American crewmen as hostages. Working out of American bases in Thailand, Ford ordered the Navy to rescue them, and the military bombed the Cambodian mainland. Marines led an amphibious assault on nearby Koh Tang Island, despite the fact that there was no clear-cut certainty of where the crew was being held. The impressive display of power ended later in the day after the U.S. Marines recovered the *Mayaguez* and rescued the crewmen, but not before 41 American servicemen were killed and 50 were wounded, a much larger number than the hostage crewmen.

The incident was meant to show that the United States had limits that could not be crossed, but it was also viewed by any as a way to boost sagging public opinion polls, which shot up over ten points in the wake of the incident. It also had the unintended consequence of the final evacuation of all military planes and the last 50,000 U.S. servicemen from Thailand. Military installations (93 total), built during the Vietnam conflict, were abandoned because Ford had not consulted the Thai government about using American bases during the *Mayaguez* Incident. The outraged response of the Thai government was to insist that the United States leave, ending American presence on the Southeast Asia mainland.

Built Ford Tough

➤ Gerald Ford played center at the University of Michigan, and his skills on the gridiron landed him appearances in the East-West game in San Francisco and a college All-Star game in Chicago in 1934.

➤ Ford was on the USS *Monterey*, a light aircraft carrier patrolling the waters around Japan in WW II. On December 18, 1943, the *Monterey* was hit by a typhoon that sunk three other destroyers. Winds up to 100 mph knocked Ford to the deck, and he was almost washed overboard.

➤ In 1974, Congress overrode four of his 15 vetoes, the highest percentage since Franklin Pierce's years of 1853 to 1857.

➤ Ford signed the Helsinki Accords, which guaranteed and recognized the Soviet divisions following World War II in exchange for basic human rights and secure boundaries. Ford felt it necessary to stabilize a peaceful Europe, but he was hammered by many conservatives for acknowledging Communist Russia.

➤ The race between Ford and Carter had a low voter turnout, but it was a narrow electoral victory, 297 to 240. Still, Ford became the first president voted out of office since Hoover in 1932.

You Betty, You Betty, You Bet

One bright spot in the Ford White House was the emergence of the modern, spunky First Lady. Other active partners had been in the White House, but Betty was the first in many ways to connect with the Baby Boomer generation. She was a refreshing paradox: She was a liberated, opinionated woman and a champion supporter of the Equal Rights Amendment, but she also was a loving homemaker who supported equally a woman's right to be a housewife or a neurosurgeon. She ruffled numerous feathers within the conservative party, but she had broad support and was respected among the masses.

Gerald R. Ford, thirty-eighth president of the United States, and wife Betty.

(Photo courtesy of the Gerald R. Ford Library)

Betty's appearance on the *60 Minutes* television show angered the rank and file of the Christian right, but her public rating polls rocketed well past those of her husband. She went on to battle two public crises with courage and honesty: a radical mastectomy and alcoholism. She spoke frankly about her operation and sickness to heighten the awareness of regular examinations for early detection. She said that women worried about their appearance shouldn't feel ashamed, and she was thrilled to learn that women across the country were lining up for breast examinations.

First Family Factuals

Betty Ford appeared on *60 Minutes* in August 1975 and shook things up with her frank answers to Morley Safer's questions. She called *Roe* v. *Wade* a "great, great, decision," and admitted that, had she been a child of the 1970s, she may have tried smoking pot. Betty also noted that she didn't favor premarital sex but that it could help lower the divorce rate and said that if her daughter Susan were having an affair, "I wouldn't be surprised. I think she's a perfectly normal human being, like all girls. If she wanted to continue it, I would certainly counsel and advise her on the subject." Susan had to address reporters to tell them that she was *not* having an affair.

In 1978, the Fords held an intervention. Betty checked into the Alcohol and Drug Rehabilitation Service of the Long Beach Naval Hospital. At first, she claimed only an addiction to medication, but in less than a couple weeks, she admitted that she was an alcoholic. Betty didn't want the news to become public and embarrass her husband, but he encouraged her to speak out and help women as she had after her mastectomy. Betty went public, and in 1982, she founded the Betty Ford Center for Drug and Alcohol Rehabilitation in Rancho Mirage, California. The center has been helping both the famous and the unknown combat their drug and alcohol addictions ever since.

Two Attempted Assassinations and a Quiet Departure

Ford went out with a relative whimper, despite the two attempts on his life in 1975 by Lynette "Squeaky" Fromme, a devoted member of the Manson family, on September 5, and Sarah Jane Moore, a civil rights activist, on September 22. His last gasp probably came when he insisted during a debate with Carter that there were no Russian troops in Poland. The exhausted president stuck to his guns when pressed on it and didn't issue a clarification for almost a week. That sealed his fate, because rumors of his presidential competency quickly resurfaced.

Ford's brief White House tenure didn't produce a lot of positive results, but he was selected because of his reputation as a decent, honest man. Even if the pardon of Nixon went over poorly, Ford had done what he felt was best to unite a bitter, divided country, and he at least deserves credit for doing what he felt was best. Besides, there is another president whose term was doomed within a few months of taking office as the country slid into the Great Depression.

From the Cornfields to the Gold Mines

Herbert Hoover was born into a Quaker family in West Branch, Iowa, on August 10, 1874. Young Hoover became acquainted with tragedy early on: His father, Jessie Clark Hoover, a blacksmith, died of typhoid fever when Hoover was 6; his mother, Huldah Minthorn Hoover, died of pneumonia less than three years later. At the age of 10, Herbert was taken in by his uncle, Henry John Minthorn, a country doctor living in the Quaker area of Newberg, Oregon. Herbert attended school at a Quaker academy and then worked for his uncle in his land settlement business in Salem while he went to a business school at night, but never graduated from high school.

Hoover Engineers a Career

Hoover then met a mining engineer in Salem who convinced him to become an engineer. The local Quaker college didn't offer engineering as a program of study, so a notable Quaker mathematician, Joseph Swain, helped get Hoover into the new tuition-free university in Palo Alto, California, named for Leland Stanford. Hoover was admitted as part of Stanford's virgin class. He worked numerous jobs during his years at Stanford, and in 1895 he graduated with a degree in geology becoming a mining engineer.

First Family Factuals

Herbert Hoover met his future wife, Lou Henry, while attending Stanford. Lou was also a geology student, and she and Hoover shared a love of the outdoors. Lou was the first woman to receive a degree in geology from Stanford.

Herbert worked his way up the ranks in an engineering office in San Francisco, taking a job for a British mining firm in charge of its gold-mining operations in Western Australia. A year later, in 1899, he became chief engineer of the Chinese Engineering and Mining Company. He and Lou were married in Monterey, and they caught a steamer for China on the same day. The Boxer Rebellion broke out in China in June 1900, and the Hoovers were trapped in Tientsin, along with other foreign families, with only a few soldiers to offer protection. Hoover directed the building of a protective wall, and he and his wife risked harm to deliver food and medical supplies to the anti-Boxer refugees who had taken cover in the compound. The Hoovers were able to flee China by German mail boat in August. After the rebellion was squashed, Hoover returned to China and reorganized his firm's interests, which quickly turned a profit.

Spanning the Globe

Hoover and his wife spent the next five years traipsing around the world—Hoover was one of the leading mining engineers on the planet, and he took commissions to reboot uncooperative mines. The Hoovers set up home base in London, and they had two children, Herbert Jr. and Allan, in 1903 and 1907. At the age of 34, Hoover was widely respected, and his pockets were lined nicely. But at the outbreak of World War I, Hoover decided to become a humanitarian.

A European Epicurean in Times of Need

Hoover had always voiced his desire to work as a public servant in some capacity, and the Great War gave him the opportunity. While he was working in London at the outbreak of the war, he was recruited by the U.S. Embassy to help Americans stranded in Europe. He organized and directed an American Relief Committee that helped some 120,000 citizens get back to the States—and he was so successful at this task that he was put in charge of the Commission for Relief in Belgium (CRB), organized to provide food, shelter, and clothing for homeless Europeans in German-occupied Belgium and northern France.

President Woodrow Wilson summoned Hoover to be the U.S. food administrator after the nation joined the war effort in 1917. Feeding the Allied soldiers was a top priority, but enough also had to be left over for civilians both abroad and at home. Hoover took the approach of a football coach, encouraging the benchwarmers to believe that they were just as important to the big game, developing an "all for one and one for all" volunteer sacrifice mentality rather than coercion or regimented rationing.

Commander in Chief Lore

Hoover spent five years working solely and diligently to spread humanitarian aide as Europe suffered through the "War to end all Wars." He resigned from all his high-paying executive positions, and he didn't accept a fee as the CRB spent $1.5 billion to assist some 10 million to 11 million civilians. The CRB even invented a special cookie to ensure that children got the essential nutrients they needed. A final fiscal report of the CRB showed that less than one half of one percent of the large amount of money they collected and spent had been used for administrative expenses.

Hoover's program was a big success—his pleas to housewives to eliminate waste dropped the consumption of food in the United States by 15 percent, and shipments tripled, which in turn helped maintain steady prices for farmers. "Hooverizing" entered the national lexicon, and families got used to meatless Mondays. After the war, Wilson sent Hoover to Europe to estimate what kind of food-distribution effort would be needed to fend off mass starvation, and the American Relief Administration (ARA) was created. The ARA fed 300 million people across 30 countries with 46 million tons of grub.

After the ARA was shut down in 1920, Hoover organized the European Children's Fund to serve the orphaned children throughout Europe.

Commerce Comes A-Knocking

Prior to the 1920 election, Hoover came out of the major party closet and announced that he had always been a Republican. In 1921, Warren G. Harding asked Hoover to be his secretary of commerce, a cabinet position that Hoover would hold for the next seven years. In typical Hoover fashion, he made his mark by expanding the role of the small office, particularly in the area of international trade. He reorganized the department in a variety of ways, which included standardizing sizes for basic items such as tires, nuts, and bolts; taking greater control of mines; regulating radio broadcasting and aviation; and increasing the role of the Commerce Department in overseas business operations.

Hoover also continued to work in the humanitarian efforts that made him famous. He was president of the American Child Health Organization, which promoted health education, vaccination, and the ever-popular hot lunch for undernourished kids. He also oversaw a massive distribution of American food during the great Russian famine of 1922 to 1923, and he was in charge of a major relief effort after the Mississippi River flood of 1927. President Coolidge sent Hoover to mobilize all available sources of aid, and Hoover set up health units and assisted more than a million people who had to flee their homes. Hoover's picture was splashed across newspapers around the country, and his well-deserved reputation as a dedicated public servant made him an instant favorite for the White House in the election of 1928.

A Big Victory Crashes to the Ground

After Calvin Coolidge announced that he wouldn't seek the nomination in 1928, Hoover was inundated with requests to run for the Republican nomination. Hoover had been planning to seek the presidency somewhere down the line, and seeing as how he was overwhelmingly selected on the first ballot at the convention in Kansas City, there was no better time than the present.

Prez Says

"In no nation are the institutions of progress more advanced. In no nation are the fruits of accomplishment more secure. In no nation is the government more worthy of respect. No country is more loved by its people. I have an abiding faith in their capacity, integrity and high purpose. I have no fears for the future of our country. It is bright with hope."

—From Herbert Hoover's inaugural address, March 4, 1929

Hoover's opponent was Al Smith, a Roman Catholic New Yorker associated with Tammany Hall who wanted to repeal the 18th Amendment and bring booze back to the people, where he (and many of his Lower East Side neighbors) felt that it belonged. At the time, many Protestants believed that a Catholic candidate would answer to the Pope, not the Constitution, and others throughout the country could think of only one word to describe Tammany Hall: corrupt. Factoring in the many—and mostly rural—regions that felt that Prohibition was a moral mandate and Hoover's effective labeling of the Democrats as state socialists, and Smith had little chance.

The campaign was bitter with overtones of religious intolerance because Smith's Roman Catholicism became a big issue with voters in the traditionally Democratic South, where Hoover carried five states. Even though Hoover gave only seven speeches, he won in a landslide, by more than six million popular votes and the most dominating electoral total up to that time, 444 to 87.

Hoover entered the White House at a time of prosperity and American pride. Here was a man who had succeeded in business, technology, politics, and of course, numerous humanitarian efforts. Unfortunately, the good feeling didn't last long, and Hoover took the full brunt of criticism for having no humanitarian solution for the direst financial calamity the United States had ever known.

Over Before it Began

President Hoover was aware that economic indicators in the United States were pointing to trouble, especially on the agricultural front. Prices had been dropping as better techniques and machinery led to excessive crop surpluses. In the campaign, Hoover promised to call a special session of Congress to deal with farm relief and restrained alterations in the tariff. The session began in April 1929, and passed the Agricultural Marketing Act a couple months later. The act aided farmers by establishing marketing organizations and arranging corporations to buy surpluses off the market to wait for higher prices. Congress also passed the Hawley-Smoot Tariff Act, signed by Hoover in June 1930, which raised agricultural duties to the highest peacetime tariff in the nation's history, which hurt international trade because other countries followed suit and raised their tariffs.

Hoover faced agricultural problems upon taking office, but in his first six months, the bull market was still in full force. However, Hoover recognized that buying stocks on margin, especially banks speculating with depositors' ducats, was a recipe for trouble, and within months he would be proved right. The stock market crash on October 29, 1929 was the unofficial beginning of the Great Depression that left millions unemployed and a nation in turmoil. Initially, Hoover assumed that it was a panic and that the crisis would pass, but his assurances didn't restore public confidence. He did take small measures like meeting with business, industry, and agriculture leaders on November 19, 1929 to discuss ideas about lessening the impact of the crash, but it was to no avail.

Hoover quickly became the point man for U.S. woes, and he has often been mislabeled as the president who did nothing during the Great Depression. He believed that aid to the unemployed and the poor should be handled by municipal governments and private charities, but he abandoned his "volunteerism" in 1932. He had hoped that businesses, participating with state and local governments, could jump-start the economy by maintaining production and increasing spending for public works, but it was an impossibility in the ugly financial climate.

Hoover urged Congress to establish the Reconstruction Finance Corporation (RFC) to lend emergency money to insurance companies, railroads, banks, and eventually directly to state, county, and city governments. Democrats had been ushered into a House majority in 1930, but Hoover refused to act on their calls to allow the government to offer assistance directly to the unemployed. Hoover was criticized for helping those at the top, using the "trickle-down" theory aiding businesses to stimulate the economy, but he was the first president to use the federal government as an active force to combat financial depression. Hoover and his administration never fathomed the enormity of the crisis and he became the scapegoat and symbol of the Great Depression as homeless people cursed his name in their *Hoovervilles*.

Hoover did have a few successes during his administration:

➤ The RFC was able to spur some public works projects, including the Bay Bridge in San Francisco, in which he helped with the engineering.

➤ Hoover signed a naval treaty at the London Naval Disarmament Conference of 1930 that placed limits on the number and size of small naval vessels and warships that the United States, Great Britain, and Japan would construct, which didn't keep the latter from invading Manchuria in 1931.

➤ He initiated the future Good Neighbor policy in Latin America by reversing interventionist policies and removing U.S. Marines in Nicaragua and eventually Haiti.

➤ He signed a treaty with Canada to create the St. Lawrence Waterway (opened in 1959) and increased the national forests and parks by five million acres.

Herbert Hoover, thirty-first president of the United States.

Knowledge Is Power

Hoovervilles was the name given to shantytown dwellings, usually made of discarded wood, cardboard, or scrap metal during the Great Depression. Newspapers became known as "Hoover blankets" and rabbits killed for food were called "Hoover hogs."

The Inevitable

Hoover was the victim of some variables beyond his control, including the massive European depression that severely wounded the vast American banking interests across the Atlantic, and a major drought in the Great Plains in the summer of 1930. On the other hand, he shot himself in the foot by harping on the fact that recovery was "just around the corner." He also made a major miscalculation by sending federal troops with tear gas to evict the small number of World War I veterans (15,000) from the "Bonus Army," which, in July 1932, demanded immediate payment for certificates that were meant to be redeemed in 1945. The soldiers were hit by the depression like many working Americans, and it added to the growing Hoover reputation that he was unable and unwilling to deal with the Great Depression. By the time he left office, some 14 million Americans were unemployed.

In on a landslide, out on a landslide—such was the single-term cycle of the Hoover presidency. FDR won the electoral election 472 to 59 and by more than seven million votes. The depression had doomed Hoover's time in the White House, and he had no chance of political survival. Ironically, Roosevelt used the RFC as the catalyst for his recovery, but Hoover deplored the governmental intervention of the New Deal and attacked it in his book *The Challenge to Liberty*.

Let's Go Hooverizing

➤ Herbert and Lou Hoover translated Georgius Agricola's *De Re Metallica* into English. Written in Latin in 1556, it was an astute analysis of metallurgical processes.

➤ Hoover refused to accept a salary for his presidency and gave all his federal paychecks to charity.

➤ Hoover was the first president of the United States born west of the Mississippi River.

➤ Hoover's famous 1928 campaign slogan (although apparently not promised by Hoover himself) was, "A chicken in every pot and a car in every garage."

➤ On November 22, 1932, Hoover invited President-elect Roosevelt to discuss the request by Great Britain for suspension of payments on its war debt.

Back Where He Belongs

Herbert and Lou returned to Palo Alto, California, and he became chairman of the board of Boys' Clubs of America. He built up the Hoover Library on War, Revolution, and Peace to 200,000 volumes, which he donated to his old alma matter, Stanford. He also criticized Roosevelt's foreign policy and pleaded for nonintervention before Pearl Harbor. During World War II he published two books regarding foreign policy, *America's First Crusade* and, with Hugh Gibson, *The Problems of Lasting Peace*. After World War II, President Harry Truman asked Hoover to travel around the world and give a summation of how global famine could be avoided. In 1947, Truman picked Hoover's brain and used his experience in government and administration by appointing him chairman of the Commission on Organization of the Executive Branch of Government.

Hoover retired from federal service at the age of 80 and wrote his *Memoirs* in three volumes. At the age of 83, he became the first president to write about a fellow president when he wrote the well-regarded book *The Ordeal of Woodrow Wilson*. He died in New York City in 1964 after passing his ninetieth birthday.

Were They Doomed from the Start?

Ford inherited a house that was burning to its embers, and he stoked the flames beyond repair with his misunderstood pardon of Richard Nixon. Hoover walked into a White House that was handed the stock market crash a few months into his term. Did the gods of fate play a cruel trick, or did each president seal his hands in cement by mishandling major turning points in American history?

Well, maybe Ford didn't run so great, and maybe we couldn't use a man like Hoover again. Still, the former should be acknowledged for trying to unite the country the best way he knew how, and the latter should be recalled for the years of humanitarian work he did outside the oval office.

The Least You Need to Know

➤ Gerald Ford was handed a precarious presidency, and it basically unraveled when he offered Nixon a pardon, even though the legal doctrine includes an admission of guilt.

➤ Ford had to deal with the impression that he was clumsy and not very intelligent, even though he was one of the most physically active presidents of all time and had graduated in the upper third of his class at the Yale school of law.

➤ Herbert Hoover was a world-class humanitarian who fed and clothed civilians throughout Europe after World War I.

➤ The Great Depression hit shortly after Hoover was elected, and he wasn't able to uplift the country's financial situation or public confidence—thus, he became the fall guy.

Chapter 20

Peanut Farmer and Jelly Belly: Jimmy Carter and William Howard Taft

> **In This Chapter**
>
> ➤ Carter country
>
> ➤ Khomeini problems, no re-election
>
> ➤ Busting trusts with little fanfare
>
> ➤ That's what third-party candidate friends are for

Men who achieved glory in the executive afterlife carried out two of the more nondescript presidencies of the twentieth century in single terms. Neither Jimmy Carter nor William Howard Taft has gone down in history as a White House legend, but both men went on to impressive post-presidential careers upon which they can hang their hat, black robe, or claw hammer. Even if they share the last two rungs on the incumbent electoral votes ladder, 49 for Carter and 8 for Taft, they can take pride in the commonality they share in the fact that food played an important role in their elevator ride to the top floor. Jimmy Carter made his fortune as a peanut farmer, and William Taft may have eaten a fortune in food as he ballooned up to 350 pounds.

Plains Peanuts

Jimmy Carter was born in the small Georgia farming community of Plains in 1924. He was raised far from the country's economic, political, and cultural epicenters, and his outsider status helped to define his oval office career in ways both positive and negative. His upbringing was by no means fancy—the wooden clapboard farmhouse had no indoor plumbing, and the modern convenience of electricity wasn't introduced until he was a teenager.

Of Carter's parents, his father, James Earl Carter Sr., was a peanut farmer and a shop-keeper who viewed the world through traditional southern segregationist glasses (although he never joined the KKK), and reportedly exited the premises whenever his wife allowed blacks in his house. His mother, Lillian Gordy Carter, was a bird of a more progressive feather. She was a registered nurse who treated all colors of her rural patients with equal compassion, and she barred her children from using the word "nigger." Carter was influenced by both Lillian's liberalism and Earl's nose-to-the-grindstone conservatism.

First Family Factuals

Jimmy's mother, Lillian, was quite a character. After Earl passed away, she accepted the job of housemother at the Kappa Alpha fraternity at Auburn University. In 1966, at the age of 68, she joined the Peace Corps and went overseas for two years to put her nursing skills to use in India.

From Sea to Shining *Sea Wolf*

Carter's family didn't have the money to send him to college, so he set his sights on the Naval Academy. After a year at Georgia Southwestern College at Americus, he was accepted at Annapolis for the following year. He spent time as a rambling wreck from Georgia Tech, taking recommended math courses (although it is unknown whether he was a "hell of an engineer") until he entered the Naval Academy in 1943. In 1946, he graduated sixtieth in a class of 820 and began a naval career. That July, he and Rosalynn Smith were married at the Plains Methodist church. They eventually had four children: John William, James Earl III, Donnel Jeffrey, and Amy Lynn.

Carter's first assignment was on a battleship, but within a couple years he was sunk—for submarine duty on the *Pomfret*.

Commander in Chief Lore

Jimmy Carter almost lost his life aboard the *Pomfret* as it made its way toward the Far East. In the nocturnal hours, the submarine was above the surface recharging its batteries when a storm hit. Carter was swept off the conning tower by a massive wave, but he was able to grab the barrel of a cannon and hold on until help arrived.

Carter was assigned to the crew of a nuclear submarine, the USS *Sea Wolf*. He had been accepted into the nuclear training program by hard-driving Admirable Hyman G. Rickover, and he took a graduate course in nuclear physics at Union College in Schenectady, New York, which became the basis upon which he later described himself as a nuclear physicist. A naval career seemed like a good bet, but in 1953, Carter was granted emergency leave to visit his father, who was dying of cancer. Jimmy decided that small, tight-knit community life was what he desired, and against Rosalynn's wishes, he resigned from the Navy and returned to Plains to take over the family farm after Earl died.

Jimmy Carter, thirty-ninth president of the United States.

(Photo courtesy of the Jimmy Carter Library)

Georgia on My Mind

Carter took over the family farm and saw it through a tough year in which the farm turned a paltry $200 profit—the family was owed considerably more, to be paid upon harvest of the crops. Still, it was the type of homespun yarn that eventually helped propel Carter to greater heights. The farm became a large operation, and Carter Warehouses became one of Georgia's big-time peanut wholesalers. Carter was a millionaire by the time he headed off to Washington.

Racial divisions were a staple of Southern politics in the 1950s and 1960s, and Carter certainly wasn't immune from the battle lines. He was the only white man in Plains to reject the offer to join the segregationist White Citizens Council, which led to a short-lived boycott of his peanut business. Later, his family stood together in supporting the right of blacks to join the Plains Baptist congregation.

Carter served on the Sumter County Board of Education, in the Georgia senate, and ran for governor in 1966. He lost to a segregationist restaurateur, Lester Maddox, a man who had made a name for himself by wielding an axe handle in his restaurant and daring blacks to try to eat there. Carter was very disappointed in himself for losing and found solace in the church. His sister Ruth, an evangelical Christian, was at his side as he was "born again" and dedicated his life to Christ. He traveled across Georgia encouraging citizens to change their lives through Christianity.

Mr. Peanut Becomes the Governor

In the 1970 gubernatorial race, Carter wasn't afraid to pander to good old-fashioned race-baiting, painting his opponent, Carl E. Sanders, as a liberal with Northern ties, which was solidified with a photo that the Carter staff circulated showing Sanders palling around with a black athlete. Carter also courted supporters of George Wallace by refusing to condemn the avowed segregationist. His questionable tactics worked, and he was elected governor in 1970. Carter did a 180-degree reversal at this inauguration and became the bell-ringer for the "New South."

Carter symbolically hung a picture of Dr. Martin Luther King Jr. in the state capitol, the first nonwhite portrait. The number of state black employees was notably increased, and school funding reform produced a more equitable distribution. He also reorganized the state government, consolidating some 300 mini agencies into 22 major agencies, and he instituted "zero-based" budgeting, a system that attempted to have state officials justify all budget requests. Carter often hinted that his policies saved taxpayers a great deal of cash, but critics pointed out that most of the money went toward his reform programs. Still, Carter had a solid record and a growing reputation as a leader of the "New South."

Prez Says

"I say to you quite frankly that the time for racial discrimination is over .... No poor, rural, weak, or black person should ever have to bear the additional burden of being deprived of the opportunity of an education, a job, a simple justice."

—From Jimmy Carter's inaugural gubernatorial speech, 1971

One More Time—Jimmy *Who?*

Georgia law dictated that Carter could not succeed himself, but he had been eyeballing the White House since 1972, halfway through his term. He basically began campaigning as he walked out of the governor's office with his catchphrase, "My name is Jimmy Carter, and I'm running for president."

Carter correctly read the Democratic tea leaves, knowing that he could position himself as the moderate among a gaggle of liberal candidates and the lone conservative, George Wallace. He also kept his positions on the issues vague, preferring to focus on his commitment to morality, integrity, and his outsider status. After the stench of Watergate and Vietnam, Carter sailed on the winds of change and won the 1976 nomination, even though he was a virtual unknown in 1975.

One facet of his campaign that didn't resonate with everyone was his constant reference to his devotion to religious faith, which is almost mandatory these days. Carter did carry 90 percent of the African-American vote and appeased some liberal apprehension by selecting Walter "Fritz" Mondale as his running mate, which also raised his standing with labor organizations. Carter's initial lead was sizable, but it shrunk as Gerald Ford kept hammering away at the Southerner's equivocations. Carter tarnished his standing amongst his fundamentalist supporters when he made the odd comment in *Playboy* that he was faithful to Rosalynn but "committed adultery in my heart many times." Ford helped Carter out by sticking to his guns in a televised debate that there was no Soviet Union domination in Poland. Carter won a close election, 40,827,394 to 39,145,977, and won the electoral vote by 297 to 240.

Carter's Presidential Triumphs and Tribulations

Carter's standard honeymoon in the White House was short-lived, and his presidency was basically strained from the moment he stepped up to the plate. Carter was a micromanager, going so far in the beginning as to review the White House tennis court reservations. He was never able to connect with Americans after he got to the White House, either—he had no overriding plan or vision, but even if he had, he was never a strong leader and had trouble communicating his ideas to Americans.

Nonetheless, spirits were high at his inauguration: He insisted on the name Jimmy at his swearing-in, and the family shunned the bulletproof limo and walked down Pennsylvania Avenue to the White House. On January 21, 1977, Carter fulfilled a campaign promise by pardoning the young men who had dodged the draft during the Vietnam conflict.

Carter's two greatest successes were both foreign policy initiatives. In September, 1977 he signed a treaty with Panama to give that country control of the Panama Canal at the end of 1999, but it wasn't ratified by the Senate until April 1978 (and Carter was on hand to turn over the sovereign reigns at the end of the century). Some conservative circles considered it against American interests, but the right of the United States to defend the canal's neutrality was written into the treaty.

Carter's greatest foreign policy triumph came in September 1978, as he negotiated a peace agreement between Israeli Premier Menachem Begin and Egyptian President Anwar al-Sadat, known as the Camp David Accords. The signing of the Arab-Israeli Peace Treaty on March 26, 1979, took place in Washington, D.C. The Camp David Accords ended the state of war between Egypt and Israel, an important step in the ever-present quest for peace in the Middle East.

Carter's Difficulties

Carter was not a president with a laundry list of accomplishments, although he did make lists of what classical music he wanted to listen to each day. From the beginning, he had problems in the domestic arena. He never established any rapport with Congress, even though both houses were Democratic. The battles with Nixon had left congressmen in an uncooperative mood, and respect for the executive office wasn't exactly sky-high at that point. Carter's outsider status left him with virtually no allies, especially in the Senate, and he overestimated the ease with which he could get legislation passed. Thus, he was never able to get the necessary support for his big-picture ideas such as national health care, or little initiatives such as a bill meant to simplify labor union organizing.

Carter also ran into personnel problems that tarnished his reputation for adherence to higher ethical standards. Bert Lance, director of the Office on Management and Budget, was an old Georgia ally who was forced to resign after charges of illegal banking activities of which he was later acquitted. Carter's brother Billy also became a headache. Besides reveling in the role of a hard-drinking redneck who added his name to "Billy Beer," Billy Carter received somewhere in the neighborhood of $220,000 to lobby for terrorist leader Muammar al-Qaddafi and his Libyan government.

Long Lines at the Gas Pumps and Inflation

The oil crisis reached its peak during the Carter era, even though he continually warned Americans that they depended too much on foreign oil. Arab oil producers had raised prices in the early 1970s, just as U.S. reliance on those sources had increased. Carter eventually scored a legislative victory by securing a program that decreased reliance on other countries for oil through conservation, alternative energy sources, and deregulation within the borders of the United States. Unfortunately, the deregulation of oil prices caused a rise in inflation, and his energy program was too complex to explain clearly and concisely. Some of the initiatives were worth pursuing, particularly the development of solar, nuclear, and geothermal power and the development of synthetic and varied fossil fuels. Unfortunately, the program was crafted without the input of the energy industry and didn't adequately address the problem at hand: long waiting lines at the gas pump.

Held Hostage

The aftermath of the 1979 Islamic uprising in Iran dogged the remainder of Carter's years in the White House, chasing away any possibility of a second term. In October 1979, at the urging of Henry Kissinger (and oil and banking magnate David Rockefeller), the former leader of Iran, the Shah (then in exile), had been allowed to seek medical treatment in the United States. The Shah had been corrupt and brutal, and his modern ideas had offended many fundamentalist Muslims. On November 4, and in response to the Shah's admission into the United States, students loyal to conservative Islamic leader Ayatollah Ruholla Khomeini stormed the United States embassy in Tehran and took the diplomats and embassy employees hostage. The American prisoners were blindfolded and paraded in front of a crowd calling for their execution. Khomeini released blacks and women, leaving 53 American hostages to endure the 444-day ordeal.

Commander in Chief Lore

Carter reached an arms-reduction agreement with Soviet Union President Leonid Brezhnev, the Strategic Arms Limitation Treaty (SALT II), in June 1979. The Senate never ratified the treaty, and it died for all intents and purposes on Christmas of the same year, after Russia invaded Afghanistan to support a Soviet-puppet government battling Muslim rebels. Carter asked the Senate to withhold any consideration of SALT II, ended any further arms-control talks, and boycotted the Moscow Olympics of 1980.

Initially, Khomeini demanded the return of the Shah, who had been put on the Iranian throne in 1953 with the help of the CIA. However, as the hostage ordeal dragged on, the Shah died in July 1980, while in Egypt, and Khomeini changed his demands. Carter froze most Iranian funds in the United States, some $6 billion, but not many reasonable courses of action were open.

In April 1980, Carter ordered a secret military rescue mission, which went over like a lead balloon. The operation was aborted after three of the eight helicopters broke down well before reaching Teheran. During the withdrawal, a chopper crashed into a transport plane over the desert, killing eight servicemen and dashing Carter's credibility. Khomeini then added insult to injury by waiting until the day of Ronald Reagan's inauguration to allow the hostages to fly out of Iran, even though Iran needed to ease economic tensions caused by the outbreak of war with Iraq and though Carter had helped secure the release of the hostages in exchange for lifting the freeze on Iranian assets.

"I Will Not Lie to You" About Jimmy Carter

➤ Carter was the first graduate of the U.S. Naval Academy at Annapolis elected to the highest office in the land.

➤ Two years before his election to president, Jimmy Carter stumped most of the panel trying to guess his identity on the television show *What's My Line*.

➤ During the Carter administration, the Departments of Education and Energy were created.

➤ Jimmy and Rosalynn Carter took turns reading the Bible aloud in bed.

➤ On December 2, 1980, Carter signed the Alaska Land Act of 1980, a law that preserved 104 million acres of wilderness area in Alaska.

The 1980 Election

The 1980 election was a landslide, to say the least. Jimmy Carter had watched as both inflation and the deficit grew, and even though unemployment dropped off in 1979, it rose again in 1980. The specter of the hostage crisis loomed over the election, and Carter spent most of his time in Washington, D.C., in case any urgent decisions had to be made with Iran. The rescue debacle, coupled with high inflation and unemployment, made his election chances slim to none. Senator Edward M. Kennedy challenged Carter from the left, and a strong coalition challenged from the right. Carter managed to become the Democratic nominee, but the Reagan-Bush ticket beat him soundly, in part by siphoning off middle-of-the-road Democratic voters who saw Carter as a failure as a president.

Poet, Carpenter, Statesman

Since leaving the White House, however, Jimmy and Rosalynn Carter have been involved in many remarkable projects. Carter has written numerous books, including *Always A Reckoning and Other Poems* and *The Blood of Abraham: Insights into the Middle East*. The Carters have long been actively involved in the building of low-income housing through Habitat for Humanity, which means that they swing a hammer rather than just a famous name. Carter founded the Carter Center of Emory University in Atlanta, where discussions and forums on human rights and democracy hold court. A program implemented through the Carter Center is helping to eradicate Guinea worm disease, which has inflicted suffering on millions of Africans.

He also has traveled around the globe promoting free elections, trying to establish peace between nations, and facilitating relief efforts. Carter even went to North Korea as an unofficial emissary to negotiate an agreement in the production of nuclear weapons, which resulted in a nuclear weapons freeze in North Korea in exchange for

Western aid to build new, efficient reactors. He isn't a saint, and his "moral" self-righteousness crusades still rankle some critics. However, his presidential afterlife has been a far greater example of the positive effect that his capabilities, beliefs, and goals can have on a large scale.

William Howard Taft, twenty-seventh president of the United States.

Law in Order

William Howard Taft was born in Cincinnati, Ohio, on September 15, 1857 to a prominent political family that still serves in public office today. His father, Alphonso Taft (1810–1891), was a lawyer and an Ohio judge, who later served as secretary of war and as attorney general in President Ulysses S. Grant's cabinet and then as ambassador to Austria-Hungary and Russia. Unlike most upper-crust Eastern families, the Tafts sent their children to public schools, and their son was both an athlete and a scholar. His wrestling prowess was outdone only by his academic rankings, usually first (or very close) in his class.

In 1878, Taft graduated from Yale, second in his class, and went on to the University of Cincinnati Law School. He graduated and was admitted to the bar in 1880. It was the beginning of a long love affair between Taft and the legal profession, although this wouldn't be fully realized until the last years of his life. Taft was appointed assistant prosecutor of Hamilton County, Ohio, in 1881, served briefly as Cincinnati's collector of internal revenue, and settled into private practice in 1883 when he partnered in a private law firm. He was appointed to the Ohio Superior Court in 1887 to fill a vacancy, but he was elected for a five-year term the following year; that was the only position he was ever elected to outside of the oval office.

In 1890, President Benjamin Harrison appointed Taft to U.S. Solicitor General, where he won a high percentage of his cases and befriended the man who later defined his future, Theodore Roosevelt. Taft didn't stay in Washington for long—he returned to the Ohio bench after Harrison appointed him to judge of the U.S. Sixth Circuit Court of Appeals. Taft viewed it as a stepping stone to his ultimate dream, a slot on the Supreme Court. During his eight years on the bench, he gained a reputation as an honest judge with a strict interpretation of the law. He also was seen as a judge who definitely leaned toward the interests of big business, but who wasn't a laissez-faire monger and who tried to incorporate a sense of fairness into his decisions.

First Family Factuals

On June 19, 1886, William Taft married Helen "Nellie" Herron, daughter of a law partner of former President Rutherford B. Hayes. He met her at a bobsledding party, and she was a driving force throughout his life. Nellie and her family had stayed in the White House as the guests of President Hayes when she was 17, and she proclaimed that she wanted to wed a man who would become president of the United States so that she could call the executive mansion home.

Philippines or Bust

Taft walked across the stage of world politics when fellow Ohioan President William McKinley appointed him to serve as head of a commission to peacefully establish a civil government in the Philippines. Taft initially wanted no part of the plan because he opposed U.S. seizure of the islands in the Spanish-American War. McKinley appealed to his sense of duty. Nellie Taft, on the other hand, wanted to get out of Cincinnati and saw it as a vertical move. So Taft agreed, but not before McKinley sweetened the pot by offering him the beloved position on the Supreme Court that he sought upon completion of the assignment.

The future president encountered trouble with General Arthur MacArthur (General Douglas MacArthur's father) and his harsh treatment of Filipinos. MacArthur was replaced, and in 1901, Taft became the island's first civil governor to help set up a democracy. He reorganized the central and local governments, improved health conditions, established schools, bolstered the infrastructure, and negotiated an agreement with the Vatican to purchase 400,000 acres from the Roman Catholic Church to distribute among the Filipinos. Taft was a popular figure in the islands who showed no trace of racial prejudice in running his colonial administration. Taft encouraged and worked toward self-reliance for the Philippines, even turning down President Theodore Roosevelt's offers of a seat on the Supreme Court so that he could see his reforms through. In 1903, the Tafts returned to Washington, D.C., after Roosevelt appointed him secretary of war—with the understanding that Taft could remain involved in Filipino affairs.

He Ain't Heavy, He's My President

Taft and Roosevelt became close friends, and his years as secretary of war were successful, for the most part. Taft was a world traveler, and he visited Panama to eyeball the progress of the construction of the Canal. He also went to Cuba to help put down a revolt and convinced Japan to accept American mediation in the peace negotiations following the Russo-Japanese War. Roosevelt had the utmost confidence in his right-hand man, but the good times didn't roll for long. Taft turned down another solicitation to join the Supreme Court. Roosevelt had basically handpicked Taft to be his White House successor anyway because he didn't think his pal would stray far from his progressive agenda.

Commander in Chief Lore

Taft was selected on the first ballot at the Republican Convention in Chicago in 1898, but not before ardent Roosevelt supporters staged a 49-minute demonstration (complete with large teddy bears) calling for their man to serve four more years in the White House. The next day, Taft received the nomination, but the cheering for the official candidate lasted a mere 20 minutes, which was noted by Nellie.

Roosevelt followed tradition and made no appearances on Taft's behalf, but it didn't matter. William Jennings Bryan became a three-time loser as he was defeated handily by Taft in the electoral vote, 321 to 162.

Taft's inauguration took place on March 4, 1909, a freezing cold morning following a brutal snowstorm. Roosevelt had already headed off to the railroad station after the inauguration, so Nellie took his seat and rode from the Capitol to the White House with her presidential hubby.

The First Golfer Drives a Wedge

Taft, a lover of golf, had a few modest successes as president, but his main dubious claim to fame was dividing the Republican Party and ensuring the election of Woodrow Wilson. Taft was not a man who found the presidency to be the pinnacle of service, and he didn't adjust to the office very well. His slow, methodical personality was in direct contrast to the popular, animated, Roosevelt, and his predecessor had been a much more polished, warm, funny public speaker. Taft also lacked the former president's charisma, which kept him from publicizing his agenda. Taft was more conservative than the progressives of the day, but he was more progressive than the conservative Republican wing, the Standpatters. Most importantly, he wasn't slick enough to forge an alliance with either side, let alone both.

Prez Says

"I am bound to say that I think the Payne tariff bill is the best tariff bill the Republican Party ever passed."

—William Howard Taft

The Payne-Aldrich Tariff

The best example of Taft's ineptness was the Payne-Aldrich Tariff Act of 1909. Taft's campaign had made tariff reduction a central point of his platform, but he fell well short of fulfilling his important promise. Taft called a special session of Congress, but the bill that was concocted was watered down, actually raised the tariffs on some products, and favored big business protectionism. As if alienating the progressive wing of his party wasn't enough, Taft put his foot in his mouth in Winona, Minnesota, on a barnstorming tour meant to convince the citizenry that it was a solid law.

Ballinger vs. Pinchot

Another division came about after Taft supported Secretary of the Interior Richard A. Ballinger against charges leveled by Gifford Pinchot, chief of the forest service. Pinchot was loyal to Roosevelt, and he claimed that Ballinger was giving away reserved Alaskan coal lands to private business interests. Pinchot was as much a symbol of a staunch conservationist as Teddy himself, so when Taft fired him and not Ballinger, it was seen as another attempt to turn his back on the progressive Republicans. Pinchot had orchestrated the insubordination, and when Roosevelt got word while tracking big game in Africa, the rift between the old friends became permanent. Ballinger's good name was besmirched, so even though the charges were unfounded, he resigned.

A Few High Marks

Taft did have a few high marks during his administration. Roosevelt is remembered as the man in the blue cape with the "S" on his tights when it comes to trust busting, but in fact, Taft's administration brought twice as many antitrust suits as the previous regime. Taft saw the creation of the Department of Labor and the parcel post, and his administration set up the Bureau of Mines in the Department of the Interior to reduce the large number of mining injuries and deaths. Taft also signed the Publicity Act, mandating that political parties make available the amounts and the benefactors of the funding of federal election campaigns.

On the foreign policy front, Taft's attempts at change were few and far between, although he did encourage "dollar diplomacy" throughout Latin America. Dollar diplomacy was basically using military threat and diplomatic pressure to open up markets to U.S. business interests, and so Taft sent Marines to Nicaragua and Cuba to see that his policies would be followed. He also tried to negotiate a treaty with Canada, which would have lowered the tariffs between the two countries and opened up relatively free trade. Unfortunately for Taft, Canada rejected it, and he didn't have the issue that he could proudly call his own.

No Chance Against the Bull Moose

By the time the 1912 election came about, Taft had little enthusiasm left for the job that he hadn't really wanted in the first place. By now, he and his old friend Teddy Roosevelt were bitter rivals, but he was still deeply hurt when he entered the 1912 presidential race. It has long been speculated that his primary reason for running was that he felt betrayed by Roosevelt and wanted to keep him out of the White House.

First Family Factuals

Nellie and William Taft began the now popular attraction of the cherry tree blossoms in the nation's capital. The Mayor of Tokyo sent them 3,000 cherry trees, like those they had seen beautifying the city in Japan. The trees were infected and had to be demolished, but more trees were sent ands successfully planted in 1912, and within a few years the trees became a springtime tradition.

Taft had the backing of the conservative Republican machine, and the Old Guard kept the Roosevelt delegates out of the process. Roosevelt split from the Republicans and formed the Progressive (Bull Moose) Party and ran for president. It was a two-man race between Roosevelt and Woodrow Wilson because Taft carried only two states, Utah and Vermont, the worst defeat ever sustained by an incumbent president. Wilson had campaigned as a Progressive Democrat, but his greatest ally was the breakup of the Republican Party, led by the breakup of one-time bosom buddies Teddy Roosevelt and William Howard Taft.

And Justice for One

Taft left Washington and started living life to his liking. At the age of 55, he became a professor of law at Yale. He was popular among the students who took his international and constitutional law classes, and he published articles and books, and gave speeches across the United States. He and Roosevelt patched things up, and Wilson asked Taft to be the co-chairman of the National War Labor Board, which mediated labor disputes and offered Taft a different perspective of organized labor.

In 1921, President Harding asked Taft to become the Chief Justice of the Supreme Court, replacing Edward D. White. For nine glorious years, Taft was able to indulge his life's ambition, and he was much more of an activist, writing about 253 opinions. He was a buffer between the adversarial conservative majority and the liberal stalwarts Oliver Wendell Holmes and Louis D. Brandeis, and Taft kept the court running smoothly instead of getting bogged down in partisan rhetoric. Although he usually sided with the conservative wing, Taft pushed Congress to pass the Judiciary Act of 1925, which gave the Supreme Court more control and leeway in deciding what cases it would hear to reduce inefficiency and backlogs. He also obtained congressional approval for a building that the Supreme Court could call home.

Never a picture of health, Taft's dream ended on February 3, 1930, when heart trouble led to his resignation at the age of 72. He died a month later on March 8 in Washington, D.C.

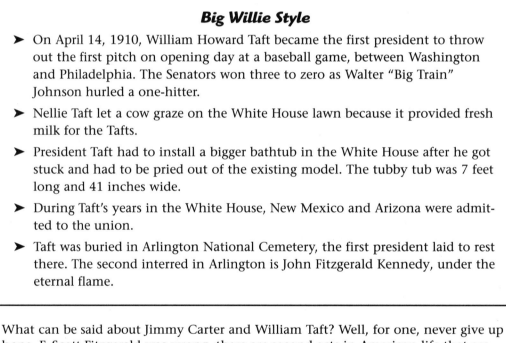

Big Willie Style

➤ On April 14, 1910, William Howard Taft became the first president to throw out the first pitch on opening day at a baseball game, between Washington and Philadelphia. The Senators won three to zero as Walter "Big Train" Johnson hurled a one-hitter.

➤ Nellie Taft let a cow graze on the White House lawn because it provided fresh milk for the Tafts.

➤ President Taft had to install a bigger bathtub in the White House after he got stuck and had to be pried out of the existing model. The tubby tub was 7 feet long and 41 inches wide.

➤ During Taft's years in the White House, New Mexico and Arizona were admitted to the union.

➤ Taft was buried in Arlington National Cemetery, the first president laid to rest there. The second interred in Arlington is John Fitzgerald Kennedy, under the eternal flame.

What can be said about Jimmy Carter and William Taft? Well, for one, never give up hope. F. Scott Fitzgerald was wrong, there are second acts in American life that are even better than rising above the office of the president of the United States of America.

The Least You Need to Know

➤ Jimmy Carter was elected as an outsider candidate who was supposed to provide a refreshing change from the Watergate era.

➤ Carter was undone by micromanaging, an economic slump, and his failure to get the hostages in Iran released during his term.

➤ William Howard Taft was elected to carry on the torch of Teddy Roosevelt's progressive Republican platform, but instead he took a more moderate stance that eventually led to a split in the GOP.

➤ Taft was not a particularly effective president, but he did bring harmony and efficiency to the Supreme Court, where he served as Chief Justice a few years after he left the White House.

Chapter 21

Death Does Its Part: John Tyler and Millard Fillmore

In This Chapter

➤ Following the Constitution to the letter—almost

➤ The president without a party

➤ How a missing Mason kickstarted the man with the funny name

➤ Fillmore was here (albeit very briefly)

Two of the more obscure and innocuous nineteenth-century presidencies in the history books came about because of the early deaths of William Henry Harrison and Zachary Taylor. The beneficiaries of their untimely deaths were John Tyler and Millard Fillmore. Neither of these two men was able to even garner the support to run for a full term, let alone win the White House outright. They both served partial terms, and that was it, although they each can lay claim to one important development in the ever-present slavery debate.

Oh, an Aristocrat, Eh?

John Tyler came into the world with the silver spoon firmly in place. He was born in 1790 on a plantation along the James River in Charles City County, Virginia (coincidentally the same county where his eventual running mate, William Henry Harrison, had been born 17 years earlier). Tyler was the son of a wealthy tobacco-planting aristocrat, John Tyler, who served as governor of Virginia from 1808 to 1811. Young Tyler went on to The College of William and Mary, followed up with two years studying law, and was admitted to the bar at age 19. Two years later, at the age of 21, Tyler was elected to the Virginia State legislature and began a long career in politics.

On Tyler's twenty-third birthday, after a nearly five-year engagement, he married Letitia Christian, daughter of another wealthy Virginia planter. They went on to celebrate 29 years of marriage and have eight children together, but Letitia later suffered a paralytic stroke and quietly died during her husband's second year in the White House. These were happier times, however. The Virginia militia Tyler joined never saw any action in the War of 1812, and he was able to get back to the business of the state.

A Strict Constitution

Tyler served five years in the legislature before ascending to the House of Representatives in 1816. The poetry-writing, violin-playing lawyer was popular in his home state, and he went along with the standard Virginian belief that government should be in the hands of the land-owners and that states' rights were of the utmost importance. Tyler's primary core belief was that the Constitution should be interpreted in the strictest sense, and he often butted heads with members of Congress over the use of the Constitution as grounds for the expansion of federal powers.

Even as the country was caught up in a wave of nationalism and leaning toward a stronger federal government, Tyler stood his ground. He voted against the Missouri Compromise of 1820 because he felt that the federal government had no right to interfere with slave owners, the select club of which he was a member. After repeatedly finding himself on the losing end of the stick, Tyler returned to his home state, serving the years 1823 to 1825 as a member of the Virginia House of Delegates and then a humdrum two-year term as the governor of Virginia from 1825 to 1827.

Tyler returned to Congress, but this time in the Senate. He initially supported John Quincy Adams, but he reviled Adams's plans to expand the federal government. Tyler voted against the protective tariff, internal improvements funded by the federal government, a national army, and the distribution of public lands to homesteaders, among other issues. He switched his loyalty to Democrat Andrew Jackson because of their shared opposition to a central bank, a plan Tyler wholeheartedly despised.

His alliance with "Old Hickory" didn't last long, however, because in his eyes Jackson went way too far in abusing federal powers. Jackson's White House counted on Tyler's Senate opposition to the national bank but probably underestimated the degree to which he would stand up for his views of the Constitution. Although he initially opposed nullification, Tyler was the only senator to vote against Andrew Jackson's 1833 "Force Bill," which gave the President the right to use military force to collect federal revenues. The bill was aimed squarely at South Carolina, which had threatened to secede over the issue of a federal tariff it felt impeded on its ultimate right to sovereignty.

Tyler voted to censure Jackson after he withdrew federal deposits from the Bank of the United States. Although Tyler loathed the federal bank, he agreed with a majority of senators that Jackson's actions were unconstitutional. Tyler's animosity toward Jackson became as strong as his strict interpretation of the Constitution. In 1836, the Virginia legislature, controlled by Jacksonian Democrats, instructed Tyler to vote for the expurgation of Jackson's censure from the Senate record, but Tyler resigned from Congress rather than go along with Old Hickory's crowd.

The Whig Cult, Preying on the Disillusioned

Tyler quickly joined the *Whig Party* because its hodgepodge of dissenting groups shared a common loathing of Andrew Jackson. In 1836, the Whigs had a master plan of running four candidates for president, thus scrambling the electoral circuitry and ensuring that there would be no majority—under this plan, the election would get kicked over to the House of Representatives. Surprisingly enough, the scheme backfired, and Martin Van Buren was a clear victor. Tyler returned to the Virginia House of Delegates from 1838 to 1840, but he scored enough Southern vice presidential electoral votes to factor into the Whig 1840 election plans.

Knowledge Is Power

The **Whig Party** was an amalgamation of small political groups that combined with the National Republican Party in opposition to Andrew Jackson's powerful Democratic Party. It was a fractured party from the outset and it never promoted a clear, concise, party platform. Harrison, Zachary Taylor, and Millard Fillmore were all loyal Whigs, but the party unraveled over the slavery issue. General Winfield Scott was the last Whig Presidential candidate in 1856.

Thirty Glorious Days as Vice President

At the Whig national convention in Harrisburg, Pennsylvania, in December 1939, John Tyler received the nomination of vice president to presidential nominee William Henry Harrison. Tyler was chosen because of his connection to voters for states' rights in the South, and to help balance the ticket with Harrison, a popular figure out West. The Whigs decided that a single ticket was the way to go, and they eschewed any distinctive platform because they had so many separate factions. Still, Tyler had always maintained a strict constitutional platform.

Although he was running on a Whig ticket, Tyler's record was often in line with the Democrats. Tyler staunchly opposed a federal bank, which the Whig majority in Congress favored. The party's brilliant campaign strategy to "keep Harrison vague and Tyler quiet" implied that he might have had too many contrary opinions. Regardless of the discrepancies, "Tippecanoe and Tyler, Too," turned out to be a winning slogan.

Tyler returned home to Williamsburg, Virginia, but a month later Harrison died of pneumonia, so Tyler headed back to Washington, D.C. At the time, the now standard process of a vice president ascending to the highest office in the land hadn't been firmly cemented, and the Constitution was fuzzy as to whether Tyler should become the official president or merely an acting president until new elections were held. Tyler rejected the idea of an "acting president," seized the day and had himself sworn in on April 6, right after he reached Washington. Tyler's actions set the precedent, but he was the subject of scorn throughout his term.

Prez Says

"For the first time in our history the person elected to the vice presidency of the United States, by the happening of a contingency provided for in the Constitution, has had devolved upon him the Presidential office."

—John Tyler, after William Henry Harrison's death

Presenting "His Accidency"

Harrison had allowed Whig leaders Henry Clay and Daniel Webster to select his Cabinet and write his inauguration speech, which ceded a great deal of power to Congress. Tyler knew that the Cabinet expected him to go along with its legislative agenda, which would require him to abandon many of his constitutional principles. This independent Virginian was not about to play ball.

Throughout his time in the White House, Tyler was referred to as "His Accidency," "Vice President—Acting President Tyler," "Ex-Vice President Tyler," and the much blunter "Executive Ass" by both the press and fellow politicians. An influenza epidemic that hit the United States was even labeled after the man in the White House.

Commander in Chief Lore

Daniel Webster visited Tyler and told him that Harrison had agreed that all decisions would be made by a majority vote. Under this plan, the president had a single vote, just like the rest of the Cabinet. Tyler replied, "I can never consent to being dictated to as to what I shall or shall not do. I, as president, will be responsible for my administration." He added that those who didn't get with the program should tender their resignations.

Jumping Ship but Holding On to Their Whigs

It didn't take long for Tyler to lose his shred of a political base, considering that his Cabinet was openly hostile. Tyler rejected the Whig program, which included tariffs. He vetoed one bill after another and alienated the Whig party leaders who had helped get him elected. In 1841, he vetoed a bill that would have re-established the Bank of the United States. Tyler felt that it was unconstitutional because it impeded states from approving bank branches within their individual borders. A second Whig banking bill, the Fiscal Corporation Bill, was passed in Congress and unhesitatingly vetoed by Tyler, amid rumors that he had previously given it his stamp of approval. With the exception of Daniel Webster, his entire Cabinet promptly resigned, and Henry Clay labeled Tyler "a president without a party."

John Tyler, tenth president of the United States.

Tyler hired conservative Democrats as secretaries within two days, and shortly thereafter the Whig caucus severed all party ties with the president. The moving and shaking gave Tyler the distinction of having more Cabinet changes than any other single-term president. Tyler was put in the position of constantly vetoing bills sent by the congressional Whigs that he never would have signed. After he vetoed a protective tariff in 1842, a House resolution called for his impeachment. Tyler signed a mildly protective tariff measure in 1842, but they still brought an impeachment vote in January 1843—it was shot down 127 to 83.

Treaties Among the Tricks

During the congressional chaos, Tyler managed to sign a couple important treaties. Webster remained a Cabinet member long enough to wrap up the Webster-Ashburton Treaty in 1842, which finally settled the Northeast Boundary Dispute, a long-standing, contentious squabble between Great Britain and the United States over the border between Maine and Canada. In 1844, Tyler envoy Caleb Cushing signed a treaty at Wanghia, China that opened the Asian country to trade with American merchants.

Enjoying Life from May to December

Tyler courted a woman, Julia Gardiner, after his wife died while he was still in the White House. He first met his future bride in 1842, at a White House reception. They began seeing each other in early 1843, and after a few weeks, Tyler proposed at Washington's Birthday Ball, but she declined. In February 1844, Tyler and a large party were floating down the Potomac River on the warship *Princeton,* and one of the guns exploded. Several partygoers were killed, including Secretary of State Abel P. Upshur and wealthy New Yorker and former U.S. Senator David Gardiner. Gardiner's socialite daughter, Julia, collapsed, and Tyler carried her down the gangplank when the *Princeton* docked. Four months later, the two were married in a private ceremony in New York City. It was a blessed affair, but Tyler caught a lot of flack from his numerous political enemies because she was 23 and he was 54.

The May-to-December romance may have seemed a bit tawdry or at least tacky, but the Tylers were happily married for more than 17 years and had 7 children, giving the proud papa 15 offspring.

First Family Factuals

Julia taught the Marine Band to play "Hail to the Chief" whenever the president appeared in public. This is still practiced today.

Texas Marks the Spot

Tyler attempted to form a third party in the fall of 1843. The primary focal point was the annexation of Texas, which had recently seceded from Mexico. Many Americans opposed the annexation because of the potential for war with Mexico (which refused to acknowledge Texas' independence), and others opposed it because they didn't want another slave state. Tyler signed the Calhoun-Upshur Treaty, an annexation treaty, with Sam Houston in 1844, but the Senate rejected it and that became the main issue of the 1844 presidential race.

Tyler had little hope of retaining the office because his newly created third party was basically a group of friends and officeholders. He toyed with the idea of running as an independent, but instead he threw his support behind James K. Polk. Tyler helped keep Van Buren and Clay from winning the election because neither of them came out strongly in favor for annexation as Polk did. In the final days of Tyler's administration, Texas was annexed by a joint resolution in Congress (suggested by Tyler), which required only a majority vote, unlike a treaty, which required a two-thirds majority, as spelled out in the Constitution. The resolution passed, and on March 1, three days before leaving office, Tyler signed the annexation bill into law. Texas was now a state, but he had done an end-around on the strict interpretation of the Constitution upon which he had staked his career.

Tyler considered himself a political outlaw, so he renamed his Virginia plantation "Sherwood Forest." Tyler came full circle, and he and Julia enjoyed the life of aristocratic farmers.

Accuracies About "His Accidency"

➤ John Tyler graduated from William and Mary at the age of 17.

➤ Tyler was a Great-great-granduncle of President Harry S. Truman.

➤ Letitia Tyler was not the White House hostess—Tyler's daughter-in-law Priscilla filled the role and presided over a large party for Washington Irving and Charles Dickens in 1842.

➤ On his final day, March 3, 1845, Tyler signed legislation admitting Florida as the 27th state.

➤ Tyler's Sherwood Forest estate has the longest wooden-frame house in the United States, a Virginia Tidewater design that is more than 300 feet long. Tyler descendants still live on the property.

Tyler had one more political moment in the sun. He was chairman of a peace conference in February 1861 that hoped to avert civil war. The conference was unsuccessful, and Tyler left more committed to the Confederacy. He urged Virginia to secede, became a delegate to the provisional Confederate Congress, and was elected to the Confederate House of Representatives. Before he could take his seat, however, Tyler had a stroke and died on January 18, 1862, at the age of 72 on "enemy" territory. Tyler may not have had a stellar presidency, but he can hang his hat on the fortitude he showed in standing firm on his views of the Constitution, and for the one action that dismissed his view: annexing Texas.

The Great Compromise: Progress or Placebo?

Millard Fillmore's administration lasted less than three years, but he still managed to oversee one of the most banal terms of any of the Presidents of the United States. The one momentous decision was the ineffective and ill-conceived Compromise of 1850.

An argument can be made that Fillmore was able to stave off the Civil War for more than a decade, but the flip side of the argument is that the Great Compromise angered Northerners beyond the point of reconciliation by forcing every American to take part in the legal slave trade.

Fillmore East Balances the Ticket

Fillmore was added to the 1848 ticket as a vice president primarily to balance the Southern war hero, Zachary Taylor, with a Northern Whig. Fillmore was a native New Yorker, and even though he had lost the gubernatorial race in 1844, it was thought that he could deliver the Empire State's crucial electoral votes. The Free-Soil Party, which was opposed to the extension of slavery, took away votes from Democratic candidate Martin Van Buren in New York, and the Taylor-Fillmore administration won a close victory and headed off to the White House.

As vice president, Fillmore presided over the Senate during the debates over the *Compromise of 1850*. It was an intense time, with Northern and Southern factions angrily arguing over the expansion of slavery in the newly acquired lands. Fillmore was personally against slavery, but he felt that it was an untouchable institution in the South. Fillmore attempted to maintain a sense of fairness in the debates, often relying on his sense of humor, but it was not a very funny issue—antislavery senators, led by William H. Seward of New York, viewed him with utter contempt.

Zachary Taylor ignored Fillmore and refused to allow him to use the spoils system to grant patronage jobs in New York. Fillmore had little political power, but he and Taylor were at odds over the Compromise of 1850. Taylor vowed to veto the bill, and Fillmore informed him that if it came to a tie, he would vote for its passage. It never came to that, however, because Taylor died of gastroenteritis (cholera) before the vote.

Knowledge Is Power

The **Compromise of 1850** was a series of resolutions drawn up by Senator Henry Clay of Kentucky. It included adding California as a free state; establishing the territories of New Mexico and Utah with the provision that they were forbidden to mention slavery while organizing, thus allowing settlers to determine whether to be a free or a slave state; and prohibiting the slave trade but continuing slavery in the District of Columbia. It also included the stringent Fugitive Slave Law, which required that runaway slaves be returned to their masters under strict legal penalty, which in effect, made every citizen complicit in upholding slavery.

Taylor-Made Presidency and a Hard Act to Follow

After Zachary Taylor's death, Fillmore accepted the resignations of all his department heads and appointed a completely fresh Cabinet. He thought the old Cabinet members were responsible for turning Taylor against the Compromise of 1850. Fillmore added concilia-tory Whigs to his Cabinet—men like himself, who cared only about preserving the Union.

Fillmore's wife, Abigail, accurately predicted that the Fugitive Slave Law would ruin him politically. The five separate measures of the Compromise of 1850 were passed by Congress and signed into law by Fillmore. The ugliest piece of legislation in the Great Compromise was a stronger Fugitive Slave Law that demanded that slaves be returned to their owners under threat of severe penalty and with no opportunity to legally defend themselves, which Fillmore wholeheartedly enforced. The Compromise of 1850 was a pro-Southern bill, and the Fugitive Slave Law basically made all United States citizens complicit in the slave trade or criminals.

The government sanction of a wholesale round-up of slaves trying to escape to freedom in the North made abolitionists more organized and militant, and made the antislavery Whigs seethe hatred for President Fillmore. In 1851, the Fugitive Slave Law was dealt with in a newspaper serial—Harriet Beecher Stowe's landmark work, *Uncle Tom's Cabin,* was reprinted as a novel and aroused Northern ani-mosity against slavery. The Fugitive Slave Law also led to intensification of the activities of the *Under-ground Railroad,* which further widened the rift be-tween North and South, and the Civil War crept ever closer to an inevitability.

Fillmore's middle-of-the-road Great Compromise staved off the Civil War for more than a decade, but it actually stoked the fiery embers between the North and the South that led to fires throughout the South. Fillmore forced the horrific Fugitive Slave Law upon American citizens who didn't think that the ownership of human beings was a reasonable proposition in the land where all men were report-edly created equal. Still, Fillmore must be given credit for believing in his cause. He called the Com-promise of 1850 the "final settlement" between the North and the South in his address to Congress in December 1851. And perhaps it was, although prob-ably not in the manner he envisioned.

Prez Says

"God knows that I detest slavery, but it is an existing evil, for which we are not responsible, and we must endure it, till we can get rid of it without destroy-ing the last hope of free govern-ment in the world."

—Millard Fillmore

Knowledge Is Power

The **Underground Railroad** was a loosely aligned group of antislavery Northerners that helped fugitive slaves escape to free states and Canada. The Underground Railroad, mostly executed by Northern blacks, grew in importance and stature after the Compromise of 1850. The fugitive slaves traveled under the cover of night with the North Star as the guide, some-times with escorts or "conduc-tors," stopping to stay with clandestine sympathizers.

First Family Factuals

While Fillmore clerked in a Buffalo law firm, Abigail continued her career as a schoolteacher. For three years, they courted by mail because he didn't have the cash to make the 150-mile trip to pay her a visit, but they stayed together and were wed in February 1826.

Knowledge Is Power

The **Anti-Masonic** Party was formed in response to the murder of William Morgan and its basic platform was opposition to the Freemasons, the oldest fraternal order in the world. The Anti-Mason Party was made up of factions of the press, churches, and the antislavery movement and survived from 1827 to 1834, winning seats in the twenty-third Congress, and William Wirt even garnered Vermont's seven electoral votes in the 1832 presidential election.

Where the Buffalo Roam

Fillmore was the polar opposite of John Tyler. He was born in a frontier cabin in Cayuga County, New York, on January 7, 1800, into abject poverty. He worked on the family farm until he was apprenticed to a clothier at the age of 14—a wool carder, to be precise. He eventually raised enough money to purchase his freedom for $30 and enrolled in a local academy, where he met his future wife, Abigail Powers, one of his teachers. It's not as steamy as it sounds—she was only his elder by a year. He went on to study law, financed by work as a schoolteacher.

In 1823, Fillmore opened a law office outside Buffalo in East Aurora, New York. In 1828, Fillmore fell into a political scandal that elevated him to the ranks of the elected. A local Mason, William Morgan, disappeared after penning an exposé that was going to reveal the hidden secrets of the fraternal order. A rumor quickly hit the streets, aided by newspaper publisher Thurlow Weed, that Morgan had been murdered by his own brethren. An *anti-Masonic* fervor gripped the community, and Weed introduced the popular lawyer to local political bigwigs, who backed his campaign as an anti-Mason and saw Fillmore serve three terms in the state legislature in Albany. Fillmore's dignified personality and conciliatory outlook made him a strong candidate in Erie County, and Weed again backed him when he was elected to the House of Representatives in 1832.

Roundabout Way to the White House

The anti-Masons melded with the Whigs, and Fillmore became a subscriber to Henry Clay's views on preserving the Union through compromise. Fillmore was defeated in 1834 but managed to get re-elected in 1836 and served three successive terms. He became chairman of the House Ways and Means Committee and marshaled the protective tariff of 1842 that raised the rates to the similar levels of 1833.

Fillmore didn't run for re-election in 1843, ran third in the race for the Whig party vice presidential nomination in 1844, and didn't serve in office again until he was elected in 1847 as the New York state comptroller. His large margin of victory made him the second most powerful Whig in New York, after former Governor Seward, and put him in the catbird seat for the vice presidential nod at the convention in Philadelphia in 1848. As comptroller, Fillmore was successful in devising a currency system that would be the model of the National Banking Act of 1863.

Building a Better Library

Fillmore had few moments in the presidential sun, but his administration authorized a naval expedition to Japan taken by Commander Matthew C. Perry. This opened relations with the Land of the Rising Sun, which had been outlawed for more than 200 years. After he left the presidency, the Treaty of Kanagawa was signed in 1854 between the two nations that opened up trading markets. Fillmore also arranged the first federal land grants for the construction of railroads.

Abigail Fillmore, a devout bibliophile and musician, also established the original White House library in the Oval Room. At her urging, Millard asked Congress for money for books and turned a large room in the executive mansion into a comfortable reading area. Abigail often invited friends over to hear their daughter Mary perform—she was accomplished on harp, piano, and guitar.

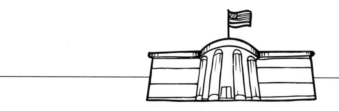

Commander in Chief Lore

Poor Millard, he can't even claim one of the great legends of his presidency. It is an oft-told tale that Fillmore installed the first White House bathtub. Alas, the story was a goof from the mind of brilliant Baltimore satirist H. L. Mencken, which is still occasionally seen in print, even after he 'fessed up to the gag in 1926 in an article entitled "The American Public Will Swallow Anything." The first tub was installed by Andrew Jackson, and it is unknown whether or not there was a Presidential rubber-duckie.

Out with a Whimper

Fillmore was a reluctant candidate for the Whig nomination in 1852, but his only goal was to ensure that the party platform included the Compromise of 1850. Fillmore was supported by Southern Whigs, but the antislavery faction was stronger and selected a war hero, General Winfield Scott because his views on the Compromise of 1850, though favorable, were not well known by the public. The Whigs were in disarray, and the party was roundly trounced in the election, and the Whigs dissolved because of the slavery issue.

Fillmore ran for president as the Know-Nothing candidate in 1856. The party was an anti-immigration, anti-Catholic group that was formed against the wave of Irish folks fleeing to the United States to escape the potato famine. It was an odd choice, considering that Fillmore had been presented (albeit reluctantly) to Pope Pius IX in Rome the year before. Fillmore carried only the state of Maryland, and his political career was over.

1856 campaign poster of Millard Fillmore, thirteenth president of the United States.

MILLARD FILLMORE,

AMERICAN CANDIDATE FOR PRESIDENT OF THE UNITED STATES.

Fillmore retired to relative obscurity in Buffalo and worked in civic affairs; he founded the Buffalo General Hospital and the Buffalo Historical Society. Abigail died in 1853, and he married a wealthy widow, Caroline McIntosh; together they lived in a Gothic mansion on Niagara Square. Fillmore made his views on national politics available, including his criticism of the Lincoln administration for an unnecessary war, but few listened. Fillmore died of a second stroke in 1874.

Neither John Tyler nor Millard Fillmore is recalled for stellar administrations, but neither of them was elected to the presidency in the first place. Tyler fans can claim that he stood up for his most tried-and-true belief, and Fillmore … well, there is that cool name.

"Fill" Us with "More" Facts

➤ Millard was his mother's maiden name, but even he found it odd. Still, he bequeathed the title on his only son.

➤ The Fillmores installed the first cast-iron cooking stove in the White House.

➤ Fillmore declined an honorary degree from Oxford University because, "I have not the advantage of a classical education, and no man should, in my judgment, accept a degree he cannot read."

➤ After retiring, Fillmore was the first chancellor of the University of Buffalo.

The Least You Need to Know

➤ John Tyler was a strict constitutionalist who butted heads with Democrats and Whigs over the expansion of federal power.

➤ Tyler used a joint resolution at the end of his term to ensure the annexation of Texas.

➤ Millard Fillmore oversaw the passage of the Compromise of 1850, which included the divisive Fugitive Slave Law.

➤ Fillmore authorized a naval expedition to Japan that opened relations with the Land of the Rising Sun, which had been outlawed for more than 200 years.

Chapter 22

Van who?

Van Buren!

A Couple of Dandies: Chester A. Arthur and Martin Van Buren

In This Chapter

➤ Custom fit for the spoils system

➤ Chester Arthur becomes his own man

➤ Why Martin Van Buren was "O.K." long before anyone

➤ Keeping the peace on the Canadian border

Chester Arthur and Martin Van Buren had two important things in common: They were both behind-the-scenes movers and shakers within their respective parties, and they were both slaves to fashion. They each had a smattering of moments in the presidential spotlight, but neither had an administration with a towering record of achievement. They looked good atop the political summit, though, and that separates them from the bulk of their peers.

Chester the Connected

Chester Arthur was born in Fairfield, Vermont, in 1829, son of William Arthur, a Baptist minister who had immigrated from Ireland, and his schoolteacher wife, Malvina.

The Arthurs moved to Saratoga County, New York, in 1839, and young Chester entered Union College in Schenectady at the age of 15. After graduating in 1848, he taught school during the day and studied law at night. In 1852, he was appointed principal of an academy near Albany and followed that by spending a final year studying law in the New York City offices of Erastus D. Culver. In 1854, Arthur passed the bar; two years later, he opened a law office in the Wall Street area of Gotham. In part to help recruit clients, he became active in local Republican circles and began to expand his circle of friends and connections.

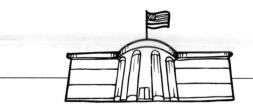

Commander in Chief Lore

William Arthur spent time teaching in Canada. Later in son Chester's political career, sneaky political adversaries circulated a rumor that he was ineligible to become president because he was a Mapleback. They claimed that Chester Arthur had taken on the place and date of birth from a brother who had died as a baby, but there was no proof to the outlandish charge.

William Arthur was a staunch abolitionist, and his son followed suit by using the law to support the civil rights of blacks. He helped a group of slaves gain freedom from a Virginia owner who attempted to move them through the free state of New York. In another case that built up his reputation, Arthur won damages for a black woman who had been kicked off a New York City streetcar because of her race—in doing so, Arthur guaranteed all blacks their rights to ride public transportation in New York City.

First Family Factuals

In 1859, Chester Arthur married Ellen Lewis Herndon of Fredericksburg, Virginia, who was living in New York City with her mother. Her father, Navy officer Capt. William Lewis Herndon had heroically gone down with his ship in a storm off Cape Hatteras after ensuring the safety of the passengers, which earned him a memorial at the Naval Academy in Annapolis.

Getting in Good with the GOP

In 1854, Arthur attended the anti–Kansas-Nebraska convention in Saratoga Springs, which was held in protest of the act that would increase the number of legal slave states. This was also the beginning of the Republican Party in New York, and in 1856 Arthur attended the original GOP convention in the Empire State. He supported candidate John C. Fremont and quickly became a ubiquitous, active, behind-the-scenes Republican Party member.

Arthur campaigned for the re-election of Governor Edwin D. Morgan in 1860, and he was repaid with an appointment to the honorary position of state-engineer-in-chief. The Civil War broke out, and in 1861

Morgan assigned Arthur to be acting quartermaster general in New York City. In his new capacity, Arthur supplied food, uniforms, and military equipment to the thousands of troops passing through the Big Apple. In 1862, Lincoln called for more soldiers, and Arthur was given the title of state inspector general of the militia and earned the rank of brigadier general. That lasted until 1863 when Morgan was succeeded by a Democrat; Arthur resigned and returned to his law practice.

Custom-Made Appointee

Arthur continued his work inside the Republican Party, and he rose up the ranks to become one of the top men in the political machine of Senator Roscoe Conkling. He vigorously campaigned for General Ulysses Grant's nomination and subsequent election to the White House in 1868. Following the long-standing spoils system, Conkling persuaded Grant to appoint the loyal Republican Arthur to the powerful position of Collector of the Port of New York. This was one of the prime jobs in Gotham because the collector was in charge of the more than 1,000 employees (all working, thanks to the Republicans) of the New York Custom House and handled the majority of all customs receipts in the United States.

Arthur was personally honest, but Conkling's machine was corrupt, and the spoils system constantly gave jobs at the customhouse to unqualified but loyal Republicans who often didn't even show up for work. Arthur held the position for eight years and earned a sizable income, but it was an operation ripe with graft, and it was also the "fueling station" for the Conkling machine. In 1877, Republican President Rutherford B. Hayes began to reform the civil service jobs given as partisan gifts, and he ordered an investigation of the customhouse. Arthur was asked to resign—when he refused, Hayes canned him in 1878, alleging that he had used tax money to reward political toadies. Arthur was certainly working in a corrupt environment and was connected to a corrupt machine, but there was scant evidence of his direct involvement, and he had a reputation as a stand-up guy.

A Stalwart of a Vice President

The 1880 Republican convention in Chicago pitted the two sides of the Republican Party, the "Stalwarts" and the "Half-Breeds," against one another. Conkling was one of the Stalwart leaders, the wing of the party that favored loyalty above all else and that supported Grant for a third term in the White House. The Half-Breeds wanted to institute more reform measures, and they supported James G. Blaine. The split was relatively even and strident in support, so there was little chance of a victory by either candidate. A Half-Breed compromise candidate, James Garfield, was finally chosen, and Arthur was chosen as his running mate to appease the Stalwarts and because there was some sympathy for the way in which he had been fired by Hayes.

The 1880 campaign featured numerous attacks by the Democrats upon Arthur's ties to the Conkling machine and its love of patronage, but the Republican ticket triumphed in a close election.

Arthur Ascends and Surprises the Stalwarts

Arthur was sworn in as vice president on March 4, 1861, and he and Garfield were quickly at odds over political appointees. Garfield appointed Conkling's rival, Blaine, as secretary of state, but he caused real problems by appointing a Half-Breed to Arthur's old job: collector of the port of New York. Conkling resigned in protest, and Arthur accompanied him to Albany to ask the state legislature to reinstate both Conkling and junior Senator Thomas Platt, who also quit in protest, but they refused. Neither Conkling nor Platt would hold public office again, although they remained active in politics. Ironically, Conkling's right-hand man, Arthur, would be president within months.

Commander in Chief Lore

Arthur made no attempts to assume the presidency during Garfield's long period of lingering between life and death, and he stayed in relative seclusion. After Garfield was shot, his assassin shouted, "I am a Stalwart of the Stalwarts .... Arthur is president now." The vice president wanted to distance himself from the lunatic who had killed the president of the United States to put the Stalwarts in charge of the spoils system. There were ugly, ludicrous whisperings that Arthur was an accomplice, but they never went anywhere.

On July 2, 1881, a deranged office seeker, Charles J. Guiteau, shot President Garfield at the Washington railroad station. Garfield hung in for 80 days, but he died on September 9. Arthur took the oath the following day.

An Honest Man Steps In

It was generally assumed that Arthur would be nothing more than a puppet of the Conkling machine, but that didn't turn out to be the case. He was an honest man who set out to fill federal positions with qualified men. He also wanted to reform the civil service system.

Arthur continued the trials, started under President Garfield, of the "Star Route" swindlers in the Post Office Department. These officials had conspired with stage-coach operators to receive large cutbacks and had stolen millions of dollars from the federal government. It came as a surprise to many because Arthur was a friend to one of the accused, yet he tried (unsuccessfully) to see that the guilty were prosecuted.

Congress was almost evenly divided with respect to party representation, so Arthur had no mandate to pass laws as he saw fit. He vetoed a graft-heavy appropriation of almost $19 million to improve rivers and harbors because it had too many special-interest fingerprints on it, but Congress overrode his veto. Congress also overrode his veto of the Chinese Exclusion Act of 1882, which would have banned Chinese laborers from immigrating for 20 years. Arthur later signed a revised bill that excluded the Chinese for a decade.

Out with the Slackers, in with the Plebes

Arthur was successful in signing the Pendleton Act into law on January 16, 1883, and it became the basis for civil service reforms. The act banished political tests for officeholders, denied jobs to known alcoholics, and added competitive tests for some federal positions. It didn't affect a large number of federal employees, but it was an important symbolic first step toward reducing nepotism.

First Family Factuals

In 1880, Chester was in Albany when Ellen became ill—by the time he rushed to her side, she was no longer conscious. Ellen died before he became president, but when he was in office, Arthur gave St. John's Episcopal Church a stained-glass window in her honor. He had it situated in the south end of the church so that he could look upon it from the White House.

Chester A. Arthur, twenty-first president of the United States.

Arthur also took a keen interest in reviving the U.S. Navy, which had gone into decline following the Civil War. Congress appropriated money for the first all-steel cruisers, and before Arthur left office it okayed funds for four more. Arthur sometimes is referred to as the "Father of the American Navy" because he took a personal interest in expanding and modernizing it—this was the beginning of the U.S. Navy's growth into a world power.

The President of Savoir Faire

Arthur has long been known as the best-dressed, most stylish man to serve in the executive office, and he went to great lengths to clean up—and liven up—the White House. "Elegant Arthur" loved to party late into the night, rarely hitting the hay before 2 A.M. He had a discerning pallet and a gourmet's love of fine food and drink. Before moving into the White House, Arthur had the executive mansion redone to match his exquisite, highbrow tastes. He also hauled out 24 wagons filled with accumulated White House junk, including a pair of Lincoln's pants. Arthur's warm hospitality and lavish parties were a far cry from the somber and sober days of the Hayes administration.

> **Prez Says**
>
> "I may be President of the United States, but my private life is nobody's damned business."
>
> —Chester Arthur's response to a temperance group who visited the White House in hopes of keeping it dry

"The Gentleman Boss" Heads Home

Arthur's popularity had risen exponentially throughout the country during his time in office. Mark Twain himself said, "I am but one in 55,000,000; still, in the opinion of this one-fifty-five millionth of the country's population, it would be hard to better President Arthur's administration." Unfortunately for Arthur, he had lost support within his own party. Many Stalwarts abandoned him after he signed the Pendleton Act, but conversely, his old ties kept the Half-Breeds from considering him one of them. The little-known Grover Cleveland had defeated Arthur's choice for governor of New York in the last election, so his political base wasn't strong, but Arthur still hoped to secure the Republican nomination. Instead, it went to his old political foe, James G. Blaine, and Arthur wasn't crushed when Blaine lost the election to Cleveland.

Arthur, "The Gentleman Boss," returned to New York City to practice law, but he was ailing from Bright's disease, an incurable kidney ailment, and didn't have the energy. Arthur died in New York City November 18, 1886.

Chestnuts About Chester Arthur

➤ Chester Arthur's stylish ways were renowned—during his presidency, he owned 80 pairs of pants and often changed clothes throughout the day.

➤ Two dismissive nicknames given to Arthur by his political enemies were "Prince Arthur" and "the Dude President."

➤ Arthur was a diehard fisherman, enjoyed walking at night, and loved English literature.

➤ Near the end of Arthur's administration, he dedicated the Washington Monument on February 2, 1885.

➤ Arthur destroyed all personal papers belonging to him and Ellen shortly before he died.

The Kid from Kinderhook

Martin Van Buren, the first president born an American citizen rather than a British subject, came into the world in 1782 in the small Dutch village of Kinderhook, New York (which would be used as the model for the town in the *Legend of Sleepy Hollow*). Van Buren's ancestors had emigrated from the Netherlands as indentured servants. His father was a tavernkeeper on the post road between New York City and Albany. At a young age, Van Buren became familiar with politicians and political debate because the family tavern served as a polling place and a popular stop for legislators. Van Buren attended the village schools until the age of 14, when he began studying law with a local attorney and then furthered his studies in New York City. He was admitted to the bar at the age of 21 and opened a law firm in 1803 in Kinderhook, where he quickly garnered a reputation as a hard-working lawyer for the community.

Commander in Chief Lore

The common term "O.K." became popular because of Martin Van Buren. As his political career advanced, "Old Kinderhook" was often used in speech and print. "O.K. Clubs" sprang up to support Van Buren, and the cry of "O.K." came to be an exuberant approval of Van Buren and his hometown. "O.K." evolved into the standard phrase of acceptance used today.

Van Buren joined the Democratic-Republican Party and frequently was called upon to take on the Federalist attorneys who dominated the county. His success rate saw his appointment to a surrogate office and his eventual election to the state senate in 1812. At the time, New York politics was split in half by two controlling factions of the Democratic-Republican party: the supporters of DeWitt Clinton, and those opposed to Clinton, known as the *"Bucktails."* Van Buren was the legislative leader of the Bucktails, and they helped get him the appointment to state attorney general.

In 1819, DeWitt Clinton assumed the governorship of New York and cleaned out all Bucktails, Van Buren included. It proved hard to keep a good Bucktail down though, and Van Buren was elected as junior senator in 1821. Before he left for Washington, Van Buren started something new in American politics: the political machine. He became the boss of the Albany Regency, which controlled the state legislature through Bucktail patronage. Throughout his time in the Senate, Van Buren was consistently recognized as the big chief of the Albany Regency, which essentially made him the absentee leader of all New York politics.

Knowledge Is Power

The main source of support for Van Buren was the **Bucktails** of Tammany Hall, the soon-to-be infamous New York City organization. The group got its name because members always sported bucktails on their hats whenever they attended political gatherings.

A Dozen Years, Half a Dozen Important Positions

Van Buren entered the Senate at a time when the Democrat-Republicans were the only party that mattered, but cracks were starting to split the foundation. Van Buren sided with the wing that didn't want a strong national government and followed the dictum that states' rights were sovereign. In the 1824 presidential election, Van Buren summoned the congressional caucus and then managed the campaign of William H. Crawford of Georgia, helping secure 41 electoral votes. What is remarkable about Van Buren's efforts is that he persuaded enough voters to cast for Crawford, landing him in third place even though the man suffered a paralytic stroke a few months *before* the caucus. The House of Representatives elected John Quincy Adams as president, not the man Van Buren wanted.

Van Buren was re-elected to the Senate in 1827, and he became the point man for the anti-Adams brigade. He jumped on the bandwagon of Andrew Jackson and was instrumental in helping unite a coalition of fractured Democrat-Republicans in a new party, called the Democratic Party founded upon Jeffersonian principles. In addition to holding together the conglomerate that would help "Old Hickory" get elected, Van Buren ran for governor of New York to help Jackson grab the 36 electoral votes of the Empire State. DeWitt Clinton had recently died, so Van Buren was able to win the gubernatorial election at the same time that Jackson soundly nabbed the presidency.

Martin Van Buren had gone from the halls of the Senate to the governor's mansion, but it didn't last long. He resigned from the office when Jackson asked him to join his Cabinet as secretary of state, although he served only a couple of months. Jackson was impressed with the way Van Buren had organized the Democratic Party in such a brief amount of time, and he wanted the dapper man from New York as part of his team.

Commander in Chief Lore

Even though Van Buren was governor barely long enough to unpack his cardboard boxes, he instituted one important banking reform. He created the Safety Fund System, which required banks to contribute to a pool that would be used as insure depositors if any of the incorporated banks went under. This was a safety net for the bankers of New York that long predated the FDIC.

Van Buren had a reputation for being a flip-flopping, double-talking, noncommitting type of politician, but he and Jackson hit it off, and Van Buren became his closest adviser. Van Buren went out of his way to ingratiate himself with Old Hickory, and Jackson was impressed by his loyalty. Van Buren really curried favor when he supported Jackson's disgraced friend Margaret "Peggy" Eaton, who had been ostracized by Washington society for rumors of sexual impropriety.

Van Buren helped shape the standard platform of the Democrats, and the dismantling of the second Bank of the United States became a central tenet. As secretary of state, Van Buren opened free reciprocal ports with the British West Indies and secured the first commercial trade agreement with Turkey.

The Beef with Calhoun

John C. Calhoun had been elected Jackson's vice president in 1828, but he never enjoyed the same type of relationship as the "Little Magician" Van Buren did. Calhoun and Van Buren had a palatable rivalry from the beginning, and Calhoun and Jackson weren't tight either, especially after Calhoun's wife led the rally to ostracize his friend Margaret Eaton. Calhoun became convinced that Van Buren was working behind the scenes to ruin his career. He wrote an article in a Washington newspaper naming Van Buren as the Machiavellian man behind the problems within the Cabinet, but Jackson was outraged that his vice president aired internal dirty laundry in a public forum. He decided that Van Buren would be his heir apparent and that he would oust all Calhoun lackeys from his Cabinet.

Van Buren resigned as secretary of state so that Jackson's purge wouldn't be so politicized. Jackson returned the favor by appointing Van Buren to be diplomatic minister to Great Britain, but Calhoun persuaded the Senate to block the appointment, and he himself cast the deciding vote. Van Buren hopped the Atlantic Ocean in advance of Senate confirmation and had to return to the United States. Ironically, this made Van Buren look like a political martyr, and the Little Magician became a sure thing for the vice presidential nomination in 1832. Jackson was furious that Calhoun had kept his trusted friend from the diplomatic post, and the popular president finagled the vice presidential nomination before Van Buren returned from Europe. The Jackson/Van Buren ticket won a resounding victory in the 1832 election. Van Buren dutifully served Jackson as one of his closest advisers and gained a morsel of revenge by presiding over the Senate that had rejected his appointment.

As Jackson's protégé, Van Buren was chosen without opposition to be the Democratic candidate in 1836 out of deference to the wishes of the beloved Old Hickory. At the convention in Baltimore, Kentucky Congressman Richard M. Johnson was given the vice presidential nomination. The anti-Jacksonians had coalesced into the newly minted Whig Party and tried the unusual strategy of nominating three separate candidates in hopes of keeping Van Buren from garnering a majority of electoral votes and forcing the election into the House of Representatives, where they felt they had a better shot. The strategy backfired, and Van Buren won 170 electoral votes to the combined candidate count of 124. He also won the popular vote by a considerable margin.

Van Buren had served in six key offices in a dozen years, but his joyride to the presidency quickly took a turn for the worse.

First Family Factuals

Very little is known about Van Buren's wife and distant cousin, Hannah Hoes, because she died of tuberculosis in 1819. The couple celebrated 12 years of marriage and had four sons who lived past infancy. Hannah was said to be "modest and unassuming," but that easily described many wives of the period. Van Buren and Hannah met in Kinderhook, and the couple spoke only Dutch at home. After her death, Van Buren never remarried, even though he was only 37 and oddly she isn't mentioned once in his autobiography.

A Panic Sets In

Van Buren told the masses at his inauguration that he had no intention of veering away from the policies of his "illustrious predecessor"—he then showed his commitment by reappointing every Jackson Cabinet member except one. The good times didn't roll, though, because within weeks the Panic of 1837 devastated the national economy, making Van Buren's inaugural note that the United States was an "aggregate of human prosperity surely not elsewhere to be found" a trump card for his political enemies.

On May 10, 1837, banks in Philadelphia and New York City closed after suspending the payment of silver and gold specie for paper money, and the rest of the country quickly followed suit. Production stopped, factories folded, companies went bankrupt, and federal and state governments weren't able to collect much revenue. Other causes were crop failures and an unfair trade balance with England. The depression outlasted Van Buren by a couple of years as unemployment rose and personal hardship became the norm. Van Buren, however, was not Franklin Roosevelt, and governmental intervention was absolutely unthinkable.

Van Buren did call a special session of Congress on September 4, 1837, but he made only two recommendations. His first idea was to establish an independent treasury system that would divorce federal funds from state banks so that tax revenue could be stored in federal treasuries, called subtreasuries, around the country and eliminate the access of state banks to the government's cash. His second initiative was to issue millions in government treasury notes to relieve the federal monetary situation. His independent treasury wouldn't become law until 1840.

Prez Says

"All communities are apt to look to government for too much. Even in our own country, where its powers and duties are so strictly limited, we are prone to do so, especially at periods of sudden embarrassment and distress. But this ought not to be. The framers of our excellent Constitution and the people who approved it with calm and sagacious deliberation acted at the time on a sounder principle. They wisely judged that the less government interferes with private pursuits, the better for the general prosperity."

—Martin Van Buren, 1837

To be fair to Van Buren, his outlook on the role of the federal government was common orthodoxy of the time. There were calls, primarily from Whigs in Congress, to aid businesses, and he was routinely criticized for being unsympathetic and heartless, but an activist federal government would have been basically a new entity. Van Buren stuck to his beliefs throughout his four years in the White House—if nothing else, it proves that "the Red Fox of Kinderhook" was not the unscrupulous opportunist of the oft-uttered conventional wisdom of the time.

Van Buren's Other Issues

The Panic of 1837 far overshadowed any other events of the Van Buren administration, but there were a few other important developments. He tried to take a middle-of-the-road approach and maintain the status quo regarding the division over slavery between the North and the South. He alienated the antislavery side because those proponents thought that the war against the Seminoles would lead to admission of Florida as a slave state; the proslavery side accurately believed that he was opposed to the annexation of Texas because he didn't want to aggravate the slavery question. During 1838 and 1839, Van Buren continued the policy of the eviction of the Cherokees by federal troops who were then forced to march along (what is now called) the Trail of Tears from their southern homelands to west of the Mississippi River into present-day Oklahoma.

On the foreign policy front, Van Buren's administration was confronted with a near war along the Canadian border in 1837. An uprising against Great Britain by Canada was roundly supported in the United States and sympathetic Americans transported materials across the Niagara River on the U.S. steamer *Caroline*. A British force took possession of *Caroline* and set it ablaze, killing an American. Retaliations were quick to follow, but Van Buren warned Americans not to start trouble that could lead them down the path to war, and he sent military personnel to the region to keep the peace.

Another skirmish over the expulsion of Canadians in a disputed region along the Aroonstoook River broke out along the Maine border in 1839. Militias lined up along the frontier, but the "Aroonstook War" had a bloodless outcome. Van Buren tactfully restored calm after sending General Winfield Scott on a peacekeeping trip to the region. Scott negotiated a truce, the United States stayed out of a war with Great Britain and the issue was settled with the Webster-Ashburton Treaty of 1842.

"Martin Van Ruin" Is Beaten by "Tippecanoe"

Van Buren received the Democratic nomination in 1840, but the Democrats were in disarray over defections and in-fighting, and the depression had hurt the president's standing with the American electorate. The Whigs nominated war hero William Henry Harrison and portrayed "Tippecanoe" as a log cabin-dwelling, hard cider-guzzling man of the people; they painted "Martin Van Ruin" as an aristocrat who drank from a silver cup. In fact, Van Buren was the self-made man and Harrison came from money, but that point was irrelevant to the voters. Van Buren lost the electoral vote by a count of 234 to 60. Although his presidency was not as enduringly influential as some others, Van Buren was more responsible than almost any other single figure for creating the Democratic Party.

Don't Ever Give Up

Van Buren actively sought the Democratic nomination in 1844, and he probably would have gotten it if he hadn't raised the ire of his iconic leader. Van Buren went on a tour of the West in late 1842 to try to mend the rifts that existed in the Democratic Party and to drum up support for his upcoming campaign. He met with Henry Clay, who was expected to be the Whig candidate in 1844, and the two made a friendly agreement to keep the hot-button issue of the annexation of Texas out of the campaign. President John Tyler had pushed the Texas annexation to the forefront of the national debate in the spring of 1844, when he presented a treaty of annexation to the Senate. On April 27, 1844, two separate newspapers printed individual letters that Clay and Van Buren had written outlining their opposition to the immediate annexation of the Lone Star state. The deal made between Van Buren and Clay outraged Andrew Jackson, who had endorsed the annexation, and he threw his considerable weight behind the nomination of James K. Polk—that dark horse candidate went on to become president.

Martin Van Buren, eighth president of the United States.

In 1848, Van Buren again took a shot at the top, this time as the nominee of the Free-Soil Party, a group formed in opposition to the extension of slavery. Van Buren didn't win a single electoral vote and received only nine popular (recorded) votes in the South—all in the state of Virginia. Van Buren did manage to pull in more than 290,000 popular votes throughout the rest of the country, particularly in the abolitionist states in the Northeast. Still, Van Buren was able to play the role of spoiler and enact a measure of revenge against the Democratic Party that had rejected him. Van Buren split the Democratic votes, pulling in ten percent of the overall popular vote (over 290,000) and pulling enough votes in New York away from Democratic nominee Lewis Cass, to allow the Whigs to carry the state and send Zachary Taylor to the White House.

Van Buren took a two-year sojourn to Europe and then returned to Lindenwald, his estate near his birthplace in Kinderhook. He worked on his *Autobiography*, which he started writing overseas, but was never completed and eventually was published with the narrative ending in 1831. On July 24, 1862, Martin Van Buren died in his home at the age of 79.

What's Up with Martin?

➤ After there was an attempt on Andrew Jackson's life, Vice President Martin Van Buren presided over the Senate with two loaded pistols.

➤ At Van Buren's inauguration, 20,000 screaming people showed up to cheer for his predecessor and stole the new president's thunder.

➤ By executive order, Van Buren reduced the federal workday for governmental laborers to 10 hours.

➤ Van Buren was only 5 feet, 6 inches, but he was always impeccably decked out in elegant clothes.

➤ Van Buren took a lump sum of $100,000 at the end of his term as president of the United States.

Neither Chester Arthur nor Martin Van Buren left office with a renowned moment of greatness, both men were dedicated to their parties and served them proudly under adverse conditions.

The Least You Need to Know

➤ Chester A. Arthur served as the Collector of the Port of New York, a powerful position that he obtained through Republican patronage.

➤ Arthur may have risen through the spoils system, but he signed the Pendleton Act into law, which was the first step in major civil service reform.

➤ Martin Van Buren was Andrew Jackson's closet adviser, serving as secretary of state and later vice president; the popular Old Hickory helped get him elected as the nominee of the new Democratic Party.

➤ The Panic of 1837 took hold shortly after Van Buren entered office, and the depression lasted throughout his term; still, he was a product of his times and refused to consider governmental intervention.

Part 5

Tomato Cans, Never Coulda' Been Contenders, and Still in Training

"Let the word go forth from this time and place, to friend and foe alike, that the torch has been passed to a new generation of Americans."

—*From the inaugural address of John F. Kennedy*

Just about all Americans alive in 1963 can recall the tragic day in November when the torch that was passed to John Fitzgerald Kennedy became the eternal flame. Some of the presidents of the United States have fallen to the only universal, inevitable, human experience, and this chapter covers those who weren't able to finish their first term and who never gave American citizens the chance to see what they envisioned for the country. It also includes the "Tomato Cans" who left a black mark on the office by doing nothing at a time when leadership was essential (as in Franklin Pierce), or who let their money-grubbing pals rob the nation blind, as Warren G. Harding did. Lastly, we take a chapter to cover the last two men who are "still in training"
—*George Bush and Bill Clinton.*

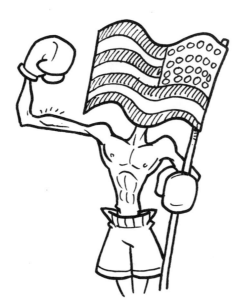

Chapter 23

'Silent Cal'

The Dull-Namic Duo: Benjamin Harrison and Calvin Coolidge

In This Chapter

➤ "Little Ben" in the big office

➤ I got the tariff, but I did not mute the rest, you see

➤ Striking out in Boston

➤ Inactivity as an art form

Benjamin Harrison and Calvin Coolidge are beloved figures in the everyday, run-of-the-mill world of tariff lovers and big business. Both men were Republicans who served in the White House, but the former primarily worked for his political handlers, and the latter refused to budge from his core belief that the government that governs least governs best (to the point of presidential inertia). Each man also had a personality that could be construed as anathema to the political process, but the crotchety codger and the silent servant managed to reach the top spot and fulfill terms that won't be recalled as the "salad days" in the oval office.

Little Ben

Benjamin Harrison was the son of John Scott Harrison, the only man in the history of the United States to be the father of one president and the son of another, William Henry Harrison. Benjamin Harrison's great-grandfather (and namesake) was one of the signers of the Declaration of Independence and a governor of Virginia. Young Benjamin was raised on a farm in North Bend, Ohio, and his political pedigree reached new heights when he was 7 and grandpa "Tippecanoe" was elected president.

Harrison was sent to a college preparatory school, Farmer's College, outside Cincinnati. In 1850, he transferred to Miami University in Oxford, Ohio, where he graduated fourth in his class of 16. During his years in school, Harrison mastered Greek and Latin, joined the Presbyterian Church, and began to shine in debate. He toyed with the idea of becoming a minister, but instead he headed off to Cincinnati to study law and was admitted to the bar in 1854.

In 1853, Harrison married his college sweetheart, Caroline Lavinia Scott, daughter of the president of the Oxford Female Institute, which eventually was added to Miami University.

The Harrisons packed up their bags and headed off to Indianapolis, not far from the site of the Battle of Tippecanoe, a prime spot for networking with the family name. After a year of working as crier of the federal court, earning $2.50 a day, Harrison opened a law firm with William Wallace, son of a former governor of Indiana. The two attorneys did well for themselves, and Harrison's reputation for legal acumen took shape. In 1857, he successfully ran as the Republican candidate for city attorney of Indianapolis and was then elected reporter of the state Supreme Court in 1860.

In 1862, Governor Oliver P. Morton commissioned Harrison as a colonel, and he raised the 70th Indiana Volunteers. Harrison had little military experience, but he was a tough taskmaster and whipped the men into soldiers. He was called "Little Ben" by his men because he stood a scant 5 feet, 6 inches tall, but he was no pushover. His division saw heavy combat during the Civil War, particularly in the notorious Atlanta campaign in the army of General William Tecumseh Sherman. Harrison proved his worth during that time and was made a brigadier general in 1865 by Abraham Lincoln for his gallantry and heroism at Peach Tree Creek after a recommendation by General Joseph Hooker.

First Family Factuals

The Harrisons lived far from the local schools, so Benjamin's father built a one-room log center of learning. Each winter, a teacher was hired to instruct his nine children in the three "R's" of reading, writing, and arithmetic.

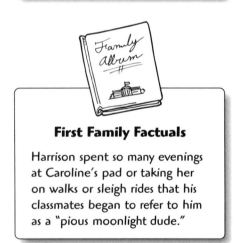

First Family Factuals

Harrison spent so many evenings at Caroline's pad or taking her on walks or sleigh rides that his classmates began to refer to him as a "pious moonlight dude."

Kid Gloves

Harrison returned to Indianapolis at the end of the war and headed back to his law practice after finishing up his term as clerk in the state Supreme Court. He became one of the leading Republicans in the state, even though "Kid Gloves Harrison" lost the 1876 governor's race to Jimmy "Blue Jeans" Williams, named for his ubiquitous overalls. Still, Harrison garnered more votes than any other Republican candidate and became the state's leading GOP man. At the Republican convention in 1880, he swayed the votes of the Indiana delegation from Blaine to Garfield. Harrison was offered a cabinet post by Garfield, but he declined because the state legislature had elected him to Congress as a United States senator.

In the Senate, Harrison followed his standard political pattern: Vote with the party, and don't rock the boat. He was an extremely talented debater, but he rarely broke ranks, even though he was more sympathetic to the problems of Indians and home-steaders against the railroad industry than most of his conservative brethren. He also supported a high protective tariff, civil service reform, and federal regulation of the railroads and trusts, and he directly criticized President Grover Cleveland's veto of pensions for Civil War veterans. "Kid Gloves Harrison" also voted against the Chinese Exclusion Act, which banned Chinese immigration to the United States for a decade.

In 1887, the Democrats took control of the Indiana legislature, and Harrison lost his re-election bid by a single vote. His attacks on Grover Cleveland, his renowned ora-torical skill, his Civil War record, and his popularity among veterans made him an A-list Republican candidate for the 1888 presidential race.

Who's the Boss?

Harrison was nominated at the Republican convention in Chicago in June 1888 on the eighth ballot over John Sherman of Ohio. Blaine had refused to run for the nomi-nation, but he cabled from Europe to let it be known that he supported Harrison, in no small part because he was much more likely to be a party puppet. Banking indus-try bigwig Levi P. Morton of New York was named the vice presidential nominee.

Harrison ran an effective "front porch" campaign and used the high tariff as the centerpiece of his platform. He also courted the votes of veterans and emphasized Cleveland's pension vetoes, lack of service in the Civil War, and policy of returning captured Confederate battle flags to the South. The Republican Party was united, or-ganized, and not afraid to get Harrison elected by any means necessary.

Down 'n Dirty

The Republican machine *assisted* Benjamin Harrison through a variety of ways to "get the vote out." The Republican party had the "Murchison Letter" written to the British minister to the United States, Sir Lionel Sackville-West, asking for his views on the upcoming election. The letter, written by a supposed former Brit who had become a naturalized American, was answered by Sackville-West and included an endorsement for Grover Cleveland. Republican Party leaders distributed copies of the response to Irish-American voters, and large numbers of the Democratic bloc switched their al-liance to Harrison because they couldn't vote for a candidate whose sympathies lay with merry old England.

The primary deciding factor in the election was New York, Cleveland's home state, which was carried by Harrison by about 12,000 votes. The margin was provided primarily through the underhanded tactics of Tammany Hall, which hated the reform-oriented Cleveland and unequivocally wanted him out of office. The 36 electoral votes of the Empire State provided the difference: Harrison won the electoral duel 233 to 168. That was fortunate for "Little Ben," because he lost the popular vote by almost 100,000 votes. In fairness to Harrison, he and Cleveland comported themselves with class and dignity and there is no evidence he had any part of Tammany Hall's backdoor shenanigans.

Commander in Chief Lore

The Harrison campaign slogan wasn't crooked, just corny. Harrison was immortalized in the song "Grandfather's Hat Fits Ben!" Those crafty Democrats got their zingers in, though, drawing cartoons that portrayed Harrison as a tiny man in the shadow of William Henry Harrison's beaver hat. The campaigning was actually fairly benign; Cleveland made only one appearance to accept re-nomination and Harrison only delivered heavily scripted addresses from his Indianapolis home. Politics is a dirty business.

Gentle, Ben

Harrison entered the White House with two large strikes against him. First, without his approval, his party had sold his administration to sects of all shapes and sizes, so he was besieged by fellows calling in their promised favors. Second, Harrison had a cold, irascible personality that didn't jibe with the give-and-take world of dealing with congressmen. A famous description of Harrison's handshake was that it was "like a wilted petunia." The problems with his demeanor forced his political handlers to pull his whistle-stop campaign engine out of the city he was visiting right after concluding his speech (and he was a fine public speaker) so that he wouldn't have to shake hands and engage in face-to-face contact with potential voters. Harrison was incorruptible and intelligent, but the former quandary made him somewhat of a figurehead, and the latter issue made him unapproachable and kept him from understanding the concerns of the average American.

Dollars for Soldiers

Harrison came into the White House at a time when Republicans controlled both houses of Congress, and significant legislation was passed during his administration. There was a large surplus when he entered office, but the extra money was quickly doled out by Congress. In 1890, Congress passed the Dependent and Disability Pension Act, which gave pensions to all disabled Union veterans, even if their injuries weren't related to the Civil War, and gave money to children, dependent parents, and widows of veterans.

Can't Trust It

In the same year, Harrison signed the Sherman Antitrust Act, which was designed to regulate the operations of corporate trusts and declared corporations that restricted commerce and trade illegal. The act was intended to keep corporations from forming monopolies, controlling the market price, and eliminating small businesses, but it ended up flawed because of its loopholes and use by big business against labor unions. The Democrats called it the "Billion Dollar Congress"—Speaker of the House Thomas Reed called it a "Billion Dollar Country!"

A New Tariff in Town

Harrison also signed the Sherman Silver Purchase Act, which increased the amount of silver the federal Treasury was mandated to purchase each month, which would help farmers pay off their debts. In part this was a compromise to get the backing of Western congressmen for an increase in the protective tariff.

The McKinley Tariff Act also became law in 1890, but it was a debacle. Duties on imports reached an all-time high of 48 percent, some foreign goods couldn't even enter the states, and new industries didn't have to worry about international competition. Monopolists, manufacturers, and merchants began raising the price of their goods, which didn't sit too well with the working-class crowd. The midterm elections saw the Republicans lose control of the House of Representatives and maintain only a slim, unstable lead in the Senate.

First Family Factuals

The White House received a much-needed facelift during the Harrison years because it had become dilapidated and was overrun with rats. A $35,000 appropriation was granted by Congress for home improvement. Among the many improvements were the installation of a new heating system, private bathrooms in each bedroom, and electric lights set in place for the first time. However, the Harrisons were frightened by the new technology and preferred using the old gaslights.

The Foreign Affairs Front

On the foreign affairs front, Harrison had a couple successes. Secretary of State (and Republican puppet master) James G. Blaine pushed for control of Samoa, which almost led to a naval conflict with Germany, but the dispute was settled without incident. The first Pan-American conference was held in Washington in 1889 and 1890, and dialogue opened up between the United States and Latin America. An old argument with Britain over seal fishing rights, known as the Bering Sea controversy, led to both countries agreeing to an international arbitration in 1892. In addition, right before Harrison left office, he sent a treaty to the Senate for the annexation of Hawaii, but Cleveland withdrew the treaty on the grounds that the American representative had acted dishonorably, and this remained a thorn in the side of Kid Gloves.

Benjamin Harrison, twenty-third president of the United States.

Tidings of the "Centennial President"

➤ Benjamin Harrison's inauguration was 100 years after George Washington's, so he was often called the "Centennial President."

➤ The first four American battleships were built during Harrison's administration.

➤ The Harrisons were the first First Family to have a Christmas Tree in the executive mansion.

➤ Montana, Idaho, Wyoming, North Dakota, South Dakota, and Washington were all added on Harrison's watch, bringing the total to 44.

➤ From 1897 to 1899, Harrison worked as counsel for the government of Venezuela in a boundary dispute with Great Britain over British Guiana. He filed an 800-page brief and, over the course of five days, delivered 25 hours of oral arguments.

Ben There, Done That

Benjamin Harrison ran again for president in 1892 and ran against Grover Cleveland one more time. However, Harrison's beloved tariff and economic policies sent many farmers, laborers, and other working class citizens to join the new Populist Party, which further hurt his re-election cause. Caroline Harrison also was gravely ill, so the president didn't campaign, and Cleveland followed suit out of deference to the First Lady's failing health. Caroline died two weeks before the election, in which Harrison was defeated by nearly 400,000 votes.

Harrison delivered a series of law lectures at Stanford University before returning to Indianapolis in 1894 to practice law. In 1896, he married Mary Scott Lord Dimmick, a widow and Caroline's niece. His two children, Russell and Mary, boycotted the nuptials in protest, but the happy new, couple would have a child of their own, Elizabeth.

Harrison wrote two books, *This Country of Ours,* about how the federal government works, and *The Views of an Ex-President,* which was edited by his widow and posthumously published in 1901. He died of pneumonia on March 13, 1901, in his Indianapolis home. The wife of the grandson of "Tippecanoe," the ninth president, lived to the ripe old age of 89, dying in January 1948 while Harry Truman, the thirty-third president, was in the White House. Her longevity is impressive, but not nearly as impressive as Benjamin Harrison's unwavering devotion to a really high tariff.

Born on the Fourth of July

Calvin Coolidge was born on Independence Day in 1872, in the village of Plymouth Notch, Vermont. He was the son of a hard-working shopkeeper. Coolidge's mother died when he was 12, and he carried her picture in the back of his watchcase for the rest of his life. He was never a very social person, but his Puritan upbringing indelibly imprinted the virtues of thrift, honesty, conservatism, punctuality, and the righteousness of God upon his psyche. Coolidge was also beset by numerous allergies that gave him a nasally voice that was both distinctive and ripe for mockery.

Coolidge attended Black River Academy in Ludlow, Vermont, but he mostly kept to himself. His spirits picked up when his younger sister Abbie, 13, joined him, but in 1890 an attack of appendicitis brought about her untimely death. Both father and son were distraught, but it went against their makeup to do much more than persevere. Coolidge wasn't able to pass the entrance examinations for Amherst College in Amherst, Massachusetts, so he spent a year at preparatory school and was admitted in 1891. He graduated cum laude in 1895 and spent two years studying law in Northhampton, Massachusetts, where he opened a law practice that he maintained until 1919. Northhampton is also where he began his long, fortuitous political career.

One day in 1904, a teacher at the Clarke Institute for the Deaf was out watering plants and looked up at an open window to see a man shaving in front of a mirror in his long underwear while wearing a brown felt derby. The teacher, Grace Goodhue,

First Family Factuals

The rascally romantic Calvin Coolidge presented his wife with a surprise in the early stages of their marriage. One afternoon, he came home with a laundry bag that contained more than 50 pairs of men's socks that needed holes mended. Grace asked her husband if he had participated in the matrimonial ceremony as a way to get his socks darned.

Prez Says

"I want your vote. I need it. I shall appreciate it."

—Calvin Coolidge's direct message as he campaigned door to door in Northhampton for election to the office of mayor

embarrassingly burst into laughter, which was the Hollywood-esque "meeting" of the future First Couple. Grace and Coolidge were married in 1905, even though they were polar opposites. Grace was warm and outgoing, had a great sense of humor, and enjoyed the company of others. Her mother didn't care for Coolidge, but who could resist the charm of his get-to-the-point proposal during a walk in the woods: "I am going to be married to you." They were married in 1905, and the following year Grace gave birth to the first of their two sons, John—Calvin Jr. came along in 1908.

Scaling the Massachusetts Political Scene

Coolidge quickly moved up the Massachusetts political ladder, starting in 1898 as a city councilman in Northhampton. He bounced from one office to another, all the way to Washington, with the exception of a 1905 race for school committeeman. He was then elected to the state legislature, where he served two years in the lower house, and he also became mayor of Northhampton, serving in 1909 and 1910. Coolidge believed in a conservative ideology, but he came from a working class background and related better to the average folks, which helped him carry the blue-collar Democratic votes.

Coolidge continued his tortoise-like, slow and steady rise to the summit. He served in the state senate from 1912 to 1915, and he became the highest-ranking Republican in the state after his election to the presidency of the Senate in 1914. His time in office was marked by his ability to get along, to remain loyal to the Republican Party, and to keep from antagonizing anyone. His ascendancy continued as he was elected lieutenant governor in 1915 and then governor in 1918.

Coolidge Squeezes Shoes

Coolidge's time in the governor's mansion was basically defined by one event, which also propelled him to the national stage even though his reaction was nowhere near as decisive as it was regarded.

In 1919, a majority of the Boston police aligned with the American Federation of Labor after their requests for higher wages and better working conditions were ignored by the city. After 19 leaders in the police unionization movement were suspended, most of the force walked out on September 9. Naturally, thugs and crooks considered this a businessman's holiday of sorts, and they took to their hobbies of rioting and looting without the burden of factoring cops into the equation. Boston's Mayor Andrew J. Peters, a Democrat, was unable to contain the chaos and called upon Coolidge to send out the State Guard. Coolidge initially declined, claiming that he didn't have the authority to intervene in city affairs—or, as many critics have claimed, that he didn't want to hurt his re-election chances by becoming known as a strikebreaker. In the interim, Peters managed to restore order to a large degree by utilizing local guard units.

On the third day of the strike, Coolidge called out the cavalry and ordered additional state troops into Boston, and the strike dissolved. He asked for federal soldiers if a general strike erupted, and he refused to allow the suspended strikers to return to work. He defended his actions in a strong reply to AFL President Samuel Gompers, who had asked the governor to reconsider what he saw as an unfair firing. Coolidge replied, "There is no right to strike against the public safety, by anybody, anywhere, anytime." His unwavering words were hailed across the United States and drew positive acclaim from President Woodrow Wilson, which thrust him into the public spotlight. Coolidge was given the credit for ending the walkout, commonly regarded as an unnecessary threat to public safety, and his name was bandied about for higher offices.

Coolidge was again elected governor, and his term in office saw the elimination of 122 state departments. He also worked for the rights of tenants, which wasn't exactly conservative dogma. The following year, 1920, saw Coolidge leave Massachusetts for Washington, D.C.

Coolidge Now

➤ Coolidge had both the first State of the Union address to be broadcast on radio (December 6, 1923) and the first radio broadcast from inside the White House (Washington's Birthday Address, February 23, 1924).

➤ Calvin Coolidge reportedly refused to hold Cabinet meetings after 4 P.M.

➤ Coolidge was the only president sworn in by a former president, Chief Justice William Howard Taft.

➤ Coolidge, a renowned skinflint, refused to buy the chair he had used at Cabinet meetings, as was customary, so Herbert Hoover and Treasury Secretary Andrew Mellon bought it for him.

Speaking Up for "Silent Cal"

Throughout his political career, Coolidge had a knack for getting people behind him, which was impressive considering that his public persona was to say as little as possible. Coolidge also hadn't produced a distinguished record in Massachusetts, but he was able to keep moving up. The vice presidential nomination was no exception because the Republican Party leaders had selected Senator Irvine Lenroot of Wisconsin to be Warren G. Harding's running mate. The word went out to the delegates that there was to be no challenge, but a revolt began when a delegate from Oregon stood up and spontaneously shouted that he was nominating Calvin Coolidge. "Silent Cal" beat Lenroot 674 to 146 and became vice president after he and Harding scored a landslide victory, 404 to 127 in the electoral college. Coolidge would become the first vice president invited to regularly sit in on Cabinet meetings and he quietly fulfilled his new role.

A Good Night's Sleep

Harding's scandalous administration and high living took a toll on his innards, and he died suddenly on August 2, 1923. Coolidge had been assured that the president was recovering, so he went home to Vermont for a visit. He was wakened in the early morning hours by his father, who gave him the news. Calvin checked on the situation with officials in Washington, and then had his father, a notary public, swear him in as they sat in a farmhouse parlor illuminated by kerosene lamps. The oath of office wasn't official, however, and it was repeated back in Washington. What was the first act of the new president? He went back to bed.

Commander in Chief Lore

Although Coolidge harped on the value of hard work, he certainly enjoyed his leisure time. Coolidge was legendary for sawing logs; he went to bed every night at 10 P.M. and rose between 7 A.M. and 9 A.M. In addition to getting at least nine hours every night, he took an afternoon nap for two to four hours. He also spent hours on his porch in a rocking chair enjoying the smooth smoke of a cigar.

Coolidge quickly turned the Harding White House from a den of iniquity to a den of tranquillity, and the public was generally clamoring for order and dignity in the executive office. Coolidge didn't clean house, though—he kept some members of Harding's

...ed the res-
...ignation
...wamp
...rosecutor
...r was rela-

All by Myself

The 1924 convention in Cleveland offered little challenge to Coolidge for president, even though there was division among congressional Republicans. He received the nomination on the first ballot in a boring convention—at least, in comparison to the raucous Democratic affair. The Democrats were split between the Northeastern, immigrant wing and the Southern, nativist wing. Al Smith of New York was a prime contender, but the Southern contingent, represented in no small part by the Ku Klux Klan, wouldn't allow a Catholic to be its nominee and pushed William G. McAdoo. A compromise candidate, John W. Davis, a conservative Wall Street lawyer, was selected on the 103rd ballot. The chaotic convention doomed the Democrats, and many of the core constituents bolted for the Progressive Party and their candidate, Robert La Follette of Wisconsin.

Coolidge's bland campaign slogan "Keep Cool with Coolidge" (cool in the calm sense, not the Fonzie sense) was more than enough to keep him entrenched in the White House because the economy was on the upswing. He was elected with 382 electoral votes, compared to 136 for Davis and 13 for La Follette. It was a bittersweet victory, though, because Coolidge lost another member of his immediate family. His youngest son, 16-year-old, Calvin Jr., died of blood poisoning after getting a blister while playing tennis on the White House lawn. It was a devastating turn of events, and the publicly taciturn president became even more remote.

Prez Says

"When he went, the power and glory of the presidency went with him .... The ways of Providence are often beyond our understanding. It seemed to me that the world had need of the work that it was probable he could do. I do not know why such a price was exacted for occupying the White House."

—From *Autobiography*, by Calvin Coolidge

Business Is Business, Round Two

Coolidge entered his second term remarking that he didn't anticipate much change, and not much change is what he brought. The Roaring '20s were marked by booze, sex, dancing, and economic prosperity, which was Coolidge's favorite part of the equation. Between 1925 and 1929, the Stock Market rose more than 200 percent, industrial production rose by 26 percent, and the national debt was substantially reduced.

Calvin Coolidge, thirtieth president of the United States, pictured with Walter "Big Train" Johnson.

The stock market crash that hit the nation in late 1929 came about because of the growth of speculative stock buying. Stocks were purchased on margin, investors had to put up very little of the value of the shares, and their brokers knew that the banks were willing to advance what they needed. The entire system spiraled past productivity, actual earnings, or worth. Granted, the crash came after Coolidge left office, and it would be unfair and irresponsible and unfair to lay the blame at his doorstep. It isn't unfair, however, to say that Coolidge was a detached boss who paid little attention to the workers' details. As long as the company prospered, he was happy, and his belief in the status quo kept him from even examining the possible downfall in the waves of speculation across the land.

Prez Says

"After all, the chief business of the American people is business. They are profoundly concerned with producing, buying, selling, investing and prospering in the world. I am strongly of the opinion that the great majority of people will always find these are moving impulses of our life ....
So long as wealth is made the means and not the end, we need not greatly fear it."

—From *Foundations of the Republic,* by Calvin Coolidge

In Touch with the Wealthy Man

Coolidge's core belief that the "man who builds a factory builds a temple" apparently didn't equate farms with any house of prayer. Western farmers didn't enjoy the same prosperity: A quarter of farms in the United States were sold to pay off debts and meet financial obligations from 1920 to 1932. A congressional coalition of Democrats and Western politicians sympathetic to the plight of the farmer introduced the McNary-Haugen Farm Relief Bill, which would have had the government purchase farm surpluses and send them abroad to raise domestic agricultural market prices. Coolidge vetoed the bill in 1927 and 1928, however, because he didn't believe in federal price-fixing.

Coolidge also wasn't a bright light in the equality debate. He did little to advance antilynching legislation. He supported the Immigration Act of 1924, which banned Japanese immigration and slowed the influx of Southern and Eastern Europeans. And he once let it be known that biology dictates that Nordics "deteriorate when mixed with other races." Although he did support the nineteenth amendment, which gave women the right to vote.

As with his domestic agenda, Coolidge didn't have much vision for groundbreaking international policy. He signed the Kellogg-Briand Pact of 1928, which renounced war as an instrument of national policy and agreed to settle all disputes by peaceful means, but it had no practical value whatsoever other than to secure the 1929 Nobel Peace Prize for Secretary of State Frank Kellogg. Coolidge also managed to protect the property rights of American oil investors who owned deposits in Mexico without incident and was in office when an international committee dealt with the mess of Germany's World War I reparations.

More Time to Rest

Silent Cal, who was actually quite garrulous in person with friends and family, announced his decision not to run in true Coolidge fashion. He handed out a 10-word statement to the press while on vacation in the Black Hills that read, "I do not choose to run for president in 1928. "His ambiguity left Republicans wondering if *they* were supposed to choose him, and he reportedly seemed perturbed at the 1928 convention when Herbert Hoover was selected. Coolidge never explained why he didn't run, but it is often speculated that he was worried about Grace's health and that he was still grieving over Calvin's death. Grace was quoted as saying that he thought a depression was coming, but there was never any concrete indication of this.

Coolidge retired to Northhampton and began writing his *Autobiography* in magazine installments in 1929 as well as articles promoting his beliefs in limited governmental interference in business practices. He died at home on January 5, 1933, after a heart attack. His reputation was sullied by the stock market crash and ensuing Great Depression, but it saw a bit of a renaissance during the Reagan administration. The Gipper hung a picture of Coolidge in the Cabinet room after removing a portrait of Thomas Jefferson. Coolidge's economic policies provided a solid block of growth, but his provincial shortsightedness kept him from noticing the warning signs of the imminent collapse.

In the end, neither Harrison nor Coolidge did much of anything, and their inactivity is a big part of their legacy. They were both honest, decent men who were happy to be there and who didn't rock the boat—heck, they didn't even pull up the anchor.

The Least You Need to Know

➤ Benjamin Harrison was the grandson of William Henry Harrison, a Civil War hero, and an accomplished lawyer before serving in the White House.

➤ Harrison was devoted to a high protective tariff, which contributed to his limited legislative success.

➤ Calvin Coolidge was president during considerable economic growth, but the "Roaring '20s" ended with the stock market crash of 1929.

➤ Coolidge is often remembered for how little his impact on the country was, but he felt that things were running smoothly and stuck to his belief in a very limited government.

Chapter 24

Back-to-Back Slacks: Franklin Pierce and James Buchanan

In This Chapter

➤ The two doughfaced presidents

➤ Personal tragedy destroys the First Family

➤ What's so civil about war anyway?

➤ Old Buck is Stuck in the Middle

Franklin Pierce served as president from 1853 to 1857, followed by James Buchanan from 1857 to 1861. These two watched this country slide into its greatest internal quagmire, and they relegated themselves to the short list of men whose time in office amounted to very little—and thus they don't have any famous monuments bearing their names.

Franklin Pierce Can't Lose

Franklin Pierce lived his life in a strange state of contradiction. On the one hand, he was a man who rose to high places without a lot of struggle, but yet his life was also deeply affected by tragedy and alienation. He tried to serve the Constitution, but he helped divide the United States into warring factions, which wholeheartedly subverted what the great document stood for in the first place. Pierce was a man who was able to make his way to the top because of his good looks, disarming personality, and staunch belief in the Democratic party, but he fell to the bottom and lived out his remaining years alone, a pariah in his own backyard.

Pierce's early political life is primarily defined by two things: the ease to which he achieved office, and his steadfast dedication to uphold the Constitution of the United States, which in his mind sanctioned the right to own slaves. He was born on November 23, 1804, in a log cabin in Hillsborough, New Hampshire, the son of a Revolutionary War veteran. His father, Benjamin Pierce, was a staunch Jeffersonian Democrat and a major influence of Franklin's political outlook. Benjamin Pierce was elected governor of New Hampshire in 1827, the same year his son began practicing law, but Franklin quickly followed in his father's footsteps. Pierce was elected to the state legislature in 1829 at age 26 and served as speaker of the lower house from 1831 to 1832.

In 1833, at the age of 29, Pierce began his career at the federal level when he was elected to the House of Representatives as a Democrat. He earned a reputation as a loyal party supporter of Andrew Jackson and stood behind the Democrats as they lobbied against a national bank. It was during these years that Pierce began voicing the unwavering stand that ultimately led to his downfall: a rabid adherence to proslavery causes. He befriended Southern, antiabolition stalwarts such as Jefferson Davis, who had remarkable influence over the Pierce's presidency as head of the War Department. It didn't take long for Pierce to become well-known as a *doughface*.

Pierce also got married during these heady days, even though his wife, Jane, hated the idea of life inside the modern Beltway. Although the two were devoted to one another, they were a classic case of opposites attracting. Jane was a shy, melancholic, deeply religious woman with a disdain for politicians. Mrs. Pierce's chronic tuberculosis kept her from joining her husband in Washington in 1835, so he spent his days hitting the taverns with the other rowdy bachelors, and Pierce eventually spent his life battling alcoholism. Still, Pierce was on the fast track upward and was elected to the U.S. Senate at age 32. Although his 10-year term was relatively uneventful, he was taken under the wing of the older Southern senators.

The Whigs took over Congress, so Pierce returned to Concord, New Hampshire, to live the quiet life that Jane always sought. Pierce even turned down President Polk's offer to serve in his Cabinet as Attorney General.

Knowledge Is Power

Doughface is a term dating back to 1830 that refers to a Northern Congressman who was sympathetic to the South and proslavery causes prior to and throughout the Civil War.

An Unfortunate Horse-Play

One offer Pierce couldn't refuse was the chance to serve his country during the Mexican War in 1846. He enlisted as a private, but Polk gave him a colonel's commission, and Pierce was quickly promoted to brigadier general in charge of volunteers, even though his only military experience up to that point had been in the militia. In June,

Pierce's New England brigade joined forces with General Winfield Scott in Puebla on a march to Mexico City. Unfortunately, the battlefield glory Pierce envisioned quickly became a source of constant mockery toward him. In August 1847, at the Battle of Contreras, southwest of Mexico City, Pierce's horse was spooked by the battlefield noises, leading to a smack in the groin against the horse's pommel. During the chaos, some of the men in his unit got scared and broke ranks. Pierce fainted and tore up his knee while falling from the horse. He reinjured the same knee the following day and fainted again in front of the troops. The Whig Party turned the situation into an act of cowardice, which would stick with him throughout his life.

Let's Be Frank About Pierce

➤ Pierce attended Bowdoin College in Brunswick, Maine, because his father felt that Dartmouth was too influenced by the Federalists. His classmates included Nathaniel Hawthorne, who became a lifelong friend, and Henry Wadsworth Longfellow.

➤ After his first term in the House, Pierce returned to Hillsborough, New Hampshire, and started a law firm. He hired an apprentice named Albert Baker and befriended Baker's younger sister, who was too sickly to attend school. The sister would gain fame later in life as Mary Baker Eddy, founder of the Christian Science religion.

➤ Throughout his career, Franklin Pierce never lost an election, only the 1856 nomination.

➤ Pierce installed the first coal-burning furnace and central heating in the White House, which had been a complaint of both previous residents and guests.

➤ Pierce is the only president in history who finished a complete term in office without making a single change in his Cabinet.

The Man of Compromise

Pierce returned to civilian life, but once a politician, always a politician. He became an elder spokesman in the state Democratic Party. He favored the Compromise of 1850 and the Fugitive Slave Law, which was not very popular in New England. The party split after the death of popular potential candidate Levi Woodbury, so the 1852 convention was divided among four candidates, led by James Buchanan and Stephen Douglas. Behind Jane's back, Pierce and his followers plotted that he could pull together both Northern and Southern Democrats, even though he wanted his name on the ballot only if the timing was perfect.

Amid sweltering heat, rising tensions, and fisticuffs, Pierce's name wasn't even brought up until the 35th ballot, and then only as a compromise candidate. However, the dark horse rode into the light on the 49th ballot, after the North Carolina delegation switched to Pierce. Senator William R. King of Alabama was the vice presidential nominee, selected primarily for his opposing geographical home. Jane collapsed when she found out, and their son Bennie wrote her expressing his hopes that his father would lose the race.

Franklin Pierce, four-teenth president of the United States.

Pierce pledged to support the Compromise of 1850 and put the slavery question to rest, which was about as likely as him turning down a victory toast. The campaign against former battlefield buddy Winfield Scott was marked by its ugliness and vapidity. Scott was well-known, but Pierce was a mystery outside of New Hampshire. Nathaniel Hawthorne wrote a campaign biography for his old friend, branding him with an *A* for *Authority*. Pierce later repaid Hawthorne by giving him the job of U.S. consul in Liverpool from 1853 to 1857 (following a trend that started when he got him a job as a Boston Customs House official in 1839).

Both candidates were similar and lacking in substance, so the race was basically an unending stream of mud, with the Whigs tagging Pierce as a coward and a drunk (and the stellar putdown, "the hero of many a well-fought bottle"). The Whigs, however, were unraveling and couldn't mend the tear between their slavery factions, so Pierce won in an electoral landslide 254 to 42. The election ushered in the rapid dissolution of the Whigs for good.

Tragedy Strikes

Pierce took office on a cold day in March 1853, following one of the saddest moments in all of presidential history. In 1843, the Pierces lost their older son, Franklin, during a typhus epidemic, and they had lost another son in infancy. Jane focused all her energies on Bennie and ensured that he had a devout religious education. As president-elect in 1853, Pierce and his family were traveling from Boston to Concord by train when the train derailed and went over an embankment. Franklin and Jane were only slightly injured, but they watched as Bennie was crushed by a beam, dying right before their eyes.

Neither of them ever got over the death of their son. Jane decided that it was God's will so that Pierce's presidency would be free of distractions, but she spent the rest of her days as a recluse. She never fulfilled any of the traditional duties of the First Lady, and she spent much of her time alone, writing letters to her dead son. Eventually, she made a few appearances, but she never showed any signs of life. Pierce thought it was a punishment from God for his sins and became consumed with guilt. He began his term in office in a fog of depression.

Out of respect to his son Bennie, Pierce kept the inauguration restrained. Jane didn't attend, there was no ball, and he refrained from taking the usual oath of office. Instead, he simply affirmed his loyalty to the Constitution. He also didn't use any notes or text—he broke tradition and spoke from memory.

Prez Says

"It is a relief to feel that no heart but my own can know the personal regret and bitter sorrow over which I have been borne to a position so suitable for others rather than desirable for myself."

—Opening words of Franklin Pierce's inauguration speech

The Man from New Hampshire Comes Undone

Pierce quickly cemented his connection with the South, reiterating his belief that the Compromise of 1850 was constitutional and that the slavery question should be put to rest. He tried to unite the halves of his voting bloc by splitting his Cabinet in the two most important positions: New Yorker William L. Marcy was named Secretary of State, and Jefferson Davis became Secretary of War. Davis quickly moved to the forefront and influenced Pierce's pro-South decisions.

The Gadsden Purchase

Early on, Pierce followed the Doctrine of Manifest Destiny and believed wholeheartedly in territorial expansion. Pierce offered $50 million for a chunk of Mexico's northern border, one of four differently priced border configurations, but it resulted only in the Gadsden Purchase, a $15 million strip across what is now southern Arizona and part of southern New Mexico. Northern congressmen opposed the Gadsden Purchase, assuming that it would become slave territory, but Pierce saw that a treaty was secured. Instrumental in the Gadsden Purchase was Davis, who wanted the proposed transcontinental railroad to run from New Orleans to San Diego.

The Ostend Manifesto

Pierce also tried to acquire Cuba through diplomatic negotiations, but a document called the Ostend Manifesto was drafted just in case. The document stated that if Spain wouldn't sell Cuba for a price not to exceed $130 million, the United States would seize the island to prevent the expected slave emancipation by Spain, which would lead to an uprising in the South. The document caused a huge uproar in Europe over the disregard for their property, and in the North over another perceived attempt to expand slavery. Pierce was forced to disclaim the Ostend Manifesto, which hurt his falling popularity and bungled any legitimate chance at adding Cuba to the American mix.

The Kansas-Nebraska Act

Senator Stephen Douglas wanted the railroad to run through Chicago because Illinois was his home state, because he had put a lot of money in the speculation of Western lands and ostensibly because new land would be available for settlers. Douglas was instrumental in crafting the Kansas-Nebraska Act, which was bartered with Southern congressmen for the repeal of the Missouri Compromise. Initially, Pierce was opposed to this deal, but Davis quickly exerted his influence, and the rest is history. Pierce himself even signed the repeal clause of the Missouri Compromise, and in May 1854, the Kansas-Nebraska bill became law.

The mini Civil War taking place in "Bleeding Kansas" ruined any chance Pierce had of re-election. Nebraskan settlers were basically in agreement against being admitted as a slave state, but it had turned ugly in Kansas. The Border War raged on as anti-slavery free-staters and proslavery "Border Ruffians" initiated violent raids against one another, widening the gap between the North and the South and greasing the rails of the Civil War.

A Venomous Antiabolitionist

Pierce became an outcast: Northern Democrats despised him, and after the Democrats faced defeat in the 1854 midterm congressional elections, Southerners knew that Pierce was unelectable. His choice to dogmatically embrace the South and his failure to establish a fairly elected government in Kansas rendered him used political goods. The Democrats dropped Pierce like an anvil in 1856. The Democrats instead chose James Buchanan, who went on to equal highs in presidential lows. When Pierce was asked what a president should do after leaving office, he said, "There's nothing left—but to get drunk." And he did.

Pierce returned to New Hampshire, but his angry rants against abolitionists (with his harshest venom spewed at abolitionist clergy) kept him from even receiving any public welcoming upon his return.

Pierce never wavered in his stance on slavery, but never thought to pull up stakes and move to Mississippi, either. He suggested Jefferson Davis to friends who wanted him to run for the 1860 Democratic nomination, after which he became an angry, outspoken critic of Abraham Lincoln. He claimed support for the Union, but he saw fit to give his last public speech against the Emancipation Proclamation. Unfortunately, it fell on the same day as news reached his audience about a great Union victory at Gettysburg. Pierce was considered by many to be a traitor; after his death in 1869, it took 50 years for a statue to be erected in his memory in his hometown of Concord, New Hampshire.

First Family Factuals

The Pierces took a long three-year trip to Madeira, Europe, and the West Indies trying to restore Jane's health. Jane took Bennie's Bible with her everywhere they roamed. She died on December 2, 1863, and the only one who came to be with Pierce was Nathaniel Hawthorne, who in turn died in 1864. Pierce fell into his alcoholic ways until the last three years of his life.

Pierce's Greatest Unintended GOP Legacy

Franklin Pierce had a couple minor successes: He brought the national debt down considerably by slashing federal spending, and he negotiated treaties that expanded trade as far away as the ports of Japan.

Perhaps Pierce's most important legacy, however, is that he unwittingly helped create a new political party, the Republicans, who elected Abraham Lincoln four years later. Western Democrats fed up with Kansas-Nebraska and Northern Democrats fed up with Pierce were part of the conglomeration of antislavery party runaways who helped create the Republican Party. How ironic, considering the small number of minority members and the large number of white Southerners in today's GOP. A meeting in February 1854 in Ripom, Wisconsin, and a mass meeting held in July of the same year, in Jackson, Michigan, were two of the early gatherings that lay claim to the formation of the Republican party.

Déjà Vu All over Again

Franklin Pierce had become too hot of a potato, so the Democrats turned to a man who had spent the last three years working in Great Britain as the U.S. envoy. Out of sight, out of mind meant that "Old Buck" James Buchanan would be acceptable to both Northern and Southern Democrats. Pierce was shoved to the sidelines, and Buchanan stepped up to promote his adherence to the constitutionality of the rights of slave owners. Let's see, a Northern Democrat "doughface" president who didn't waver in his antiabolitionist stance and stood idly by as the country slid ever closer to Civil War—sounds like someone else, doesn't it?

Lancaster Law

Buchanan was the last president born in the eighteenth century, in a one-room log cabin near Mercersburg, Pennsylvania. He went on to college at the age of 16, and was practicing law by the time he was 21. Buchanan was a stellar attorney and became quite prosperous in Lancaster within a few years. He volunteered for the War of 1812 and marched to Baltimore to help defend the city from England, fresh from the torching of Washington. He saw little action, though, and he returned to Lancaster in time to win the legislative seat in 1814 as a member of the Federalist Party.

During these years, Old Buck fell in love and got engaged to Ann Coleman, the daughter of an extremely rich iron-mill owner. He and Ann got into a quarrel and she broke off the engagement. The details of the argument have never been known, but rumors have said that Ann thought he was marrying her for money and that Ann's father didn't approve. Whatever the reason, Ann became despondent and died soon thereafter of a possible suicide, although the circumstances remain mysterious to this day. The family refused to allow Buchanan to attend the funeral, and he was never engaged again, although he did carry on flirtations with other women.

Commander in Chief Lore

Later in life, Buchanan revealed that he had sealed documents in New York City that would explain why the relationship with Ann had dissolved. He had sent them to Gotham along with financial papers and other documents to keep them from Confederate troops. After he died, the material was found with a letter ordering its contents burned without being opened, and his wishes were respected.

After consecutive terms, Buchanan returned to private practice and rolled merrily along, winning case after case and amassing $8,000 a year by the age of 27, a fortune back in his day. He was elected to Congress as a Federalist in 1820, and he switched loyalties to the Democrats four years later. Buchanan spent a decade in the House of Representatives and was contemplating retirement when President Andrew Jackson tapped him to be the U.S. diplomatic representative to Russia. Buchanan lived in

Saint Petersburg from 1832 to 1834 and negotiated the first trade treaty between the two countries. He then returned and was elected to the U.S. Senate, where he served for the next 11 years.

Facts About Bachelor No. 1

➤ James Buchanan was kicked out of Dickinson College in Carlisle, Pennsylvania, after his first year for insubordination and excessive partying. He was reinstated after he pledged to work hard and stay out of trouble, and he kept to his word: He graduated the following year at age 18.

➤ In 1846, Buchanan negotiated the Oregon Treaty with Great Britain that gave the United States most of the territory in Oregon country below the northern boundary of the 49th parallel.

➤ Buchanan respected and agreed with James Madison's views on how the Constitution should work, and he helped ensure that Madison's notes on the 1787 Constitutional Convention were given to the federal government to be printed.

➤ Led by South Carolina in December 1860, seven Southern states seceded on Buchanan's watch and met on February 4, 1861, to begin the formation of the Confederate States of America.

If at First You Don't Succeed ...

Buchanan became one of the leading Northern Democrats with a Southern soul. He chaired the Senate Foreign Relations Committee and adamantly supported Andrew Jackson and Martin Van Buren. He spurned offers from Van Buren to be attorney general, and by Whig President John Tyler to be an associate justice of the Supreme Court. Yet Buchanan was a top-notch lawyer renowned for his thoughtful compromises and sincere efforts. What if Old Buck had become a member of the Supreme Court instead of the President of the United States? It isn't a stretch to say that he would at the very least have been able to keep from becoming a key scapegoat in the ugliest conflict in the short history of the United States.

Buchanan wanted the 1844 nomination, but it went to James Polk. Buchanan diligently campaigned for Polk, who in turn named him secretary of state. He followed the Manifest Destiny credo and made the final arrangements for the annexation of Texas, the straw that stirred the drink that became the Mexican War. Buchanan returned to his estate, called Wheatland, near Lancaster, after he failed to win the 1848 nomination.

Buchanan worked toward the 1852 nomination, but he struck out during the holding pattern between fractions of the Democratic Party. He had been a front-running candidate, but Pierce was chosen because he was an unknown and appealed to both Southerners and Northerners because of his adherence to a proslavery platform. These were the exact same qualifications that would get Buchanan to the White House four years later.

Old Buck Stops Here

In 1853, Buchanan became a diplomat once again, as Pierce appointed him U.S. envoy to Great Britain. He gained notoriety by helping draft the Ostend Manifesto, which did major damage to Pierce's presidency. Ironically, the Ostend Manifesto was so popular among Southerners that it helped put Buchanan in the forefront for the 1856 nomination.

James Buchanan, fifteenth president of the United States (1856 campaign poster).

JAMES BUCHANAN,
DEMOCRATIC CANDIDATE FOR PRESIDENT OF THE UNITED STATES.

Knowledge Is Power

A **lame duck** is an elected official that continues to hold political office while waiting for an elected successor to be inaugurated.

Buchanan was personally opposed to slavery and found it morally wrong, which wasn't even the standard of many abolitionists. Still, he also felt that it was constitutional and believed that the federal government's primary role was to protect the interests of the Southern states from abolitionists, whom he held in contempt.

Buchanan's Ill-Fated Inauguration

Buchanan was elected in 1856 primarily because he could get elected. He had no ties to "Bleeding Kansas" because he had been in Great Britain, but his proslave leanings were known enough to appease the Southern contingency. He entered the White House at 65 years of age—and promptly shot himself in the foot. In his inaugural speech, he announced that he would serve only one term, which made him an instantly weak, pseudo-*lame duck* president at a time when this country needed strong, clear leadership.

The Dred Scott Case

In his address, Buchanan called for both sides of the slavery issue to wait for a ruling by the Supreme Court in the Dred Scott case, which would settle the tense situation in Kansas. Two days later, the decision was announced by Chief Justice Roger Taney that Scott was not free because blacks were "so far inferior, that they had no rights which a white man was bound to respect." The Supreme Court added that it was illegal to limit slaveholding in the territories because it violated property rights and that Congress did not have the authority to regulate anything that was in direct contrast to the Constitution. Taney went on to argue that free blacks could never be U.S. citizens, even if they were in states that allowed them to vote or if they were native sons.

The decision infuriated Northerners and abolitionists, and Lincoln hinted that there might have been a conspiracy involving Buchanan and Taney. It turns out that Honest Abe was right: It was discovered years later that Taney had informed Buchanan of the decision before the inauguration. The vote was seven to two, but Buchanan asked a friend from Pennsylvania, Justice Robert Grier, to join the Southern judges in their effort to end Congress's attempts at limiting slavery, the farthest reaches of the decision. Obviously, this is a clear breach of ethics, but it also was woefully naive of Buchanan to think that this would pacify both sides and usher in his dream of the happy medium between North and South.

The Dred Scott case was one of the rallying points for the new Republican Party, and the Civil War quickly became an inevitability. Lines in the sand were being drawn, and the slavery debate reached a fevered pitch. Buchanan even went as far as to push Congress to recognize the proslavery capital of Lecompton, Kansas, and its constitution, even though it had been voted down by the majority of residents of the territory. Popular sovereignty had given way to Buchanan's attempts at conciliation. His explanation was that he thought the Southern states would secede, or take up arms, but the majority of Southerners most likely would have accepted an honest vote.

Zealots in Zion

Buchanan never really had one shining moment as president. His greatest successes came in his life prior to the presidency in various other political personas, particularly his years as a diplomat. In 1857, he used force to end what he thought was a Mormon rebellion at the Zion (promised land) in Utah. It was reported that the Mormon settlers followed only the rules of Brigham Young and the church, not the rulings of three federal judges sent by Pierce. Buchanan sent 2,500 troops to force a new governor upon the Mormons, who mobilized their own army. Reportedly, two federal forts were torched, army wagon trains were attacked, and Mormon zealots killed 120 immigrants on their way to the coast. Further bloodshed was averted and order was

restored to the territory after meetings with the states-manlike Young, but Buchanan's later stance that it was unconstitutional to use federal force against the seceding states rang hollow.

John Brown's Raid at Harper's Ferry

The John Brown standoff at Harper's Ferry brought the sectional conflict to the brink of explosion. Brown had seized the federal arsenal in Virginia in hopes of building a safe haven for escaped slaves in the Appalachian Mountains. He also wanted to start a slave revolt, but Buchanan sent Robert E. Lee and a company of Marines to handle Brown and his supporters. Brown was wounded and captured along with six followers, and ten of his men (including two of his sons) were killed in the battle. Brown was hanged within six weeks, but his claim that his efforts were in the name of God made him a martyr for abolitionists. The Brown incident also united Southern militias to form and appropriate arms, and the threat rang forth that if a "Black Republican" were elected in 1860, secession would immediately follow.

Buchanan's Numbered Days Come to an End

Democratic voters were split between Buchanan's vice president John C. Breckinridge and Douglas, while some switched their allegiance to John Bell, nominee of the Constitutional Union Party, whose platform was to preserve the Union. Buchanan refused to back Stephen Douglas, which further split the Democratic vote and Lincoln easily became the sixteenth President of the United States. Buchanan could do nothing as the United States became two entities. At his final annual address to Congress, on December 3, 1860, Buchanan continued to blame abolitionists for driving the nation to the boiling point. He stuck to his theories of compromise and did nothing as secession took place, believing that any overt act would initiate a civil war. Buchanan didn't think the South had the right to secede, but neither did the North have the right to force them to refrain, which wasn't the strong leadership the country needed.

Buchanan was able to stave off the conflict throughout his time in the White House. He idly watched as Southern militias seized federal property in the Confederate states, but he still held out hope that a compromise could avert a civil war. It was a do-nothing policy that remained unchanged by Lincoln, until shots were fired on Fort Sumter. To his credit, Buchanan was deeply affected by the secession, almost passing out when he heard the news, but he refused to waver from his belief in a compatible resolution for both sides.

On March 4, 1861, Buchanan left office and told Lincoln, "If you are as happy in entering the White House as I shall feel on returning to Wheatland, you are a happy man indeed."

Like Pierce before him, Buchanan lived out his remaining years in infamy. Many Northerners held him personally responsible for allowing secession, which begat the Civil War. The Senate even tried to censure him for "sympathy with the conspirators and their treasonable project," but it failed by a small margin. As the war raged on, Buchanan was publicly insulted in Lancaster, and there were threats on his life. Still, he never wavered from his belief that abolitionists caused the Civil War, and he remained against the Emancipation Proclamation. His main weakness was a failure to grasp the depth of anti-South and anti-slavery sentiments in the North. Buchanan also believed, "History will vindicate my memory." Unfortunately, he was wrong.

Not That There's Anything Wrong with That

One last long-standing rumor that must be addressed is the question of Buchanan's homosexuality. Massachusetts Representative Barney Frank himself called him the nation's only gay chief executive, but is there any truth to it? It's hard to say, because Buchanan had the letters regarding the situation with Ann destroyed. It is true that he was the only White House bachelor, but it also was said that he was very flirtatious, even though he never considered marriage after his engagement to Ann.

Assuming that we did indeed have a gay president has its strongest argument in Buchanan's relationship with William King, Pierce's vice president for a few weeks. The two men were roommates in Washington for 16 years, and King was often referred to as "Aunt Fancy" or "his wife." There is stronger evidence that King was gay and that he never attempted to hide his effeminate behavior or his uncommonly flashy wardrobe. King also wrote that he missed Buchanan greatly when he served as an ambassador in Paris.

It will never be known whether Buchanan and King had a homosexual affair. A credible case can be made that the men were in love, but there is no evidence of any physical manifestation. There were never any hints, rumors, taunts, or innuendoes that sex was a part of their relationship, so if they were having an affair, it was of the heart rather than the body. Buchanan may have had homosexual inclinations, but whatever his orientation, in the long run, it doesn't change the fact one bit that he really wasn't a very good president.

First Family Factuals

Buchanan's niece Harriet Lane acted as First Lady during his presidency. She erased the gloom of the Pierce years with flowers, lavish parties, class, charm, and unbridled enthusiasm. Later in life, she donated a large sum of money to Johns Hopkins Hospital in Baltimore for invalid children, and the clinic she endowed serves thousands of children every year.

Could Anyone Have Made a Difference?

Probably the best thing that can be said about the terms of Franklin Pierce and James Buchanan is that there probably weren't any good men for the job. Both dominant parties, the Whigs and the Democrats, were divided over slavery, so to the White House went men who weren't about to rock the slave ship. One could speculate all day as to why both presidents found slavery undeniably constitutional, but they were unbending in their belief systems. Pierce and Buchanan certainly weren't ones to poll their constituents to see how they should vote, because they were both way out of touch. Morally, their slavery stance leaves a lot to be desired, but they did have the moxie to see it through to the bitter end.

Of the two, Buchanan was probably far more suited to the presidency, but it is somewhat bewildering that he refused to see the writing on the wall and abandon (or at least stop capitulating to the South) his misguided compromise vision. Perhaps an argument could be made that border states such as Delaware, Kentucky, and Maryland refrained from joining the Confederacy because of his policies, but there is no evidence—only conjecture. Pierce was undone by horrific personal tragedies and the deepening of his alcoholism, which, regardless of his White House years, is more than one family should have to endure.

In the end, it was an awful period for White House leadership. It was a time when great courage, intelligence, and foresight were needed, but this would have to come via a man named Lincoln. Maybe Pierce and Buchanan's ineffectiveness did the nation a great favor—the Civil War ended slavery, and it had to come some time. Effective presidential leadership may have been able to work out a suitable compromise for the majority of Americans—except for the ones who were bought and sold, that is.

The Least You Need to Know

➤ Northerners Franklin Pierce and James Buchanan staunchly adhered to a Southern proslavery platform that pushed the United States closer to civil war.

➤ Pierce and his wife watched their last son die in an accident on a train, and the family never recovered.

➤ Buchanan thoroughly believed that a compromise between the North and the South could be reached, and so he did nothing as secession began.

➤ Neither Pierce nor Buchanan was very effective, but the rift over slavery was going to happen at some point, no matter who was in Washington.

Chapter 25

With Friends Like These: Warren G. Harding and Ulysses S. Grant

---

In This Chapter

➤ The mysterious happenings in the smoke-filled room

➤ I'm a little Teapot Dome scandal

➤ The Vicksburg victory

➤ Getting fried with a little help from their friends

A famous passage from the William Butler Yeats poem "The Municipal Gallery Revisited" says, "Think where man's glory most begins and ends, and say my glory was I had such friends." Apart from coincidentally being quoted by George McGovern in his 1972 concession speech, these lines are fitting to use for the infamous reputations of Warren G. Harding and Ulysses S. Grant. Fitting, that is, if the Yeats poem is judiciously edited and the word "glory" is replaced by "failure."

Getting the Scoop on a Young Republican

On November 2, 1865, Harding was born as the first of eight children on a farm in Blooming Grove, Ohio, to George and Phoebe Harding. When Harding was 10, the family moved to nearby Caledonia, where he attended school, played coronet in the village band, and worked as a printer's devil to help set type and run the presses of a small weekly newspaper. In 1879, Harding enrolled at tiny Ohio Central College in Iberia and graduated two years later.

In 1882, George Harding packed up the family belongings and moved to Marion, Ohio, in hopes of building a more lucrative homeopathic medical practice. Warren slowly followed behind on the family mule after he eventually gave up teaching. He tried his hand at selling insurance, studying law, and teaching school, but none of them held much interest for him. His passions lay in hanging out with his friends, shooting pool, playing poker, or organizing and playing the helicon in the Marion's People Band.

Eventually Harding drifted into the newspaper business and got a job at the *Democratic Mirror*. He quickly resigned (or he may have been fired) because of his enthusiasm for the 1884 Republican presidential candidate James G. Blaine, which didn't agree with the editor's politics. Harding and a couple friends then scraped up $300 and bought a local newspaper that had gone bankrupt, the *Marion Star*. The town was growing, and the newspaper went from a minuscule blip to an unqualified success. Within five years, the *Marion Star* was one of the Buckeye State's accomplished small-town dailies. Harding bought out his two friends and started a separate *Weekly Star* that was unabashedly pro-Republican.

Commander in Chief Lore

There was fierce competition for advertising dollars, so Harding jumped into the standard mudslinging campaigns that editors waged toward one another in the pages of their newspapers. One rival paper suggested that Harding was part black. The gossip surrounding the Hardings had been thrust upon them years back: Harding and his siblings were taunted by the other schoolchildren for having African-American blood. He was even confronted in the street by his future father-in-law, who profanely called him a "nigger" and threatened to kill him. The rumblings about Harding's black ancestry followed him throughout his political career, all the way to the White House.

A Lady's Man Comes Out of the Closet

In 1891, Harding married the divorcee Florence "Flossie" Kling DeWolfe, five years his senior and the daughter of Marion's wealthiest citizen. She was headstrong, domineering, and a nag, and Harding and his toadies called her the "duchess." Florence loved and admired Harding, and he cared for and respected his wife, but he wasn't in love with her and carried on two long-running affairs. One of his lovers was Carrie Phillips, the wife of his good friend James Phillips, a Marion businessman. Florence probably didn't know of their torrid shenanigans because the couples saw each other quite frequently and traveled abroad together, but she eventually found out everything.

In 1920, after the Republican convention, Harding's handlers gave the Phillipses $20,000 and a monthly stipend to leave the country for a while on a long vacation. Harding's other affair began in 1917 with Nan Britton, a woman 31 years his junior, who fell in love with him when she was a high school student back in Marion. He visited her in New York City, and she made trips to the White House. Their favorite hot spot was a small coat closet near the oval office, where she and President Harding made love. Florence almost caught them once, but a Secret Service agent gave Harding a heads-up by banging on the closet door.

Apart from his sexual affairs, Harding had long-running love affairs with his "Ohio Gang," as they would come to be known. Florence took over most of the business side of the *Marion Star*, so Warren's primary duty was to be his own best public relations firm and handle the local Republicans. He joined all the right clubs, lodges, and fraternal organizations; served as director of the Marion County Bank; and became a trustee at the Trinity Baptist Church. Harding was friendly and easygoing, a man's man who loved dirty jokes, whiskey-and-sodas, late night poker games, and the backslapping camaraderie of political meetings. The combination of his affable personality, dynamic public speaking skills, and ownership of a newspaper voicing Republican ideology made him a natural favorite of party bigwigs.

First Family Factuals

In 1927, four years after Harding's death, Britton wrote a kiss-and-tell-all book, *The President's Daughter*, which detailed their affair. The book also claimed that Harding recommended her for a job at U.S. Steel and had fathered Britton's baby, Elizabeth Ann, born in 1919. There is little evidence that her story was true (it's speculated that he was sterile), and much of the book was fabricated. Still, people around the country—historians included—believed (and some continue to believe) Britton's account, and the book was a huge hit. Mercifully, Florence was spared the details and embarrassment because she died in 1924.

From Columnist to Candidate

In 1898, Harding was elected to the Ohio state Senate. His popularity rapidly grew, and he caught the attention of Harry Daugherty, an influential lawyer with clout in the Republican Party. Harding was known as a harmonizer between the fractious elements of the GOP, and he became floor leader in his second term. In 1903, Daugherty helped get Harding elected to the post of lieutenant governor by enlisting the Cincinnati machine. In 1910, Harding ran for governor (Daugherty was his campaign manager), but he was badly beaten.

Harding returned to the *Marion Star* for two years, until he was called upon by fellow Ohioan President Taft to deliver Taft's nominating speech at the Republican National Convention for his second term. Harding's address was shouted down by Roosevelt supporters and he left the stage to chants of "We Want Teddy!" He continued to be politically active, and Daugherty saw to it that he got the Republican nomination in 1914 for the U.S. Senate, an election he won handily.

As with his record in the Ohio legislature, Harding's time in the Senate was undistinguished, to say the least. He stuck with the Republicans pretty much down the line, introduced no measures of any significance or bills bearing his name, spent plenty of time hitting the town with drinking buddies, and wasn't afraid to skip at least one out of every two roll calls. It is a testament to his convictions that he voted primarily for political purposes, which meant casting a "yes" vote for Prohibition and, to his credit, women's suffrage, by absentee vote. He also supported President Wilson's World War I measures, until he helped submarine the country's place in the League of Nations.

Five the Harding Way

➤ Warren G. Harding was the first president to be broadcast on radio; his speech at the dedication of the Francis Scott Key memorial at Fort McHenry on June 14, 1922, was carried by a Baltimore radio station.

➤ Harding's appointment of Albert Lasker as head of the Shipping Board was the first high-profile appointment of a Jew.

➤ Harding received 61 percent of the vote, the largest percentage that had been won by a candidate and almost as many popular votes as the two candidates combined just four years earlier. Why? Women were able to vote for the first time, and they overwhelmingly supported the handsome senator from Ohio, in no small part because he supported suffrage.

➤ Florence insisted that her husband refrain from chewing tobacco in public as executive officer, but cigars were acceptable.

➤ Harding died happy because Florence was reading an article in the *Saturday Evening Post* with a positive view of his policies.

The Legend of the "Smoke-Filled Room"

When the time came to nominate a candidate for the 1920 presidential election, Harding was probably not at the top of anyone's list except for Daugherty. It was assumed that Teddy Roosevelt, having made amends with the Republicans, would run for the presidency, but his death in 1919 left things up in the air. The main candidates were General Leonard Wood and Governor Frank Lowden, of Illinois.

Daugherty, however, correctly predicted that neither candidate would be able to win a majority, and a compromise would have to be made—enter alternative candidate Warren G. Harding. Reportedly, both he and Florence were wary of deserting the life of a senator, but they put full effort into the front-porch campaign that was forthcoming.

At the Republican convention in June, Harding got only 65½ votes on the first ballot, and his tallies went down from there. The conventioneers were still at an impasse on Friday night, and they called it a day. At the Blackstone Hotel, in a liquor-soaked, "smoke-filled room," Harding was accepted as the best of the "second-raters." Around 2 A.M. (just a few minutes earlier than Daugherty had guessed), Harding was summoned and told that he would likely be nominated when the convention reconvened. They asked if there was anything in his background that would keep him from becoming president. He spent 10 minutes by himself mulling it over and answered that there was no reason that he couldn't be president, probably due to the fact that his personal affairs and supposedly African-American roots had never come up in his other campaigns. Harding was finally nominated on the tenth ballot and Calvin Coolidge was chosen as his running mate.

Commander in Chief Lore

Harding said in a speech, "America's present need is not heroics but helping, not nostrums, but normalcy ...." He had meant to say "normality," but he butchered it. The phrase "Back to Normalcy" became his campaign slogan, though, and it was a hit with voters who wanted a change from the activist style of Woodrow Wilson.

Harding was the right man for the times because the national mood was swinging away from the progressive Wilson administration. A depression had set in, isolationism was growing in popularity, and many people were still angry that the United States had gotten involved in World War I—and all of that favored the Republicans. Harding ran a bland front-porch campaign and spoke in tepid generalities, but the country was looking for a caretaker, not a crusader. He easily whomped his Democratic opponent, James M. Cox.

Warren G. Harding, twenty-ninth president of the United States (pictured with his dog "Laddie").

Corruption Takes Control

Harding appointed some respected men to his Cabinet, including Secretary of State Charles Evans Hughes and Secretary of Commerce Herbert Hoover. He also filled it with friends such as Attorney General Harry Daugherty and those who had political ties to heavy campaign donors such as Secretary of the Interior Albert B. Fall. Much of the business of Harding's administration took place at the late-night poker sessions frequented by Daugherty, Fall, and shady Harding friend Jesse Smith. The "Ohio Gang" would meet at the "Little Green House" at 1625 K Street in Washington, D.C., and curry favors through dubious deals. There is no evidence that Harding was aware of the back-alley agreements, and he never stole a penny, but his naiveté and willingness to accept the *advice* of his friends, not to mention his own self-indulgences, kept him from recognizing the rampant corruption that surrounded him, and even later when he became aware of some of the corruption he kept his mouth shut out of loyalty.

Harding was a conservative following a public mandate for less federal government interference, but he did have a few accomplishments of which the administration could be proud:

➤ He called the Washington Conference for the Limitation of Armament in 1921 to 1922, which resulted in several treaties and ended the country's costly naval defense race with Great Britain and Japan. The conference also led to the destruction some of the existing weapons of war, including battleships.

➤ He reversed Wilson's policy of excluding blacks from federal posts.

➤ He convinced the steel industry to shorten the 12 hour work days.

➤ He created the system for a national budget and appointed Charles G. Dawes of Chicago as director of the Bureau of the Budget.

➤ He signed the treaties that formally ended World War I.

➤ He was the first president since the Civil War to deliver a civil rights speech on Southern soil, to a racially segregated audience in Birmingham, Alabama. He promoted racial equality, but never took any legislative steps.

The Harding administration will always be remembered first and foremost for the corruption that bled through the veins of his inner circle. In March 1923, Charles R. Forbes, the head of the Veteran's Bureau and card-playing pal of Harding, resigned his post and went to Europe. A subsequent investigation found that the Medal of Honor winner and his accomplices had bilked the federal government out of millions of dollars in a scheme that looted war surplus supplies and sold them at cut-rate prices to private enterprisers, and overpaid on government contracts for a hefty kickback. Forbes sent his resignation from Europe, but he was eventually brought back to the United States and sentenced to prison. The attorney for the Veterans Bureau, Charles F. Cramer, who bought the house Harding owned as a Senator and had profited along with Forbes, put a bullet in his head.

Prez Says

"I want to see the time come when black men will regard themselves as full participants in the benefits and duties of American citizenship .... We cannot go on, as we have gone on for more than half a century, with one great section of our population ... set off from the real contribution to solving national issues, because of a division of race lines."

—From a speech by Warren G. Harding on October 26, 1921

Et Tu, Daugherty?

Other scandals began to surface, and Harding ordered Jesse Smith out of the nation's capital. Smith was basically the bagman for Daugherty's "Department of Easy Virtue." An investigation showed that Daugherty was making money by allowing illegal alcohol to be taken from the federal bar and by expediting a claim through the Alien Property Bureau for a large price tag. On May 29, 1923, Smith returned to Washington and shot himself in the head. There are accounts that he was right-handed and the bullet entered his left temple, promoting arguments that he was murdered.

A Last-Gasp Effort

Harding went on a speaking tour across the country in the summer of 1923, called his "voyage of understanding." By the time he reached Kansas City, he met with Mrs. Albert Fall and probably got the scoop on the ugliest scandal yet to emerge: the Teapot Dome scandal. He had made it to Alaska—the first president to do so—but the scandals were already taking their toll on his health. He had a heart condition, and the constant touring and speaking made him sick. Harding took to bed rest in San Francisco, but he died of a possible embolism or a stroke on August 2, 1923. Thousands of mourners lined the tracks to watch the presidential funeral train on its way back to Washington, D.C and at the time of his death his national popularity was very high.

Harding died before he learned all the ins and outs of the Teapot Dome scandal, in which Secretary of the Interior Albert B. Fall accepted bribes of more than $400,000. Fall was given the gift of graft from two oil tycoons, E.L. Doheny and Harry F. Sinclair, in exchange for leasing naval oil reserves in Elk Hills in California and Teapot Dome in Wyoming. In 1929, Falls was convicted of bribery and was sentenced to prison. Harding may not have known what was taking place underfoot, but had become an unwilling accomplice when he signed an executive order that turned over control of the reserves from the Navy Department to the Department of the Interior and Mr. Fall. In big-money politics, apparently that's what friends are for.

First Family Factuals

Florence Harding wouldn't allow an autopsy of her husband, so an exact cause of death is unknown. Rumors began circulating that she, or someone else, might have poisoned Harding to keep him from testifying against his friends. The notion that Florence was responsible gained prominence in the book *The Strange Death of President Harding*, written by a convicted perjurer, Gaston Mean, in 1930.

Innocuous Beginnings

Ulysses S. Grant was born on April 27, 1822, in a two-room cabin in Point Pleasant, Ohio. His father was a successful tanner and farmer, and the Grants moved the family tanning business to Georgetown, Ohio, in 1823. "Lyss" attended local schools but didn't display an overly impressive scholarly aptitude. As a boy, however, he gained a reputation as a master horseman, and adults from all around the area would bring him their unruly horses to break to saddle. He even outrode the trick ponies that came through with the circus, once reportedly while getting scratched on the neck by a monkey that an angry ringmaster had thrown on him. At West Point, Grant set a high jump record on horseback that stood for 25 years.

Prez Says

Grant called the Mexican War "one of the most unjust ever waged by a stronger against a weaker nation. It was an instance of a republic following the bad example of European monarchies, in not considering justice in their desire to acquire additional territory."

—From Ulysses Grant's *Personal Memoirs*

Grant's father secured an appointment to the U.S. Military Academy at West Point. He was an average student, graduating 21 out of a class of 39, but he built relationships with many cadets who would become generals in the Civil War. Grant had no great desire to be a military man—he hoped for a job as a mathematics instructor at West Point, but he was assigned to the 4th Infantry and was sent to Jefferson Barracks, near St. Louis, Missouri. He served at various posts along the southwestern frontier, and in 1845 he joined the command of General Zachary Taylor and fought in the Mexican War. Grant learned military strategy from Taylor and then General Winfield Scott, and he earned two citations for bravery in combat, even though he was personally opposed to the war.

Commander in Chief Lore

Grant's given name was Hiram Ulysses, but a snafu somehow listed his name as Ulysses Simpson (his mother's maiden name) Grant when he enrolled at West Point. Grant liked the name and didn't say a word, in part because he hated the initials that had been on his trunk: H.U.G. Grant put the "U" in front because he didn't want to be known as "Hug," but the mix-up gave him a name he liked better and led to his West Point nicknames "Uncle Sam" and eventually "Sam."

After the Mexican War, Grant returned as a brevet captain to St. Louis and married Julia Dent, daughter of a wealthy, slave-owning planter, and the sister of a West Point classmate. He and Julia were very much in love throughout their life together, and he got very lonely when he was apart from her. Grant was assigned to posts in Detroit, Michigan, and Sackets Harbor, New York, but in 1852, he was transferred to the West Coast to Fort Vancouver in Oregon Territory. This was followed by time at Fort Humboldt in California.

Getting to the Bottom of the Bottle

Grant has long had a reputation as a rummy, a drunkard of whom Abraham Lincoln supposedly said, "I wish you would tell me the brand of whiskey that Grant drinks. I would like to send a barrel of it to my other generals" (Lincoln denied ever saying this). However, Grant's boozing has been, at the least, overblown and often totally fabricated. Other than a famous bender during the time of the Vicksburg campaign, Grant mostly abstained throughout the Civil War. In the last 20 years of his life, he almost never touched a drop, and there is only one credible story of public inebriation—at the Swing 'Round the Circle in 1866.

During the years 1852 to 1854, Grant did drink to excess with some regularity because of the extreme loneliness he felt being apart from his wife and children. He was morose and unhappy, failing in his attempts to raise extra money to bring his family out West. His behavior and attitude led to a forced resignation by his commanding officer. Grant's drinking was problematic from 1852 to 1854, but he seemed to have curbed his appetite for liquor, and the legends of him being a battlefield boozehound are mostly tall tales.

Nowhere to Go but Up

At the age of 32, Grant left the Army, reunited with his wife and family in St. Louis, and built a log cabin called "Hard Scrabble" on a plot of land given to the couple as a wedding gift by the bride's father. For four years, Grant gave farming his all, but he was a washout and sold the farm at auction in 1858. It got so bad that he had to pawn his watch one Christmas for money to buy his family presents. He then tried his hand at real estate in St. Louis, but he floundered at that as well. In 1860, he accepted a job working with his brothers as a clerk in a leather store they ran in Galena, Illinois. In April 1861, Lincoln called for volunteers to fight in the Civil War—fortunately for the flailing Grant, he reached astronomical heights in the blink of an eye.

Knowledge Is Power

The **Battle of Shiloh** in Southwestern Tennessee in 1862 was a major Confederate attack through the unfortified Union lines, and Grant was unprepared. The Union soldiers fought the Confederate soldiers in a bloody battle, and the casualty figures brought a cloud over Grant's sterling reputation. Phony rumors spread that he had been drunk and that his negligence caused the bloodiest conflict on American soil up to that point. Lincoln was pressured to drop Grant, but he defended him, saying, "I can't spare this man, he fights."

Civil War Hero

Grant quit working at the store, donned his musty uniform, and helped put together a company of volunteers from Galena. He wrote a letter to the Illinois governor and was hired to organize the state's voluntary regiments in Springfield. He whipped a defiant regiment into shape and successfully led them into combat against pro-Confederate rebels in Missouri.

On August 7, 1861, President Lincoln commissioned Grant brigadier general of volunteers, headquartered at Cairo, Illinois. His first major victory came in February 1862, when he captured Fort Henry and Fort Donelson in Tennessee, both Confederate posts guarding the Cumberland and Tennessee Rivers. Utilizing the country's original ironclad gunboats, Grant led the charge that saw the first two important Union successes, including the surrender of 14,000 soldiers at Donelson. Grant also uttered his famous declaration to a Confederate general who asked his terms of capitulation, responding, "No terms except an unconditional and immediate surrender can be accepted." Ulysses "Unconditional Surrender" Grant was promoted to major general of volunteers and rose to national prominence. But Grant's fortunes dipped just two months later at the *Battle of Shiloh.*

Vicksburg

In the fall of 1862, Grant began plotting the advance on the Confederate stronghold along the Mississippi River at Vicksburg, Mississippi. He tried a conventional advance, but the soldiers were repeatedly repulsed, and he had to devise a new strategy. Grant had a longstanding superstition about retracing his steps. He always wanted to go forward, so retreating and regrouping didn't appeal to him. Instead, he marched his army south of Vicksburg and moved eastward. It was a daring maneuver because Grant cut himself off from Northern supplies and communications, but it led to his capture of the capital city of Jackson on May 14.

After Jackson, Grant's army turned west toward Vicksburg, and he defeated the Confederate troops under the command of Lieutenant General John C. Pemberton. After the Confederates were forced back into Vicksburg, Grant isolated the city from reinforcements and supplies in a six-week siege. On July 4, 1863, Pemberton surrendered 30,000 men to Grant, at the same time as the Union victory at Gettsyburg, Pennsylvania. Grant had led a colossal Union triumph because it knocked out a large Confederate unit and gave the North control of the Mississippi River.

Supreme Commander

Grant became a hero throughout the North, and Lincoln made him major general in the regular army and gave him command of all Western armies. He then launched a counter-offensive with 60,000 troops to regain control of Chattanooga, Tennessee. After three days of fighting at the Battle of Chattanooga, the Confederate armies retreated, and Grant opened the way for an invasion of the deep South. On March 9, 1864, Grant was given the revived rank of lieutenant general, which had been previously bestowed only upon George Washington and Winfield Scott; then on March 12, Lincoln made him supreme commander of all Union forces. Grant organized the communications and developed a grand strategy for winning the Civil War. He ordered simultaneous attacks on the Confederate armies in hopes of forcing them to surrender through combat and a loss of supplies. He also planned to drive a stake through the heart of the Confederacy by having his Western commander, William Sherman, capture Atlanta.

Prez Says

"I have always regretted that the last assault at Cold Harbor was ever made. I might say the same thing of the assault of the 22nd of May, 1863, at Vicksburg. At Cold Harbor no advantage whatever was ever gained to compensate for the heavy loss we sustained."

—From Ulysses Grant's *Personal Memoirs*

In may-June 1864, Grant engaged Robert E. Lee in the Wilderness campaign (named because it took place in dense Virginia woodlands). The Union army suffered heavy casualties, 60,000 for the month and 7,000 on a single day of fighting at Cold Harbor on June 3. Grant was wearing down the enemy, but the massive losses sullied his reputation and earned him the nickname "the Butcher."

Grant Leads the Union Victory

Grant's armies entrenched Lee's armies in Petersburg, Virginia, and instituted a siege that lasted from June 1864 to April 1865. While Grant applied pressure and basically starved out Lee's men, Sherman and the other Union leaders successfully carried out their missions. Lee was forced to abandon Petersburg and Richmond in early April, but Grant cut him off and made it clear that further resistance was futile and could wipe out his entire army. On April 9, Lee surrendered to Grant at the village of Appomattox Court House, Virginia. Grant's terms were generous—he went so far as to share Union rations with the Confederate soldiers. Seventeen days later, Sherman accepted Confederate surrender, and the Civil War was over.

Grant was a hero, a man respected by soldiers and officers who had devised a winning military strategy but who was smart enough to adapt as combat situations dictated. Had his life ended here, he would be a 100 percent American icon, but the call to the White House damaged his historical legacy.

From Hero to Goat in Eight Short Years

Grant was on top of the world. The residents of Galena built him a house, Philadelphia gave him a mansion, and New York City gave him a gift of $105,000. In 1866, he became the second man (after George Washington) to be made a full general. He oversaw the demobilization of the army and helped administer and publicize President Andrew Johnson's Reconstruction acts, even though they weren't in total agreement. Johnson and Grant then had a falling out over the suspension of Secretary of War Edwin M. Stanton who was dismissed in February 1868. Grant filled in for Stanton, but when Congress failed to uphold the suspension, Grant resigned. Grant was abiding by the decision of the Senate, which fell under the Tenure of Office Act of 1867, which forbade the president from removing federal office holders without Senatorial approval. Johnson publicly accused him of bad faith, and Grant joined the Radical Republicans and supported the impeachment of the president. Although Grant was never political, his was the only name presented at the Republican Convention and was unanimously nominated on the first roll call.

Grant won the 1868 presidential election over Horatio Seymour of Indiana by an electoral count of 214 to 80. In seven years, Grant had gone from a store clerk to a war legend to the President of the United States.

Ulysses S. Grant, eighteenth president of the United States.

A Shaky Start

Grant was unsuited for the executive office, and his military brilliance didn't translate to political success. He approached the presidency like a troop, handing out orders to his trusted friends and exhibiting little understanding of how government works. Grant's trust in others would be his greatest undoing, but he hurt his own cause by giving federal positions to friends and family (40 members of the Grant clan were able to use the federal government to their benefit through jobs and access). He hired a pal from Galena, Major General John A. Rawlins, as secretary of war; a wealthy New Yorker who had lavished gifts on him, Alexander T. Stewart, as secretary of the treasury; and Adolf E. Borie, a Philadelphia native who had helped him buy a house as secretary of the navy. Stewart was rejected because of a big conflict of interests, and Borie quit because the job took up too much time. One notable appointment by Grant was Secretary of State Hamilton Fish and he made sound choices for Attorney General, Postmaster General and Secretary of the Interior.

Grant's Gaffs

Grant wanted to help enfranchise blacks in the South, but violent organizations such as the Ku Klux Klan had begun terrorizing blacks and keeping them from the polls.

Grant supported the Force Acts of 1870 to 1871, which made it a federal crime to interfere with civil rights and upheld the constitutional rights of all citizens to vote. He enforced the law with federal troops only once, though, in South Carolina, and a totally segregated South quickly became a reality. To be fair, Reconstruction hadn't worked, the Northern states were reticent to send troops into the South again, and this was a problem that demanded clear, visionary, political leadership, which wasn't Grant's forte. Grant did float an odd, naive plan to annex Santa Domingo (now the Dominican Republic) and send the former slaves there to start an all-black state. He thought it was one of his strongest ideas, but it was rebuffed by the Senate.

Grant also followed a standard conservative approach to economics and early on signed an act that pledged payment in gold or coin to those who owned government bonds, "greenbacks" that had been issued to finance the Civil War. The gold reserves were low, and the price of "greenbacks" dropped well below a $1 gold coin. The balance was shaken by one of the numerous scandals during the Grant administration, when two speculators, Jay Gould and James Fisk, started a sizable financial crisis. They attempted to corner the gold market by buying up a large chunk of the gold for sale on the New York City Gold Exchange and spreading the word that Grant wouldn't put reserves up for sale. When Grant got wind of the scheme, he acted decisively, putting $4 million in reserves up for sale and canning the lower officials who had been bribed. Still, the stock market came to halt on Black Friday, September 24, 1869, and the price of gold plummeted. Grant was widely blamed for the fiasco, even though he was unaware of the plan.

First Family Factuals

Julia Grant loved her time in the White House and wanted to keep on being First Lady for a third term. Grant, however, used military strategy to get out of running for president in 1876 by launching an offensive and sending a letter to the Republican Convention saying that he was finished before telling his wife. The sneak attack was effective, even if it ticked off his wife, because Ulysses knew that he wouldn't have been able to say no to Julia's wishes.

Grant's Gains

Grant did have a few moments of glory. The South *was* brought back into the Union, even if it was at the expense of African-Americans. He brought inflation under control as well, and the country weathered the Panic of 1873 even though it was lengthy and caused plenty of suffering. Fish also negotiated the Treaty of Washington with Great Britain in 1871, which solved the question of what to do about the damage caused by British-built ships such as the *Alabama,* used by the Confederacy in the Civil War. The $15.5 million settlement was awarded to the United States by international arbitration and helped strengthen ties between the United States and England.

Hero of Appomattox and His Unheroic Underlings

In 1872, Grant was re-elected by a substantial margin, 286 to 66 in the electoral tally, but it was not a productive four years. Scandals broke out one after another, and even though Grant was never implicated in any of them, the unethical members of his party and on his staff reflected poorly on him. Grant also remained loyal to many of those involved in dirty business instead of cleaning house, and this dampened his formerly regal prestige. The illegal stock-buying deal of the Credit Mobilier scandal saw his first vice president, Schuyler Colfax lose his job for alleged bribery from his Speaker of the House days and many Republicans were implicated in the scandal.

Grant's secretary of war, William Worth Belknap resigned after being impeached in the House for defrauding Indians and the government of a reported $100,000, and Grant's minister to Brazil, James Watson Webb, shook the Brazilian government down for the same fee. Although he was never convicted, Navy Secretary George Robeson pocketed more than $300 grand in shady contract deals, and Julia Grant's brother-in-law, James F. Casey, lined his pockets after corrupt handling of the New Orleans Customs House. Other scandals arose as well, but Grant stood by his friends—he even testified on behalf of his private secretary, Orville E. Babcock, who was tried as part of the Whiskey Ring that had swindled the government out of millions in liquor taxes. Grant's intercession saved Babcock from conviction, even though earlier he had said in regards to the Whiskey Ring "let no guilty man escape."

I'll Grant You That

➤ Ulysses S. Grant was always unsettled by the sight of blood and used to char his meat so that he wouldn't see bloody residue.

➤ Grant was a light smoker, but after his cigar-chomping victory at Donelson, he was sent thousands and began smoking up to 20 cigars a day, which probably contributed to his throat cancer.

➤ The Grants were supposed to attend the show at Ford's Theater with the Lincolns on the night of the assassination, but Julia didn't care for Mary Todd and so they went to Burlington, New Jersey, to see their kids instead.

➤ Grant wasn't dedicated to the long work day, to the delight of slackers everywhere—10 A.M. to 3 P.M. was good enough for him.

➤ Who's buried in Grant's Tomb? Ulysses and Julia, in New York City's Riverside Park overlooking the Hudson.

A Warm Welcome

The Grants set sail on a tour of the world, and he was treated like the hero of the Civil War. In 1880, the Republican Party pushed for his nomination for president, but he was deadlocked with James G. Blaine, and the convention went with a dark horse, James Garfield.

As par for his lifelong course, Grant had monetary troubles after he invested $100,000 in a New York City brokerage firm—the firm went belly up, and his partner was sent to prison. Grant even had to sell his military memorabilia, and an attempt by supporters to have him restored to the rank of general, which he had turned down in order to run for the presidency, met political opposition and was not approved until 1885.

By that time, Grant was afflicted with throat cancer. He moved to Mount McGregor, near Sarasota Springs, New York, for his health and diligently wrote down his recollections of the war to provide financial stability for his family. Mark Twain published his *Personal Memoirs* at an unprecedented 75 percent of all domestic sales for the Grants, and it eventually paid Julia nearly half a million dollars. Grant died on July 23, 1885, a week after he finished the book, which has become one of the finest war commentaries ever written.

Getting Fried with a Little Help from Their Friends

Harding and Grant usually rank No. 1 and No. 2 at the bottom of the list of the men who have served as President of the United States. Whether that is fair is always open for debate, but both men would probably agree with Harding's summation of life in the White House: "My God, this is a hell of a job! I have no trouble with my enemies, but my damn friends, they're the ones that keep me walking the floor nights."

The Least You Need to Know

➤ Warren Harding was elected by a considerable margin as a conservative answer to the progressive years of Woodrow Wilson.

➤ Harding was undone by his corrupt cronies, with the most egregious example being the Teapot Dome scandal.

➤ Ulysses S. Grant was a great Civil War leader, successfully orchestrating the victory at Vicksburg and accepting the surrender of Robert E. Lee.

➤ Grant was also undone by scandals, and he and Harding are generally ranked at the bottom of the list of Presidents of the United States.

Chapter 26

Trouble at the Top: Andrew Johnson and Richard Nixon

In This Chapter

➤ Making suits and passing laws

➤ Avoiding impeachment by the slightest of margins

➤ Nixon's campaign theme: "Better Dead Than Red"

➤ The plumbers bring down the White House

Andrew Johnson and Richard Nixon left the White House in much worse shape than when they entered it. Johnson's failed Reconstruction programs and his questionable near-impeachment set the country on course for a century of segregation, and it almost cost him his job. Nixon called it quits when it came to light that he was using the Constitution of the United States like a dishrag, and he left Washington, D.C., in a state of disgrace unmatched by any other executive leader in American history.

The Tailor's Apprentice

Andrew Johnson was born into abject poverty in Raleigh, North Carolina, in 1808. Johnson was only three when his father died after saving a friend from drowning. His mother, Mary McDonough Johnson, began washing and weaving clothes in their tiny cottage to support the family. She remarried, but the family's financial picture never improved, and they had no money for the four Johnson boys to get a private education (public schools did not yet exist). At the age of 14, Johnson was apprenticed to a tailor so that he could learn a trade and bring in extra cash for the family.

Johnson became the only President of the United States who never spent a day in formal schooling. His education began as a tailor's apprentice as he sat and stitched, listening to local citizens who came to read to the men as they sewed. Johnson frequently borrowed their books and gradually taught himself to read and write, exhibiting an independent determination that would be one of the hallmarks of his political career. Johnson fled to Laurens, South Carolina after seeing his name in print in connection with a childhood prank (throwing rocks and wood at someone's home).

Johnson returned to Raleigh and tried to get out of his indenture, but he was denied. He then convinced his family to head westward to start a new life. They packed up their meager possessions in a two-wheel cart pulled by a blind pony and moved to Greeneville, Tennessee. The town didn't have a tailor, so Johnson became Greeneville's new tailor. In 1827, he nailed a sign above a small shop that simply stated, "A. Johnson, Tailor."

The tailor shop turned into a successful business in a relatively short amount of time, and it became a center of local political bull sessions. Johnson's zeal for learning hadn't subsided, and he joined a debate society at a local college. Every Friday night, Johnson would walk four miles to engage in political, philosophical, and theoretical deliberations with the students. Johnson's business also brought him into contact with affluent customers and other artisans, known as "mechanics."

Johnson was a tailor during the time of Andrew Jackson, and in 1828, the local Greeneville tradesman supported Johnson's run for alderman. In 1834, the same supporters of the fledgling Democratic Party elected him mayor. Johnson basically followed the standard Jacksonian platform and got a reputation as a fiery orator and a skilled debater. These qualities helped him speak his mind, but they also marked an intense stubbornness that rendered compromise a dirty word and put those who dared disagree with him in enemy camps.

First Family Factuals

In 1827, 18-year-old Johnson married 16-year-old Eliza McCardle. She, too, came from humble roots: Her father had been a shoemaker, and when he died, her mother took to making quilts to support them both. Eliza had spent some time in a private academy, so she helped her husband improve his reading and writing and also taught him arithmetic. She continued the tradition of reading to Andrew while he worked, and the happy couple's marriage lasted until his death in 1875.

Union, Yes!

Johnson continued his rise up the political ladder when he was elected to the state legislator in 1835; he served until 1837 and then returned to serve from 1839 to 1841. He became known as a champion of the working man, and a deep-seated prejudice against aristocrats shaped his political agendas. In 1841, Johnson was elected to the state senate in Tennessee and angered slave owners by futilely trying to abolish a law that gave them enhanced representation.

In 1843, he was elected to the first of his five terms as a member of the U.S. House of Representatives. Johnson supported the Jacksonian belief that the Constitution took precedence over everything—states' rights included—and this often put him at odds with other Southern legislators. In the House, he was successful in passing a homestead bill that gave 160 acres of public property to any family who cultivated the land for five years, but it failed in the Senate until 1862. He voted against the tariff and "extravagant" expenditures such as the Smithsonian, and he supported the Mexican War and the Compromise of 1850.

The Whig legislature *gerrymandered* Johnson out of federal office, but it didn't slow him down: He simply returned to Tennessee and won the gubernatorial election in 1853.

Johnson served two terms as governor and encouraged the legislature to pass a tax that supported Tennessee's first public school system, set up a public library, and oversaw the founding of a state board of agriculture.

Knowledge Is Power

Gerrymandering is the restructuring of electoral districts to give the majority political party an advantage in a larger percentage of districts, while concentrating the minority party base in fewer districts. The term dates back to 1812, when a bill was signed by Massachusetts Democratic-Republican Governor Elbridge Gerry, who gerrymandered districts to gain an advantage over the Federalists.

To the Upper Chamber and Beyond

In 1857, the Tennessee legislature elected Johnson to the U.S. Senate, which prompted his response, "I have reached the summit of my ambition." In 1860, Johnson's name was kicked around as a possible Democratic nominee for the upcoming election, but the party split behind two candidates, Senator Stephen A. Douglas and Vice President John Breckinridge.

Up until this point, Johnson had basically followed the standard Southern positions on the slavery issue, including the vile Fugitive Slave Law, but not enthusiastically because his district had few slave owners (Johnson being a notable exception). The slavery debate and potential secession were the primary topics of the day, and Johnson supported the proslavery Southern candidate Breckinridge. His true stance, however, was the preservation of the Union, and he spoke out against both secessionists and abolitionists. He reportedly said, "When the crisis comes, I will be found standing by the Union."

First Family Factuals

In April 1862, Jefferson Davis imposed martial law upon Eastern Tennessee and gave the Northern supporters 36 hours to leave. Eliza was sick, so she was allowed to stay, but the Johnson household was commandeered, and she and her eight-year-old son had to seek refuge with a relative. In September, she was given permission to cross rebel lines to be with Andrew. It took her weeks to reach Nashville, and by the time she got there, she was suffering from illness and extreme exhaustion.

Johnson was the only Southerner in Congress to denounce secession, and he proudly proclaimed his Jacksonian views from the floor of the Senate two days before South Carolina left the Union. Johnson was the only Southern senator to remain in Washington, D.C., even after his home state of Tennessee joined the Confederacy. President Lincoln named Johnson military governor of Tennessee with the rank of brigadier general of volunteers after Union troops seized the central and Western regions in March 1862. The state's loyalties were still split, however, and Confederate troops would not be quelled for two more years. Lincoln envisioned Johnson setting up a pro-Union civilian government, but he wasn't able to accomplish the tough task until 1864.

A National Tragedy Elevates Johnson

Along with most of the North, Lincoln was now in Johnson's corner, and the delegates selected him to be vice president in 1864. The National Union Convention balanced the Northern Republican Lincoln with a Southern "War Democrat," and they defeated General George McClellan by a considerable margin.

Commander in Chief Lore

On the night of Lincoln's assassination, Johnson was also supposed to be killed at the hands of Booth associate George Atzerodt. Atzerodt rented a room right above the vice president at the Kirkwood House, a hotel on Pennsylvania Avenue, but after stalking the vice president, he chickened out and got drunk instead. Atzerodt was hanged along with three other coconspirators in the assassination plot. Johnson was awakened with the news that Lincoln had been shot and quickly went to his bedside to see for himself that the president was not going to recover.

Johnson contracted typhoid fever near the end of the campaign and was feeling ill the night before the inauguration, but he still reportedly celebrated with a hefty dose of booze. The next morning he was shaky, so he calmed his nerves with a few whiskey eye-openers. He then delivered a babbling, rambling, semi-incoherent speech that embarrassed himself and his friends and tagged him as an alcoholic in opposition circles. Lincoln stood by Johnson and said, "I have known Andy Johnson for many years; Andy ain't a drunkard." Six weeks later, Lincoln was shot dead and Johnson became president.

Johnson retained all of Lincoln's Cabinet, even Secretary of State William Seward, who had been knifed in his bed during the ugly night of April 14, 1865.

"Seward's Folly" Is America's Gain

Johnson's presidency was a failure through and through, but he did have a couple foreign policy successes during his truculent years in the White House. Seward scored a major coup by purchasing Alaska from the Russians for a cool $7.2 million. At the time, the purchase was mocked as "Seward's Folly," or (even better) "Seward's Icebox," but no one was laughing when the beautiful "Last Frontier" brought Americans oil, gold, and pristine wildlife.

Seward also used the Monroe Doctrine to remove European influence from the Western Hemisphere. During the Civil War, French Emperor Napoleon III sent troops to Mexico and set up Austrian archduke Maximilian as the Mexican "Emperor." Johnson approved Seward's plan to apply pressure by sending 50,000 soldiers to the border. The threat did the trick—the French troops pulled out, but the French government abandoned Maximilian and he was court-martialed and shot by the Mexican republicans.

Andrew Johnson, seventeenth president of the United States.

The Radical Case for Johnson's Impeachment

Johnson's administration was defined by a single issue: Reconstruction. Johnson favored a mild reconstruction of the Confederate states and believed that a handful of aristocratic Southerners had been behind secession. His plan to rebuild the South was lenient toward rebel soldiers and basically ignored the concerns of the newly freed slaves. He offered amnesty to all who would take an oath of allegiance to the Union, except for the wealthiest plantation elite and Confederate leaders. After a scant 10 percent of a particular state voting population had taken the oath, a state government could be elected solely by whites. All Johnson demanded was that the states abolish slavery, repudiate Confederate debt, ratify the thirteenth amendment, and disavow secession ordinances. Johnson didn't address black suffrage, however, and felt that voting practices should be left up to the individual states. Once the state met his requirements, they would be allowed to rejoin the Union and resume congressional representation.

The South Is Reconstructed with the Same Blueprints

Johnson's Reconstruction was based, like Lincoln's, upon the theory that the Confederacy was never officially recognized, so a few small changes rather than fundamental shifts were all that was needed to restore the Union. Although Lincoln had pursued a conciliatory policy toward the South, he understood Northern anger at what the Confederacy had wrought, and it is hard to imagine him following such a weak and doomed course of action.

Lincoln was also a humanitarian and didn't share Johnson's unabashedly bigoted views, which included a reference to the "barbarism" of blacks in his 1867 address to Congress. Johnson had no respect for African Americans and did nothing as Black Codes were instituted. The Codes restricted the kinds of jobs blacks could hold, barred them from owning land, and allowed for them to be arrested, fined, or rented to whites if they were "unemployed" (which meant if they didn't sign labor contracts with their former masters). It was basically business as usual for the South—in fact, the Black Codes were written in such a way that an amended form of slavery existed if African Americans didn't abide by the new rules of the South.

Needless to say, Johnson's Reconstruction efforts didn't sit well with the Republican congressional leaders who favored a radical reconstruction. His policies were welcomed in the South, where many had feared severe punishment, but Southerners simply were able to re-elect the elite old guard, not the working-class artisans that Johnson had expected. The Radical Republicans were furious and correctly assumed that the freedmen's constitutional rights would not be recognized, although this should have been mandatory for readmittance to the Union.

Running Afoul of the Radicals

The Radical Republicans entrenched themselves for a long, bitter battle with Johnson. The Civil Rights Act of 1866, which granted citizenship to all former slaves and voided the black codes, was passed, becoming the first bill to ever override a presidential veto. Its protection of blacks was incorporated into the Constitution with the fourteenth amendment, which was ratified in 1868. Congress also overrode his veto passing the Freedmen's Bureau Act (which extended the life of the bureau that assisted the former slaves politically, educationally, and proprietarily) and the District of Columbia Suffrage Act franchising residents of the nation's capital.

Johnson now viewed those who opposed him in Congress, whether radical or moderate, as the enemy. He went on a speaking tour, hoping to connect with the masses in the East and the Midwest, but the "swing around the circle" was a dismal failure. Hecklers provoked his hot temper, rumors circulated that he was an alcoholic and was unsuited for the presidency, and bloody violence arose at the hands of the Ku Klux Klan—all this hurt his cause. The Radical Republicans added congressional seats in the 1866 election and passed the Military Reconstruction Acts of 1867, which instituted military rule over civilian rule in the South until the region enfranchised blacks and ratified the fourteenth amendment.

The Radical Republicans passed the Tenure of Office Act in 1867, which banned the president from dismissing any federal officials without Senate approval. During the break in session, Johnson removed his secretary of War, and Radical supporter Edwin M. Stanton, and appointed Ulysses S. Grant, who turned the office back over to Stanton after a few months. Stanton was again removed by Johnson, who ignored the action by barricading himself in the War Department office with armed guards on February 28, 1868.

"High Crimes and Misdemeanors"

Three days after Stanton's defiance of Johnson's attempt at removing him, a resolution of impeachment was passed in the House of Representatives. The Constitution states that any President of the United States can be impeached and convicted of "treason, bribery, or high crimes and misdemeanors." The House of Representatives plays the role of prosecutor, and the Senate plays the role of judge. The committee had seven Radicals on it, and they voted to impeach Johnson on 11 counts, most of which centered upon the violation of the Tenure of Office Act. The Senate trial was presided over by Chief Justice Salmon P. Chase.

Although the Radical Republicans were voting to impeach because Johnson opposed their politics

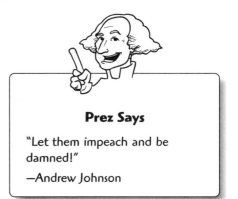

Prez Says

"Let them impeach and be damned!"

—Andrew Johnson

(opponents would claim that they mainly wanted a black voting base in the South), they were still on the right side of the American dictum that "all men are created equal." The impeachment trial was very close on all three counts—one vote kept the conviction of the mandatory two-thirds majority at bay. Republican Senator Edwin Ross was the final "not guilty" vote, which he had kept a secret until the moment of decision, and he made the final tally 35 to 19 to the first vote on the eleventh article of impeachment, which was a catch-all item that included much of what was in the other 10 articles. Johnson was acquitted by a single vote, after seven Republicans voted with the Democrats. Ten days later, Johnson was acquitted of two other articles of impeachment by the same tally and the rest of the articles were never brought to a vote. Johnson and the Radical Republicans remained deadlocked throughout his administration, so he served out his years in the White House passively.

The Real Deal on Andrew Johnson

➤ As Governor, Andrew Johnson made a suit for the governor of Kentucky, a former blacksmith, and was given a shovel and tongs in exchange.

➤ Johnson was once dragged out of a train by pro-Southerners in Lynchburg, Virginia, who kicked and spit on him, but let him go before living up to their town's name.

➤ An unfounded and unbelievable charge made by the Radical Republicans during the time of impeachment was that Johnson had played a part in Lincoln's assassination.

➤ Johnson was the last president to skip his successor's inauguration.

Johnson hoped to be the Democratic nominee in 1868, but it was not to be. He blasted the Republican Congress for unconstitutional practices, and he turned out to be right on one count: The Supreme Court overturned the Tenure of Office Act in 1926. He returned to Tennessee and felt vindicated in 1874 when he became the only former president elected to the U.S. Senate. He took his congressional seat on March 5, 1875, but he suffered a stroke and died in July of the same year while visiting his daughter in Tennessee.

Sewn from Quaker Oats

Richard Milhous Nixon was born in 1913 on a lemon farm in Yorba Linda, California. His mother, Hannah, was a devout, gentle Quaker, and Nixon eventually enrolled at Whittier College, a Quaker institution. At the age of 9, the Nixons moved to Whittier, California, where his father opened a gas station/general store. Richard and his older brother, Harold, worked at the store whenever they weren't in class. Harold died from tuberculosis, ending one of the only close relationships Nixon had throughout his life and the disease would also claim the life of younger brother Arthur.

After Whittier, Nixon received a scholarship to Duke University and graduated third in his class in 1937. Nixon spent most of his time there immersed in his studies and was not as active in campus politics as he had been at Whittier, although he was elected president of his graduating class. He returned to Whittier to be a small-town lawyer after his goal of getting a job with the Federal Bureau of Investigation was shot down.

Pat and Nixon were married on June 21, 1940, and they drove down to Mexico in a car filled with canned food for their honeymoon. After the outbreak of World War II, Nixon went to Washington, D.C., and worked in the tire-rationing section of the Office of Price Administration. He later said that this eight-month job soured him to the federal bureaucracy. In 1942, much to the chagrin of his mother, he broke from Quaker teachings and received a navy commission as a lieutenant. He was assigned to the Naval Air Transport Command and spent the war years in the South Pacific; he left in 1946 with rank of lieutenant commander.

First Family Factuals

Nixon auditioned for a local theater company after seeing the beautiful new teacher in town, Thelma Catherine Ryan, known as "Pat" because she was born late on the eve of St. Patrick's Day. Never suave, Nixon told her that he wanted to marry her upon their first meeting. Pat wasn't overly impressed with Nixon at first, however. Nixon was dogged in his effort, and he even drove her to Los Angeles for dates with other men, killed time until her evening was over, and drove her back home.

An Anti-Communist Crusader Is Born

Nixon was persuaded by California Republicans to campaign against Democrat Jerry Voorhis in the Twelfth Congressional District. Nixon crafted the aggressive take-no-prisoners campaign style that would become a benchmark of all his political races. He bluntly aligned the New Deal Democrat Voorhis with Communists because he felt that he had to do this to win, even though the charges were built on shaky connections. Nixon had no record to speak of, so Voorhis became defensive and lost the election, and Nixon entered the House of Representatives in 1947 along with the first Republican majority since the Hoover administration.

Nixon went to Europe as part of the Herter Committee to study the post-World War II economies. The bipartisan group supported the Marshall Plan, and foreign aid would become part of his later policies.

The most plum freshmen assignment Nixon received was on the House Un-American Activities Committee, which was designed to root out Communists in the government, the entertainment industry, schools, and other areas of American life. Testifying before this committee, *Time* magazine editor Whittaker Chambers named Alger Hiss, former state department official and secretary general of the UN charter meeting, as one who was actively involved in prewar Communist circles in Washington. Nixon relentlessly pursued the case, even as Hiss repeatedly denied any involvement in Communism. Nixon kept the heat on, even though President Truman himself dismissed the case against Hiss. Eventually, after much legal wrangling, Hiss was convicted on a perjury charge, and the biggest winner was Nixon. He now had a national reputation as an ardent enemy of Communism during a time when the Cold War took center stage in American life.

Commander in Chief Lore

Nixon was given a seat on the Education and Labor Committee along with another congressional rookie, John F. Kennedy. The Taft–Hartley Bill was the committee's centerpiece, and years before the renowned television debates, Nixon and Kennedy bantered over the merits of the bill in a public forum in McKeesport, Pennsylvania. Nixon said, "I had the better of the argument because most of those present, as employers, tended to be on my side in the first place."

Nixon parlayed his success into a United States Senate seat in 1950. He ran against popular liberal Democrat Helen Gahagan Douglas and used the same tactics that had helped elevate his career. As the Soviets extended the Iron Curtain in Europe and Joe McCarthy red-baited in the United States, Nixon painted Douglas as a Communist sympathizer. He passed out "pink sheets" listing her votes with New York Vito Marcantonio, a Communist. Nixon neglected to list all the other names who had voted with Marcantonio on bills that had easily passed, but it worked. Despite criticism of Nixon's questioning of the "pink lady's" loyalty to the United States, he won the election by nearly 700,000 votes.

Playing Checkers for Eisenhower

Nixon toured the country making speeches to local Republican organizations in 1951, and his popularity kept growing. General Dwight Eisenhower received the Republican nomination in 1952 and asked Nixon to be his running mate. At the age of 39, Nixon was on a ticket with one of the most beloved and admired men in the country, but it almost unraveled right off the bat.

The (then) liberal *New York Post* ran a front-page story accusing Nixon of having a personal slush fund that had been set up by wealthy Californians who would presumably expect favors. Eisenhower wanted a clean, moral administration, and instantly politicians (even a few Republicans) demanded that Nixon be dropped from the ticket. In reality, the fund was strictly for political purposes, and there was no evidence of financial improprieties by Nixon. Still, the rumors had done damage, and Eisenhower had a decision to make. Nixon decided to defend himself on national television, and 55 million viewers, the largest audience up to that date, tuned in on September 23, 1952 to hear what became known as the Checkers speech. Nixon announced his innocence and gave full disclosure of his and Pat's nominal assets. He also added a brief note about one gift that the Nixon family had accepted—a dog.

Nixon encouraged viewers to let the Republican Party know what their thoughts on Nixon's status should be, and he left the studio thinking that he had flopped. He was wrong. The speech hit a chord with the public, and overwhelming support poured in for Nixon. Eisenhower kept him on the ticket, and they coasted to wins in both the 1952 and the 1956 presidential elections. Richard Nixon had been in politics for a whopping six years before he became vice president of the United States.

Prez Says

"One thing I should tell you .... We did get something, a gift .... It was a little cocker spaniel dog, in a crate that had been sent all the way from Texas—black and white, spotted, and our little girl, Tricia, the six-year-old named it Checkers. And you know, the kids love that dog and I just want to say this right now, that regardless of what they say about it, we are going to keep it."

—From the "Checkers" speech by Richard Nixon, September 23, 1952

Keeping Busy in Times of Peace

The vice presidential office has never offered a plethora of activity for its inhabitants. Coupling the detached Eisenhower Era with the relatively stress-free 1950s didn't leave Nixon a lot of options for growth, but he expanded his duties and played a greater role than his predecessors. He traveled to more than 50 countries as an emissary, visiting Moscow in 1959 and ending up in a debate of the merits of democracy and communism with Nikita Khruschev on television, which is known as the Kitchen Debate because it was held in a display of an "American house."

Nixon was the front-runner for the Republican nomination in 1960, and he received all but 10 of the delegates' votes on the first ballot at the Chicago convention. His opponent was John F. Kennedy, and the television era changed the landscape. The two candidates squared off in a series of four debates that helped spread Kennedy's telegenic personality in areas of the country where he wasn't well-known. Nixon regretted his decision to eschew makeup—his mother called to see if he was "feeling all right." The young, good-looking, vibrant Kennedy was made for television, however, and the debates were key to his victory. It was a very close election—around 112,800 popular votes, one tenth of 1 percent of the total, separated the two men. There was solid evidence of fraud in both Texas and Illinois, but in a classy move on Nixon's part, he didn't ask for a recount and conceded the election—he even sent Kennedy his regards.

Commander in Chief Lore

In spring 1958, Nixon was on a tour of South America, which turned ugly. In Caracas, Venezuela. rock-throwing, Communist-led protesters pelted the cars carrying the vice president and his aides near the Caracas airport and tried to turn over his car. Mobs in Lima, Peru spat on Nixon, but his cool demeanor in the face of danger earned him points for courage when he returned to the United States and helped his political career down the line.

Nixon went back to California and wrote a book about his career, called *Six Crises*, and joined a Los Angeles law firm. In 1962, he ran for governor of California, but this time anti-Communist rhetoric wasn't enough. He lost the gubernatorial race and blamed the media. In an angry tirade, he gave the press a tongue-lashing that ended with this pronouncement, "You won't have Nixon to kick around anymore, because, gentlemen, this is my last press conference." It appeared as if the political career of Richard Nixon was over.

Back from the Dead

Nixon moved to New York City and joined a successful law firm, but he continued to campaign for Republican candidates in 1964 and 1966. He re-established his congressional connections and quickly became a favored candidate, representing a middle-of-the-road conservatism popular amongst the rank and file, particularly in the emerging Sun Belt. Nixon dominated the primaries and won the nomination on the first ballot at the convention in Miami. He selected Spiro Agnew, the governor of Maryland, as his running mate. Nixon put himself to the right of the liberal

Democrats and their candidate, Hubert Humphrey, and to the left of the radical American Independent Party and their nominee, George Wallace. The strategy worked: Nixon won 32 states and 301 electoral votes en route to the presidency.

Richard M. Nixon, thirty-seventh president of the United States on the 1968 campaign trail.

(Photo courtesy of the Richard M. Nixon Library)

The Vietnam War Rages On

The most pressing issue facing the nation in 1968 was the Vietnam War, which Nixon had basically sidestepped in the campaign, besides making simple overtures that he would bring U.S. soldiers home. He gradually withdrew troops, reducing the number from 550,000 in 1969 to around 30,000 in 1972.

Nixon's "Vietnamization" plan increased the responsibilities and training of the South Vietnamese army while reducing the number of American troops. Nixon also expanded the Vietnam War into Cambodia in 1970 by authorizing an attack on Communist troops in the country. Protests in the United States intensified, which led to the nightmarish shooting and killing of four unarmed student protesters on the campus of Kent State University in May 1970. Congressional opposition to the expansion into Cambodia also escalated on the grounds that it was unconstitutional. Only Congress has the power to declare war on another country, so congressmen passed a measure that cut off all funds and combat troops in Cambodia. In 1973, a Senate investigation reinvigorated the Cambodian controversy when it was discovered that secret bombing raids had targeted Cambodia

Prez Says

"I would rather be a one-term President and do what I believe is right than to be a two-term President at the cost of seeing America become a second-rate power and to see this Nation accept the first defeat in its proud 190-year history."

—From a speech by Richard Nixon on April 30, 1970

as early as 1969 without the approval of Congress (or the American citizenry). In 1971, the United States also began providing air and artillery assistance in a South Vietnamese invasion of Laos.

In May 1972, Nixon reordered air strikes against Hanoi and the mining of the Haiphong Harbor, which had been temporarily halted. Peace negotiations between Assistant for National Security Affairs Henry Kissinger and North Vietnamese negotiator Le Duc Tho went nowhere, and the most intensive two-week bombing campaign of all, known as the "Christmas Blitz," began in December.

Peace talks resumed in Paris, and Nixon called off the bombing. A cease-fire was signed and went into effect on January 23, 1973. The agreement provided for the withdrawal of the 25,000 remaining American troops from South Vietnam in the next 60 days and attempted to build a framework for the Vietnamese factions to work toward reconciliation. However, the North and the South soon began fighting again. Nixon also secured the release of nearly 600 U.S. prisoners of war, and the bombing of Cambodia ended in August 1973. Nixon had followed through on his promise of bringing about the "era of peace," and his popularity was at its pinnacle, even though more than 20,000 extra American soldiers had died between 1969 and 1973. It could have been a major sigh of relief for the United States, but a new domestic controversy soon reared its ugly head.

China, Russia, and the Middle East

A major highlight of the Nixon administration was an improvement in U.S. relationships with China and the Soviet Union. Nixon flew to Communist China in February 1972, a trip that was broadcast back to the United States and that gave many citizens their first glimpse behind the "Bamboo Curtain." The trip was a success, and relations were improved in terms of trade and culture. The trip came after the United States withdrew its objection to the inclusion of the People's Republic of China in the United Nations in August 1971. China was admitted to the United Nations that October. In May 1972, Nixon made a visit to Moscow, where he completed talks that had begun three years earlier and signed a number of treaties. The treaties between the Americans and the Soviets limited strategic nuclear weapons, opened up trade, improved environmental protection, and outlined steps to ensure a peaceful co-existence. Nixon addressed the Russian people on television and said, "We shall sometimes be competitors, but we need never be enemies." Russian Premiere Leonid Brezhnev returned the favor and came to the United States for another round of summit meetings and signed, among other things, a nuclear nonaggression pact. Relations between the two superpowers were generally improved during the Nixon administration, and the Strategic Arms Limitation Treaty (SALT) was a significant first step toward arms reduction.

A fourth war between select Arab states and Israel broke out in October 1973, and pressure to end the fighting came from both the United States and the Soviet Union. Kissinger intervened and averted a potentially ugly situation. Nixon received a warm reception when he visited the Middle East in 1974.

Domestic Concerns (Minus the Big One)

Nixon followed a relatively conservative domestic agenda. In 1969, the Supreme Court demanded that schools be desegregated immediately, but Nixon asked for the institution of busing at the minimum allowed by law. Recession set in early in Nixon's first term, and inflation and unemployment were both on the upswing. The president raised interest rates and reduced government spending to try to lower prices, but the measures had little effect. In 1971, Nixon reversed his course and announced a new policy that controlled prices and wages, reduced the number of federal employees, and devalued the dollar by suspending the convertibility of foreign-held dollars into gold. Throughout 1972, the economy improved, but inflation would be a problem for the duration of his time in the White House.

Nixon pushed a broad conservationist program, which included a billion-dollar effort to clean up the nation's lakes and rivers, the establishment of federal clean air standards and an act that encouraged recycling. He also ended the draft and steered anti-crime measures that were largely ineffective. Nixon made good on his promise to add conservative judges to the Supreme Court, such as Warren E. Burger, of Minnesota, Lewis F. Powell Jr., of Virginia, and William H. Rehnquist, of Arizona. He regretted appointing Harry A. Blackmun, a conservative who would do a 180-degree turn and become a liberal justice; Blackmun even wrote the majority opinion in the monumental *Roe* v. *Wade* case in 1972.

Tricky Dick Trivia

➤ Richard Nixon was the first president to visit all 50 states.

➤ Nixon was the first president-elect to wait eight years between losing an election and winning the White House, and the first to defeat a different opponent than the one who previously had defeated him.

➤ Nixon had a swimming pool outside the White House filled in to provide more room for journalists (Ford dug up a new pool).

➤ President Nixon spoke to astronauts Neil Armstrong and Edwin "Buzz" Aldrin after they became the first men to land on the moon, saying, "For one priceless moment in the whole history of man, all the people on this earth are truly one ...."

➤ In June 1970, Nixon signed into law an act that lowered the voting age from 21 to 18; the act was ratified by the states the following year and became the twenty-sixth amendment to the Constitution.

Watergate Breaks; Nixon Resigns

The worst presidential mess the United States has ever dealt with began slowly but accelerated as the foundation of the White House increasingly crumbled throughout 1972 through 1974 . Nixon had a commanding lead in the 1972 election and could lay claim to the fact that international relations were improving and that the economy was turning the corner. Kissinger also boasted that peace was at hand with the Vietnam War, even though there was no cease-fire yet. The Democratic Party was still in the state of upheaval that had started with President Johnson's retirement and the assassination of Robert Kennedy. Still, Nixon's imminent paranoia kept him on edge, and he wanted to ensure a victory. He set up a campaign organization, called the Committee to Re-elect the President (aptly called CREEP). In June 1972, five burglars were arrested after a break-in at the Democratic National Committee offices at the Watergate complex in Washington, D.C. The burglars, who had brought bugging equipment into the DNC offices, were "plumbers" working for CREEP. One of the men turned out to be James W. McCord, a former CIA agent and the security chief of CREEP.

The term "plumbers" referred to the men in CREEP whose role was to plug any "leaks" in light of the publishing of the "Pentagon Papers" in *The New York Times* and other newspapers. The "Pentagon Papers" were documents that detailed governmental fraudulence in the policies regarding Vietnam, beginning in the Truman administration. They were provided by Daniel Ellsberg, a former Department of Defense researcher who had worked on the exhaustive report and was now opposed to the Vietnam War. The "Pentagon Papers" showed a pattern of deception on the part of the American Presidents and became a rallying point for the anti-war movement. Ellsberg was indicted on conspiracy and espionage charges for taking the documents. The charges were dismissed when it was discovered that the "plumbers" had placed illegal wiretaps on Ellseberg's telephone and broken into the office of his psychiatrist looking for information they could use to smear his reputation.

Coverup and Investigations

After the arrest at the Watergate, a coverup began, even though the general public wasn't initially interested and Nixon's White House Press Secretary Ronald Ziegler famously called it a "third-rate burglary attempt." Behind the scenes, though, pressure was mounting. Hush money payments were made, and it was revealed in August that more than $100,000 in deposited Nixon campaign checks had been discovered in the bank account of one of the burglars.

Two *Washington Post* reporters, Bob Woodward and Carl Bernstein, kept the heat on in their investigative reports, and it became clear that the coverup reached high levels of the oval office. A Senate committee on Watergate was convened in February 1973, chaired by North Carolina's Sam Ervin, and an investigation was led by Archibald Cox. Testimony from members of Nixon's inner circle led to the embarrassing resignations of all but one of his top officials, including White House Chief of Staff H. R.

Haldeman, White House Special Assistant John Ehrlichman, and Attorney General Richard Kleindienst.

The hearings and investigations detailed numerous scandals, and disturbing revelations became an almost daily event. The clandestine illegalities included a large cash contribution to CREEP by a financier under SEC investigation, the use of federal cash for improvements to Nixon's estates in California and Florida, an attempt by Nixon to evade paying taxes by falsifying details of a gift of vice presidential papers to federal archives, and Nixon's attempt to keep the FBI from investigating the Watergate break-in. And, as if Nixon didn't have enough headaches, Vice President Spiro Agnew was forced out of office after it was revealed that he had taken bribes of more than $100,000 as governor of Maryland in return for favorable construction contracts, but he was able to plea bargain and was ultimately convicted of tax evasion.

Commander in Chief Lore

Another Watergate-era revelation that came out was that the Nixon administration had an "Enemies List" that was written up to "use the available federal machinery to screw our political enemies," according to a White House memo. The list included: African-American Representative John Conyers of Michigan who had a "weakness for white females," Bill Cosby, Paul Newman, Jane Fonda, Tony Randall, CBS newsman Daniel Schorr, a host of academics, McGovern supporters, journalists, businessmen, liberals, and upwards of 200 other prominent American citizens with whom the administration hoped to get even with in due time.

Caught on Tape

As the Senate hearings moved forward, the question "What did the president know and when did he know it?" became the centerpiece. On June 25, 1973, fired White House Counsel John Dean implicated the president in the coverup. On July 16, White House aide Alexander Butterfield said that an oval office taping system had been installed at Nixon's request. Nixon stonewalled the release of the tapes under executive privilege, which cast a major shadow over his presidency. Calls began to be made for his resignation or impeachment.

On October 20, Nixon ordered Archibald Cox to cease his attempts to subpoena the tapes; when Cox refused, Nixon ordered acting Attorney General Elliot Richardson to fire him. Richardson resigned in protest, and the "Saturday Night Massacre" convinced many previous Nixon supporters that he had something to hide. House Democrats then took up an inquiry into impeachment.

Nixon released some tapes, but they were edited, and one tape had an 18½-minute void that sound experts concluded had been purposely erased. In June 1974, the Watergate grand jury named Nixon an "unindicted coconspirator" in the coverup. On July 24, the Supreme Court ruled eight to zero against Nixon's claims of executive privilege, and the House voted to introduce three impeachment articles.

On August 5, Nixon released the remaining tapes, and his participation in the Watergate coverup was confirmed. On August 8, Nixon gave up the siege mentality and became the first President of the United States to resign.

Later Years and Looking Back

Nixon was unexpectedly pardoned by Gerald Ford, but without Nixon acknowledging his guilt. He was disbarred in New York for obstructing justice, but he never served any jail time, unlike 19 of his former associates. Nixon wrote his memoirs and finished eight more books, including *No More Vietnams* and *Beyond Peace*. David Frost interviewed Nixon in 1977 and he admitted to "mistakes" of judgment on Watergate, but denied being involved in any impeachable offense. Nixon rehabilitated his reputation to a degree and was consulted by Bush and Clinton on post-Cold War Russia. He never escaped the black cloud of Watergate, though, and the disgrace he brought to the executive office will always be in the first line of his biography. Nixon died after a stroke in 1994 and was buried next to his wife at the Nixon Library in Yorba Linda, California.

Andrew Johnson's reputation has been improved in the history books because he stood up to Congress and strengthened the presidency, but his Reconstruction policies played a major role in setting back true civil rights for another hundred years. His impeachment may have been unfair and an abuse of Congressional power, but he still allowed the South to entrench racist regulations. Nixon, on the other hand, brought unnecessary shame on the White House, even if the exact details of what part he played will never be known. Apart from all his other illegal or suspicious behavior, the Watergate break-in was an attempt to undermine a national election, to cheat democracy, and to treat the Constitution of the United States with contempt.

The Least You Need to Know

➤ Andrew Johnson was the only Southern leader to stand by the Union during the Civil War, which elevated him to Abraham Lincoln's vice president.

➤ Johnson's lenient Reconstruction policies and blatant disregard for congressional intent led to an impeachment trial by the Radical Republicans, and he remained in office by a single vote.

➤ Richard Nixon brought about the end of the Vietnam War, but not before expanding it into Cambodia.

➤ Nixon resigned before an impeachment trial could begin after his complicity in the coverup of the Watergate break-in was revealed.

Chapter 27

What We'll Never Know: William Henry Harrison and John F. Kennedy

---

In This Chapter

➤ The birth of the campaign ditty

➤ Why you should always wear your hat

➤ Kennedy wins the "eyeball-to-eyeball" stare-down

➤ Staying off the grassy knoll

One of the interesting aspects of the history of the men who have served in the White House is that there are always links, whether personal, political, or philosophical. William Henry Harrison and John Fitzgerald Kennedy might not seem to share obvious links, but they do share some. Both men changed the fundamental way that presidential campaigns are run, and both men were robbed of their chance to leave as much of a mark on the development of the United States as they might have otherwise.

A Slogan Is Born

William Henry Harrison was born on February 9, 1773, on the family plantation of Berkeley, in Charles City County, Virginia. He studied under tutors until he began attending Hampden-Sydney College, but he left to study medicine at the University of Pennsylvania under renowned physician Benjamin Rush. After his father's death in 1791, Harrison chose the life of a military man and received an ensign's commission in the First U.S. Infantry.

At Home in Indiana

Harrison fought in the Battle of the Fallen Timbers in 1794 and received an official commendation for his service. He resigned from the army and was appointed secretary of the Northwest Territory in 1798. The following year, he traveled to Washington, D.C., as the delegate of the Northwest Territory to Congress, and he successfully lobbied to separate the land from Indian Territory. He went on to become the territorial governor of Indiana from 1800 to 1813 and made a name for himself by defeating the Indians at the battle of Tippecanoe in November 1811. As governor, Harrison followed Thomas Jefferson's initiative, which allowed him to make treaties with the native peoples. His instructions were to take their lands but keep their friendship—unsurprisingly, this didn't happen. Eventually, Harrison led a militia against a confederation of Indians under the Shawnee Chief Tecumseh, whose people were not about to allow for any more friendly takeovers of their lands.

Tête-à-Tête With Tecumseh

Tecumseh and his one-eyed brother Tenskwatawah, called the Prophet, founded a village referred to as Prophetstown at the point where Tippecanoe Creek runs into the Wabash River. Tecumseh envisioned an independent Indian Nation between the Ohio River, the upper Great Lakes, and the upper Mississippi River near central Indiana. Tecumseh ventured from tribe to tribe rallying support for his one united Indian state, which could only become a reality if the advance of Anglo-American settlement was halted. In actuality, the number of Indians in the region had dwindled to roughly 40,000, and more than half a million Americans resided in the Northwest Territory.

Tecumseh was attending a gathering of Southern Indians in Alabama in October 1811, so Harrison took the opportunity to move a thousand militiamen to within a mile of Prophetstown at the mouth of Tippecanoe Creek. Prophet attacked just before dawn on November 7, but the militia held the tribe at bay. Harrison launched a bayonet counterattack, and the Indians fled. Harrison and his men burned Prophetstown on November 8, and his attack was reported as a clear-cut triumph. It was much closer to an inconclusive defensive stand, but it was the beginning of the erosion of the allied Indian powers. It also made Harrison a nationally recognized Indian fighter and bestowed the nickname "Old Tippecanoe" upon him.

Old Tippecanoe reported that the Indians had been armed with English weaponry, a rallying point that helped make the War of 1812 an inevitability. Harrison was appointed brigadier general in command of the

First Family Factuals

Captain William Henry Harrison secretly married his wife, Anna Symmes Harrison, on a day when her father, a respected judge, was out of town. Judge Symmes didn't want his daughter to have to deal with the hardships of a military life, but the two went to a justice of the peace behind his back. It worked, though—they were married for 46 years.

U.S. Army to defend the Illinois and Indiana territories. Harrison and Tecumseh, fighting with the British in Canada, eventually faced each other at the Battle of the Thames River in Ontario. This time, Harrison's troops soundly trumped their rivals, killing Tecumseh in the process and effectively crushing the federation of the Indians.

Whig-ing Out

Harrison set himself up on a farm at North Bend, Ohio, and was elected to the Ohio House of Representatives shortly thereafter. He followed this by successfully running for the Ohio Senate and then the U.S. Senate. In 1828, President Andrew Jackson appointed him ambassador to Colombia, but Harrison was called back after only eight months, which was for the best because he had alienated himself from Colombian President Simon Bolivar by cooperating with his rival. Harrison returned to his farm, which had fallen into financial strife because of excessive debts.

The *Whig Party* decided that it needed a candidate similar to the popular, twice-elected war hero Andrew Jackson. Harrison was selected to run as one of the Whigs regional candidates. At the Whig convention in Harrisburg, Pennsylvania, Harrison was chosen to be the party's candidate by unit rule, a process in which state delegates selected a committee of three to meet with other states, forming a Committee of the Whole. The state delegates, meeting separately, gave instructions to the members of their committee, who later voted as a unit in the Committee as a Whole. The process gave Harrison 148 votes, a clear majority.

In 1839, Harrison began campaigning as a man of the people. He publicized his poor, rural background and portrayed himself as a man's man raised in a log cabin who enjoyed drinking hard cider (which flowed quite freely at the campaign rallies). This approach totally obscured the fact that he actually had a background as a wealthy plantation owner and had owned slaves, which was a divisive issue among the Whigs.

Harrison's campaign was marked by his lack of focus on the issues and a reliance on slogans, songs, picnics, and parades. The legendary catchphrase "Tippecanoe and Tyler, too" was about as deep as the Whig candidate went. The Whigs were content to portray Van Buren as an aristocrat who worried only about the rich, while Harrison was painted as the everyman who wasn't accustomed to the life of privilege, even though he lived in a 22-room manor in Ohio and Van Buren was a self-made man. The idea of being outside the political establishment is nothing new, and Harrison parlayed the idea into the presidency. This became the popular ditty of the campaign.

> "What has caused this great commotion, motion
> Our country through?
> It is the ball a-rolling on,
> For Tippecanoe and Tyler, too, Tippecanoe and Tyler, too.
> And with them we'll beat little Van, Van, Van;
> Van is a used-up man."

William Henry Harrison, ninth president of the United States pictured on a campaign banner from the 1840 Election.

Harrison amassed 234 electoral votes to Van Buren's 60, and the role of the sound byte was cemented in American politics.

Telling the Truth About Tippecanoe

➤ William Henry Harrison was the son of Benjamin Harrison, a signer of the Declaration of Independence, a member of the Continental Congress, and a governor of Virginia.

➤ Anna Harrison was the original First lady to receive a pension, a grant of $25,000.

➤ Almost a million more voters turned out for the 1840 election than the one in 1836. Both Harrison and Van Buren were the first candidates to attain more than a million votes (1,274,624 to 1,127,781).

➤ William Henry Harrison Jr. died an alcoholic at the age of 35. His widow, Jane, and their children were looked after by the president, and Jane served as official White House hostess during his brief tenure.

➤ Harrison was the first president to lie in state at the Capitol.

Tippecanoe and the Wicked Flu

William Henry Harrison was inaugurated on March 4, 1841, in Washington, D.C. He rode hatless to the Capitol on a white horse as it rained cats and dogs upon him. He then proceeded to deliver the lengthiest inaugural speech on record, clocking in at an hour and 45 minutes. The speech was centered on the idea that federal power was too strong, and he vowed to limit his executive power by serving a single term, using the veto sparingly, and eschewing patronage as a way to strengthen his political base.

Harrison said little about the economic crisis other than that he opposed a wholly metallic currency. The driving rainstorm didn't let up, and the newly elected president caught a severe cold. He never recovered, and by March 27 he was bedridden. William Henry Harrison became the first president to die in Washington, D.C., on April 4, 1841, only a month after the inauguration. Ironically, Anna was sick when her husband went to Washington, and her doctors advised that she wait until May before joining her husband in Washington, D.C. She never occupied the White House.

It is hard to speculate on what Harrison's presidential ambitions were because his campaign revealed little and his party had no discernible platform. Perhaps his legacy as president can be summed up in the four-word rhyme that has influenced campaigns of all shapes and sizes, "Tippecanoe and Tyler, too."

Prez Says

"The only legitimate right to govern is an express grant of power from the governed."

—From William Henry Harrison's inaugural address

Confrontations in the Castro District

John F. Kennedy is too often discussed and recalled for his sexploits, the tantalizing "conspiracy" surrounding his assassination, and the unfathomable sadness and frequent corruption regarding the family at-large. It is unfortunate, because he was president at a time of great social and international change, and his role in shaping the 1960s and beyond shouldn't be overlooked.

A Month in April: The Cuban Failure

After Fidel Castro assumed power in Cuba and took control of U.S. assets and properties, President Eisenhower imposed a trade embargo. That didn't phase Castro. Instead, he turned his country over to Marxism, which sent many Cuban refugees to the United States. Eisenhower enlisted the CIA in covert preparations and training of exiles for an invasion of Cuba. Numerous Castro assassination plots were reported, including a plan to use exploding cigars and the "Samson Scheme," in which Castro would be poisoned, his beard would fall out and thus his image would be gravely tarnished and he would lose the support of his people. When Kennedy came into office, he approved of the invasion.

On April 17, 1961, a troop of more than 1,000 anti-Castro exiles made an amphibious assault on Cuba, but they weren't able to establish a beachhead at the Bay of Pigs. Castro's forces met the troops, so they never made inroads into the interior of the island. CIA air support also never materialized—over 100 American deaths were reported, and the surviving exiles were thrown into prison. Kennedy took full responsibility for the bungled, embarrassing debacle. He refused to negotiate with Castro, but he encouraged private enterprises to come to a settlement. Eventually, the 1,000-plus exiles were returned to the United States in exchange for a ransom of medical supplies and other goods. Kennedy caught heat from both sides for the Bay of Pigs fiasco—right-wingers felt that he should have sent Marines to do it right, and left-wingers didn't see that it was necessary at all.

Fourteen Days in October: The Cuban Success

The most intense moments of the Kennedy presidency, and the closest the Cold War rivalry came to escalating, took place during two pressure-packed weeks in October 1962. In the previous year, Cuban Dictator Fidel Castro had announced that his nation was Communist and going to form alliances with the Soviet Union and China. Russian Premiere Nikita Khrushchev began supplying his Cuban comrades with nuclear missiles, well within striking distance of the United States. Khrushchev denied that he was sending weapons to the small island off Florida, but on October 16, Kennedy was shown aerial reconnaissance photographs taken by spy planes of the construction of Soviet missile bases. Kennedy held secret meetings with his military advisers to formulate a plan of attack. On October 22, Kennedy went on national television and delivered a strong message that took the Monroe Doctrine into the atomic age. He ordered a naval and air blockade, and demanded the dismantling of all Russian bases and the removal of all weaponry.

Prez Says

"It shall be the policy of this nation, to regard any nuclear missile launched from Cuba against any nation in the Western Hemisphere as an attack by the Soviet Union on the United States."

—John F. Kennedy, October 22, 1962

For several days, the waters were eerily calm as Kennedy and Khrushchev relayed communications back and forth through diplomatic channels. After exchanging notes over a couple days, Khrushchev agreed to dismantle and remove the nuclear missiles from Cuba and allowed for American onsite inspection. Kennedy then called an end to the blockade. Cuba refused to allow the inspection, but aerial photography confirmed that the dismantling of the missile bases was taking place.

It was later revealed that Kennedy gave the Soviet Union his assurances that he wouldn't invade Cuba and would remove the missiles in Turkey aimed at Russia. Both superpowers exhaled—as global thermonuclear war had been avoided. This was generally considered the major accomplishment of Kennedy's administration, and he received international credit for standing tall against Communist aggression. In the famous words of Kennedy's Secretary of State Dean Rusk, "We're eyeball to eyeball, and I think the other fellow just blinked." Kennedy's refusal to blink was an important stand for the West, and some felt that it had prevented the outbreak of World War III.

"Most Likely to Succeed"

John Fitzgerald Kennedy was born into the wealthy family of Joe and Rose Kennedy in Brookline, Massachusetts, on May 29, 1917. His father was one of the richest men in the country and had served in several appointed positions in the Roosevelt administration. Kennedy moved to New York City and attended public school until he was sent to Canterbury School, a Roman Catholic private institution in Connecticut. Later, he graduated from Choate Preparatory School and spent the following summer studying at the London School of Economics with socialist professor Harold Laski, but he had to cut it short after an attack of jaundice.

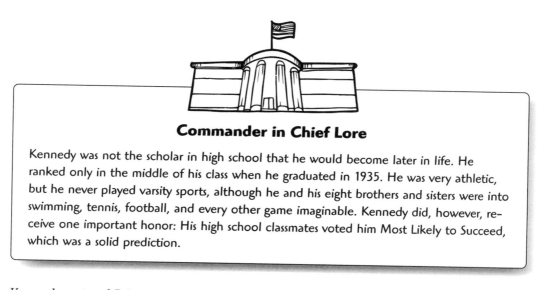

Commander in Chief Lore

Kennedy was not the scholar in high school that he would become later in life. He ranked only in the middle of his class when he graduated in 1935. He was very athletic, but he never played varsity sports, although he and his eight brothers and sisters were into swimming, tennis, football, and every other game imaginable. Kennedy did, however, receive one important honor: His high school classmates voted him Most Likely to Succeed, which was a solid prediction.

Kennedy entered Princeton in 1935, but jaundice again forced him to drop out. The next year, he followed in his father's footsteps: He stayed true to his ivy-covered Massachusetts roots and joined his older brother Joe at Harvard. Kennedy was an average student until his senior year, when he wrote a thesis about Great Britain's appeasement policies of Germany before World War II that had led to the Munich Agreement of 1938. He had the luxury of seeing and discussing diplomatic relations firsthand when he visited his father who was serving as ambassador to Britain. He expanded his honors thesis into a book titled *Why England Slept,* which became a bestseller in 1940, the same year Kennedy graduated *cum laude* from Harvard.

The Saga of PT 109

After World War II broke out, Kennedy volunteered for the U.S. Army, but he was rejected because of a back injury he had suffered playing football in college. He spent the summer of 1941 doing strengthening exercises and was accepted by the Navy in September. In 1943, his father helped him get out of the office and onto a PT-boat in the South Pacific as a lieutenant.

In August, PT 109 was rammed by a Japanese destroyer and sunk off New Georgia in the Solomon Islands. The boat was sliced in half, and the 10 survivors clung to the wreckage trying to stay alive. Kennedy rallied his men to swim to a nearby island and even saved a wounded sailor, pulling him by a strap on the man's jacket in his teeth. Kennedy spent the next few days swimming standard routes hoping to find an American ship. He came upon some friendly islanders who took a message carved on a coconut to a nearby navy base.

First Family Factuals

At 36, Kennedy married a beautiful young socialite and photographer for the Washington *Times-Herald,* Jacqueline Lee Bouvier, who was 12 years his junior. Her class, style, love of the arts, and high living made her one of the most popular First Ladies and a cultural icon. They had three children: Caroline, John Jr., who died in a plane crash in the summer of 1999, and Patrick, who died of an infection within 48 hours of his birth.

Kennedy received the Purple Heart and the Navy and Marine Corps Medal, but he contracted malaria and had a recurrence of his back injury. His military career was over. He then went to work for the Hearst newspapers as a reporter and covered the organizational meeting of the United Nations. He changed careers again after the death of his brother Joe in World War II, who had planned on a political career.

"The Poor Little Rich Kid"

Kennedy immediately set out at the age of 28 to win a seat in Congress. He moved to Boston and began campaigning for the 11th Congressional District of Massachusetts, which included his old stomping grounds of Cambridge. Utilizing a strong organization, made up primarily of family members and friends, Kennedy beat out nine candidates for the nomination and lived down the tag "poor little rich kid" in the process. He easily won the congressional seat in the solidly Democratic district and headed off to Washington, D.C. During his six years in the House, he supported Democratic domestic programs and most of President Truman's "Fair Deal." He also backed the Truman Doctrine, but he was a staunch Cold Warrior and joined Republicans in criticizing the administration for not doing all it could to stem the tide of communism in China.

The Family Helps Elect Senator John Kennedy

In 1952, Kennedy ran for the Senate against incumbent Republican Henry Cabot Lodge Jr. and defeated him by more than 70,000 votes, even though Eisenhower carried Massachusetts. Kennedy again used his family members to full advantage, and his younger brother Robert served as campaign manager.

During his first two years as a senator, Kennedy primarily pushed for legislation that was favorable to Massachusetts industries. He worked toward bringing New England senators together as a voting bloc for their common interests. As a freshman, he was assigned to the Government Operations Committee, which was chaired by the notorious senator from Wisconsin, Joseph McCarthy, who was a friend of the Kennedy family. By the time Kennedy entered the Senate, McCarthyism was on everybody's lips. Kennedy's status as a fence-sitter and his failure to renounce McCarthy lowered him in the eyes of liberals in the Democratic Party. Kennedy had reportedly planned to vote for censure and had wanted to speak out against McCarthy, but he was in the hospital when the vote was taken.

Commander in Chief Lore

Kennedy's back finally had to be operated on, and he spent a long, painful convalescence after spinal operations in October 1954 and February 1955. While he was laid up, he wrote *Profiles in Courage,* a series of portrayals of American politicians who had risked their careers taking courageous stances. Kennedy won the Pulitzer Prize in 1957 and raised his national awareness, especially among the literary elite, and led to Eleanor Roosevelt's alleged description of him as "more profile than courage."

Kennedy took a step to the left when he returned to the Senate. He supported the compromise civil rights legislation in 1957 and spoke out in favor of accepting the 1954 school desegregation ruling. In 1957, he was appointed to the Senate Foreign Relations Committee and raised a minor flap when he supported Algeria's right to independence from France. He also encouraged economic aid to underdeveloped nations and voiced his concerns that a "missile gap" had developed and that Russia was moving ahead in the development of atomic weaponry. He won the 1958 Massachusetts senatorial election by a whopping 874,000 votes and spent a good portion of his time in 1958 to 1959 trying to reform labor legislation. Some of his ideas were incorporated into the 1959 Landrum-Griffin Act, which guaranteed the rights of unions to speak, assemble, and elect officers.

The Television and the Politician Merge

Kennedy had been eyeing the oval office since 1956, when he campaigned for the vice presidential slot on the Adlai Stevenson ticket. He lost the nomination to Senator Estes Kefauver of Tennessee, but Kennedy's profile continued to rise. His family began to organize and prepare for the 1960 presidential campaign, which was again managed by Robert. Kennedy had won seven primary victories by the time the Democratic Convention convened in Los Angeles in July. Pundits still wondered whether a Roman Catholic could ever be elected president; liberals wondered whether he was a conservative in sheep's clothing; and all kinds of people wondered whether he was too young. He received the nomination on the first ballot and persuaded his closest rival, Lyndon B. Johnson, to be his running mate. It was a good strategic move because Johnson could deliver more Southern states, and Kennedy never would have triumphed without Texas.

The 1960 campaign was the first to feature televised debates, and this was to Kennedy's distinct advantage over the untelegenic Richard Nixon. Kennedy's sophistication allayed fears that he wasn't mature enough to be president, and he reiterated his devotion to the separation of church and state, not the Pope. Kennedy laid out a generally centrist "New Frontier" agenda that seemed liberal compared to Nixon. Kennedy's calls for expanded civil rights helped him carry the liberal and black votes. It was a razor-thin outcome: Kennedy won by a mere 113,000 votes out of nearly 69 million votes cast, one tenth of 1 percent of the total. The electoral count was 303 to 219, and there was strong evidence of voter fraud in Illinois, but Nixon didn't press the issue. Kennedy was inaugurated on the snowy day of January 20, 1961.

Prez Says

"In the long history of the world, only a few generations have been granted the role of defending freedom in its hour of maximum danger. I do not shrink from this responsibility—I welcome it. I do not believe that any of us would exchange places with any other people or any other generation. The energy, the faith, the devotion which we bring to this endeavor will light our country and all who serve it—and the glow from that fire can truly light the world.

—From the inaugural address of John F. Kennedy, January 20, 1961

Home Happenings

Kennedy broke precedence by appointing his brother Robert to his Cabinet as attorney general. Two years later, his younger brother Edward "Teddy" would be elected to the U.S. Senate, the only time three members of the same family have held high federal positions. He also appointed Republicans to two other positions: C. Douglas Dillon as secretary of the treasury, and Robert McNamara as secretary of defense.

A Stifling Congress

Kennedy had made overtures to enacting broad New Frontier legislation, but he was often stifled by the 87th Congress. He was able to pass some of his agenda in the first year, including a housing bill, an increase in minimum wage, aid to economically depressed areas, and the creation of the Peace Corps. Kennedy appointed a brother-in-law, R. Sargent Shriver, to direct the agency, which sent American volunteers all over the globe in humanitarian service. The idealism of building international bridges through helping people in foreign lands meshed with the activist 1960s, and the program has become a respected national achievement.

Kennedy failed to achieve many of his goals, however, because even though his party had a majority in both Houses, Southern Democrats often went along with Republicans in blocking legislation that they didn't like—and this was almost anything to do with civil rights. Congress shot down Kennedy's Medicare bill and also a bill to create a new Cabinet post, the Department of Urban Affairs, in part because he wanted to appoint a black economist as secretary. Kennedy's capital gains tax cut and civil rights legislation were passed, but they were compromised and then delayed.

Commander in Chief Lore

Kennedy was successful in convincing Congress to appropriate more than $1 billion to ensure that the United States beat Russia in landing the first man on the moon. During his term, NASA began Project Mercury to gauge the effects of high-gravity launch, reentry on human astronauts and weightlessness in space. In May 1961, Alan B. Shepard Jr. became the first American in space and the following February John Glenn became the first American in orbit. Kennedy didn't live to see his ultimate goal of a moon landing accomplished, but American astronauts beat the expressed 1970 deadline by a little under half a year.

Too Cautious on Civil Rights?

Civil rights was an especially tricky area for Kennedy because he had always taken a moderate stance, which wasn't going to work anymore. He sent troops to the

University of Mississippi and to the University of Alabama to ensure integration, and he voiced support for the end of discrimination in federally funded projects.

Kennedy has been criticized for dragging his feet on civil rights, though, and for taking a cautious approach to an issue that demanded passion (not too mention his taciturn support of J. Edgar Hoover, who ignored the Mafia that "didn't exist" while wiretapping Dr. Martin Luther King Jr.). Kennedy did give an important speech in June 1963 that precipitated the historic March on Washington, asking Congress for across-the-board equality. A comprehensive civil rights bill didn't pass until after his death.

International Interests

In addition to addressing the situations in Cuba, Kennedy dealt with other international issues. He was concerned about the spread of communism in Latin America, so he sponsored an aid program for the development of the Americas. The Alliance for Progress was launched in 1961, and although the results were mixed, it raised the prestige of Kennedy and the United States.

Knowledge Is Power

Built in 1961, the **Berlin Wall** was a concrete fortified wall—12 feet high and 103 miles long—that sealed off East Berlin from West Berlin and was maintained by the Communist forces in East Germany. The Berlin Wall was erected ostensibly to prevent military aggression from the West, but in reality it was to keep the workforce from fleeing the East. The Berlin Wall became irrelevant in 1989 when Hungary allowed passage to West Germany through their country, and it was jubilantly demolished on November 9. In 1990, the Federal Republic of Germany became one united nation again.

Another Brick in the Wall

Kennedy had a rough time dealing with Khrushchev all around, beginning with a meeting in Austria in 1961. Khrushchev was angry over the Bay of Pigs fiasco, and he was openly hostile toward Kennedy. No significant agreements were reached, and there was no resolution of the main issue of keeping access routes to Berlin open to the West. In response that August, the Communists constructed the *Berlin Wall,* and Kennedy sent soldiers into Germany to keep the Allied route to West Berlin open and accessible. Khrushchev never signed an agreement with East Germany for control of Berlin, so cooler heads prevailed. However, the Berlin Wall didn't come down for almost three decades. In June 1963, Kennedy gave a stirring speech at the Berlin Wall saying, "All free men, wherever they may live, are citizens of Berlin, and, therefore, as a free man, I take pride in the words 'Ich bin ein Berliner.'"

A Limited Test Ban Treaty

One Cold War success between superpowers came on August 5, 1963, when the United States, the Soviet

Union, and Great Britain signed a limited test ban treaty. There had been an unofficial international ban on testing nuclear weapons in the atmosphere because of the potentiality for contamination. Russia resumed atmospheric tests in 1961, and Kennedy reluctantly followed suit. Kennedy then initiated talks with Russia, which led to the test ban treaty and the first limitations on arms in the Cold War. The treaty eventually included most nations in the world, and Kennedy considered it his most important achievement.

A Penalty for Early Withdrawal?

In Southeast Asia, Kennedy continued the containment policy, and the threat of Communist China convinced him that defenses needed to be fortified. In 1961, Kennedy increased the number of advisers in South Vietnam from 700 to 15,000. He made mention that it was "their war" (referring to the South Vietnamese) to win or lose, but the oft-floated idea that he was getting ready for American withdrawal appears to have been exaggerated, at best.

In 1963, McNamara requested the withdrawal of 1,000 U.S. military personnel that year if the "situation allows," and Kennedy mentioned a small withdrawal shortly before his death, but that seems to be as far as any impending withdrawal went. There were no firm plans for the removal of U.S. personnel, and nobody in Kennedy's inner circle mentioned getting out of Vietnam without a victory. The popular notion is often used by conspiracy theorists to explain why Kennedy "had" to be killed, but that is a giant leap. Even Robert Kennedy, who became an outspoken critic of the war down the line, was in no way advocating the evacuation of Vietnam in 1963.

A JFK Joint

➤ At 43, John F. Kennedy was the youngest president of the United States ever *elected*, Teddy Roosevelt was 42 when he *assumed* the office.

➤ Kennedy was the first president to witness the firing of a Polaris missile aboard the USS *Observation Island* off the coast of Florida in November 1963.

➤ John and Jackie Kennedy were the first White House couple born in the twentieth century.

➤ Jackie Kennedy led a major White House restoration that uncovered many items throughout its history and restored rooms such as the Lincoln Bedroom with the proper furnishings of the time. After she finished, she gave a guided tour on television, and the number of sightseers at the White House increased dramatically.

➤ Kennedy's Arlington National Cemetery gravesite is marked with the eternal flame.

John Fitzgerald Kennedy, thirty-fifth president of the United States, with Caroline and JFK Jr. in the Oval Office.

(Photo courtesy of the JFK Library)

Staying off the Grassy Knoll

The events of November 22, 1963 are ingrained in the ugly annals of American history. The Kennedys visited Dallas on a speaking tour. Enthusiastic crowds greeted his open-air motorcade as it wound through downtown Dallas. At 12:30 P.M., shots were fired from the Texas School Book Depository, hitting Kennedy twice, first in the neck and then in the head. Kennedy was rushed to Parkland Memorial Hospital, where he was pronounced dead at about 1:00 P.M.

Less than two hours later, Johnson took the oath of office as Mrs. Kennedy looked on in her bloodstained dress. She arranged for her husband's funeral as his body lay in state in the U.S. Capitol rotunda. On November 25, representatives of around 100 nations attended the funeral of Kennedy, and millions watched it at home on television. An estimated one million people lined the streets as the funeral procession made its way to Arlington National Cemetery.

The assassin was Lee Harvey Oswald, an ex-Marine, who was killed by nightclub owner Jack Ruby on November 24. The Warren Commission was convened to investigate Kennedy's assassination, and members concluded that Oswald was the lone gunman and was not part of a conspiracy. In 1979, the House Select Committee on Assassinations concluded the opposite, but all the conspiracy theories would be a book unto themselves, so let's leave it at that.

William Henry Harrison and John F. Kennedy share one undeniable trait: The United States never got the chance to find out what type of president either would make, because of an unlucky illness and an unconscionable assassination.

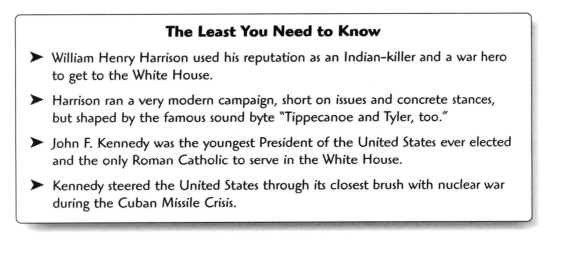

The Least You Need to Know

➤ William Henry Harrison used his reputation as an Indian-killer and a war hero to get to the White House.

➤ Harrison ran a very modern campaign, short on issues and concrete stances, but shaped by the famous sound byte "Tippecanoe and Tyler, too."

➤ John F. Kennedy was the youngest President of the United States ever elected and the only Roman Catholic to serve in the White House.

➤ Kennedy steered the United States through its closest brush with nuclear war during the Cuban Missile Crisis.

Chapter 28

What Might Have Been: James Garfield and Zachary Taylor

In This Chapter

➤ Garfield, one congressional cat

➤ Splitting the difference between the "Stalwarts" and the "Half-Breeds"

➤ War is hell, but it paves the way to 1600 Pennsylvania Ave.

➤ The inverse doughface

Of all the presidents who went to the giant oval office in the sky without the opportunity to leave their mark on this fledgling nation, a case could made that the most intriguing leaders were James Garfield and Zachary Taylor.

It is strictly speculation to make the assumption that Garfield and Taylor would have gone on to become great—or even good—presidents. It isn't a stretch, however, to say that they both had more fortitude and vision than many of the Milquetoast officeholders in the second half of the nineteenth century. Unfortunately, an indigested radical and radical indigestion kept the history books from ever being filled with admirable words about what Garfield and Taylor had done for the United States.

Last Log-Living Leader (Literally, Like Lincoln)

On November 19, 1831, James Abram Garfield became the last of a hearty, long-forgotten breed: U.S. presidents born, and raised in log cabins. Garfield's was a one-room dwelling on the family farm in Orange township, Ohio. His father died when Garfield was 2, but his mother, Eliza Ballou Garfield, was determined to keep the farm alive even though she was heavily saddled with debt. She sold 50 acres to pay off the bill, and she and her four children endured a hardscrabble existence on the remaining 30 acres. Garfield spent the first 16 years of his life working, offset only by the time he spent in school and in his studies—reading became one of the loves of his life.

Garfield attended local schools from the age of three, until he decided to become a seafaring man in his late teens. He found work on a canal boat, but life on the waterways wasn't all that he had envisioned. His next employment consisted of driving horses and mules that were pulling boats along the Ohio Canal. He was not well versed in the art of swimming, and the 14 times he fell off the tow path and nearly drowned helped convinced him that he might not be cut out for this line of work. He came down with a fever, returned home and his mother and a local teacher convinced him a life of letters might be more his speed.

In 1849, with his mother's monetary assistance, Garfield entered Geauga Seminary, but the money ran out and he had to earn extra cash as a carpenter. Following his parents, he was also baptized into the church of the Disciples of Christ. Religious instruction played an important part in Garfield's life because preaching helped him hone his renowned oratorical talents. In 1851 he enrolled at the Western Reserve Eclectic Institute, which later became Hiram College, a school founded by the Disciples of Christ.

Commander in Chief Lore

Garfield spent three years studying at the Eclectic Institute. He became proficient in both Greek and Latin, and he earned money as a janitor and through tutoring other kids at district schools in Warrensville and Blue Rock, Ohio, including his future First Lady. Even more impressive than learning the ancient languages, however, was Garfield's ability to simultaneously write Latin with one hand and Greek with the other. Ironically, at the Eclectic Institute, he became a talented and persuasive debater and speaker, and started lay preaching, but had no time for politics and the "total disregard of truth in all their operations."

Garfield then went on to Williams College in Williamstown, Massachusetts. Two years later, he had a degree with honors under his belt, and he returned to Hiram as a professor of Greek and Latin. At 26, he became president of the school and continued to spread the good word in the Disciples of Christ Church. In 1858, Garfield married

Lucretia "Crete" Rudolph, whom he had met at Geauga Seminary, but they didn't become friendly with each other until they were both enrolled at the Disciples school in Hiram. Crete was a shy, reserved woman, the exact opposite of her gregarious, sociable husband, which wasn't always the case when Garfield was alone with his thoughts. Their early years together were not happy ones; they later referred to them as the "years of darkness," which was also Garfield's description of a long bout with depression early in his adult life. These devout bibliophiles did share a love of the arts, though, and they took pleasure in reading together, taking in the theater, and soaking in the sweet symphonic sounds of local concerts.

Gentleman Preacher to Citizen Soldier

By the time the North and the South were knee-deep in the bloody mess of the Civil War, Garfield had become a lawyer and a Republican member of the state senate in Ohio. His speech skills—further developed as a lay preacher for the Disciples of Christ—coupled with his sharp debating abilities, helped his campaign considerably.

He used those same powers of persuasion to raise troops for the Union Army when the Civil War broke out in 1861. The students of the Eclectic Institute formed a company that was attached to the 42nd Ohio Infantry Volunteers, and Garfield was elected lieutenant colonel and, later, a commanding colonel of the regiment. Garfield led a brigade into eastern Kentucky in 1862 and drove the Confederate troops out, which earned him the commission of brigadier general of volunteers at the age of 30. He saw action in the second day of fighting at Shiloh and also took part in the battle of Corinth. Garfield then became chief of staff to Major General William Rosecrans and distinguished himself at the *Battle of Chickamauga*.

At the Battle of Chickamauga, Garfield's bravery in delivering a message, even after his horse had been shot out from under him, earned him the battlefield promotion to major general.

> **Knowledge Is Power**
>
> The **Battle of Chickamauga,** on September 19 and 20, 1863, was one of the major engagements of the Civil War. The battle was fought at Chickamunga, Georgia, about 12 miles south of Chattanooga, Tennessee. The Union lost, but their quick regrouping helped them win the Battle of Chattanooga, a strategic point coveted by both the North and the South. Combined, more than 34,000 soldiers were killed or wounded in the Battle of Chickamauga.

Our House, in the Middle of D.C.

Garfield was elected to the House of Representatives in 1862, while still on active duty. In December 1863, at the urging of Abraham Lincoln, Garfield began serving in the House, where he stayed for 17 straight years, still a record for a man who would go on to the presidency. He joined the Radical Republican group, which was against Andrew Johnson's lenient policy in dealing with the South and wanted to penalize the Confederacy through actions such as the seizure of rebel soldiers' property, but worked for reconciliation between the Congress and the President. Ultimately, Garfield supported the Radical Republicans call for extending the vote to blacks and backed the impeachment of President Johnson. His animosity toward the South never waned—at the convention in Chicago where he was nominated for president, he said (in regards to amicable relations with the South) "that it shall be admitted, forever and forever more, that in the war for the Union, we were right and they were wrong."

Garfield rose up the ranks to serve on committees such as the House Ways and Means, Appropriations, Military Affairs, and Banking and Currency. He eventually became minority leader of the Republicans in the House. Two scandals tainted his time in the House, but neither was ever conclusively proved, so his career train never went off-track. Garfield was listed among the men alleged to have taken bribes to stall a congressional investigation of the Credit Mobilier, a corrupt construction company that had made illegal profits from government contracts during the building of the Union Pacific Railroad. (Credit Mobilier billed the government $50 million dollars over the cost of the actual construction.) In 1873, an investigating committee found no evidence that Garfield took bribes for political favors, and he wrote a 30-page personal defense.

Commander in Chief Lore

The amount of the supposed bribe Garfield took was $329 dollars, and the number 329 began showing up throughout the United States during the campaign of 1880. Garfield's political opponents put the number everywhere to remind voters that his name had been mentioned in the bribery scandal, even though he had never been charged. They even put 329 on the steps of his house in Washington.

Garfield also allegedly took a retaining fee for his legal services from a company that was trying to get the paving contract in Washington, D.C. The fee was supposedly unconnected to the company's business with the government and wasn't illegal or improper, and other reports say it was just a rumor in the first place, but either way, it never kept his fellow Ohioans from sending him to the House. In June 1880, Garfield went to the Republican Convention in Chicago, where the party was divided down the middle. New York Senator Roscoe Conkling headed the "Stalwarts," and Maine Senator James G. Blaine headed the "Half-Breeds." The primary division between the groups was over patronage and how the appointment of federal positions should be handled. The Stalwarts wanted control of New York appointments and supported the return of Ulysses S. Grant, while the Half-Breeds felt that all decisions should come from Washington and wanted Blaine as the candidate. Garfield didn't take either side—he backed the secretary of the treasury, a fellow Ohioan, John Sherman.

Garfield attempted to secure delegates for Sherman, but although he was modestly successful, he was backing the wrong horse. Garfield gave a rousing speech on Sherman's behalf, but he didn't mention his candidate's name until 15 minutes into it, so there were rumblings that he was looking out for himself. Because of his friendship with both men, Garfield was selected as a compromise between the Sherman supporters and the Blaine faction on the thirty-sixth ballot. On the sixth day, he became the Republican nominee for president. It was the first time that a president-to-be was present at his own nomination.

James A. Garfield, twentieth president of the United States.

The campaign was very close; Garfield's support (lukewarm, at best) of a protective tariff was the primary difference between him and Democrat General Winfield Scott Hancock, a political neophyte selected because of his heroism at the Battle of Gettysburg. Garfield won in the electoral college 214 to 155, but there was a virtual tie in the popular vote because the Greenback-Labor Party had siphoned some votes.

Garfield was inaugurated on March 4, 1881, becoming the twentieth President of the United States. For the first time, a president's mother attended the swearing-in ceremony, and Garfield's first act was to plant a kiss on his mom.

Going Postal

Garfield's inaugural address emphasized the need for black suffrage, universal education for children to combat the outrageous illiteracy rate, and the need for civil service reform. Since the days of Andrew Jackson, political offices had been filled by unqualified political patrons who had gotten their jobs through the spoils system. This was the same wedge issue that had divided the Stalwarts and the Half-Breeds, and there was resentment when Blaine was appointed secretary of state and the Stalwarts were ignored when other important posts were filled. Conkling resigned his Senate seat in protest, but it made no difference—Garfield's choices were approved by Congress.

Commander in Chief Lore

Guiteau stalked Garfield for a few weeks. Three times he was armed and within close range of the president, one of the times he was going to shoot, Garfield, but he was with a sickly Crete, so Guiteau aborted the plot. Guiteau also visited the Washington jail where he would be incarcerated, to satisfy his need for a comfortable home. Lastly, he arranged for a handsome cab to give him a lift to jail so that he could avoid a lynching at the hands of an angry mob. When Guiteau finally shot Garfield, he used a .44 British Bulldog because he thought it would look nice in a museum display.

Garfield had never been a strong proponent of reforming the spoils system, but in the spring in 1881 he began exposing the Star Route frauds, an attempt by Western post office employees and mail carriers to cheat the government. Garfield's calls for reform were signed into law in 1883 under the Pendleton Civil Service Act, but the measure gained its popularity primarily because of his death.

A religious fanatic, lawyer, and Stalwart backer, Charles J. Guiteau, had been pestering the State Department for an appointment as consul in Paris. Guiteau felt that he deserved the position because of his work for the Republican Party, and he wanted his piece of the spoils system. In May 1881, Guiteau even cornered Blaine, who sternly rebuffed him. Guiteau exacted his revenge on the morning of July 2 at the Potomac and Baltimore railroad station—he shot Garfield twice, once in the arm and the second time in the back.

Guiteau is commonly believed to have been acting out of the anger he felt for not getting the position he sought, but that isn't the case entirely. He did scream his affiliations with the Stalwarts, but Guiteau was also a mentally unstable man who believed that God had told him to shoot the president. Garfield never lost consciousness as he was whisked away to the White House.

Ignorance Is Bliss

Garfield died 80 days later, and it was his medical staff that ensured that he had seen his final days. The X-ray had not yet been invented, and sterilization was still just a theory, so Dr. Willard Bliss (and his surgical assistants) began searching for the bullet with his finger and an unsterilized instrument. Garfield was close to death. The doctors mistakenly thought that the bullet had pierced the liver, but the navy general surgeon instead punctured the liver with his own finger. Garfield hung on, drinking milk and brandy until Alexander Graham Bell rigged up a metal detector to search the president's body. The detector located something much deeper than expected; it was the metal spring under the mattress. (Actually, Bell's device may have worked, had they only been aware of the new invention, the coil spring mattress and put Garfield on the floor.) The doctors continued to search for the bullet, turning a small, harmless three-inch wound (the bullet was lodged four inches from the spine in a protective cyst) into a 20-inch canal that grew more infected by the day.

Garfield was taken to a seaside cottage in Elberon, New Jersey, where he died on September 19 as a result of blood poisoning and subsequent bronchopneumonia from the unsterilized probing. Crete had maintained an 80-day vigil by his bedside. Guiteau tried to argue in court that the doctors had killed Garfield (a solid argument), but he was found guilty and hanged on June 30.

In the aftermath, Dr. Bliss gave a public apology, but he still billed the government $10,000. On a positive note, Garfield's death led to an outcry against the spoils system, and the Pendleton Act was signed into law in 1883. The Civil Service Commission was established to mete out federal positions based on merit instead of connections, of which Charles Guiteau had none.

Garfield of Dreams

➤ James Garfield was the first left-handed president.

➤ Garfield had an affair in New York City with a married woman, which broke his wife's heart. She forgave him, however, and their marriage got stronger from that point forward. Years later, she told her children that her cold upbringing had been tough for her passionate husband to handle.

➤ Garfield was the first American citizen to receive a day of mourning in the royal courts of Europe.

➤ Garfield's son, James Rudolph, went on to serve as secretary of the interior under Teddy Roosevelt.

Rough and Humble Beginnings

Zachary Taylor will always be remembered first and foremost as a legendary man of war, a valiant leader who never lost a single battle. Taylor was born on November 24, 1784, and was raised on the family plantation on the Muddy Fork of Beargrass Creek, which ran basically parallel to and a half-mile south of the Ohio River in what is now Louisville, Kentucky. His father, Richard, had served as an officer during the American Revolution, and George Washington had appointed him collector of customs for the Port of Louisville. Although the family was wealthy and prominent in the area, schools in rural Kentucky were few and far between. Taylor had no formal education, and he learned mainly the practicalities needed for sustaining life on the farm. His father hired private tutors on occasion and Taylor attended rudimentary local schools, but never on enough of a regular basis to offer more than a primitive education, although his parents were both educated and may have offered additional instruction at home.

First Family Factuals

The Taylors had five daughters and a son, although two of the girls died in infancy. Their son, Richard, went on to become a lieutenant general in the Confederate Army; Sarah, their eldest daughter, married Jefferson Davis. The union took place against Taylor's wishes, and Sarah died three months later. Taylor and Davis did not reconcile until Davis distinguished himself at the Battle of Buena Vista.

War! What Is It Good For? (The Presidency)

Little is known about Taylor until he turned 23 and enlisted in the U.S. Army, other than that he lived at home and presumably worked on the plantation, which most likely featured tobacco as the primary crop. Later in life, Taylor rarely spoke or wrote about his early years, so his youth was lost long ago to the bluegrass.

In 1808, Taylor received a commission in the Army, Seventh Infantry, with the influential help of his father's cousin, Secretary of State James Madison. In 1810, he married Margaret "Peggy" Mackall Smith, a pipe-smoking, devout Episcopalian from Maryland who obviously didn't mind that Zachary had never joined a church. She also didn't mind the hard life of a military bride, always on the move and often living in quarters that would make a hobo uncomfortable.

By 1810, Taylor was promoted to captain. This was the beginning of a 40-year military career.

War of 1812

On September 4, 1812, Taylor temporarily vaulted up to the rank of major for his acumen in fending off Indian attacks at Fort Harrison in the Indiana Territory.

Shawnee Chief Tecumseh attacked Fort Harrison with an 8 to 1 advantage, but Taylor successfully defended the fort and received widespread publicity.

Taylor's defense of Fort Harrison was always recalled by his supporters as proof of his fortitude. Taylor's rank was reduced after the War of 1812, however, when Congress streamlined and reduced the size of the U.S. Army and the number of officers by retaining those who had their rank before the war began. Taylor resigned and returned to civil life, but his rank of major was reinstated in less than a year, and he returned to the military life that would be his world for 33 years—he eventually resigned only to become President of the United States.

Commander in Chief Lore

Taylor awoke shortly before midnight on September 4, 1812, to find that Native Americans had opened fire and torched the blockhouse where the provisions were kept. Taylor decided to throw off the roof that connected the blockhouse and keep the open end completely soaked. The barracks caught fire throughout the night, but Taylor's plan kept Fort Harrison from sustaining any serious damage, and repairs were made the following day.

The Black Hawk War

Taylor spent 19 years at various military posts, including stops in the states (or eventual states) of Minnesota, Louisiana, Mississippi, Arkansas, and Oklahoma. He became a full colonel in 1832 and was stationed at Fort Crawford in Prairie du Chien, Wisconsin, in June 1829. He assumed command on August 5, 1832. He commanded a regiment in the Black Hawk War, against an alliance of the Sac and the Fox Indians, led by the ambitious leader, Chief Black Hawk. The war started when white settlers shot and killed two of five peace emissaries sent by Black Hawk, who was trying to lead a faction of the Sauk peoples back to their lands in Northwest Illinois.

As Black Hawk and his followers made their way through Wisconsin, Taylor was part of a three-month campaign to chase the elusive Native Americans through the wilderness. The final defeat came at the Bad Axe Massacre, where many followers of Black Hawk was killed—most were felled at the hands of the Army, but others drowned trying to cross the Mississippi River or were killed by their Sioux enemies as they reached the western bank. Chief Black Hawk escaped, but he either surrendered to or was captured by the Winnebagos and was turned over to Taylor.

Battles with the Seminole Indians

In November 1837, Taylor was sent to Florida to fight the Seminole Indians. Although he participated in the second war with the Seminole for three years, his victory at the Battle of Okeechobee on Christmas Day was the most successful. Taylor relentlessly pursued the Native Americans from Fort Gardiner, near Kissimmee Lake in south central Florida, to the Everglades. It was a bloody fight on the shores of Lake Okeechobee, and U.S. casualties (26 dead and 112 wounded) were larger than those of the Seminoles, but the power of the white soldiers left an indelible imprint on the Seminole Indians, hundreds of whom went on to surrender to Taylor. The Second Seminole War, however, continued until a negotiated settlement was reached in 1842.

The future president received the thanks of current President Van Buren and a promotion to brigadier general, and he was put in command of all the troops in Florida. Taylor also picked up his famous handle, "Old Rough and Ready," which referred in part to his blunt, down-to-earth frontier manner and in part to his slovenly dress. He preferred civilian clothes to military garb even on the battlefield.

Commander in Chief Lore

In an amusing anecdote, Taylor found an old military uniform, cleaned it up, and added a sword and sash for a visit from Commodore David Conner, an American naval officer. In deference to Taylor's well-known informal manner, however, Conner showed up in civilian duds. The conversation was awkward, and afterward Taylor discarded his uniform and vowed to stick to his comfortable guns.

In 1841, Taylor was put in command of the entire Southwest Department of the Army. Not a big fan of Florida, Taylor requested to be stationed in Louisiana. The War Department granted his wish, and for five placid years his headquarters were in Baton Rouge. He and Margaret purchased plantation land in Mississippi and in Jefferson County, Louisiana. The Cypress Grove plantation in Louisiana was a 2,100-acre place, and Taylor was the master of more than 100 slaves but was basically an absentee owner. Margaret and her daughter, Betty, remodeled a cottage at the Baton Rouge headquarters and turned it into a homey abode, where they stayed while Taylor went to Mexico.

Mexican War (1845–1847)

Taylor was sent down to Texas after Congress passed a resolution to annex the Lone Star State on June 23, 1845. President Polk wanted the territory between the Rio Grande and the Nueces River, and parts of what is now New Mexico, California, Nevada, Utah, and Arizona. Mexico wasn't selling, so Polk decided to simply take what he wanted by force. Taylor was ordered to march troops down to the Rio Grande and to mix it up if they came under attack, which was an inevitable after they left their position in Corpus Christi.

The Mexican War was on. Taylor won two battles right away, the Battle of Palo Alto and the Battle of Resaca de la Palma, which sent the Mexican army back across the Rio Grande. Across the United States, Taylor was hailed as a military giant. Polk promoted Taylor to major general, but presidential jealousy soon reared its ugly green head.

In September 1846, Taylor lead a major assault into northern Mexico, even though he was ready to retreat to a quiet life. As great a military man as Taylor was, he was no hawk. He once called war a "national calamity, to be avoided if compatible with national honor," and he said of the Mexican War, "I want nothing more than to see this campaign finished and the war brought to a speedy and honorable close." He was never consulted about commanding the operations in Mexico, but he followed his orders as served, like a true soldier.

He captured the city of Monterrey by sending half his army to attack from the rear while he made noise and diverted the city's attention to the east. The Mexicans surrendered, but Taylor didn't fleece them. A few of his liberal terms included allowing the losing men to return to the interior of Mexico, letting the officers keep their side arms on private property, and keeping American troops from advancing beyond the mountains where the Mexicans were to retire, pending government approval.

Zachary Taylor, twelfth president of the United States, pictured on horseback at the Battle of Buena Vista.

Taylor's heroics became the stuff of legend, and Rough and Ready clubs sprang up throughout the United States. Polk, however, was not one of his fans. The president was livid at the terms of the settlement and was jealous of Taylor's rapidly rising popularity and of the fact that the Whigs were maneuvering to make Taylor their candidate in the 1848 election. Polk, a Democrat, sent most of the men under Taylor's command over to General Winfield Scott, who had orders to attack the Mexican coast at Veracruz, but also to try to get the celebrity war-winner out of the spotlight.

His plan backfired. Mexican General Antonio de Lopez de Santa Anna heard about the ploy and decided to march north toward the Rio Grande, attack the undermanned Taylor army, and force Scott to forget about his invasion and retreat to the aid of his countrymen. Both Polk and Santa Anna were thwarted by Taylor at the Battle of Buena Vista on February 22 and 23, 1847. Taylor's 5,000 men defeated between 15,000 and 20,000 Mexicans in a brilliant victory. Taylor kept moving his troops to counter Mexican advances and was constantly one maneuver ahead of the enemy. The horse-drawn light artillery sprinted from position to position, firing like madmen, which stalled the forward thrust of the attackers. Taylor inspired his men through his own courage—he never left the heavy fighting and constantly stayed astride his white charger, even staying put after enemy fire punctured his coat.

Taylor had disobeyed his orders in advancing so far, and Polk blamed him for the loss of 267 American lives, even though the army's bravery at the Battle of Buena Vista saved the president's political behind. The American citizenry was enraptured by Taylor and he returned as the presidential front-runner.

Taylor-Made Truths

➤ Peggy Taylor was basically an invalid during her stay at the White House, although friends and family frequently visited her room. Her daughter Betty Taylor Bliss was in charge of the official state dinners and gatherings.

➤ Taylor refused to accept letters that arrived "postage due," so he didn't pick up the notification by the Whigs that he was their candidate. The letter sat in a Baton Rouge post office for weeks, until he received a replicate letter from the chairman of the convention and returned his official acceptance.

➤ Taylor's only substantial vice was his love of chewing tobacco, and he had a reputation for being a marksman spitter.

➤ Taylor was elected during the first presidential election to be held in all the states simultaneously.

Shopping for a Whig

As noted throughout the book, the Whigs were a fractured party whose primary unifying issues were to get one of their men elected and their opposition to the

Democratic Party. Taylor's popularity and loose Whig ties were all the party needed to cement his position as their top contender. Taylor's military life had kept him constantly on the move, so he hadn't established a permanent place of residence and thus had never registered or exercised his right to vote. Taylor's initial response to a Whig supporter who approached him with the idea of making a run for the White House was, "stop your nonsense and drink your whiskey."

In June 1848, the Whigs nominated Taylor at their convention in Philadelphia and named Millard Fillmore as vice president to appease the Northern Whigs, who were a bit wary of the Southern slave owner. The reluctant candidate was so popular that all worries were set aside—even the fact that Taylor had no discernible platform and vowed to be president of the people, not of the party. It was the same strategy that got William Henry Harrison elected, and lightning struck twice. The war record of Old Rough and Ready and his plainspoken, unpretentious ways resonated with the electorate.

The Question for the Ages

Taylor was sworn in on March 5, 1849, and delivered one of the shortest inaugural addresses of a newly minted president. He made no mention of his plans for the nation, but he did express his desires "to perpetuate that Union which should be the paramount object of our hopes and affections." Taylor had hoped to open his administration as the first nonpartisan president, but the spoils system was too strong, and things stayed business as usual.

The primary issue in Taylor's term was slavery. Although he was a Southerner and a slave owner, Taylor was never convinced that it was the only way to live, and he didn't want slavery expanded into states that didn't rely on cotton as the cash crop. In 1849, Californians decided that they wanted to be a free state and asked for admission to the Union, which angered the Southern states because that would upset the balance. Taylor felt that it should be up to the state itself—and if the state desired to be free, there was no need for compromises because that was the will of the people. Naturally, this didn't sit well with proslavery extremists who treated the Missouri Compromise as sacred text, because Southern California was below the infamous line of demarcation. Southern Congressmen started rumblings about seceding from the Union. Taylor made no bones about his Jacksonian beliefs, that he would employ all means necessary to squash any uprising against the Union.

Prez Says

"If it becomes necessary, in executing the laws, he would take command of the army himself, and that, if they were taken in rebellion against the Union, he would hang them with less reluctance than he had hung deserters and spies in Mexico!"

—Taylor's response to three Southern Whig Congressmen who made the mistake of mentioning secession

Taylor's unequivocal stance against granting concessions to the South kept the moderates plans at bay. The Missouri Compromise of 1850 was only a pipe dream until after Old Rough and Ready died.

Making Friends with Daddy's Enemy

One significant act in Taylor's administration was the Clayton-Bulwer Treaty, which was signed shortly before he died. It was a treaty with Great Britain that ensured the neutrality of Central America. The treaty ensured that neither the U.S. or Great Britain would occupy, colonize or otherwise exercise hegemony over Central America and set the wheels in motion for a canal to be built in Nicaragua that was later scrapped in favor of the Panama Canal. It also helped initiate the long-standing friendship between the United States and Great Britain, whom Taylor's father had fought against in the Revolutionary War. Still, Taylor's legacy is predominately defined by his fiery congressional speeches against the extension of slavery.

Death Is a Bowl of Cherries

On July 4, 1850, Americans became independent from Old Rough and Ready. Taylor, 65, attended the laying of the cornerstone of the Washington Monument and spent hours in the hot sun soaking in one patriotic speech after another. Overexposed in the heat, Taylor returned to the White House and tried to cool down by consuming iced milk and cherries, neither of which agreed with him. That night, he suffered severe abdominal cramps, developed acute gastroenteritis (cholera morbus), and died several days later. It was a common ailment of the time that arose from poor sanitation and made eating raw fruit or fresh dairy a risky summer proposition. Daniel Webster said that Taylor's death in 1850 prevented the outbreak of a civil war.

There have always been historians who attribute Taylor's death to another cause, arsenic poisoning. In the early 1990s, Taylor's remains were exhumed, and Kentucky's medical examiner took hair samples and fingernail tissues. The investigation showed that Taylor had less arsenic in his system than would have been needed to poison him because most human bodies have traces of arsenic. Still, acute arsenic poisoning wouldn't leave long-term evidence because only small doses over time would penetrate the bones. It is highly unlikely, but conspiracy theorists can't spend *every* day on John F. Kennedy.

In the final assessment, both Garfield and Taylor weren't in office long enough to leave much of an impact, but each president showed his mettle in his brief tenure. Garfield at least floated the idea that the spoils system wasn't the most equitable way to fill governmental positions, and Taylor steadfastly declared that the extension of slavery was a threat to the Union and was not in the country's best interest, even if he owned many slaves himself.

The Least You Need to Know

➤ James Garfield was a congressional workhorse, serving 17 consecutive years until he reached the White House.

➤ Garfield was elected as a compromise candidate between factions of the Republican party that differed in opinion on the standard spoils system. He addressed the issue of reforming civil service, but an assassin who felt entitled to a position because of his party loyalty killed Garfield early in his term.

➤ Zachary Taylor was a brilliant, popular military man who served for more than 40 years and never lost a battle, including a major engagement in the Mexican War in which his troops were vastly outnumbered.

➤ Taylor wholeheartedly believed that the extension of slavery wasn't good for the Union, and he spoke out against any compromise between the North and the South, even though he was a slave owner.

Chapter 29

Too Soon to Know: George Bush and Bill Clinton

In This Chapter

➤ Unleashing a desert storm

➤ Read my lips: no second term

➤ "The comeback kid" wins the White House

➤ Impeachment trial, part two

It is entirely possible that either George Bush or Bill Clinton will be gazing upon the first administration of the twenty-first century with pride and thinking of it as an extension of his administration. It is also possible that the political winds will blow either George W. Bush or Al Gore into the air of forgotten candidates with such pretenders as James G. Birney, Alfred Landon, and John Anderson. Whether or not the familial or political ties keep Bush or Clinton's legacy alive, at some point in the not-so-distant future, they will both be relegated to the history books. It doesn't seem very likely, however, that the last two presidents of the twentieth century will be illuminating the pages with the highlights of their years in the White House.

From the Silver Spoon to the Flying Cross

George Herbert Walker Bush was born in Milton, Massachusetts, in 1924 into a wealthy family and was raised in exclusive Greenwich, Connecticut. Bush's father, Prescott, became an investment banker and eventually a partner in the Wall Street firm Brown Brothers, Harriman and Company. Prescott Bush went on to serve a decade, 1952 to 1962, as a moderate Republican senator from Connecticut.

First Family Factuals

Just like in the movies, George Bush got engaged to his high school sweetheart (although they attended different schools) before heading off to war. Barbara Pierce was the daughter of a magazine publisher, and the couple was wed a couple weeks after Bush returned from the Pacific in January 1945. The Bushes had six children: George, John Ellis (Jeb), Neil, Marvin, Dorothy, and Robin, who died at the age of three of leukemia. Bush said later in life that Robin's death was one of the toughest periods in his life.

Bush attended Philips Academy in Andover, and after graduating in 1942, he enlisted in the Navy. At 18, he was one of the youngest fighter pilots, and his plane was shot down over the Pacific Ocean during a bombing raid on the island of Chichi Jima. Neither of the other two men aboard the plane survived, but Bush was able to stay afloat for a few hours until he was rescued by a passing submarine. He received the Distinguished Flying Cross and continued his flying missions, totaling 58 in all before being sent home at the end of 1944.

Bush entered Yale in 1945 and graduated Phi Beta Kappa in three years with a degree in economics and a secret handshake courtesy of his membership in the exclusive clandestine Skull and Bones society.

He took a chance after graduation—he spurned his father's banking firm and instead used connections to get into the oil business in Texas. In 1953, Bush was co-founder of the Zapata Petroleum Corporation and became president of its subsidiary, the Zapata Off-Shore Company in 1954. Four years later, the company became an independent entity, and Bush moved the headquarters to Houston and stayed on as president until 1964. The company was on the cutting edge in manufacturing off-shore drilling equipment, and Bush was a financially secure millionaire at a relatively young age, so he turned his attention to politics.

The Elected Years

Bush began his long political career as chairman of the Harris County Republican Party and didn't wait long to seize the day: He ran for the U.S. Senate in 1964. Although he lost, he had a strong showing in what was a predominantly Democratic state at the height of the Lyndon Johnson era. In 1966, he became the first Republican to represent Houston in Congress when he was elected from an affluent district to the House of Representatives.

Bush had catered to the ultraconservative John Birch types in 1964 and lost, but when he changed tactics in 1966 and ran as a more moderate Republican like his father, he won a seat in the House. This attempt to straddle both the conservative and the moderate wings of the Republican Party haunted him later in his career, however, and it was never totally clear where his allegiances lay. He generally supported conservative positions, but occasionally he voted for moderate (some would say liberal) initiatives such as the 1968 Fair Housing Act, which was ridiculed in his home district.

Bush went on to play a prominent role in national and international politics for the next 18 years—without winning a single election.

The Appointed Years

In 1971 Bush was tapped by Richard Nixon to be the U.S. Representative to the United Nations, a post in which he served for two years. Upon his appointment, Bush had little foreign-policy experience, but it was a great opportunity for gaining experience and insight into international diplomacy. Bush's next position also came at the behest of President Nixon, and he served as chairman of the Republican National Committee (RNC). This was a thankless position, however, because the Watergate scandal was intensifying almost by the day and Bush had to both show support for his party's president, and keep the RNC's nose out of the dirty fund-raising business. In early August 1974, Bush sent Nixon a formal letter asking him to resign, which became a reality a few days later.

As compensation for not nominating Bush vice president, Gerald Ford asked him to choose where he wanted to serve his country, and he made the interesting choice to be Chief of the U.S. Liaison Office in the People's Republic of China. The United States didn't even have formal diplomatic relations with China, but in the year he spent there, Bush helped facilitate the burgeoning relationship between the two countries that had started under Nixon. Ford then recalled Bush and put him in charge of the Central Intelligence Agency in 1976, which took a severe beating during the Watergate revelations. A good portion of the general public was astounded by the level of covert operations that remained shrouded in secrecy under the guise of "national security." Bush drafted an executive order regulating the CIA, and he appeared before congressional committees more than 50 times between 1976 and 1977 and instituted a variety of reassessments and reforms.

The Hand-Picked Years

After Ford lost the White House, Bush returned to Houston, but he started organizing a long-shot presidential campaign. He took a more moderate stance than his main opponent, Ronald Reagan, even ridiculing his plan to cut taxes, increase military spending, and balance the budget as "voodoo economics." Bush had a brief moment of success when he pulled an upset in the Iowa caucus, but it was clear that Reagan would be the nominee before the convention. Afterward, the two candidates mended their fences: Reagan got complete assurances from Bush that he would support his much more conservative platform. Bush was named the vice presidential candidate and probably helped assuage moderate Republicans and conservative Democrats, but it didn't make a lot of difference: The Reagan ticket rolled in 1980 and became an unstoppable juggernaut in 1984.

Bush was a loyal vice president and engaged in the standard global travels, but also had more hands-on responsibilities. He attended Reagan's Cabinet meetings and national-security briefings, and he chaired task forces on terrorism and drugs. The quantities of narcotics seized significantly increased, but treatment was basically an afterthought, and critics abounded. Bush even assumed presidential powers for eight hours while Reagan underwent cancer surgery. Bush also got caught up in the web of the Iran-Contra scandal when he denied knowing the details of the arms-for-hostages deal, even though he was in attendance at meetings with key officials in which the topic was discussed. Later, Bush said that he had opposed the Iran-Contra scheme, but there was little concrete evidence to back him up.

The Presidential Years

Bush went into the 1988 election with the benefit of having been a loyal soldier to the very popular Reagan, but he constantly had to defend his conservative credentials. He had also subordinated himself to Reagan, so he was somewhat of a question mark to voters—it wasn't even clear whether he was more of a Texan or a New Englander because he spent most of his leisure time at the family home in Kennebunkport, Maine. Bush knew that economic gains of the 1980s favored the upper crust, so he called for a "kinder, gentler America" in his acceptance speech at the Republican Convention in New Orleans. Bush withstood the criticism that arose after he chose the little-known Senator Dan Quayle as his running mate and when the press reported that he had used family influence to serve in the Indiana National Guard during the Vietnam War.

Bush's opponent was Massachusetts Governor Michael Dukakis, and the campaign was one of the more negative in recent years. Bush attacked his opponent for his refusal to support the saying of the Pledge of Allegiance in schools, for the pollution in the Boston Harbor, for being a card-carrying member of the American Civil Liberties Union, for planning to reduce the production of major weapons, and for possibly raising taxes. One effective political ad that came under fire as a race-baiting play upon white fears was the "Willie Horton" spot, which featured a black man who had committed murder while out on a furlough from a Massachusetts prison. Bush also promised not to introduce any new taxes, which later came back to haunt him.

Dukakis never connected with the people and ran an relatively ineffective campaign, although he had a much better showing than the two previous Democratic candidates. Neither candidate was ever able to focus the campaign on their substantive issues. Bush won by a comfortable electoral margin, 426 to 111, and captured about 53 percent of the popular vote. Bush's success didn't help the Republicans, though, because Democrats had majorities in both Congressional houses. Bush made the White House more accessible and informal than it had been under Reagan, however, and he jogged through the streets of Washington, D.C., almost every morning.

Prez Says

"The Congress will push me to raise taxes, and I'll say to them: read my lips, no new taxes."

—George Bush's repeated 1988 campaign pledge

George Bush, forty-first president of the United States, pictured walking down Pennsylvania Avenue with Barbara after the Inauguration on January 20, 1989.

(Photo courtesy of the George Bush Library)

The Foreign Upside

Bush entered the White House with a strong network of relationships with numerous world leaders that he had developed during his days in the United Nations and emboldened under Reagan. Bush certainly had many more foreign affair achievements than domestic successes, and during his administration, numerous oppressive regimes fell. Bush supported sanctions against South Africa, but after meeting with both reform president F. W. De Klerk and freed nationalist hero Nelson Mandela; he lifted the sanctions as apartheid began to be dismantled.

Bush also sent troops to Panama in December 1989 to help in the overthrow of Panamanian President Manuel Noriega after he nullified a losing election. Noriega had been convicted of international drug trafficking in February 1988, but was still in power. Critics of Bush pointed out that Noriega had worked with the CIA for years, including the time he was in charge, and the Panamanian dictator had become an enemy only upon conviction. The United Nations General Assembly voted 75 to 20 (with 40 abstentions) against the invasion as a violation of international law, but Panamanians overwhelmingly supported it. Noriega was captured within a few days and was extradited to the United States to stand trial—eventually he was convicted on drug and racketeering charges.

Bush stood firm in his stance to recognize China, even as the student protests in Tiananmen Square were being crushed. He also spoke out against the brutal military crackdown, but he came under fire from human rights activists for maintaining relations and refusing to add sanctions.

He had greater success in dealings with Mikhail Gorbachev, and relations between the United States and the Soviet Union entered a new realm with the fall of communism. Bush offered his help in establishing a Soviet democracy and proposed an unexpected reduction of U.S. troops in Allied Europe. Like the rest of the country, however, Bush could not have known how quick and violence-free the democratic transformation of Eastern Europe would be. Only the removal of the Marxist regime in Romania led to heavy bloodshed.

As the Berlin Wall started to come down in November 1989, Bush tactfully restrained from making grand pronouncements about the evils of communism. He supported newly elected Russian President Boris Yeltsin, who defeated a coup attempt that tried to remove Gorbachev from power. Bush waited until Gorbachev's retirement was official to officially recognize Yeltsin's Russia and the surrounding independent republics. The two presidents agreed to cut nuclear weapons in the spring of 1992.

Bush's Shining Hour: The Gulf War

In August 1990, Iraqi leader Saddam Hussein launched a sneak attack on neighboring defenseless Kuwait to seize its rich, oil-producing regions. After invading Kuwait, Hussein was within striking distance of Saudi Arabia and 25 percent of the world's oil reserves. Bush reacted swiftly and severely, ordering sanctions and an economic embargo against Baghdad within hours and lining up other countries in an organized diplomatic alliance against Iraq called Operation Desert Shield. Bush maneuvered around the U.N. Security Council, which was unprecedented because it was the first time the United Nations had approved military action—*Operation Desert Storm*—outside of its own flag or its own enforcement powers. Iraq offered to settle for a chunk of Kuwait, but Bush demanded total withdrawal and was supported by the United Nations. On January 12, 1991, Congress ended its heated debate and gave full authorization to use military action to liberate Kuwait. On January 15, the removal deadline passed, and aerial attacks on strategic Iraqi military and communication targets began.

Operation Desert Storm restored the Kuwaiti government with only 149 American soldiers killed and 141 allied deaths. Bush's stated objective was never to remove Saddam Hussein, however, and he was criticized for ending the offensive before the Iraqi dictator was ousted. It was an organized, effective military display in the first major international crisis after the

Knowledge Is Power

The multinational invasion of Kuwait called **Operation Desert Storm** started on January 17 with four weeks of an intense air campaign. The ground troops began rolling across the desert toward Kuwait City, and allied forces were able to drive the Iraqis out because they put up little resistance and couldn't match the advanced technological weaponry.

Cold War, and Bush was hailed as a hero, even if some of the luster of the Gulf War has worn off because of repeated incidents with Hussein.

The Domestic Downside

After the Gulf War, Bush's approval ratings were astounding, above 90 percent, but the numbers soon dropped faster than a New Year's resolution over the domestic economic situation. As early as 1990, Bush had to drop his pledge of "no new taxes" because of the massive federal budget deficit. Bush attempted to build a bipartisan deficit reduction plan, but the compromise was killed in the House, primarily by conservative Republicans. The government was close to shutting down over a lack of funds, so Bush had to assemble a majority to pass a budget and adhere to Democratic demands that included a marginal tax hike and the elimination of the upper-class exemptions that were central to "Reaganomics." Bush couldn't get a cut in the capital gains tax, so he was abandoned by many congressional Republicans. In 1990, a minor recession set in, but its aftermath became the center of the 1992 campaign as unemployment crept up amid a wave of corporate, white-collar layoffs.

In other domestic situations, Bush made minor progress but was never able to capture the public's fancy with a single issue. In 1991, Bush proposed a North American Free Trade Agreement (NAFTA) between the United States, Mexico, and Canada. A draft of the trade-free continent agreement was signed by the three countries in 1992 and was sent on to each individual legislature. Bush also took part in the first Earth Summit in June 1992 in Rio de Janeiro and signed a global warming treaty, although he was criticized by environmentalists for weakening the original treaty and for undermining the summit by not taking a leading role in world-wide environmental issues. Bush also took his economic lumps because his administration initiated the mammoth bailout of the government-supported Savings and Loan banks, which had lost billions through mismanagement and fraud.

One George Bush in Hand

➤ At Yale, Bush was a first baseman on the collegiate team that twice won the Eastern Regional Championship in 1947 and 1948 and lost in the first College World Series in 1947.

➤ Bush became the first vice president to be elected, and to lose a re-election, since Martin Van Buren.

➤ Bush appointed the second African-American, Clarence Thomas, to the Supreme Court, but Thomas wasn't confirmed until after tense hearings featuring accusations that he sexually harassed Anita Hill, a former member of his staff.

➤ After retiring, Bush fulfilled a lifelong goal and parachuted out of an airplane twice.

It's the Economy (and the Bull Moose Effect)

From the amazing highs of the post-Gulf War euphoria to the lows of the 63 percent of the electorate who voted against him, Bush ran the gamut during his administration. He was first and foremost a foreign policy president, but the recession was lingered on, and Arkansas Governor Bill Clinton painted Bush as a president who ignored average Americans. The Republican votes were also split by third-party candidate Ross Perot, whose primary goal was to reduce the federal deficit to spur the economy. Perot captured 19 percent of the popular vote, primarily at the expense of Bush. As the campaign came to a close, Bush appeared to be making up ground on Clinton, but he got 370 electoral votes on Election Day, to Bush's 168.

In retirement, Bush wrote his memoirs and stayed out of the spotlight. His son Jeb was elected governor of Florida, and George Jr. was elected governor of Texas, but George Jr. now has his sights on the biggest trophy of all in the 2000 election: president.

Have a Little Hope

William Jefferson Blythe was born in the small rural town of Hope, Arkansas, on August 19, 1946. His father died in an automobile accident three months before his son was born, and his wife, Virginia, left the boy with his grandparents while she was in Louisiana studying to be a nurse.

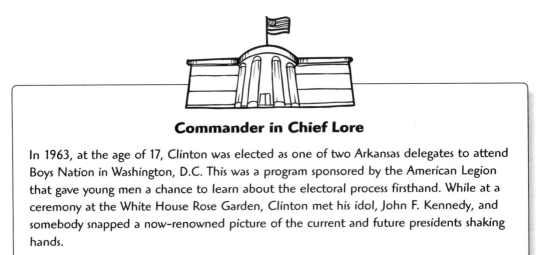

Commander in Chief Lore

In 1963, at the age of 17, Clinton was elected as one of two Arkansas delegates to attend Boys Nation in Washington, D.C. This was a program sponsored by the American Legion that gave young men a chance to learn about the electoral process firsthand. While at a ceremony at the White House Rose Garden, Clinton met his idol, John F. Kennedy, and somebody snapped a now-renowned picture of the current and future presidents shaking hands.

Virginia remarried Roger Clinton when young Bill was 4, and the family moved to Hot Springs, Arkansas, where another child, Roger, was born. Bill Blythe immediately began answering to Bill Clinton, but his name wasn't legally changed until he turned fifteen. Clinton's stepfather was a heavy drinker and a gambler who played with the family finances, and he often was physically and verbally abusive to the family. Clinton was very close to his mother and occasionally protected her from Roger. (Later in his political life, he shared the details of his dysfunctional upbringing while campaigning.)

Clinton went to a Hot Springs Catholic school for a couple years before transferring into the public education system. Always a conscientious student, he got high marks, was active in student offices, and made the all-state band as a tenor saxophonist.

Clinton enrolled in Georgetown University in 1964 and majored in international studies. He covered school costs by interning in the office of Senator William Fulbright, an Arkansas Democrat and chairman of the powerful Senate Foreign Relations Committee. After graduating, Clinton received a Rhodes scholarship and attended Oxford University in England in graduate studies. The year was 1968, and the Vietnam War was polarizing the United States. Clinton joined the thousands of students protesting American involvement. He secured a deferment and eventually became the first president who hadn't served in the military since Franklin Roosevelt, even though his draft number was selected near the end of the conflict. In 1970, Clinton entered Yale Law School, where he met another young go-getter, Hillary Rodham, and the two traveled to Texas together to work on the McGovern campaign in 1972.

First Family Factuals

In 1974, Clinton returned to teach law at the University of Arkansas at Fayetteville. All the while, Hillary was busy working on the congressional impeachment staff investigating Nixon's role in Watergate.

Hillary joined the law school staff at the University of Arkansas after the hearings wrapped up, and she and Bill were married in October 1975.

Never Too Young to Be Governor

Clinton first ran for office in 1974 in an enthusiastic grass-roots campaign to unseat a popular Republican who had been in office for quite some time. Clinton lost in a surprisingly close race, but more importantly, he got the attention of state Democrats and was elected attorney general in 1976. Two years later, he ran in the gubernatorial election on a platform to improve Arkansas's educational system; at 32, he became one of the youngest governors in American history.

In his first term, Clinton appointed a young staff and attempted to pass a variety of legislative initiatives. He succeeded in getting a compromise tax passed to fix the shoddy highways, but it was politically costly because it came out of the pockets of car owners whose fees were increased. He failed in an attempt to consolidate schools and eliminate some rural districts, and he took a lot of heat when President Carter ordered more than 18,000 Cuban refugees to an old U.S. Army post in Arkansas. Some of the refugees escaped, and a riot broke out. The incident hurt Clinton because he had campaigned as a friend and ally of Carter.

Clinton spent the next couple years working in a private Little Rock firm and preparing for the next election. He campaigned hard and was re-elected, earning the nickname "the Comeback Kid." He campaigned for the votes of African-Americans and carried more 95 percent of their votes, and that set a precedent that would remain through his years in the White House.

Clinton spent the next 10 years of his life in the governor's mansion (1983–1992). He appointed Hillary to head an education commission, and she traveled around the state, holding meetings in all 75 counties to get ideas on how to improve the state's educational system. In 1983, Clinton called a special legislative session to try to win passage of his broad reforms. He proposed raising taxes across the spectrum to pay for a variety of measures, including higher teacher salaries, college scholarships, extra art and music programs, better math and science classes, and a more equitable financial distribution to the poorer districts. Clinton also made eighth-graders pass a standard exam before advancing to high school, and mandated teacher and principal competency tests. Within a decade, graduation rates and the number of students going on to college increased.

From a Little Rock Comes the Big Cheese

Clinton left the governor's mansion in 1992, by which time he had established himself as a national presence. He served as chairman of the Southern Growth Policies Board in 1985 to 1986 and the National Governor's Association in 1986 to 1987, and he gave the nominating speech for Michael Dukakis in 1988 at the Democratic Convention. The speech was a disaster, but there were no long-term effects, and Clinton became head of the Democratic Leadership Council in 1990 to 1991. The council was made up of a group of moderate-to-conservative Democrats, and Clinton became one of the prominent leaders of the shift from the liberal elements of the party to the center.

George Bush seemed unbeatable after his strong leadership during the Gulf War, so some prominent Democrats opted not to run—that made Clinton instantly one of the front-runners. He lost the New Hampshire primary to Paul Tsongas but went on to secure the Democratic nomination in New York City. Early in the summer of 1992, some polls had him in third place behind Bush and Perot, but Clinton didn't let the long odds slow him down. He selected a popular running mate, Al Gore, even though both men came from similar backgrounds and the decision didn't help his cause in any region of the country.

Prez Says

"There is nothing wrong with America that cannot be cured by what is right with America."

—From Bill Clinton's inaugural speech, January 20, 1993

Instead, the Clinton/Gore ticket campaigned as a young, energetic team from the "New South" whose policies would lift the country out of the recession.

Bush tried to portray Clinton as too inexperienced in foreign policy matters and too willing to raise taxes, and conservative opponents labeled him a draft-dodger and a drug user, eliciting a response that he "didn't inhale" when he smoked pot. Clinton constantly hit the drumbeat about ending the Bush administration recession, and it worked. Clinton won the electoral election handily, although he got only 43 percent of the popular vote.

Commander in Chief Lore

Clinton and Gore took their message to the people, tooling around the country in a bus and promoting their plan for universal health care, middle-class tax cuts, and a reduction in military spending—basically an anti-Reaganomics platform. They stopped everywhere and participated in town meetings, met with local reporters, and scored extensive media coverage. They also tried to connect with the Baby Boomers and younger voters with the Fleetwood Mac ditty, "Don't Stop Thinking About Tomorrow," as their campaign song. Clinton sat down with Larry King and Phil Donahue and even played the saxophone on the old *Arsenio Hall Show*.

Clinton's Domestic Life

Clinton came into office with a wide-ranging legislative agenda and a Democratic Congress, but he wasn't able to capitalize. However, he was successful in fulfilling his campaign pledge to appoint more women and minorities as Cabinet members than any president in history, including Attorney General Janet Reno, Secretary of Commerce Ron Brown, and Secretary of Housing and Urban Development Henry Cisneros.

Clinton had announced that he was going to end the legislative deadlock, and right away he was able to overturn abortion restrictions and sign an act that gave workers the right to unpaid leave to deal with familial issues such as childbirth. He was stifled, however, on his campaign promise to allow homosexuals in the military after a firestorm of criticism form military officials. He settled on the "don't ask, don't tell" compromise, which may have been the best he could do, but he was derided by both liberals and conservatives for being too ambiguous.

Clinton didn't stray far from his budgetary promises, although middle-class tax cuts weren't a reality for three years. In 1993 and 1994, he called for reducing the deficit by $500 billion through spending cuts and a series of new taxes, which passed by the slightest of margins in both the House and the Senate. His greatest failure in the early years of his first term was his inability to follow through on his plan to guarantee health care for all Americans from cradle to grave. Clinton made the unprecedented move of appointing Hillary as the unpaid head of the President's Task Force on National Health Care Reform. A massive 240,000-word proposal for universal health insurance was presented to Congress in October 1993, but it never made it through Congress for a vote. An effective campaign convinced the public that the proposal was too complicated and expensive, and the Clinton administration was never able to reach a compromise with congressional Republicans.

Patriot's Day Tragedies

Two horrific events took place during Clinton's first term, on Patriot's Day (April 19) in both 1993 and 1995. The first tragedy was in Waco, Texas, where a group calling themselves the Branch Davidians were stockpiling weapons. A botched raid by the Bureau of Alcohol, Tobacco, and Firearms lead to a gun battle and the ensuing deaths of four government agents and six Davidians. A 51-day standoff ended when federal tanks broke down the walls and fired tear gas into the compound. A fire engulfed the Branch Davidians retreat and some 80 members were killed, including a group of children. Critics have claimed that the government was the aggressor. Two years later, the Alfred P. Murrah Federal Building in Oklahoma City was devastated by an explosion from a bomb left by Timothy McVeigh, partially in response to the Waco raid. 169 people were killed in the worst act of terrorism on American soil, and McVeigh was sentenced to death in connection with the bombing.

Other events during Clinton's first term included the signing of NAFTA in 1993 and the General Agreement on Tariffs and Trade (GATT), a world trade agreement. Clinton broke with union organizations, though, and anti-free traders have complained that American jobs are constantly shipped to countries with cheap labor. A World Trade Organization (WTO) was created to govern commerce and was greeted with large, raucous protests at the WTO Seattle conference in late 1999. A hard-fought crime bill also banned the sale of some assault weapons and appropriated funds for 100,000 more police officers.

In 1994, Clinton suffered a major setback when Americans began to see him as a traditional liberal, and they responded by voting in Republican majorities in both the House and Senate. The strident conservatives set an agenda titled the *Contract with America,* but very few of their bills became law. Ironically, it was Clinton's willingness to stand up to Republican spending cuts in areas such as Medicaid, Medicare, and education that registered with voters and resulted in upward approval ratings. On August 22, 1992, he signed a comprehensive welfare reform bill that shifted the responsibility to the states and limited lifetime benefits to five years. By the end of

1999, the welfare rolls had drastically shrunk, but there has been criticism that the available jobs are low-paying and that a reduction in recipients doesn't address the roots of poverty.

Clinton's Mixed Bag of Foreign Situations

Clinton's foreign policy initiatives in both terms were a mixed bag: A few initiatives worked out well, but others were dismal failures. In Haiti in 1994, Clinton sent U.S. troops to reinstate democratically elected president Jean-Bertrand Aristide. Before things got ugly, a delegation led by Jimmy Carter was able to convince military junta leader Raoul Cedras to surrender the government and leave the country. In North Korea, tension was high when the Communist dictatorship broke the Nuclear Non-proliferation Treaty by preventing inspectors from seeing whether they were manufacturing plutonium, one of the main ingredients in nuclear weapons. There were whispers of the specter of war, but again Carter intervened, and an agreement was reached to allow the return of the inspectors in exchange for building safer plants and reactors that reduced plutonium.

In 1994, Clinton sent troops to Kuwait after Iraqi leader Saddam Hussein, who had remained in power after the Gulf War, again threatened the country. Clinton then ordered air strikes against the Iraqis two years later to force compliance with the peace agreement, and again in 1998, after Hussein refused to allow United Nations weapon-inspection teams access. The major foreign policy achievement of the Clinton administration, however, was the brokering of a historic peace agreement in Northern Ireland by his representative, George Mitchell. It remains to be seen if the peace accords will become a full reality, but it was a major breakthrough in Irish relations.

Big Scandals, Big Money

From the time of Clinton's 1992 campaign, it seemed as if he was always shrouded in scandal. Opponents claimed that he had no use for the truth and that there had to be something to all the allegations that were answered in double talk and legalese. Supporters claimed that there was an organized effort against President Clinton and asserted that the mere sign of smoke doesn't necessarily mean there is fire. Whatever side of the fence sounds accurate, one thing that cannot be denied is that Clinton never suffered any irreparable political damage.

Talk of scandals was cheap, ranging from the ludicrous to the benign, but it would take a whole other book to examine them all. Instead, let's examine the two big ones.

Whitewater

Questions arose about a failed Clinton investment in an Arkansas real-estate venture called the Whitewater Development Corporation. The Clintons lost money on the deal, but their partners managed later to buy a small savings and loan, which went bankrupt and received a federal bailout. The impropriety questions arose as to whether then Governor Clinton used his influence and power to assist his partners in either venture.

The Whitewater affair was investigated by Independent Counsel Kenneth Starr, and hearings were led by Senator Alphonse D'Amato, but both closed without any charges against either of the Clintons.

Commander in Chief Lore

Clinton agreed to give sworn testimony concerning his role in the Whitewater mess. He became the first sitting president to forgo executive privilege and answer questions under oath. Clinton's answers were that he and Hillary were investors, but they weren't actively involved in any of the financial wrangling and knew of no illegal behavior.

Lying Under Oath Scandal

Independent Counsel Starr then looked into a civil lawsuit filed against President Clinton by a former Arkansas state employee, Paula Jones. Jones claimed that Clinton had sexually harassed her while he was governor. While Starr's office was investigating the matter, a sexual dalliance between Clinton and a young White House intern, Monica Lewinsky, came to light. That became topic no. 1 in newspapers across the country in January 1998. While under oath for the Jones civil case, Clinton adamantly said that he did "not have sexual relations" with Lewinsky. Physical DNA evidence to the contrary surfaced, however, and in August 1998, Clinton admitted to "inappropriate" relations with Lewinsky, which led to the charges of perjury, or lying under oath.

In November, the House Judiciary Committee began impeachment hearings, which resulted in outlining four articles of impeachment. The committee had a majority of conservative Republicans, and they decided on an all-or-nothing strategy—they ignored the Democratic compromise of a censure resolution. In December 1998, the entire House, which serves as the prosecution in an impeachment case, voted affirmatively on two articles of impeachment: obstruction of justice and perjury. The trial got underway in January 1999, and a few weeks later President Clinton was acquitted in the Senate by a count of 55 to 45 on the charge of perjury and 50 to 50 on the charge of obstruction of justice, neither of which was close to the two thirds needed for a presidential ouster.

It's the Economy, Stupid

Throughout the Clinton Impeachment saga, the president's approval ratings remained high and actually rose a couple times. The reasons seem to be twofold: First, the average person didn't think that a sexual affair—even lying under oath about one—rose to the level of "high crimes and misdemeanors." Whether that was out of cynicism or sincerity, Clinton had the public's support, and the House Republicans didn't.

William Jefferson Clinton, forty-second president of the United States.

The second reason is much simpler to understand: To paraphrase Clinton himself, it's the economy, stupid. People didn't want to interrupt the huge wave of prosperity that had begun in Clinton's first term and continued through the end of the twentieth century. In 1997, a major tax cut took place, but a solid plan also emerged to balance the federal budget. Wall Street topped the mythical number of greatness, 10,000, unemployment reached its lowest peak since the days following World War II, and the new technology-based economy was creating tremendous wealth. Critics are quick to point out that gap between the rich and the poor also widened substantially, but the economy was certainly on much stronger ground than it had been when President Clinton entered office in 1993. In 1998 and 1999, there were actually large surpluses, and rumors began surfacing of a plan to pay off the entire federal deficit, a trick that had been performed only once, back in the heady days of Andrew Jackson.

413

> ### *Meet Bill Clinton*
>
> ➤ Clinton was the first President of the United States born after World War II.
>
> ➤ Clinton took the controversial step of formally recognizing and lifting the trade embargo with former American enemy Vietnam.
>
> ➤ Clinton made the first two Supreme Court appointments by a Democrat since the 1960s, Stephen G. Breyer and, the second woman, Ruth Bader Ginsburg.
>
> ➤ Clinton became the first sitting president to be sanctioned for contempt of court.

It is too early to state what kind of legacy George Bush or Bill Clinton will leave behind—it takes at least a decade of post-presidential analysis to begin forming a consensus. It suffices to say that both men will always have their detractors—the former because his major crowning achievement was undermined by a dubious economy, and the latter because his major crowning economy was undermined by a dubious achievement.

> ### The Least You Need to Know
>
> ➤ George Bush organized a strong coalition in the Gulf War, but couldn't lift the country out of a recession.
>
> ➤ Bill Clinton steered the country through its greatest economy on record, but he will always live with the stigma of impeachment.
>
> ➤ Whomever is elected President of the United States will always have his (or her) supporters, opponents, and, most important, a place in the historical record.

Index

B

C

N

U–V